The Dynamics of War and Revolution: Cork City, 1916–1918

THE DYNAMICS OF WAR AND REVOLUTION:
CORK CITY, 1916–1918

John Borgonovo

CORK UNIVERSITY PRESS

First published in 2013 by
Cork University Press
Youngline Industrial Estate
Pouladuff Road, Togher
Cork, Ireland

British Library Cataloguing in Publication Data
A CIP catalogue record for this book is available from the British Library.

ISBN-1-909005-82-2

Typeset by Tower Books, Ballincollig, County Cork
Printed by Grafo in Spain

www.corkuniversitypress.com

This work is dedicated to my father
Roy Remo Borgonovo,
who passed away shortly before its completion.
He was a good man, a wonderful father,
and loved history.

Contents

Acknowledgements

A number of people made this book possible. My PhD dissertation at UCC could not have been completed without financial assistance secured by the School of History. Thanks to Professor Dermot Keogh, Gabriel Doherty and Dr Hiram Morgan for helping secure that assistance.

I am grateful for the assistance received from the staff at Q-1 in the Boole Library, UCC; Gregory O'Connor and the staff at the National Archives, Dublin; Commandant Victor Laing at the Bureau of Military History; Brian Kirby at the Capuchin Provincial Archives; Kieran Burke and the team at the Cork City Library Local Studies Department; Brian McGee, Michael Higgins and Peter McDonnell at the Cork City and County Archives; and Dan Breen at the Cork Public Museum. Special thanks are due to Andrew Bielenberg for allowing me to pick his brains on economic policy; and Donal Ó Drisceoil who is an oracle on Cork labour and commercial history.

Thanks also to Gabriel Doherty who was an insightful supervisor of my PhD dissertation. I also received assistance and support from my fellow PhD students at UCC including Donal Corcoran, James Ryan and Sarah-Anne Buckley. I am grateful for hospitality afforded me during my research trips by Niall and Dr Catherine de Barra, Chris and Claudia Murray, and Andrew Daly. Brendan O'Shea and Gerry White provided me with hours of thought and debate about this subject. Throughout the past number of years, I have been sustained by frequent chicken dinners from Kevin and Caoimhe Kiely of Preghane House, Kinsale, and Sunday brunches by Conal Creedon and Fiona O'Toole, of Coburg Street, Cork.

Special recognition is also due to my devoted siblings and nephews, my loving mother Roberta, and my late father Roy, who pushed me to finish in time for him to see my PhD conferment. Sadly, that deadline was missed.

Abbreviations

AFIL	All-For-Ireland League
AOH	Ancient Order of Hibernians
CBS	Christian Brothers School
CDC	Cork District Council (Cumann na mBan)
CDTC	Cork District Trades Council
DDSSF	Discharged and Demobilised Sailors and Soldiers Federation
DI	District Inspector (RIC)
DORA	Defence of the Realm Act
GAA	Gaelic Athletic Association
ICA	Irish Citizen Army
IDA	Industrial Development Association
INAA	Irish National Aid Association
INAVDF	Irish National Aid and Volunteer Dependents' Fund
IRB	Irish Republican Brotherhood
ITGWU	Irish Transport and General Workers Union
LGB	Local Government Board (Ireland)
MP	Member of Parliament
MWFL	Munster Women's Franchise League
NUR	National Union of Railwaymen
NV	National Volunteers
PLG	Poor Law Guardians
RM	Resident Magistrate
RIC	Royal Irish Constabulary
UCC	University College Cork
UIL	United Irish League
UTLC	United Trades Labour Council
YMCA	Young Men's Christian Association

Tables

A Note on
Language

When reading this study, the reader will note a myriad of personalities, organisations, and acronyms. I have attempted to find
consistency in the use of language in my text, with the explanation
below intended to alleviate any confusion.

The Irish Party features very prominently in this narrative. While
the term 'Redmondite' or 'Redmondism' can denote adherence to John
Redmond's particular brand of constitutional nationalism (generally
more conciliatory and imperial), I have used the term as it was
employed during the period – to refer to followers of the Irish Party
led by Redmond. To reduce confusion, I continue to employ this term
even after the point when Redmond died and John Dillon had become
party chief. Some historians use 'Irish Parliamentary Party' to describe
the Redmondite organisation, but I prefer the shortened 'Irish Party',
as the former can confine the party to members elected to the House of
Commons. Occasionally I also employ as synonyms 'Hibernian',
'Mollies' or 'Mollie Maguires' for Irish Party adherents, which were
popularly used in Cork at the time. The Irish Party used the United
Irish League as its constituency organisation. As a result, the United
Irish League (or UIL) is used interchangeably with the Irish Party.

William O'Brien's political organisation was the All–For–Ireland
League. I have shortened it to the AFIL, and occasionally call its adherents 'All For's' or O'Brienites. The 1914 Irish Volunteers were properly
named the Irish National Volunteers, but I utilise the former term, to
denote the continuity of that organisation (especially its leadership
and core) with its second generation that appeared in 1915. National
Volunteers (or NV) refers to the organisation that emerged in October
1914 and swore allegiance to John Redmond. On the Republican side,
the terms separatist and Republican are used interchangeably.

In Cork, numerous residents shared surnames, which was often
confusing. As a result, inhabitants were differentiated by nicknames or
abbreviations. Further complicating matters, some separatists changed

their names to Irish (for example: William Roche became Liam de Róiste). I have chosen the form of name most frequently used during this period of study. For example: Florrie O'Donoghue, Donal 'Óg' O'Callaghan, JJ Horgan, Jerry Lane, Paddy Meade, Annie Walsh, and Sean O'Hegarty.

This study focuses on the city of Cork. The terms Cork, the city, and Cork city are all used to describe the city of Cork. When referring to the County of Cork (beyond the city), the word county is included.

Introduction

Baggers and gents, and the captains of ships,
Ashmen and clerks in the bank,
Doctors and waiters that live by your tips
Brewers exalted in rank.
The Quakers and barmaids, and Masters of Art
Dentists and scavengers, too
Life's but a farce, and each of your parts
Fate has selected for you.
D.C. Kelleher, 'Cork's Own Town', 1920[1]

On 4 September 1921, the Cork Harbour Board commissioners attended their weekly meeting at the Cork Customs House, to be followed by an elaborate luncheon. The commissioners included many of the city's most prominent commercial leaders, primarily railway directors, shipping agents and large merchants. Recently they had been joined by a handful of elected Sinn Féin officials. During this meeting, one such Sinn Féin commissioner, Robert Day, stormed into the ornate Board Room. He announced that members of his Irish Transport and General Workers' Union had hoisted a red flag over the Customs House and would now run the Port of Cork themselves as a workers' Soviet. 'It is true that I am Day, the ex-driver of a one-horse van,' he told the startled commissioners, 'but now I am a Harbour Commissioner and Town Councillor . . . I have got every worker in the city of Cork behind me.'[2] After a day of negotiations, Day's men vacated the Customs House, as an Irish Republican Army (IRA) squad replaced their red flag with a tricolour to reflect the port's allegiance to the revolutionary parliament, Dáil Éireann.[3] The IRA headquarters in Cork took instructions from Florrie O'Donoghue, one of the top IRA commanders in the country. Five years earlier, O'Donoghue had been an anonymous shop assistant in a tiny drapery on Cork's North Main Street, with little money or prestige and ineligible to vote under the pre-1918 franchise. This book will attempt to explain the launch of the

1

Irish Revolution, a period in which previously marginalised young men like Robert Day and Florrie O'Donoghue briefly ruled Ireland.

The conventional War of Independence narrative begins with the Home Rule crisis; acknowledges initial enthusiasm for the First World War; jumps to Easter 1916 and its executions; tips its cap to 1918's conscription crisis and general election; then pushes off from Soloheadbeg. Little explanation is offered for the seemingly sudden swing in public opinion after the Easter Rising. Scholars generally rush past 1917 and 1918, eager to come to grips with flying columns and Black and Tans. Yet an entirely new political movement came to pre-eminence in 1917. It produced an unprecedented nationalist mobilisation in 1918 that protected young Irish men from mandatory military service, a striking exception among the First World War's European combatants. With less formality than Russia's Treaty of Brest, Ireland unilaterally withdrew from the war that summer. Sinn Féin's triumph in the 1918 general election merely punctuated the startling change in Irish political allegiance. This study will attempt to explain that tectonic popular shift, by analysing events in the city of Cork during the thirty months following the Easter Rising.

Prior to David Fitzpatrick's 1986 Trinity College Workshop, Ireland's First World War role was largely neglected.[4] Since then, numerous innovative scholars have pushed well beyond the suspension of Home Rule, to encompass the war's cultural, sociological, economic, religious and political dimensions in Ireland.[5] 'It was the outbreak of the Great War,' offers George Boyce, 'that first seemed to postpone, but then hastened, the opportunity for revolutionary conspirators to turn their dreams into reality.'[6] As the war dragged on month after month, war mobilisation built up social, economic and political pressures in Ireland. According to Senia Paseta and Adrian Gregory, Ireland experienced 'the politicisation of almost every facet of civilian and military involvement in the war effort and the augmentation of already existing political tensions under wartime conditions.'[7] As Ben Novick puts it, 'The Easter Rising should be seen not as a transformative moment, but rather as a moment of intensification – a fulcrum upon which public opinion pivoted.'[8] Wartime social and economic mobilisation weighed heavily on ordinary citizens across Europe. The Irish public grew increasingly disenchanted with these burdens. Charles Townshend argues of the British perspective, 'The single-minded pursuit of victory – or avoidance of defeat – came to replace the complexities and nuances of normal politics.'[9] This tunnel vision produced government policies with little consideration of their impact on Ireland. To their detriment, British politicians deferred to the military such sensitive political questions as whether to enrol the National Volunteers into the British Army, continue the Easter Rising executions, or expand conscription in 1918. Each misstep drove opinion towards republicans, who skilfully seized their opportunity.

The War of Independence has received extensive attention from impressive senior scholars such as Charles Townshend, George Boyce, Tom Garvin, Michael Laffan, Michael Hopkinson and David Fitzpatrick, who in turn inspired valuable local studies by Joost Augusteijn, Peter Hart, Fergus Campbell, Marie Coleman and John O'Callaghan among others.[10] Important speciality studies have recently been produced by Patrick Maume, Michael Wheatley, Anne Dolan, Johnathan Githenes, Jerome aan de Wiel and Ferghal McGarry.[11] However, a gap remains in the literature regarding the latter stages of the First World War, post-Easter 1916. Michael Laffan's *The Resurrection of Ireland* answered many but not all critical questions of this period. Additional exploration is needed to explain 1917–18, the much neglected first of Frank Gallagher's *Four Glorious Years*.

Some historians still view the First World War and revolution in Ireland separately, as if confined neatly within their own respective boxes. Scholars must discard the prism of political allegiance when examining Ireland and the First World War. The Easter Rising and the Conscription Crisis are as important to Ireland's First World War experience as Gallipoli and the Somme. Recent scholarship by Thomas Hennessy, Ferghal McGarry, Nuala Johnson, Charles Townshend and Ben Novick has offered specific insight into how the Great War and the revolution fed off each other.[12] This study will follow this incorporative approach, to illustrate the dynamism of war and revolution in Cork city between 1916 and 1918.

Parameters

When my father was a teenager, he accidentally blew up a chemistry laboratory during an experiment he had successfully conducted numerous times before. As he picked glass shards from his face he asked himself, 'how did that happen?' Deconstructions of the Irish Revolution are reminiscent of that ill-fated experiment. Irish counties that experienced intense revolutionary activity from 1916 to 1921 only shared a couple of common social factors: most notably, traditions of political and agrarian violence; a vibrant cultural revival movement; and a large population living above the poverty line. Different levels of these ingredients were mixed with countless other variables. Results differed not just from county to county, but often from parish to parish. This natural variation mandates local surveys to explore areas with different geographies, demographics and levels of revolutionary activity. Only by the compilation of numerous micro-studies will we truly understand the Irish Revolution.

This study explores events in Cork city, a locale Joe Lee called 'pivotal to the struggle nationally'.[13] Transforming popular opinion will be apparent in street protests, public controversies, social concerns, police activities and the state of political parties. Charles Townshend wrote, 'Politics is not merely a matter of ideas but also, above all, of organisation.'[14] Revolution occurred because republicans seized the opportunities presented by public discontent. As a result, special attention will be paid to the republican structures of Sinn Féin, the Irish Volunteers and Cumann na mBan in the city.

Easter 1916 offers a recognisable watershed that also clearly demarks Cork separatism from its pre-Rising version. To clarify the events of 1916–18, two chapters will contextualise the city's political landscape prior to the rising. The study omits the Home Rule impasse, but readers should consider its affect on the polarisation and militarisation of Irish politics. Peter Hart's *The IRA and Its Enemies* includes some material on Cork city, but largely concentrates on events in the Bandon Valley during 1920–22.[15] This book touches on Cork's Easter Rising experience, already expertly covered in Gerry White and Brendan O'Shea's *Baptised in Blood*.[16] Analysis has been incorporated into a rough chronological narrative, though some events are referenced more than once. This study generally ignores the European context of the First World War, especially the nationalist revolutions that broke out in the Austro-Hungarian Empire.

John Horne's edited collection, *State, Society, and Mobilisation in Europe during the First World War*, discussed how different states 'remobilised' public opinion in favour of the war effort during 1917 and 1918.[17] This process promoted government policies that often had unintended and destabilising consequences in Ireland. As Horne explained, 'political legitimacy remained central to the process of national mobilization.'[18] State legitimacy was seriously damaged by the Home Rule crisis, but eroded further with the Easter Rising executions, declarations of martial law and general suppression of anti-war sentiment. Readers should consider the disappearance of popular consent for the war effort in Ireland, which was best indicated by the nearly universal rejection of military conscription in 1918.

Some of the characters mentioned in this narrative are familiar: nationalist icons William O'Brien, Terence MacSwiney, Mary

MacSwiney and Tomás MacCurtain; and lesser-known figures like J.J. Walsh, Liam de Róiste, Florrie O'Donoghue, Seán O'Hegarty, Cathál O'Shannon, J.J. Horgan, Maurice Healy and Bishop Daniel Cohalan. More obscure personalities will be introduced, such as radical trade unionist John Good; republican opportunist Jerry Lane; cagey Redmondite Willie O'Connor; genial philanthropist Sharman Crawford; bemused political prisoner Tadhg Barry; and the shrewd newsagent Nora Wallace. The identities of many determined participants have been lost to history: Irish Volunteers coolly drilling on a busy street; a besieged police stenographer demanding the return of his notebook; a sailor covertly unfurling a tricolour from a ship carrying John Redmond; women outside Cork women's prison serenading Cumann na mBan prisoners; patriotic businessmen hoisting Union Jacks the day of the 1918 Armistice; a lone figure climbing atop the courthouse to grab the scales of justice; 'separation women' cheering for the Munster Fusiliers amid a republican procession; a grubby newsboy orator inspiring a mob attack on police. Their actions capture the essence of the Irish Revolution: ordinary people in extraordinary circumstances boldly declaring their political allegiance. This study shows the early stages of a mass movement composed of countless individuals and contributions. Collective action cannot always be precisely explained, but it can be documented and considered.

Existing scholarship has addressed most of the subjects mentioned in the forthcoming chapters: military recruiting levels; civilian war support; public reactions to the Easter Rising; the growth of republicanism; the decline of the Irish Party; intensification of industrial unrest; sexual policing; rising agrarian disturbances; and conscription opposition. However, these themes have largely been analysed in isolation. This book attempts to synthesise many strands of the war into a single local narrative. That account will demonstrate the global conflict's destabilising effects and explore the popularisation of anti-government sentiment in 1916–18. In doing so, it will hopefully illuminate a process that culminated a few years later with marginalised men like Florrie O'Donoghue and Bob Day briefly in control of the city of Cork.

I. Cork Political Life prior to Easter 1916

The 'Rebel City' of today was not known as such during the early part of this century: it was known throughout the length and breadth of the land as 'Rotten Cork' and 'Khaki Cork' – names which made every honest Nationalist in the city blush with shame.

Commandant P.J. Murphy, 1953[1]

In 1916, Cork city was Munster's principal commercial centre and the third largest city in (pre-partition) Ireland. The city borough had a population of 76,632 and about another 20,0000 people lived in the suburban 'liberties'.[2] Catholics accounted for 88 per cent of the city population, with Protestants (primarily Church of Ireland) and a small Jewish population making up the difference.

Geographically, Cork city was built into the bowl of a small river valley, in a wetland that gave the place its Irish name, Corcaigh. The city centre rests on reclaimed marshland on the flat of the valley, with residential neighbourhoods carved into each side of the bowl. Two branches of the River Lee flow through the city centre, emptying into the river's estuary known as the Upper Harbour. Water comprises the city's eastern border, while farmland surrounds the other sides. The city contains numerous bridges, steep hills and narrow laneways. Three main boulevards form the commercial centre of Cork: Patrick Street, the Grand Parade and the South Mall.

The Cork economy supported limited heavy industry, with some shipbuilding, linen manufacturing, brewing and distilling.[3] Numerous small factories manufactured a myriad of goods for domestic consumption, such as shoes, stationery, books and clothing.[4] Many women worked in the local textile industry, as well as for upholstery and tailoring manufacturers.[5] Cork acted as a regional retail centre, with the large drapery establishments giving the city a distinctive look.[6] A provincial transport hub, Cork served as a terminus for six railways and its busy port accounted for about 9 per cent of Irish livestock exports.[7] Though the city's world famous butter trade had been battling extinction for fifty years, many foods were processed in Cork, including butter, bacon and flour. Farmers consumed locally produced agricultural goods, such as machinery, seeds and fertiliser.[8] Construction and saw milling were also important sources of employment.[9] The British military had a significant economic presence, with roughly 100 civilians working at Victoria Barracks, while nearby Queenstown (renamed Cobh in 1920) hosted one of the Royal Navy's largest bases.

There was intense poverty in Cork. In his 1915 sociological survey, Fr A.M. MacSweeney reported 35 per cent of city residents 'in a chronic state of want', suffering from hunger, possessing a single set of clothes and often residing in tenements.[10] Another 14 per cent of the population were unskilled labourers living a 'hand-to-mouth' existence. Housing remained a pressing issue, with over 16,000 people (20 per cent of city residents) inhabiting homes classified as either unfit or barely fit for human habitation.[11] The city's high density ensured, in the opinion of historian John B. O'Brien, 'an atmosphere bordering on the claustrophobic', to which he attributes Cork's culture of intense political rivalries.[12] Like many European cities, Cork had public health concerns: in 1915 infant mortality was 132 per 1,000 births, while tuberculosis deaths numbered 2.88 per 1,000 (a total of 283 deaths).[13] Cork's widespread economic distress drew generations of city men into the British Army and Royal Navy, a practice that became particularly relevant during the First World War.[14]

Cork enjoyed a tradition of political radicalism, especially among shop assistants, skilled labourers and small shopkeepers. They generally preferred national over economic issues.[15] In the 1860s, Cork was a Fenian stronghold boasting up to 4,000 members, comprised mainly of artisans and unskilled labourers.[16] Charles Stewart Parnell represented the city in Westminster from 1880 to 1891 and spoke to monster meetings during the Land League and Home Rule campaigns.[17] Separatist politics remained part of mainstream Cork public life, reflected in large demonstrations against the Anglo-Boer War; warm civic receptions for republican radical O'Donovan Rossa; and the election of numerous ex-Fenians to Cork Corporation.[18] Constitutionalists marched alongside unrepentant Fenians during the annual Manchester Martyrs commemoration, a popular public procession.[19]

In 1916, Cork was a provincial British port city, with little to distinguish it except for a past reputation for butter, a penchant for street rioting and nostalgia for failed rebellion. There was no indication that within a few years the city would become synonymous with guerrilla violence, dramatically reclaiming its medieval moniker 'Rebel Cork'.

All-For-Ireland League

A political anomaly, Cork city was one of the few areas of Ireland not fully controlled by John Redmond's Irish Party. Since 1908, Redmondites and the All-For-Ireland League (AFIL) had furiously struggled for dominance across the county. The AFIL was the creation of William O'Brien (MP), a dynamic hero of the Land War, once considered Parnell's possible heir.[20] An impressive propagandist, thinker and orator, O'Brien fell short of political greatness, betrayed by a brittle personality and faulty political judgement. In the twentieth century, O'Brien rekindled some of his old magic and built the United Irish League (UIL) into a national force for agrarian agitation. The triumph proved short-lived as John Redmond's followers transformed the UIL into an Irish Party shell and cast O'Brien into the political wilderness. Cork city served as O'Brien's lifeboat, buoyed by a strong following of strident nationalists, trade unionists and the urban poor. Searching for allies, O'Brien reconnected with the brilliant but isolated Tim Healy. Out of favour since the Irish Party reunited in 1901, Healy departed with his 'Bantry Gang' faction (mainly cousins from west Cork), whose politics veered towards right-wing Catholic nationalism. Healy formed an unlikely alliance with O'Brien's socially progressive programme that urged 'Conference, Conciliation and Consent' with Unionists.[21]

Despite clerical opposition, O'Brien and Healy built a strong electoral coalition in County Cork composed of their personal followings, urban labour, advanced nationalists and D.D. Sheehan's radical Irish Land and Labour Association (formed from farm labourers and small farmers).[22] Cork resentment of the Irish Party's Dublin orientation likely contributed to the AFIL's success, as did tactical support from the city's unionists. The city AFIL boasted nine branches, its own marching bands and the daily *Cork Free Press* newspaper financed by O'Brien's millionaire wife, Sophie.[23] During the (second) 1910 general election, the All-For's swept County Cork, winning nine of ten constituencies. O'Brien and Maurice Healy (a talented jurist, like his brother Tim) seized the two city seats. In 1911, the AFIL also secured majorities on both Cork Corporation and Cork County Council. The AFIL/Irish Party election campaigns were notably violent, even by Irish standards, routinely producing brawls, stone-throwing and attacks more akin with nineteenth-century faction fights than twentieth-century popular politics.[24] Suffragette Susanne Day satirised Cork's polling day chaos in her book *The Amazing Philanthropist*:

The number of voters who subsequently went to the polls without bandage or sticking-plaster adjoining their heads was small. The public houses ran out of porter, the hospitals ran out of lint and bandages, the streets were impassable for nights altogether, the big drum of the Cork Exchange Band was smashed to fragments and the Gallows Green trombone was in bed for three weeks. The O'Brienite candidates marched to victory – their majority being substantially increased by a solid Unionist vote given on the sound principle that when dog eats dog, the fox comes by its own.[25]

The AFIL lacked a coherent ideology and ultimately lost a war of attrition with the Irish Party. The 1913–14 Home Rule crisis delivered a devastating blow to the AFIL. Horrified by possible partition, O'Brien and Healy opposed the Third Home Rule Bill, bewildering long-time nationalist supporters.[26] Amid the rise of Edward Carson and the Ulster Volunteer Force, the AFIL's policy of unionist conciliation fell out of step with the electorate. The Irish Party eclipsed the AFIL in the 1914 local elections. At the outset of the First World War, the All-For's condition turned terminal as much of its rank-and-file recoiled from its leadership's vocal support of recruiting.[27] Now losing money hand over fist, the daily *Cork Free Press* became a weekly. Though a potential catalyst for future anti-Redmond sentiments in Cork, the AFIL was scarcely breathing by Easter 1916.[28]

The Irish Party in Cork

In 1916 the Irish Party was ascendant in Cork city. Triumphant in the 1914 local elections, Redmondites secured a strong Corporation majority of 33 councillors agaist 12 for the AFIL (and eleven independents) and seized a twenty to twelve majority on Cork County Council.[29] The Redmondites won the Cork lord mayorship and began to purge All-For's from municipal government employment.[30] The 'Mollie Maguires' (as they were popularly known) eagerly awaited the next parliamentary election to drive a stake through the heart of their nemesis William O'Brien.

The Irish Party's Cork city organisation was powerful, flexible and multi-faceted. Five branches of the UIL served as the party's constituency organisation, answering to a city executive.[31] The UIL worked hand-in-hand with the Ancient Order of Hibernians (AOH), the national fraternal order run by Redmond's lieutenant Joseph Devlin. The Cork AOH should be viewed as an arm of the Irish Party, as 'one of the first principles of the Order' was its support for John Redmond.[32]

The Cork city AOH boasted eight divisions (branches) and two women auxiliary divisions.[33] During the pre-war years the order expanded rapidly in County Cork, attracting 1,000 new members in 1912 alone, bringing the total to 4,000.[34] The Cork AOH also formed the Hibernian Boys' Brigade, which boasted 400 boy scouts.[35] A special AOH committee worked with the UIL to ensure Hibernians filled local government patronage jobs.[36] The Order often issued voting directions to Hibernians in public office and occasionally to AOH magistrates hearing cases.[37] It encouraged members to join the Irish Volunteers, so the militia would be commanded by 'officers loyal to Mr Redmond and the Irish Party'.[38] In Cork city, the AOH was not an ally of the Irish Party but an elite within the party. Senior Hibernians directed the Irish Party in a manner that was comparable to the Irish Republican Brotherhood's role within the separatist movement.

The Irish Party retained its own armed militia: the Cork City Regiment of the National Volunteers (NV), which was led by senior Redmondites.[39] The city's NV commander Henry Donegan flatly stated: 'the Volunteers are for the purpose of supporting the Irish Party.'[40] Divided into four companies, the city NV mustered 220 poorly armed members during a 1915 mobilisation.[41] Declining since early 1915, by Easter 1916 the Cork NV maintained a skeletal organisation armed with 100 single-shot rifles.[42]

The Redmondites enjoyed a powerful mouthpiece in the *Cork Examiner*, the city's largest daily newspaper. Its editorials were stridently pro-Redmond and equally hostile towards William O'Brien and Edward Carson. Publisher George Crosbie owned another Cork daily, *The Evening Echo*, which likewise maintained a pro-Redmond stance. Crosbie was a member of the city's UIL Executive, the National Volunteers Executive and the AOH Watch Committee.[43]

Like Crosbie, Cork's other senior Redmondites displayed striking organisational overlap between the UIL, AOH and National Volunteers.[44] Coroner J.J. Horgan served on both the UIL and AOH national executives and was a captain in the Cork city National Volunteers. Henry Donegan was the UIL election agent, a senior member of the AOH and commanding officer of the city National Volunteers. Thomas Byrne was the chairman of the Cork NV, president of the Central Ward UIL branch and secretary of the AOH Second Degree Order. Jeremiah McEnery served on the executives of the Cork NV, Cork city UIL and the AOH County Board, while R.H. Geary sat on the executives of the Cork city UIL, AOH 2nd Division and Hibernian Boys' Brigade. Overall, at least twelve of the nineteen members of the 1917 UIL Executive held offices in the city AOH, while the two Redmondite lord mayors of this study (T.C. Butterfield and Willie O'Connor) were also Hibernians.[45]

The Redmondite political machine in Cork city thrived on patronage.[46] The UIL Executive controlled the public bodies in charge of various public institutions, such as the schools, hospitals, the port, the workhouse and the lunatic asylum. These governing committees exercised strong economic leverage through their management of planning, contracts and staff hiring and promotions. Though historian James McConnell has downplayed the corruption of the Irish Party during this period, studies of local government are necessary to determine the depth of this problem elsewhere in Ireland.[47] Beyond ordinary jobbery, Cork suffered from institutional corruption through predatory food prices charged by politically connected wholesalers and the controversial management of the workhouse.

The Irish Party leadership was upper-middle class, primarily composed of merchants and professionals. Former Lord Mayor Henry O'Shea owned a large bakery; George Crosbie published newspapers; ex-MP Augustine Roche was a wine merchant; Alderman Henry Dale a corn merchant; former Lord Mayor Sir Edward Fitzgerald, a builder; Lord Mayor Thomas Butterfield a dentist; and High Sheriff Henry Tilson a stockbroker. A large number of solicitors roamed the party's upper ranks, including Henry Donegan, Willie O'Connor and the ruling triumvirate of coroners William Murphy, James McCabe and J.J. Horgan. Coroner Murphy served as chairman of the Cork city UIL Executive, while coroner McCabe acted as the executive secretary. Both Murphy and McCabe were essentially backroom operators, in contrast to the dynamic and young coroner John J. Horgan, who represented Cork city on the UIL National Directory.

Educated at the elite Clongowes Wood College, J.J. Horgan was a man of many talents, who attained international celebrity for his handling of the *Lusitania* inquest in 1915. He was born into politics, as his father (also a coroner) managed Charles Stewart Parnell's Cork city base. While a young man, Horgan was active in the Gaelic League, the industrial revival movement and Daniel Corkery's Cork Dramatic Society.[48] John Redmond thought highly of the urbane and intelligent Horgan, who seemed destined to hold high office in a Home Rule Ireland.[49]

Just how powerful were the Redmondites in Cork city in 1916? The Irish Party organisation peaked during the 1914 nationalist mobilisation over the Home Rule crisis. UIL strength in Cork city and county slowly dropped in 1915. Membership dues submitted by six AOH divisions in Cork city similarly tend downwards after the beginning of the war. The decline should be attributed to an easing of tensions with Ulster, the passage of Home Rule onto the statute book and disenchantment with the prolonged war.

TABLE 1.1

RIC Report of UIL Organisation,
Cork City and East Cork, 1911–16

Quarter	Branches	Members	£ Raised
Q1 1911	52	3471	222.01.1
Q1 1912	57	3880	202.04.0
Q1 1913	59	3616	262.18.6
Q1 1914	61	3794	374.06.6
Q1 1915	55	3692	105.03.0
Q1 1916	52	2832	14.00.0

Source: RIC Crime Special Branch Reports, PRO 904/20,
      Kew National Archives

TABLE 1.2

Combined Membership Dues of Six
AOH City Divisions, 1911–16, in £

Year	Total
Q4 1911	15.16.03
Q2 1912	17.06.09
Q2 1913	17.19.06
Q2 1914	17.04.04
Q2 1915	13.19.03
Q2 1916	10.04.06

Source: U389a/5, Cork City and County Archives

The Redmondite political machine was sharpened by the two contested 1910 general elections and the 1914 local elections. These campaigns were characterised by thorough canvassing, extensive registry work and spectacular processions, along with frequent stone-throwing and police baton charges.[50] The Irish Party had weakened by 1916, but still possessed money, patronage networks and media dominance. Confidently, Redmondites waited for their moment to begin governing a Home Rule administration within the British Empire. The party remained a daunting political power, which made its subsequent collapse four years later that much more dramatic.

Labour

From 1905 to 1915, Cork's labour movement was debilitated by internal discord. Deep divisions existed between skilled and unskilled workers; national and amalgamated unions (affiliated to British-based trade unions); party politicians and non-interventionists; and supporters of the AFIL and UIL. A tiny branch of the Irish Socialistic Republican Party appeared in Cork from 1897 to 1902, but fell victim to public indifference and sustained clerical hostility.[51] The more mainstream Cork Labour Party first ran local candidates in the 1898 municipal elections, elected city mayors in 1899 and 1900 and secured five corporation seats in 1905 and six in 1908.[52] However, labour was consumed by the AFIL/UIL split, with most labour councillors flocking to William O'Brien's banner.[53] In the city suburbs, the AFIL/UIL feud also struck the agricultural labourer movement, as the Land and Labour Association divided into a pro-AFIL organisation led by D.D. Sheehan and a weaker Irish Party-allied group headed by P.J. Bradley.[54]

Another deep fissure occurred in 1909 following the traumatic Cork dock strike, which can be viewed as a successor to the 1906 Belfast dock strike and a precursor to the Dublin Lockout of 1913. James Larkin had formed the Irish Transport and General Workers Union (ITGWU) in December 1908, emphasising syndicalism, organisation of unskilled labourers and the creation of an Irish trade union distinct from Britain.[55] The ITGWU made strong inroads in Cork, attracting 800 new members, encouraging labour militancy and bringing over the local branch of the National Union of Dock Labourers (a British union).[56] In April 1909, Cork experienced a series of stoppages, some violence against non-unionised workers and a tramway strike that briefly paralysed the city.[57] The following month saw a walkout by 300 builder labourers and the first Labour Day gathering in recent memory, which Larkin addressed.[58] However, action taken by a new ITGWU-allied dock workers' union brought disaster.

In June 1909, quayside coal porters downed tools to protest against mechanisation.[59] When replacement workers were introduced, dock workers, carters and warehouse workers refused to touch goods unloaded by non-union hands. In a forceful response, major employers locked out involved sectors, intending, in the words of one police official, 'to fight the matter to a finish'.[60] The acerbic Sir Alfred Dobbin, Cork's answer to William Martin Murphy, formed the Cork Employers' Federation which vowed to dismiss all strikers and create an employers' blacklist of perceived troublemakers. For two months, strikes and employer lockouts affected between 5,000 and 6,000 workers, as the city experienced a 'state of unrest' and frequent clashes between strikers and police.[61] Workers attacked goods wagons and threw merchandise into the River Lee, while female union supporters assaulted women replacement workers on the streets and in their homes. Police reinforcements, newspaper hostility, a lack of cooperation from other unions and frequent prosecutions of labour pickets wore down the ITGWU.[62] The strike collapsed after seven weeks, resulting what Cork police officials termed 'complete victory for the masters'.[63] The Cork ITGWU branch was destroyed and its leadership purged by employers. Dublin Castle also prosecuted James Larkin, Cork ITGWU organiser James Fearon and two branch officials under the dubious charge of fraud, for having accessed funds raised by the ITGWU's dock workers' branch before it defected from the National Union of Dock Labourers. (Larkin received a one-year sentence and his colleague Fearon served six months, which contributed to his nervous breakdown.)[64]

Beyond eliminating the ITGWU in Cork for three years, the Cork dock strike ruptured the city's trade union movement. Fourteen craft unions that refused to support the dock workers' strike formed a breakaway trade union body, the Cork District Trades Council (CDTC).[65] It aligned with the Irish Party and subsequently opposed the ITGWU during the 1913 Dublin Lockout. The United Trades Labour Council (UTLC) largely supported the Cork dock strike, retained a more egalitarian membership and drifted into an AFIL orbit. Rather than pursue a clear labour agenda, the rival trades councils acted as combatants in the fierce AFIL/Irish Party rivalry. Cork labour stopped contesting elections on its own terms, as trade union officials stood instead as members of the AFIL or Irish Party. In the 1911 and 1914 municipal elections, only a single independent labour councillor was returned.[66] The 1909 dock strike also created the powerful Cork Employers' Federation, which coordinated city wage levels, supported businesses during disputes and moved aggressively against labour organisers. A final legacy was the Irish Citizen Army, the inspiration for which James Larkin attributed to his experience with the violent Cork dock strikers.[67]

Craft unions dominated the UTLC, with two notable exceptions. The National Union of Railwaymen (NUR) led by republican socialist John Good, organised unskilled workers and pushed for an independent Cork Labour Party. After imploding in 1909, the ITGWU returned to Cork in 1912 and made limited inroads among unskilled labourers. It likewise supported a separate labour party.[68] During 1914, the ITGWU established a Cork branch of the Irish Citizen Army, setting up a rifle range in the basement of the union headquarters. However, the local Citizen Army only attracted about forty members and collapsed after six months.[69] Both the NUR and ITGWU later became closely associated with the city's republican movement.

The Cork Labour Party re-launched itself in 1913, despite divisions about whether to stick strictly to labour issues or intervene in popular politics. To the relief of labour activists, the UTLC and CDTC amalgamated in late 1916, forming the Cork District Trades and United Labour Council (hereafter called the Cork Trades Council).[70] Unified and acting as the Cork affiliate of the Irish Trades Union Congress and Labour Party, local trade unionists erected a solid public platform. Labour quickly became an active and influential voice in Cork.

Unionists

Roughly 11 per cent of city residents were Protestant (Church of Ireland accounted for 8.6 per cent) and the community retained significant commercial and political power in Cork.[71] Local Protestants maintained their own distinct social structure of schools, hospitals, clubs, youth groups and support services.[72] Much of the city's large factories, shops, railways and banks were owned and/or managed by Protestants and both the Cork Chamber of Commerce and Cork Employers' Federation were considered unionist bodies. In 1916 the city and county high sheriffs were Protestants, as was the city engineer, the town clerk, the head librarian, the chief of the Fire Brigade, the Cork Asylum Board solicitor, the city treasurer and the chairman of each of the Public Works Committee, the Water Works Committee, the Carnegie Library, the County Technical Instruction Committee and the Fitzgerald Park Committee.[73]

Despite the presence of the Cork County and City Unionist Association, city unionists usually stood for office as independent or 'commercial' candidates without a formal party behind them.[74] Protestants tactically voted for the AFIL in city elections, though with little enthusiasm. By 1914, only three of the city's fifty-six corporation councillors were unionists, though unionists retained a healthy presence on other public bodies.[75] Protestant political expression was not confined to unionism, as two leading Cork Redmondites were Protestant Home Rulers: High Sheriff Henry Tilson and National Volunteer commander Maurice Talbot-Crosbie.

During the Home Rule debate, a chasm opened in Cork unionism between pragmatists amenable to a Home Rule settlement (led by Sir Stanley Harrington, Sharman Crawford and Richard Beamish) and militants rejecting any change to the Act of Union (headed by Dan Williams, Sir John Harley Scott and Sir Alfred Dobbin). Publisher H.L. Tivey supported the 'no surrender' faction and his daily *Cork Constitution* newspaper proved unceasingly hostile to nationalists throughout the war. Reporting a mob lynching of an American pacifist in 1917, Tivey headlined the story 'Just Desserts', which reflected his strident editorial orientation.[76]

Republicans and Other Advanced Nationalists

William O'Brien characterised Cork's separatists in the decade prior to the Easter Rising as 'an inestimable handful of diamonds'.[77] With only slight overstatement, one activist attributed Cork's Gaelic revival to ten or twenty families, who 'went into everything that looked national.'[78] Siblings like the Walshs (Annie, Eitne, Susan, James and Thomas), the MacSwineys (Terence, Mary, Annie and Seán), the Conlons (Seán, Eily, May and Lil), the Duggans (Peg, Bridget, Sarah and Annie) and others immersed themselves in various cultural and political organisations since 1900. Many separatists also entered the movement under their own steam, including the city's two most prominent republicans, Tomás MacCurtain and Liam de Róiste. They found a dynamic community of intelligent, motivated and experienced activists toiling in relative obscurity.

Amid a national cultural revival, the Cork Dramatic Society emerged from the Gaelic League. Inspired by Dublin's Abbey Theatre and the American Little Theatre Movement, Daniel Corkery founded the company in 1904 as a forum for locally written works. Using the Gaelic League hall (An Dún), the society staged plays by an impressive array of writers, including Corkery, Lennox Robinson, T.C. Murray (both later associated with the Abbey), novelist Con O'Leary and Terence MacSwiney. Numerous future republican leaders could be counted among society alumni, such as Seán O'Hegarty, Mary MacSwiney, Seán MacSwiney, Seán Milroy, Margaret Buckley, Bridget Duggan and Diarmuid Fawsett.[79]

In the sporting sphere, the Gaelic Athletic Association dominated organised sports in the city. By 1914, there were twelve Cork hurling clubs, eleven Irish football clubs and three camogie teams, compared to four cricket teams, three rugby clubs and seven soccer teams.[80] Hurling and Gaelic football matches routinely drew thousands to the Cork Athletic Grounds and the Cork County Board enjoyed a reputation as one of the most efficient bodies in the GAA. In 1909 separatist reformers, led by J.J. Walsh, Tadhg Barry and Michael Mehigan, took

charge of the county board. They modernised the association by introducing turnstyles, transparent accounting, referee standardisation and
systematic parish organisation.[81] Tadhg Barry produced the country's
primary hurling manual and managed its second-ever camogie team.
County board president J.J. Walsh rode his GAA success to a corporation seat in 1914, the only republican elected.[82] Numerous republicans
retained links with the Cork GAA, including camogie-playing
Cumann na mBan activists and several Gaelic footballers who later
emerged as guerrilla leaders.[83] However, GAA membership did not
necessarily correlate into advanced nationalism, as illustrated by the
name of the city's leading hurling club, Redmonds. Republican
Cornelius Murphy claimed that 90 per cent of Cork GAA members
remained aloof from politics.[84]

The city's Gaelic League started humbly in 1899, with twenty students in the home of Tadhg 'Seandun' Omurchadha, to accommodate
women barred from Irish classes in the Catholic Young Men's Society
rooms.[85] Within five years a core of school teachers helped build a
healthy organisation that included six active branches, two halls on
Queen Street (the 'Grianán' and 'An Dún'), an Irish teaching college in
the village of Ballingeary and a weekly Irish-language column in the
Cork Examiner.[86] The city Gaelic League enjoyed an eclectic intellectual
membership that included novelist Daniel Corkery; republican propagandist P.S. O'Hegarty; Capuchin College rector Fr Augustine;
University College Cork (UCC) president Bertram Windle; Augustine
Roche, MP; Brother Aloysius, Superior of the Presentation Order; and
Redmondite politician J.J. Horgan.[87]

Much of the city's revolutionary era leadership can be traced to the
Gaelic League including Liam de Róiste, Tomás MacCurtain, Mary
MacSwiney, Terence MacSwiney, Donal Óg O'Callaghan, Tadhg Barry,
Seán O'Hegarty, Margaret O'Leary and Diarmuid Fawsitt. In 1910, a
fierce dispute arose within the Cork League, when constitutionalists
denounced republicans for associating the league with politics.[88] The
republicans responded by forming the O'Growney branch, which
became a centre of separatist activities.[89] Robert Langford recalled that
branch members 'were interested and active in every forward national
movement'.[90]

Later in 1910, O'Growney branch activists founded a Cork
'sluaighte' of the republican boyscouts, Fianna na hÉireann.[91]
Headquartered in An Dún and organised by an Irish Republican
Brotherhood (IRB) cadre (Seán O'Hegarty, Tomás MacCurtain and
Tadhg Barry among others), the Fianna started with a cluster of Baden-
Powell Boy Scout defectors and grew to an estimated thirty members

in 1913 and eighty by early 1916.[92] Each Fianna scout pledged 'to work for the Independence of Ireland, never to join any of England's armed forces and to obey his superior officers'.[93] The scouts took Irish history and language lessons and laid wreathes on Fenian graves during the annual Manchester Martyrs commemoration.[94] In their distinctive blue shorts, green shirts, saffron scarves and slouch hats, the Fianna were less popular than the city's other scouting groups: the AOH Boys' Brigade, the Baden-Powell Scouts, and the Church of Ireland Boys' Brigade.[95] Similar to patriotic scouting groups across Europe, the Fianna learned map-reading, marching, first aid, camping, Morse code and knot tying. They also participated in more subversive activities, like marching through the city followed by police detectives, taking rifle target practice, distributing seditious leaflets and egging a cinema screen showing a British Army recruiting film.[96] The Fianna produced many guerrilla fighters prominent during 1920–21, some of whom did not survive the conflict.[97]

The re-emergence of militant republicanism in Cork can be directly traced to the 1898 centenary commemorations of the 1798 Rebellion; and a mass pro-Boer meeting in 1899 hosted by the Cork Transvaal Committee.[98] A few young separatists engaged with these events were recruited into the Cork Young Ireland Society, mainly composed of aging ex-Fenians who organised the annual Manchester Martyrs commemoration.[99] These not-so Young Irelanders focused on raising funds to build Cork's National Monument (completed in 1906 and dedicated to the rebels of 1798, 1803, 1847 and 1867).[100] Impatient younger members eventually left and formed the Celtic Literary Society, which J.J. Horgan quipped was 'more revolutionary than literary'.[101]

The Celtic Literary Society affiliated with John O'Leary's separatist Cumann na Gaedheal organisation. It attracted key figures like Liam de Róiste, Terence MacSwiney, Tadhg Barry, Seán O'Hegarty and Edward Sheehan.[102] Members promised 'to strive for the establishment of an Irish Republic', protested against King Edward's 1902 visit to Cork and successfully lobbied to rename streets and bridges after separatist heroes.[103] The society's rooms on Washington Street also hosted a Cork branch of Maude Gonne's women's separatist organisation, Inghinidhe na hÉireann, the forerunner of Cumann na mBan.[104] The RIC later reported that 'these societies worked hand in hand'.[105]

The Celtic Literary Society established the Cork Industrial Development Association (IDA) in 1903.[106] The association intended to improve local manufacturing in order to create more jobs in Ireland, forge economic links beyond Britain and stymie endemic emigration.[107] Initial reactions were cold: 'Many businessmen and shop keepers treated it as a joke,' recalled J.J. Horgan, 'or regarded it as a combination designed to destroy their trade.'[108] Eventually the movement featured prominent constitutionalists and commercial figures. Co-founder Edward Lorton, a republican and president of the Boot and Shoe Operators' Society, encouraged trade union involvement. Two prominent republican socialists, John Good and Tadhg Barry, joined the association leadership, which was driven by their separatist colleagues Liam de Róiste and Diarmuid Fawsitt and assisted by republicans like P.S. O'Hegarty, Seán O'Cuill, Terence MacSwiney and Tomás MacCurtain.

The Cork IDA encouraged similar organisations in Kilkenny, Limerick, Belfast, Dublin, Nenagh and Galway to form the National Industrial Conference.[109] The Cork activists designed and patented the 'Made in Ireland' trademark, claimed to be the first of its kind in the world.[110] The Cork IDA's annual Irish Industrial exhibitions incorporated Gaelic League singers, dancers and musicians to express a distinctly Irish-Ireland identity.[111] The organisation remained (nominally) non-political and non-sectarian and its standing committee included representatives from the (Protestant) Young Men's Christian Association (YMCA) and Church of Ireland Christian Young Men's Association.[112] Beyond promoting Irish-made goods, the Cork IDA also denounced overseas imitations, such as 'Irish lace' made in France, 'Ould Paddy Number One Whiskey' distilled in England and 'Donegal Tweed' produced in India.[113]

The Cork IDA aggressively pursued overseas investment opportunities for Cork by distributing commercial information material in Singapore, Australia, South Africa, Argentina, the United States and Canada.[114] In 1916 and 1917, the organisation attracted three major international developments to the city. British shipbuilders Furness, Withy and Company bought Passage West and Rushbrooke shipyards; and Manchester automobile manufacturer Trafford agreed to construct a lorry factory nearby.[115] Most spectacularly, Henry Ford built his first European factory in Cork, through a deal brokered by the Cork IDA and its secretary Diarmuid Fawsitt (with assistance from Liam de Róiste).[116] Around the same time the IDA secured regular visits from the American Moore and McCormack Shipping Line and a renewal of the Cunard Line service to Queenstown.[117] Rather than attempt to pull a 'Green Curtain' over Ireland, separatists looked both inside and outside the country for economic opportunity.[118] They sought international trade links with the Americas and Europe to develop a distinctly Irish economy that was free of British dominance. Though the Cork IDA's achievements were modest, it acted as a precursor to the later

Industrial Development Authority and showed an alternative economic path for Ireland after 1921.[119]

In the background of all this activity was a rejuvenated Irish Republican Brotherhood (IRB). At the turn of the century the Cork IRB had dwindled to one inactive circle comprised mainly of elderly veterans of the 1867 Fenian Rising. By 1908, the reorganised IRB Supreme Council tasked P.S. O'Hegarty with reviving the Cork brotherhood. O'Hegarty found the surviving Cork membership unimpressive and its leader P.N. Fitzgerald uncooperative.[120] Determined to make a clean break, O'Hegarty swore in his brother Seán and instructed him to rebuild 'The Organisation' from scratch. Seán O'Hegarty selectively approached activists in the Gaelic League, GAA, IDA and Sinn Féin.[121] Once established, the new Cork IRB remained completely separate from the 'old' IRB circle still operating in Cork, whose members 'were not now deemed up to standard'.[122] The old IRB circle continued as a fraternal organisation, but remarkably its members remained unaware of the new IRB in Cork.[123] In 1947, Cork IRA and IRB leader Florrie O'Donoghue interviewed 84-year-old John Good, a member of the bypassed IRB circle. 'He thought theirs' was the last survivor of the group [the IRB] in Cork,' wrote O'Donoghue. '. . . In the circumstances I did not say anything which would demolish a cherished belief.'[124]

From 1909 to 1916, the IRB operated from the O'Growney branch and numbered no more than twenty members.[125] One IRB brother recalled, 'Its personnel were a group of men whose national opinions were well known to each other and many had worked for years in various organisations.'[126] Among O'Hegarty's first recruits was Tomás MacCurtain, his close collaborator during the ensuing decade.[127] While the IRB promoted its members in various separatist organisations, it also supported committed republicans who remained outside the brotherhood. For example, neither Liam de Róiste nor J.J. Walsh were IRB brothers, while Terence MacSwiney only served in the organisation from 1915 to 1916. The IRB's purpose was strategic, to keep separatist organisations moving along a republican trajectory.

O'Growney branch members formed the nucleus of the Ancient Order of Hibernians American Alliance, a possible IRB front that acted as a republican counterpart to the Redmondite AOH. Familiar names like Tomás MacCurtain, John Good, Tadhg Barry, Diarmuid Fawsitt, Donal Óg O'Callaghan and Micheál Ó Cuill organised a branch of thirty-five members.[128] Robert Langford described the brotherhood as the base of 'all anti-British and anti-recruiting activity at that period', including a protest against King Edward's visit to Ireland in 1911.[129] In that episode, the group formed a Vigilance Committee to prevent Cork

Corporation submitting a loyal address to the king.[130] When the corpo-ration approved the loyal address (by a vote of twenty-seven to fifteen), separatists in the visitors' gallery unveiled an enormous black flag and later leafleted the city and draped black sheets over the National Monument.[131] In 1909, the group joined a national protest against the execution of Indian nationalist Madan Lal Dhingra in London, for his assassination of Indian colonial administrator Sir William Wyllie. Posters and leaflets reading 'Ireland Honours Madan Lal Dhingra, who was proud to lay down his life for the cause of his country' were covertly distributed in Cork, Skibbereen and various parts of the country, most likely through IRB sources.[132]

A Cork branch of Sinn Féin existed from 1906 to 1911, but died out shortly before the First World War. The Celtic Literary Society, Inghinidhe na hÉireann and the Cork Young Ireland Society merged to form a Sinn Féin branch in 1906, overcoming considerable internal debate about Arthur Griffith's dual-monarchy programme (Terence MacSwiney, among other republicans, refused to join the party). Called the Cork National Council branch of Sinn Féin, members organised a few other clubs in County Cork.[133] Branch leaders Tadhg Barry, Seán O'Hegarty and Liam de Róiste steered Sinn Féin away from municipal politics, despite overtures from the AFIL.[134] Sinn Féin, however, never caught on in the city and evolved into a kind of an Irish-Ireland interest group. 'There was a lack of enthusiasm,' recalled Liam de Róiste. 'It was difficult to keep the Cork Branch of Sinn Féin going. Tadhg Barry, secretary, was often despondent.'[135] Republicans grew disenchanted with the party's Dublin leadership, questioning its commitment to Westminster abstention and criticising covert amalgamation talks with the AFIL.[136] Branch chairman Seán O'Hegarty unsuccessfully attempted to dissolve the branch in early 1911 and he subsequently withdrew with Tomás MacCurtain and other hardline republicans.[137] The city branch apparently disappeared entirely by 1913, though local police continued to refer to the republican movement generically as 'Sinn Féin'.[138]

Cork's republican movement resembled similar Gaelic revival groupings in Dublin and Belfast.[139] It featured major national figures like Diarmuid Lynch (the most senior IRB leader to survive the Easter Rising), P.S. O'Hegarty (influential IRB and Sinn Féin writer), Margaret Buckley (future national president of Sinn Féin), Seán Milroy (Sinn Féin director of elections in 1917–18); and Frank Gallagher (future Sinn Féin propaganda director). By 1916, city separatists boasted a deep leadership bench with years of experience.

For the most part, the republican elite came from the petty bour-geoisie of small shop owners, artisans, shop assistants, clerks and low-level civil servants. A remarkable group of activists was educated at the South Monastery, a Christian Brothers' secondary school that attracted ambitious working-class students.[140] Conversely, few notable members can be traced to Cork's two prestigious Catholic secondary schools, Presentation College and Christian Brothers College, which drew from the middle and upper classes. Prior to 1916 there was also little direct separatist engagement with University College Cork faculty and students. This indicates the failure of separatism to appeal to the comfortable Catholic middle class in Cork.[141]

Though Cork separatists were small in number, they enjoyed a rich social life of dances, concerts and picnics where young men and women interacted without supervision, a rare opportunity in Irish society.[142] This helped sustain them during fifteen years of political marginalisation. Among the notable republican couples were Eitne and Tomás MacCurtain, Maura and Terence MacSwiney, Liam and Nora de Róiste and Madeleine and Seán O'Hegarty.

In the city, a few leaders dominated. The highly intelligent Diarmuid Fawsitt served as secretary of the Cork IDA and co-founded the Irish Volunteers, but he could be mercurial and difficult to work with.[143] Ballyvourney native Liam de Róiste was probably the city's best-known separatist, recognised as an industrious intellectual and Irish language expert. Bookish and thin-skinned, he lacked the common touch. GAA organiser J.J. Walsh cut a more dashing figure, but he could be domineering, impulsive and shallow. The humour of sad-faced Tadhg Barry secured his personal popularity, but his socialism was out of step with other separatists. Terry MacSwiney was a prodigious worker, good public speaker and capable organiser. However, he was also aloof, gentle and never particularly popular with the movement's rank and file.[144] Behind blazing eyes and a severe moustache, Seán O'Hegarty possessed the brains, presence and decisiveness for leadership but lacked the tact.[145] Cork's pre-eminent republican leader was the bright, charismatic and shrewd Tomás MacCurtain, who impressed all he met. One colleague recalled, 'He had the stature of a world statesman but was constrained by circumstance to operate on a small stage.'[146] Balancing warmth with pragmatism and foresight, the cherubic MacCurtain generated accolade and fierce devotion until his violent death in 1920.

The Irish Volunteers

The 1913 Home Rule crisis presented separatists with a tremendous organising opportunity, which they gladly exploited. Responding to drilling by the Ulster Volunteer Force, Eoin MacNeill launched the Irish Volunteers organisation in Dublin, which took off with strong republican support. Three weeks later, local separatists called a public meeting to inaugurate the group in Cork, under the signature of Diarmuid Fawsitt (Cork IDA), J.J. Walsh (GAA) and Liam de Róiste (Gaelic League).[147] In the background, IRB leaders Tomás MacCurtain and Seán O'Hegarty served as meeting secretaries and organisers. Invitations were issued to Irish Party and AFIL representatives, but both parties refused to formally participate. As the meeting started, AOH members (led by Irish Party councillor John Horgan) occupied the first six rows of the City Hall auditorium. Eoin MacNeill and Sir Roger Casement addressed the gathering, with MacNeill's remarks producing bedlam. Explaining that the arming of the Ulster Volunteer Force cleared the way for the Irish Volunteers, MacNeill called for three cheers for 'Carson's Volunteers'. This sparked a seemingly pre-arranged assault by the Hibernians, who stormed the platform, attacked the speakers and brawled wildly with meeting organisers. One AOH member knocked J.J. Walsh unconscious with a chair and more serious damage was only prevented by a handy Fianna lad who hit the house lights, causing the Hibernians to flee in the darkness.[148] When the lights returned, de Róiste renewed the meeting from atop a chair, amid defiant cheers and singing from supporters, who passed up hundreds of membership slips. 'Such was the blood-baptism of the Volunteers,' mused J.J. Walsh years later, 'in what up to then we were pleased to call Rebel Cork.'[149]

The Cork Volunteers initially numbered about 150 and drilled under an ex-British Army sergeant in the O'Growney branch head-quarters, An Dún. By April 1914, the organisation had secured its own meeting hall and paraded in the Cork Corn Market. The same month, the Cork Cumann na mBan was founded. City organisers launched Volunteer companies around County Cork and by early May the movement had made considerable headway. That month, John Redmond approved Irish Party participation and within weeks his fol-lowers took a majority position on its national Provisional Committee. At this stage, the organisation's membership was composed of arti-sans, labourers, shop assistants and clerks, along with a smattering of professionals (mainly accountants and salesmen). That same demo-graphic was still apparent in the city Volunteers in 1920, with the exception of the UCC students, who did not join the organisation in numbers until 1917.

TABLE 1.3

Cork City Irish Volunteers Occupations,
July 1914[150]

Occupation	Number	Per cent
Shop Assistant	19	9%
Artisan	79	37%
Un/Semi-Skilled	52	24%
Clerk	24	11%
Shop Keeper	15	7%
Teacher	3	1%
Professional	18	8%
Merchant	4	2%

Sample: 214

Source: Irish Volunteers Cork City Corps Rolls, Liam de
Róiste Papers, U271A, CCCA

Beginning in late May 1914, AOH members flooded into the County Cork Volunteers, assuming charge of numerous branches in the process.[151] AOH leaders lamented their failure to seize the Cork city organisation, but boasted, 'judging by the numbers in which our men are joining[,] this Corps too will be properly led and directed under officers loyal to Mr Redmond and the Irish Party.'[152] Having received Redmond's blessing, the Cork city Volunteers jumped from about 250 to roughly 1500 members by late summer.[153] Irish Party supporter Captain Maurice Talbot-Crosbie (ex-British Army) took command of the city unit, while five Redmondites joined the Cork Volunteer Executive Committee. However, the executive formed a 'military council' composed of five IRB leaders (MacCurtain, Seán O'Hegarty, Seán O'Sullivan, Seán Murphy and Patrick Corkery), that kept a republican hand firmly on the tiller.[154]

Cork's Irish Volunteers drilled throughout the uneasy summer, until the unexpected outbreak of war in Europe. The conflict drove an immediate wedge between moderate and militant Irish nationalists, with the vast portion of public opinion supporting the former. Though an obscure minority in August 1914, the separatists found themselves masters of the city four years later.

II. Cork and the First World War, 1914 to Easter 1916

. . . They have mistaken a momentary apathy for acquiescence
Terence MacSwiney, 1914[1]

On 4 August 1914, Great Britain declared war on Germany. During the ensuing days in Cork, crowds crushed into the train station to see off hundreds of reservists called up for active service. A newspaper reporter observed that 'in the working class quarters of Cork, there is scarcely a home that has not been affected'.[2] Three weeks later, 1,000 citizens attended a recruitment rally at Cork City Hall organised by unionists and the AFIL, which promised Britain 'the manhood of Ireland'. 'It would not do to say they were willing to fight for Poland, or Belgium, or France,' argued William O'Brien, 'but they had got to say they were willing to fight for England.'[3]

Split in the Volunteer Movement

As Irish unionists and nationalists unified to face the war crisis, pressure grew on the Irish Volunteers to offer their services to the government. Speaking to the House of Commons on 3 August 1914, John Redmond promised to 'defend the coasts of our country' with the Irish Volunteers and the Ulster Volunteers.[4] The following week, Prime Minister Asquith announced the War Office's intention to arm and train the Irish Volunteers, which Redmond quickly confirmed.[5] Indicative of the rapidly evolving situation, the Cork Volunteers received a £5 donation from Major General John Keir, commander of the British Army's 6th Division in Cork.[6] However, for constitutional nationalists, War Office cooperation came with a price. As the RIC Cork county inspector explained to Dublin Castle, 'a large number of them [Cork Volunteers] will not in any way assist the Government unless and until Home Rule is placed on the statute book.'[7]

Within the Cork Volunteer leadership, republicans and Redmondites split over the decision to serve in the war. Tomás MacCurtain

25

(representing the republican faction) and Captain Maurice Talbot-Crosbie (on behalf of Irish Party officials) exchanged acrimonious letters in the *Cork Examiner*, offering the pros and cons of war participation.[8] On 30 August 1914, 1,000 Volunteers gathered at the Cork Corn Market to determine the organisation's war policy. After listening to spokesmen from each side, an officer asked (pro-war) Talbot-Crosbie if the Volunteers would be made to serve 'in any part of the world that Great Britain sends them to'. Talbot-Crosbie promised they would not be deployed overseas without John Redmond's approval. This satisfied nearly all the Volunteers, who hoisted Talbot-Crosbie onto their shoulders and triumphantly paraded from the market. Just seventy men remained standing with the dejected republican officers.[9]

Two political militias now operated in Cork – the Irish Party-affiliated National Volunteers (NV), and the much smaller Republican Irish Volunteers. The latter group returned to the familiar margins of Cork's body politic, though it retained a clear message and most of the militia's committed officers. Senior Irish Party officials now commanded the National Volunteers, and intended to use their new organisation to implement Redmond's vision of a Home Rule Ireland.[10]

Historian Brian Girvin provides a handy summation of the Irish Party's rationale for participating in the war: 'it would confirm and secure Home Rule, and that it might find the basis for consensus among Irish people once the conflict ended.' Such attitudes were apparent in Cork. Irish Party leader J.J. Horgan remarked in 1914, 'They should stand or fall together, and in that way Ireland would look forward to the success of English arms.'[11] The *Cork Examiner* believed that since the Irish people had proved 'they may be relied upon in any emergency', the government should move quickly to settle the Home Rule impasse.[12] A Cork AOH circular warned that 'the betrayal and disappointment of the hopes of the Irish people in the matter of self-government would be an act of sheer lunacy by any Government'.[13] In Mid-September the policy seemed to work, as the Home Rule Bill was moved onto the statute book, though implementation was delayed for a minimum of one year. The *Examiner* argued that war service presented Ireland with an opportunity to 'make good the promise given her leader now that she has been given self-government'.[14] The AOH County Board brokered no internal criticism of the new policy, warning: 'members holding opinions contrary to those expressed by the Irish Party . . . should be asked to consider their position as members of the Order.'[15] Across the party divide, William O'Brien, MP, wrote, '. . . it is not Belgium's war, but Ireland's own war for her very existence the 'recruiting sergeants' are endeavouring to obtain recruits for.'[16] His newspaper celebrated the enlistments of AFIL members, noting that additional recruits would make them 'blissfully secure as to the future of Home Rule'.[17]

Cork Self-Mobilisation

First World War scholars use the term 'self-mobilisation' to describe voluntary participation in the war, as individuals joined the armed forces and/or contributed to the civilian war effort.[18] Within the city's nationalist community, self-mobilisation initially achieved limited success but (like other war-weary combatants) showed clear signs of deterioration by 1916.

The Cork public almost fully backed the war effort for the first twelve months of hostilities. In April 1915, the Cork RIC reported, 'with the exception of a small gang of Sinn Féiners . . . the bulk of the people in the Riding were in sympathy with the British Empire in the war,' and in June believed 'a large majority' sympathised with the Allies.[19] In this period brass bands and crowds often accompanied recruits to the railway station.[20] Anti-recruiting activity was limited to occasional covert distribution of posters, pamphlets and 'mosquito press' newspapers by republicans.[21] Speaking in Cork during September 1914, James Larkin denounced the war to an audience of 1,000, but drew just 300 the following month when he stopped on his way to America.[22] (He blasted, '. . . In God's name never take the dirty Saxon shilling for remember[,] he who does is a traitor to Ireland.')[23] Anti-war sentiments did not sit well in Cork. At the outset of the war, O'Brienites 'beat hell out of' three republicans distributing anti-war pamphlets outside an All-For-Ireland League meeting, landing all three in the hospital.[24] 'There were incidents when people spat into our collection boxes,' recalled one pre-Rising IRA veteran. 'There was one solitary Volunteer in Douglas; he was almost a pariah and dare not wear his equipment when leaving home.'[25] Another republican described the Irish Volunteers in County Cork during this period as 'little communities of Trappist monks in a pagan country'.[26]

During 1914 and 1915, public bodies (controlled by the Irish Party) vocally supported the war. When the postal authorities transferred republican town councillor J.J. Walsh out of Ireland in November 1914, Cork Corporation refused to condemn the action.[27] (Redmondite councillor J.F. O'Sullivan claimed 'Sinn Féin' was 'only supported by a few political cranks'.)[28] In early 1915, the corporation stripped the freedom of the city from German Gaelic scholar Kuno Meyer, after he urged captured Irish soldiers to join Casement's brigade.[29] Despite shouts of 'felon setter' from Alderman and ex-Fenian Paddy Meade, the motion passed by twenty-three votes to three, in what writer Daniel Corkery called 'the lowest point reached in their national helot-like public carping'.[30] The same month, corporation Redmondites bestowed the freedom of the city on the outgoing lord lieutenant, Lord Aberdeen; the Cork NV provided an honour guard during his ensuing visit.[31] Much of the Irish Party elite attended a 1915 testimonial dinner for County Cork war hero Michael O'Leary, VC.[32] Two weeks later, at a 1915 St Patrick's Day luncheon, George Crosbie 'celebrated Irish loyalty during the present crisis', while coroner McCabe congratulated Irish soldiers fighting to secure 'the liberty of Ireland'.[33]

Enlistments into the British military flowed from the city of Cork in 1914 and most of 1915.[34] Overall, 6,272 men from County Cork joined the military in the first year of the war, and a further 2,088 enlisted from the city alone from August 1915 to August 1916.[35] Though recruiting data cannot be discerned for the city itself after mid-1916, an estimated 6,000 to 7,000 Cork residents served in the British forces by war's end. Military recruiting totals for County Cork were about average for Ireland, but figures within the city were on the higher end of national figures.

Previous scholarship has explored motivations for enlisting, which included a desire to validate Irish Home Rule aspirations through military service, British Imperial pride, economic necessity, a spirit of adventure, family traditions of military service, and peer pressure.[36] Economic need seemed an important enticement in Cork, especially as the conflict dragged on. War Office newspaper advertisements in 1915 told enlisting workers to ask their employers to keep their positions open ('all patriotic employers are helping their men to join'),[37] and emphasised separation allowances for dependents, death benefits and (curiously) disability pensions for maimed servicemen.[38] By mid-September 1916, over 3,000 Cork servicemen dependents received separation allowances and pensions.[39]

Army enlistments briefly jumped in May 1915, after the liner *Lusitania* was torpedoed about thirty miles from Cork Harbour.[40] In the following days, stunned survivors wandered about the city's hotels, while the *Cork Examiner* ran graphic photos of corpses and gut-wrenching inquiries about missing loved ones.[41] Public bodies vigorously condemned the sinking, such as Cork Corporation ('the foul and dastardly act'), Cork Poor Law Guardians (PLG) ('the most fiendish murders'), Cork AOH ('an insult to civilisation'), the Cork National Volunteers ('the brutal murder'), and Cork District Asylum ('a crime that shocked humanity').[42] At the *Lusitania* inquest, coroner J.J. Horgan suggested the coroner's jury return its famous verdict of 'wilful and wholesale murder' against 'the officers of said submarine and the Emperor and Government of Germany'.[43] Five years later, his verdict was echoed by a Cork coroner's jury that indicted the British prime minister and other high officials for the assassination of republican lord mayor Tomás MacCurtain.

TABLE 2.1

Ratio of Men Available for Military Service to Men Enlisted, in Irish County and City Districts, October 1916

Area	Ratio	Area	Ratio	Area	Ratio	Area	Ratio
Belfast Boro	0.20	Carlow	1.40	Kilkenny	2.03	Clare	2.98
Armagh	0.82	Kings	1.53	Limerick	2.06	Leitrim	3.56
Monaghan	0.82	Queens	1.55	Westmeath	2.15	Galway	3.81
Londonderry	0.90	Kildare	1.57	Louth	2.16	Roscommon	3.83
Dublin Metro	1.03	Tyrone	1.73	Sligo	2.43	Donegal	4.11
Antrim	1.05	Waterford	1.75	Wexford	2.46	Mayo	5.03
Down	1.06	*Co Cork*	*1.94*	Meath	2.70	Kerry	5.16
Fermanagh	1.24	Wicklow	1.95	Cavan	2.71		
Tipperary	1.26	Longford	1.97	Dublin Co	2.72		

Source: Statement Giving Particulars of Men of Military Age in Ireland, 1916, HC
    XVII.581, CD 8390, Parliamentary Papers

Government coercion should feature in any discussions of First World War enlistment. Under Defence of the Realm Act (DORA) regulations, the government could imprison citizens, confiscate literature, and suppress publications discouraging recruiting. In late 1914, Terence MacSwiney's anti-war newspaper *Fianna Fáil* was shut down after just three months in operation.[44] Acting on instructions from Dublin Castle, the Post Office transferred three senior Irish Volunteer leaders in their employment from Cork to England. Both J.J. Walsh and P.S. O'Hegarty reluctantly accepted the move, but Seán O'Hegarty refused it.[45] He was then dismissed from the postal service and served with a DORA order giving him twenty-four hours to leave Cork city and east Cork or face possible life imprisonment. For the next two years O'Hegarty worked as a labourer in the Ballingeary area of west Cork. Government power gently but firmly pushed Irishmen towards the front line throughout this period.

All four Cork daily newspapers maintained strong support for the war and encouraged recruiting. Future IRA leader Florrie O'Donoghue recalled that in this period he was exposed only to 'unquestionably pro-British' publications.[46] The papers closely monitored battlefield progress and celebrated British and Allied victories when they occurred (or were reported to have occurred). Approving stories detailed the meritorious service of local men fighting in exotic locations across the globe.

As Lord Kitchener raised his citizen armies in early 1915, the War Office launched a major recruiting campaign in Cork.[47] Colourful parades and emotional appeals enticed young men. 'Sustained and intense, with the glamour and the glory emphasised in a thousand ways,' remembered O'Donoghue, 'it took many a young lad with no better appreciation of issues than I had, so completely off his feet that the appeal was irresistible.'[48]

During the 1915 recruitment campaign, Cork speakers repeatedly warned of a German invasion. Justice of Peace J.D. Kelleher believed the Germans would soon arrive on Irish shores;[49] Francis Lyons demanded the Irish 'help repel the attacks of the German barbarians';[50] and UCC Professor A.E. Moore argued, 'the way to prevent the invasion of Ireland was by sending over to the fighting line every fit man and that at once.'[51] Cork recruiting speeches also exploited public anger over German atrocities in Belgium (both real and imagined) which had been emphasised in the controversial Bryce Report.[52] UCC student St John Giusani asked residents to envision themselves as Belgians, 'with the German hordes roaming about Cork with children stuck upon their bayonets'.[53] Captain R.E. Roberts (a National Volunteer leader) claimed Germans 'murdered and maltreated the clergy and women and children of that country', and Church of Ireland Reverend A.E. French announced Germany's supposed execution of 300 Belgian priests.[54] A War Office advertisement in the *Cork Free Press* ominously asked Irish women, 'Have you thought what they would do if they invaded Ireland?'[55] Adverts in the *Cork Examiner* denounced Germany, 'which glories in the desecration of churches, the violation of women, and the murder of children'.[56]

Beyond emphasising alleged German crimes against Catholic priests and churches, Cork recruiters repeatedly claimed German soldiers sexually assaulted nuns in Belgium. The Earl of Bandon warned of 'anti-christ' Kaiser Wilhelm's rampaging troops: 'They violated the nuns; they put children up on the point of their bayonets and carried them through the streets of Belgium.'[57] The Irish Party's Tom Kettle claimed Cork republicans would greet German invaders with the words, 'you broke your pledge in Belgium; you murdered priests; you violated nuns . . . Come, then, and set Ireland free.'[58] J.D. Kelleher argued that if the Germans came to Ireland they would 'torture and shoot priests, outrage nuns, burn their churches, and rob rich and poor alike'.[59] Crown clerk D.J. O'Connell spoke of 'nuns driven out, and the greatest horror of all, their purity violated'. He continued, 'Fifty Belgian nuns who have come to this country were violated by these brutal men.'[60]

Recruiters also expressed contempt for the city's 'Sinn Féiners'. Captain Philips called them 'worms, not men', while Lieutenant Maurice Healy used the more palatable 'shirker' label.[61] Tom Kettle mocked Cork republicans by shouting, 'Three cheers for the Cork revolutionary cowards and slackers.' He accused them of applauding for Germany as corpses from the *Lusitania* were carted through the streets of Queenstown.[62] Despite such insults, outnumbered Cork republicans seldom disrupted early recruiting meetings.[63]

Most nationalist politicians did not openly join the recruiting effort. James McConnell has detailed the general aloofness of Irish Party MPs from recruiting. In Cork similar attitudes were visible further down the political food chain.[64] Only three of the Irish Party's thirty-three town councillors directly participated in the recruiting effort (J.F. O'Riordan, M.J. O'Riordan and Henry Tilson). A survey of fourteen Cork city recruiting meetings during 1914–15 found two local Irish Party officials speaking on the platforms (Tilson and J.F. O'Riordan), comprising one of twenty members of the UIL Cork City Executive.[65] The UIL triumvirate of coroners McCabe, Murphy and Horgan likewise never appeared on a Cork recruiting platform. When the Cork City and County Recruiting Council formed in March 1915, only Lord Mayor Henry O'Shea, J.F. O'Riordan and Henry Tilson joined the largely unionist committee, despite direct appeals to leading Redmondites J.J. Horgan and Henry Donegan.[66] J.J. Horgan did covertly assist the recruiting council by suggesting a speaking tour by Inchageela native and Victoria Cross winner Sergeant. Michael O'Leary.[67] (While Michael O'Leary proved a recruiting success, authorities dispensed with the services of his father after he complained to a Macroom audience, 'The Irish never got their rights from England, but the Irish fought her battles.'[68]) However, Henry Donegan (a senior Irish Party official and the new commander of the city NV) believed that if he and Horgan explicitly participated in the recruiting drive, they would 'bring disrepute' and 'cause a stampede' of members out of the National Volunteers.[69]

Military-aged Redmondites, such as J.J. Horgan, Thomas Byrne, Eugene Gayer and Henry Donegan, failed to join the colours. Of thirty-three town councillors, one (J.F. O'Riordan) enlisted, and none of the twenty-one members of the UIL Executive served. Captain Maurice Talbot-Crosbie was the only senior leader of the Cork National Volunteers to enter the British Army. Overall, just five of the twenty-seven Cork city National Volunteer officers in 1915–16 served in the war.[70] A republican later mocked two leading military-aged Redmondites, 'They'd shed all others' blood but not their own.'[71]

The senior All-for-Ireland League leadership participated more directly in the recruiting campaign. Party leaders William O'Brien and Maurice Healy spoke at a recruiting meeting at the outset of the war. Healy's wife was involved in the voluntary war effort, and his son Maurice Jr., a city solicitor, enlisted and appeared on recruiting platforms in 1915.[72] Virtually alone among prominent public officials in County Cork, the AFIL's D.D. Sheehan (MP for Mid-Cork and head of the Irish Land and Labour Association) enlisted, along with three sons who were educated at Christians College in the city. Sheehan served with distinction on the Western Front, but lost two sons in action with the Royal Flying Corps and had his daughter wounded while a nurse on the Western Front.[73] However, similar commitment to the war was not apparent below the AFIL top rank. AFIL councillors and branch officials in Cork did not enlist, recruit or engage with the voluntary war effort. Like the Irish Party, the AFIL rank and file supported the war, but did not embrace it.

Catholic Church leaders were even more ambivalent about the war. In his 1915 Lenten pastoral letter, Cork's critical Catholic bishop T.A. O'Callaghan described the situation as 'the darkest and saddest in all human history', which he attributed to European governments 'casting off the yoke of Christ'.[74] His successor, Bishop Daniel Cohalan, linked Irish war participation with Home Rule, arguing, 'all that support would fail if the hopes of the people failed.'[75] Throughout the conflict, neither O'Callaghan nor Cohalan participated in recruiting efforts, and none of the city's Catholic clergy appeared on recruiting platforms.

Church of Ireland clerics, on the other hand, supported the war and spoke at Cork recruiting rallies. Cork's Bishop Dowse encouraged young Corkmen 'to find their way to the nearest recruiting officer'.[76] 'War is very awful,' warned the Church of Ireland Dean of Cork, but there was something worse, '. . . cowardice, betrayal, selfishness, and refusing the call to duty'.[77] During the war, Church of Ireland congregations, but not Catholic churches, celebrated intercession services to pray for Britain's victory.[78]

Voluntary war work in Cork retained a pronounced unionist identity, utilising Church of Ireland structures and attracting few nationalists.[79]

Primarily unionists comprised the Cork Women's Emergency Committee, which provided clothing to Irish regiments, and the Cork
Committee of the National Relief Fund (to raise money for the dependents of reservists).[80] Nationalists were noticeably absent from other
war-assistance organisations, including the Cork Soldiers' Institute, the
Red Cross Collection Committee, the Munster Fusiliers' Aid Society, the
Tipperary Club, and the Soldiers' and Sailors' Free Buffet (which served
over 440,000 meals to troops at the local rail station from 1914 to 1918).[81]
Cork's (Protestant) YMCA managed the Cork Soldiers' Institute (a servicemen's club), a railway hostel for servicemen, and the troop
entertainment hut at Victoria Barracks.[82] The Cork city branch of the
Volunteer Training Corps (a War Office home guard for men ineligible
for military service) was organised by the Church of Ireland Young
Men's Association, and described by police as 'primarily Unionist'.[83]
There is little evidence of corresponding voluntary war work by Cork
Redmondites or participation by Catholic Church structures. A notable
exception was a committee to assist fifty Belgian war refugees relocated
to Cork, which drew republican Mary MacSwiney, Catholic priests, and
town councillors who later sympathised with Sinn Féin.[84]

The National Volunteers

The Irish Party intended for the National Volunteers to be treated as
the embryonic army of the new Irish Home Rule state.[85] This reflected
Redmond's desire to use the war to express Irish nationality, so, in
George Boyce's words, 'Ireland would take her place as a Home Rule
Government in the United Kingdom, and as a nation equal with the
other nations of the British Empire.'[86] In those first few months, the
government could have used the National Volunteers to build robust
support for the war across Ireland.[87]

At the war's outset, diverse bodies such as the Cork Church of
Ireland Young Men's Association, the University College Cork student
body, and the suffragist Munster Franchise League formed their own
National Volunteer branches (the suffragettes started an NV Ambulance
Corps).[88] Unionist ex-army officers with double-barrelled names flocked
to the Cork NV, including county sheriff Philip Harold Barry, Colonel
James Grove-White, Colonel A.H. Wood, and Colonel Standish-
Harrison.[89] In the city NV, Captain H.W. Bowher (ex-Suffolk Regiment)
became inspecting officer, while the new commanding officer was
Jeremiah Smith-Sheehan, an elderly gentleman adventurer who fought
with the Papal Army, French Zouaves, Spanish Carlists, and 'in several
Argentine revolutions'.[90] County Cork inspecting officer Captain R.E.

Roberts (ex-Royal Engineers) tactfully pointed out the 'want of the right class of men' among the Cork NV officers, and urged a reversion to Ireland's natural ruling order: 'No pains ought to be spared to get men of a better social status,' he sniffed, '– gentlemen in plain words.'[91] A similar feudalistic attitude was also seen in the mobilisation of rural military auxiliaries in Britain and within the Ulster Volunteer Force.[92]

The *Cork Examiner* warned the government that failure to deploy the National Volunteers or form a distinctly Irish corps in the British Army (similar to Australia and Canada) would 'diminish and frustrate the patriotic desire of the Irish National Volunteers to play their part in the great struggle against German aggression'.[93] Yet, it became increasingly clear to the Irish Party that instead of National Volunteers guarding Irish beaches, the government wanted nationalists in khaki, fighting in France as part of the British Army. During September 1914, Joseph Devlin told Cork National Volunteers that compared to the Ulster Unionists, 'there were five times as many men willing to die, if necessary, for the principle of Irish nationality.'[94] Speaking before 5,000 city Redmondites at an NV review during November 1914, Willie Redmond accurately promised, '. . . If the day comes when the honour of Ireland requires her sons to go abroad, I will not beat around the bush. I will say, those of you willing to go abroad, follow me and I will go with you.'[95]

Despite these pleas, Irish Party adherents did not rush into the military. In 1915, 378 National Volunteers from Cork city and east Cork joined the British Army, 17 per cent of the total recruits received in the area.[96] However, with an estimated 5,300 NV members in that region, the enlistment figure accounted for only 7 per cent of NV members, well below the national average of 17 per cent.[97] Enlistment percentages from the Cork city NV Regiment may have been slightly higher, but hardly impressive.[98] Writing to the press in March 1915, NV adjutant W.T. Daunt reported that 60 out of 500 members had joined the British forces since the war's outbreak.[99] Unionists scoffed at the modest contribution of the city NV.[100] 'Cork for generations to come,' wrote 'A Brigadier', 'will be branded with the stigma of having had a thousand trained men, of whom only 60 were willing to fight for the country when called for.'[101]

Gerry White and Brendan O'Shea have explored the Cork NV's attempt to act as 'Ireland's Army of Defence', which culminated in the formation of an NV 'bridge guard'.[102] During January 1915, the NV provided armed nightly patrols for two local railway bridges, despite O'Brienite jibes against the 'Molly Watchmen' and 'The heroes of the night watch'.[103] NV officers told police they were 'anxious to do all they can to assist the government', and reported that when the patrols started many lapsed members returned to the NV ranks.[104] However, the military disbanded the bridge guard just four weeks later, as Brigadier-General Hill explained he would not 'allow citizens who do not belong to the Crown forces to bear arms in defence of the realm'.[105] Redmondite University College Cork president Sir Bertram Windle complained to Prime Minister Asquith: 'Nothing could do them more harm or act more effectively against the growing sense that Ireland is part of the Empire than to tell them in so many words that they are not trusted even to look after a few bridges in the city in which they live.'[106]

By February 1915, NV commander Henry Donegan reported 'an all round feeling of slackness. Men tell my officers too – that it is getting on their nerves to appear in uniform.'[107] Appealing for War Office sponsorship, he plaintively asked his headquarters 'if Kitchener will ever see that he is ignoring the best fighting race in the world'[108] The following month, Colonel East, commanding the British Army's Cork Recruiting District, advised National Volunteers to join the army. He theatrically warned that in the event of German invasion, the NV would be considered unlawful combatants and 'the Germans would shoot any man captured'.[109] As invasion fears waned, the rationale for the NV evaporated. Members also worried that the organisation could be classified as yeomanry or militia, which would make members eligible for military service. This anxiety furthered the NV decline.[110] By the end of 1915, the Cork NV had become largely a skeleton force.

Changing Public Opinion in 1915 and Rising Conscription Fears

In December 1915, Tom Kettle spoke at a recruiting rally of 5,000 on Patrick Street. Braving calls of 'slacker' and 'coward' from the audience, 200 republican hecklers brought the meeting to a standstill.[111] John Redmond had intended to attend the same meeting, along with the Lord Lieutenant and William O'Brien, but he first checked with the city UIL Executive. ('When I am ready to meet Carson etc,' wrote Redmond, 'it seems to me absurd to refuse to stand on the same platform as O'Brien.')[112] J.J. Horgan waved him off, arguing that the appearance would 'do no possible good to recruiting'.[113] 'Our people here have given generously of their best,' continued Horgan. 'There is not one of us who has not some near relative in the firing line.' To Horgan, the growing threat came from Cork's 'Sinn Féiners':

> The fear of conscription has drawn many of our people into their
> ranks and I have no doubt whatever that if conscription is sought

to be enforced here there will be serious trouble. I am quite sure that the best aid to recruiting in Ireland would be a definite statement by the Government that conscription will not be applied to us, but it seems to me that the Government are heading in exactly the opposite direction.[114]

TABLE 2.2

Irish Catholic Monthly Enlistments, Pre-Rising*

Year	Month	Total	Year	Month	Total
1915	May	3,598	1915	Nov.	3,436
1915	June	3,260	1915	Dec.	2,073
1915	July	2,011	1916	Jan.	1,779
1915	Aug.	2,448	1916	Feb.	1,281
1915	Sept.	2,145	1916	March	771
1915	Oct.	1,413	1916	April	827

Source: John Redmond Papers, MS 15,259, NLI
* Months are four-week periods, starting at the 15th of the prior month and ending on the 15th of the listed month.

TABLE 2.3

County Cork Annual Enlistments, First and Second Years of the War

Period	Total
Aug. 1914–Aug. 1915	6,272
Aug. 1915–Oct. 1916	2,088

Source: Statement Giving Particulars of Men of Military Age in Ireland, 1916, HC XVII.581, CD 8390, Parliamentary Papers

Long casualty lists, unthinkable just two years earlier, were now commonplace as Irish troops entered killing grounds in Flanders, Salonika, and especially Gallipoli.[115] By war's end the local toll included an estimated 1400 residents who perished in the inferno.[116] Recognising mounting military manpower shortfalls, public fear of conscription mounted. During 1915 senior RIC officials warned that mandatory military service would face serious opposition from 'Sinn Féin and Redmondites', including physical resistance from republicans.[117] At a Cork anti-conscription meeting in January 1916, 1,500 listened to Fr Michael Flanagan threaten, 'Unless England altered a great deal she would be an enemy . . . and the harbours of Ireland might become submarine bases.'[118] The platform included familiar separatists like Tomás MacCurtain, Terence MacSwiney and John Good, but also four Capuchin priests, previously uninvolved in politics.

Despite initial enthusiasm, Ireland had never fully self-mobilised for the war effort, preferring, in the words of Charles Townshend, 'mental neutrality'.[119] Irish enlistments remained far lower than the rest of the United Kingdom, with just 6 per cent of available males joining the colours from 1914–1917, against 24 per cent in England, 22 per cent in Wales, and 24 per cent in Scotland.[120] Ireland also failed to match the Dominions' enlistment rates of 19 per cent for New Zealand, Canada's 13 per cent, Australia's 13 per cent, and South Africa's 11 per cent.[121] When examining Southern Ireland's low enlistments, David Fitzpatrick argues that they 'had more to do with inadequate market research than political alienation', owing to the government's failure to successfully leverage Irish social organisations.[122] However, this does not adequately explain why nationalist institutions required such special attention, or why the population underperformed compared with the rest of the empire. Keith Jeffery offers a more nuanced view of Irish enlistments, recognising a political dimension to Ireland's low recruitment but placing it within the context of war weariness elsewhere.[123] 'The progressive (though not consistently so) unwillingness of Irishmen to serve Britain and, by extension the Empire,' he wrote, 'may say as much about the contemporary attitudes to the war throughout the British Isles as it does about political circumstances in Ireland.'[124] While perhaps underestimating Irish reluctance to serve the crown, Jeffery does offer an intriguing perspective on the second half of the First World War. Ireland had an anti-government tradition, an ambivalent political ruling class, a talented separatist leadership ready to exploit new opportunities; institutions in place to mobilise opposition, and a catalyst in the Easter Rising. This raises the question: had they possessed similar elements, would other parts of the British Empire have experienced as much anti-government turmoil as Ireland?

British social and economic mobilisation for total war required more frequent government intrusions into Irish affairs. The growing war burden fed longstanding Irish suspicions of government coercion, propaganda and unfair treatment of Ireland. Already, Cork magistrates chafed under DORA regulations, refusing in February 1916 to punish republicans Thomas Kent and Terence MacSwiney for 'very violent, disloyal utterances'.[125] As war opposition increased, experienced republican organisers directed it into anti-state organisations like Sinn Féin, the Irish Volunteers and Cumann na mBan. The harnessing of anti-government sentiment had begun prior to the 1916 Easter Rising, but rapidly accelerated afterwards.

Though politically isolated at the start of the war, the Irish

Volunteers constructed a tight body dedicated to resist conscription or any attempt to disarm them. Police noted increasing support for the movement in Cork during 1915.[126] By the year's end, the Cork city Volunteers numbered about 300, organised into four companies.[127] Primarily working- and lower middle-class, the Volunteers retained a single solicitor and few university-educated members.[128] Activists possessed little of the economic and social clout that authorities assumed was necessary for successful political mobilisation. After the Easter Rising, the Cork RIC described the Irish Volunteer movement:

> It received no support from any influential people from its inception up to the rebellion. It was principally composed of shop assistants, clerks, artisans, labourers . . . It was piloted by advanced extremists or failures in various walks of life in which they started. A great number in the ranks were young men under 21 years, amongst whom the reading of the pernicious literature that was being circulated had such a deleterious effect.[129]

Though dismissed by police, Cork republicans possessed vibrant political organisations in Sinn Féin, the Irish Volunteers and Cumann na mBan that allowed for quick and decentralised expansion. When public opinion shifted after The Rising, republicans with speed and sureness seized their fleeting opportunity to form a mass movement. Much of their subsequent success can be attributed to the presence of a critical mass of advanced nationalists, created in obscure meeting rooms over the better part of two decades.[130]

Though inferior in class terms to their nationalist competitors, the republican cadre was comprised of experienced and devoted activists who well understood the art of political organising. They knew how to run meetings: to send invitations and agendas; appoint secretaries and chairs; create action items, and keep minutes. They could plan demonstrations: publicise the event; appoint practised speakers; create a spectacle; and use the meeting to advertise upcoming activities. They could fundraise: organise flag days and door-to-door canvases; run concerts, picnics and raffles; appoint competent treasurers and manage accounts. They could control publicity: write pamphlets and leaflets; distribute literature; and publish their messages in newspapers, books and pamphlets. They could manage organisations: establish chains of command and lines of communication; delegate tasks; create rules, workflows and structures; and recognise and promote talent from within their ranks. They had built up networks of sympathisers to secure housing, office supplies, transport, communications, food and printing services. Republicans held this invaluable material on the eve of the Easter Rising.

The shifting public mood was evident at the Cork St Patrick's Day celebration in March 1916. Traditionally the city procession was a cross-party and inter-religious affair. The previous year (1915), the *Irish Times* reported a church parade by 'a large number of soldiers in khaki, who wore the shamrock profusely'.[131] This year the British Army asked the Parade Committee to allow 6,000 troops to march in the procession.[132] The committee (composed of both Redmondites and republicans) rejected the military request, including a counter-proposal to parade only Irish soldiers and sailors.[133] Despite protests from war supporters and a boycott by two unionist groups, constitutionalist public officials joined the 4,000-person procession, along with 250 National Volunteers.[134] However, they were overshadowed by the imposing spectacle of 1,000 well-drilled Irish Volunteers, many carrying rifles and pikes.[135] This proved the republicans' final outing before their famous, if ill-fated, Easter Rising mobilisation.

III. The Rising and After

This much we can judge: never again can we get back to the conditions that existed before the storm burst; its effects will remain, either in the shaping of facts or the stimulation of inspirations. Ireland cannot be the same.

Liam de Róiste, May 1916[1]

In Cork, the Easter Rising planted a seed in many young minds that eventually blossomed into physical-force republicanism. Apolitical draper's assistant Florrie O'Donoghue was one of those affected.

> For me, as for thousands of others, the Rising was an illumination, a lifting of the mental horizon giving glimpses of an undiscovered country. It created an interest more intense and absorbing than anything in my previous experience. It raised questions so vital and immediately personal that study of them became an imperative necessity. Out of what kind of Ireland, unknown to me, had it come? What manner of men were these who had put their names to the brave, inspiring words of the Proclamation? What was this idea of national freedom for which they had fought and sacrificed themselves?[2]

The Aborted Rising in Cork

The rebellion itself was a disaster for Cork's Irish Volunteers. The episode has been expertly covered in Gerry White and Brendan O'Shea's *Baptised in Blood*, so a brief summary of Cork events will suffice.[3] Two weeks before Easter, senior Volunteer leaders in Cork were informed of the intended insurrection. They were instructed to march to the Cork/Kerry border on Easter Sunday and protect the offloading of 20,000 rifles from a German vessel disguised as the Norwegian steamer *Aud*. Rifles would be dispersed to Volunteer units in Limerick, Clare and Galway, who would form a protective shield south of the Shannon River. In the hills and mountains of Cork and

40

Kerry, Volunteers would defend the lower end of a parimeter. Besides drawing the British military away from Dublin, the deployment would create a refuge for retreating Dublin insurgents, who could conceivably take up guerrilla operations in the Cork and Kerry mountains. However, these plans depended on the arrival of the German arms ship. The Rising leaders issued no backup instructions, and the units themselves were so poorly armed that any other action would be doomed to failure.

In the days leading up to the Rising, Cork Volunteers noted hushed meetings, collections of arms and explosives, and the presence of armed guards in the Volunteer Hall on Sheares Street. Further suspicion was aroused the day before the Easter Sunday mobilisation, when men were issued first aid packets and encouraged to attend confession. At a céilí, a senior Volunteer officer indiscreetly boasted that in a week's time, he 'hoped to be dancing on the plains of Kildare'.[4] Yet events in Dublin and Kerry overtook Cork republicans.

On Holy Thursday, the *Aud* arrived off the Kerry coast three days early, confusing both Irish Volunteers and the Royal Navy, who were awaiting her arrival (the British military knew the landing date from its interception of messages between Berlin and the German embassy in Washington DC). British warships finally intercepted the *Aud* on Good Friday evening and escorted her into Cork Harbour. Approaching Queenstown Saturday morning, the *Aud*'s crew raised the ensign of the Imperial German Navy and discarded their civilian garb. Taking to their lifeboats, the uniformed Germans cheered loudly as a scuttling charge sent their vessel to the bottom of Cork Harbour. Breakfasting on his terrace, British admiral Lewis Bayly watched the dramatic event unfold beneath his eyes.[5]

Also on Good Friday, police arrested Sir Roger Casement a few hours after he disembarked from a German submarine at Banna Strand, near Tralee, Co. Kerry. Known to be recruiting Irish POWs for the German military, Casement's arrest electrified the country when news of it spread on Saturday. The same day (Saturday), Irish Volunteer commanding officer Eoin MacNeill issued public and private instructions to all units cancelling the Easter Sunday mobilisation. The Cork Volunteer officers assumed The Rising was postponed until a special message from Dublin (representing the Clarke/Pearse faction) ordered them to proceed with their previous plans. Though their mission had been made obsolete by the capture of the *Aud*, the Cork Volunteers decided to continue with their Easter Sunday mobilisation timetable. It seems Volunteer commanders anticipated combat, and intended to resist any interference from police or troops.

On a rainy Easter Sunday, Irish Volunteers rendezvoused at different assembly points around the county. From Cork city, 160 men took the train towards Macroom to meet gathering units.[6] Over a thousand Volunteers were armed with about 200 (mainly) obsolete rifles, along with assorted pistols, shotguns and homemade bombs and pikes.[7] Recently it has been suggested that the County Cork mobilisation was poorly attended.[8] However, precise unit-by-unit figures show a healthy turnout of 68 per cent from parade strength.[9] Among city Volunteers, only 143 appeared from a total of 300. The turnout figure, though, nearly matched the number of rifles held by the city Volunteers (of the 143 men who left Cork, 132 held rifles).[10] This suggests city companies fielded only Volunteers who owned rifles (Volunteers bought, held and maintained rifles as personal weapons). This would be consistent with the leaders' knowledge that no additional arms would be forthcoming, and their over-abundance of unarmed men in the mobilisation. Tomás MacCurtain also ordered specific city officers to remain behind, probably intending them to rebuild the organisation after its certain defeat.[11]

Just as the Cork Volunteers departed their headquarters, another message arrived from Eoin MacNeill in Dublin cancelling their action. After disembarking from a train at Crookstown, Volunteers marched in pouring rain to Macroom where they and other assembled units were dismissed by MacCurtain. Unclear as to what was occurring in Dublin, MacCurtain told his men to stay on guard and be ready to move immediately.[12] When the Cork Volunteers learned of fighting in Dublin on Monday, they seemed to have initially thought it was an unauthorised outbreak, probably confined to the Citizen Army and an IRB faction surrounding Tom Clarke. Armed guards were posted at the Sheares Street Volunteer Hall, and officers prepared to resist any attempt by the crown forces to disarm them.

During the next week, MacCurtain struggled with a terrible choice: to pit his poorly armed men against professional British soldiers, without benefit of surprise and in support of Dublin Volunteers acting on their initiative; or to sit out a once-in-a-generation patriotic fight, and face accusations of cowardice. 'Tomás was a very practical man, and he would not undertake a thing that he believed had not a reasonable chance of success,' recalled his brigade adjutant Pat Higgins. 'In plain language, the two of them [MacCurtain and MacSwiney] thought the Dublin crowd were daft.'[13] Ultimately the Cork Volunteer leaders took no action, encouraged by Catholic Bishop Daniel Cohalan, Lord Mayor T.C. Butterfield, and the tactful British Army intelligence officer, Captain Wallace Dickie, who restrained the city's military commander from attacking Sheares Street. Under a compromise brokered by Bishop Cohalan, the Volunteers agreed to temporarily surrender their weapons to a neutral third party (Lord Mayor Butterfield), and retrieve them when fighting concluded in Dublin.

Following days of fierce internal debate, the Cork Volunteers reluctantly handed over their rifles. 'We were all young and inexperienced,' recalled one Volunteer. 'It was no longer a case of being arrested – it was a case of being shot.'[14] After the Dublin insurgents surrendered, the military in Cork was ordered to seize the rifles and arrest Volunteer leaders. As the handcuffed Volunteers marched into Victoria Barracks, neighbourhood women (presumably related to British soldiers) shouted, 'bayonet the bloody bastards!'[15] Liam de Róiste described his comrades' dejection. 'So far as we were concerned, Easter Week, 1916, was ended – with heart burnings, disappointments, and some bitter feelings. The hour had come and we, in Cork, had done nothing.'[16]

An outside commentator laughed at the 'Cork Comedy' and questioned how the locale ever earned the name 'Rebel Cork'.[17] The city's Easter experience matched the farce of Dublin but without the accompanying tragedy and heroism. Outside Volunteer Hall on Easter Monday, a mob of angry pro-British civilians shouted insults until a Volunteer punched their ringleader, arguably the only blow struck in Cork during the entire week.[18] Inside the hall the next day, MacCurtain faced down mutinous subordinates by hopping onto a table and daring them to shoot him.[19] Amid finger-pointing, Mary MacSwiney castigated the Citizen Army 'rabble' for ruining the Irish Volunteers, while City Battalion commander Seán O'Sullivan smashed a photo of 'the traitor' Roger Casement with a bayonet.[20] The city's contribution to the Dublin fighting was Micheál Ó Cuill. Disgusted with the inaction, he and his revolver made their way to Dublin, only to be arrested just as the insurgents surrendered.[21] (O'Cuill was bestowed with the lifelong title, 'the man who walked to Dublin'. In fact, he took a train to Naas, and covered only a few remaining miles on foot.)[22] As guns were surrendered to the lord mayor, many dissenting Volunteers handed over dummy wooden rifles, then smuggled away their real weapons for safe-keeping.[23] One Volunteer turned in a fake rifle but emerged with a functioning pistol, having used his access to Butterfield's office to palm the lord mayor's revolver.[24]

Redmondites did not escape embarrassment. At the outbreak of the rising, Cork National Volunteer leaders offered the militia's services to local police, but nothing came of it.[25] J.J. Horgan later expressed relief that 'we kept many young fellows out of this insane outbreak'.[26] When the NV assistance proposal came to light a few months later, the O'Brienite *Cork Free Press* gleefully condemned 'the readiness of the Molly Volunteers to do or die against their fellow countrymen under the banner of the Royal Irish Constabulary'.[27] It is unclear if the National Volunteers rank and file would have been willing to take the field against the Irish Volunteers, but the scenario remains intriguing.

Public Reaction

Confusion reigned in Cork in the days following the Dublin outbreak. Initial reports from Dublin suggested riots rather than combat, and it was unclear if the participants extended beyond the ITGWU's Citizen Army. Only after the surrender did Cork residents grasp the scope of the rising. The common response of Cork's civic leaders was to condemn the rebellion, decry the execution of rebel commanders, and blame the outbreak on Ulster unionists and the government's failure to deliver Home Rule.

Denunciations of the Dublin rebels came from across the city's political establishment. The Cork Employers' Federation convened a special meeting 'to humbly convey to His Most Gracious Majesty the King the expression of unfailing loyalty'.[28] Writing privately, William O'Brien, MP, called the Dublin insurrection 'heartbreaking folly'.[29] Before the guns fell silent in Dublin, the pro-Redmond *Cork Examiner* remarked, 'If these misguided individuals are under any delusion that the people of Ireland are going to support them in their hare-brained schemes they little know how they miscalculate.'[30]

The Cork Harbour Commission offered 'its sincere loyalty and devotion' to the king.[31] However, three of the commissioners submitted a corollary attributing the outbreak to Sir Edward Carson's example.[32] Other Cork constitutionalists emphasised that the Ulster Volunteers first took up the rifle during the Home Rule crisis of 1913–14. The O'Brienite *Cork Free Press* denounced Carson, who began 'the whole mad policy of taking what you want by force', and called for the Ulster Volunteer Force to feature in any rebellion inquiry.[33] Among five separate editorials linking the Dublin outbreak with Carson's intransigence,[34] the *Examiner* mused, 'The wanton delays, the procrastination, the unresponsive attitude of Ulster, have had its effect, and have produced an ebullition of disorder.'[35]

Reporting to his superiors, Redmondite J.J. Horgan explained:

> The reasons for the wretched rebellion are as clear as daylights
> . . . They are
> 1. The way which Carson and Co. were permitted to break the
>   law with impunity.
> 2. The distrust of Ireland and the tinkering with Home Rule.[36]

Cork County Council held a stormy meeting on 29 April, the day the rebels surrendered. The councillors tendered their support to 'His Majesty the King and the Government in the conduct of the present war'. They also ascribed the outbreak to 'the differential treatment given to Sir Edward Carson by the Government'.[37] Fermoy councillor O'Gorman argued, 'The Orange Party under the leadership of Sir Edward Carson were permitted to land arms and to defy the law . . . All that was a game at which two could play . . .'[38]

Cork Corporation did not meet until two weeks after the start of the rising, thus fortuitously (and probably deliberately) preventing a motion on the outbreak. Bishop Cohalan initially remained silent about the rebellion, but he later applauded MacCurtain's conduct and criticised military interference with a chaplain ministering to Thomas Kent the night before his execution in Cork's Victoria Barracks.[39] (Kent was defended at his court-martial by Irish Party leader coroner James McCabe, indicating sympathy on his part.)

The Executions

On 3 May 1916, the British government began to shoot prominent rebels. A police intelligence report explained the response in Cork: 'At first people generally condemned the actions of the rebels; but after the execution of the leaders public opinion among the Nationalists suddenly swung around into one of sympathy with them.'[40]

Civic officials promptly and clearly condemned the executions, even as they were going on. This contradicts the popular perception that the protracted nature of the executions created the sympathy for the rebellion. Cork city's political elite immediately denounced the executions, indicating that any capital punishment, however brief, would have triggered strong opposition. Cork's public bodies also criticised the arrest of hundreds of advanced nationalists uninvolved in the Dublin rebellion.

Before the executions began in Kilmainham Gaol, the *Cork Examiner* cautioned against government over-reaction to the 'mad enterprise', suggesting, 'Amnesty in this case would not be generous. It would only be just.'[41] After the first executions, the *Examiner* argued, 'Clemency is more likely to alienate any sympathy from these humiliated and beaten men than any drastic or severe measures.'[42] The paper advocated amnesty again two days later.[43]

As the executions continued, the Cork Poor Law Guardians demanded their cessation, arguing, 'a policy of terrorism will not succeed in this country, and will only serve to exasperate and embitter feeling.'[44] By 9 May, an additional six prisoners had been executed, including Fermoy separatist Thomas Kent shot in Cork's Victoria Barracks. 'Is it not time, therefore, that the putting into effect of the extreme penalty should cease,' asked the *Examiner*.[45] The *Cork Free Press* suggested the government's actions should be 'deplored even more than the mad rising which occasioned it'.[46]

On 10 May, Bishop Cohalan, Lord Mayor Butterfield and the city's Irish Party leadership appealed to Prime Minister Asquith and John Redmond to end the executions, arguing they were 'extremely preju-dicial to the peace and future harmony of Ireland'.[47] The same day the conservative Cork Harbour Board likewise asked for a halt, to prevent 'untold consequence to the country'.[48]

On 11 May, the Cork District Trades Council and Cork Corporation protested against the executions.[49] Councillor Con O'Sullivan com-pared the harsh treatment of the Dublin rebels with the mercy shown to Boer insurgents after their 1914 rebellion. The corporation argued that 'further executions and indiscriminate arrests will only embitter public opinion in Ireland'. Showing the rebellion's newfound popu-larity, the councillors also celebrated their fellow councillor J.J. Walsh, sentenced to death for his role in the rising (commuted to ten years' hard labour). They paid 'tribute to his self-sacrifice and congratu-late[d] him on having his name placed on the roll of Irish Patriots'.[50] Sympathetic local citizens searched for ways to help the imprisoned Volunteers, which apparently caused hucksters to cash in on that sen-timent. Before his arrest, Tomás MacCurtain warned in the press, 'at present no collection is being made, and nobody in the city has any authority to solicit monies on their behalf.'[51]

Politicians' persistent petitions and resolutions indicate that public opinion was running towards the rebels, especially after the executions began. The American consul in Queenstown reported that the execu-tions produced 'an emotional revulsion against England which amounted to hysteria'. In this environment, he explained, Sinn Féin quickly became the 'general symbol of devotion to Ireland and defi-ance of England, repudiating parliamentarianism and Redmondism as futile and feeble'.[52]

Public Opinion and Prisoners

The authorities had seized seventy-four separatists in County Cork, including Irish Volunteer leaders Terence MacSwiney and Tomás MacCurtain. In Cork, the Poor Law Guardians, Trades Council, Bishop Cohalan, the Cork City UIL Executive and the AOH called for a release of those who had been mistakenly detained.[53]

Prime Minister Henry Asquith's flying visit to Cork on 18 May 1916 did little to dissipate the anger. Asquith met privately with Redmondite leaders and Bishop Cohalan, but revealed little. On Empire Day, 24 May 1916, the *Cork Constitution* noted the absence of any flags flying on Patrick Street.[54] By the end of May, the RIC county inspector observed of the city, 'There is, however, a prevailed feeling of disloyalty and sedition; and the rebellion has had the effect of stirring up all the old bad feeling which all patriotic men hoped the Great War would kill out.'[55]

Yet shifting public opinion should not be overstated, as indicated by reactions to Sir Roger Casement's execution in July. The *Cork Examiner* awkwardly argued for Casement's clemency, as 'he was not mentally responsible' owing to previous exposure to tropical diseases.[56] A few civic leaders signed a petition for Casement's reprieve, but labour, clerical, Irish Party and AFIL leaderships failed to back the effort.[57] Of the public bodies, only the Poor Law Guardians adjourned to 'mark our sense of horror and detestation at the murder of Sir Roger Casement . . . it is another instance of the perfidy and hatred of the English towards Irishmen and Ireland.'[58] Casement's supporters on the PLG Board, though, passed their protest before most other Guardians arrived.[59] The reluctance of public officials to intervene on behalf of Casement was likely influenced by rumours of his sexually explicit diaries, pushed by government officials. Outrage over Casement's execution was most palpable in the AFIL's *Cork Free Press*, which prominently covered his trial and suggested his hanging 'only succeeded in multiplying a thousand fold the men who are ready to come forward and die for the same ideal'.[60] During these months, the *Cork Free Press* ran foul of the military, police and press censor, with General Sir John Maxwell labelling the newspaper 'distinctly seditious'.[61]

Humanitarian assistance offered Cork residents a safe way to express support for the rebellion, while providing separatists with a mechanism to harness the energy released at Easter. A few weeks after the Rising, Dublin Lord Mayor James McGallagher established a 'Mansion House Fund' for the relief of the hundreds of civilian casualties from the fighting. The fund was also available to the families of killed and arrested Volunteers.[62] During June, Cork Lord Mayor Butterfield organised two flag days on behalf of the Mansion House Fund.[63] 'From an early hour in the morning till late in the evening,' the *Cork Constitution* wrote of the second effort, '. . . flags were sold by the thousands, and again and again the collectors' supplies had to be renewed.'[64]

Cork politicians unified behind the new Irish National Aid Association (INAA) to assist insurgents' dependents.[65] The INAA's Cork Provisional Committee reflected diverse nationalist support, featuring top Redmondite and AFIL leaders, along with senior Irish Volunteer officer Seán O'Sullivan and Cumann na mBan leader Birdie Conway.[66] The branch launch at City Hall on 29 June 1916 bridged the bitter Irish Party and AFIL divide.[67] Most Redmondite leaders attended, while coroner William Murphy sent a £35 cheque and a note explaining his support of both constitutionalism and the families of men who 'gave up their lives for a principle'. The absent Bishop Daniel Cohalan also forwarded a donation. Speaking to the gathering, AFIL MP Maurice Healy called for assistance for the rebels' dependents and denounced the internment of 'innocent' men.

While prominent constitutionalists and labour officials supported the Cork INAA, the branch was over-represented by republicans. Members included prominent Irish Volunteer officers who escaped arrest (Seán O'Sullivan, Tadhg Barry, Donal Óg O'Callaghan); Cumann na mBan leaders (Birdie Conway, Muriel Murphy, Annie MacSwiney and Eileen Walsh); and remnants of the old city Sinn Féin branch (Liam de Róiste, Edward Sheehan and Diarmuid Fawsitt). Republicans influenced the branch committee through the simple tactic of attending its weekly meetings.[68]

During July 1916 the Cork INAA printed fundraising posters, planned flag days, collected door to door, and helped launch other fund committees throughout County Cork.[69] By mid-August the INAA had forwarded £500 to Dublin.[70] Later that month, Dublin's various relief funds amalgamated (the INAA, the American Irish Distress Fund and the Irish Volunteers' Dependents' Fund), forming the tongue-twisting Irish National Aid and Volunteer Dependent's Fund (INAVDF).[71] Over the coming months, the INAVDF organised concerts, dances and other events, expressing clear support for the rebellion in the process. These activities helped spread the republican message to a receptive public, at a time when government repression made it difficult to do so.

'No Mollies Here': Partition Uproar

The British government attempt to end the Home Rule impasse caused a second seismic political event in Cork.[72] In June 1916, Asquith despatched David Lloyd George to Ireland to find a settlement acceptable to nationalists and unionists. After intense negotiations, Lloyd George produced a compromise to immediately implement the Home Rule Act, but with an amending bill that would temporarily omit six of the nine Ulster counties. A final settlement would be negotiated after the end of the war. Planned partition sparked bitter protests from all the city's political tribes.

At a special meeting, Cork city and county unionists condemned their proposed abandonment to a southern parliament. They decried partition as an 'accentuation of existing difference' and a 'reward for disloyalty and outrage'.[73] The Cork Women's Unionist Alliance deemed it 'surrender to the forces of disloyalty', while the *Cork Constitution* argued it would encourage 'further disloyalty and popular turbulence'.[74]

With his political position deteriorating, John Redmond wanted to deliver Home Rule at almost any cost. However, partition proved highly unpopular, even within Cork's Irish Party. Just weeks before the deal was announced, the AOH Cork County Council called partition 'calamitous for the entire country'.[75] It promptly backtracked when the solution was supported by Redmond and AOH president Joseph Devlin.[76] At a meeting of the Cork County Council, Redmondites defeated a defiant AFIL motion that argued, 'it would be infinitely better for us to remain as we are for fifty years' rather than accept the proposal.[77] Irish Party councillors, though, recognised the 'unjustifiable and . . . needless pandering to the Northern Orangemen', but insisted that partition was 'the price of peace'. At a corporation meeting, confused Redmondites called for an all-Ireland conference to defeat partition, while simultaneously reaffirming loyalty to 'the honesty, wisdom, and statesmanship of Mr. John Redmond and the Irish Parliamentary Party'.[78]

The AOH County Board criticised the party's political drift, noting Joseph Devlin's 'garbled' public stance. It advised party leaders to 'move boldly' to explain the new political situation.[79] Writing for the Cork UIL, J.J. Horgan asked Devlin to 'lay the position of affairs fully before the country'.[80] John Dillon tried to reassure the beleaguered Cork Redmondites: 'It is quite natural that there should be much difficulty in getting Irishmen to agree to the proposal – but there can be no doubt as to the tactical necessity of doing so.'[81]

The RIC County Inspector reported, 'The Home Rule movement is much disdained and partition generally condemned.' He also recognised malaise among city constitutionalists and the dislike of partition, assuming it would be accepted without 'any enthusiasm'.[82] The following month, police noted declining public support for the Irish Party and its 'weak-kneed' leaders.[83] City republicans exploited the situation, jeering the government's surrender to the Ulster unionists and even citing 'treachery' to the thousands of Irish nationalists serving in the British forces.[84] Republican Patrick Brady asked pointedly, 'What about the 150,000 Irish who were induced to join the army on the plea that it was for Ireland they were to fight?'[85]

For AFIL leader William O'Brien, opposition to partition was consistent with his 'consent, conference, and conciliation' mantra. It was also good politics, offering a potent wedge issue against John Redmond. O'Brien denounced 'the abominable proposal to split our country', and privately cautioned the government of its unintended consequences.[86] 'I have warned both Lloyd George and Carson in the plainest possible language,' he wrote, 'that partition in any shape, permanent or (as it is farcically called) 'temporary' would hand over the country to the Sinn Féiners.'[87]

Moving quickly to tap into the public anger, O'Brien and fellow AFIL MP Maurice Healy called a meeting at City Hall to protest against 'the dismemberment of Ireland'.[88] The 23 June demonstration was O'Brien's first public appearance in Cork since the Dublin rising.[89] When the meeting opened, a large section of the audience disrupted the proceedings.[90] Wearing tricolour pins, they drowned out speakers with songs such as 'Who Fears to Speak of Easter Week'. Leaflets passed out during the meeting accused O'Brien of being 'a silent witness' to the Dublin executions, and promised 'there is material for another insurrection, if necessary, to defeat partition'.[91]

Taking to the podium, O'Brien waited minutes for the booing to subside slightly. As he began speaking, hecklers drowned him out, which sparked fistfights in the hall. 'Even in England and in the English House of Commons they give me some fair play,' O'Brien pleaded. 'Shall I receive none from the men who are desecrating that name of Irishmen?' The din became deafening, driving O'Brien back to his seat.[92]

Maurice Healy followed O'Brien, but he could not be heard, even at the press table. Protesters forcibly reminded Healy of his 1914 appearance on a British Army recruiting platform, crying out, 'recruiter' and 'where's your Union Jack?' Alderman John Forde tried to keep the proceedings going, but he could not be heard over the uproar. A newspaper reported Forde's reflexive blaming of the discord on the AFIL's perennial enemies, John Redmond's 'Molly Maguires': 'The noise continued, and Alderman Forde, turning suddenly to the side from which the interruptions mainly came, said – 'There it is, the cry of "Up the Mollies", there it is now.' This indictment was hotly denied amid cries of 'There are no Mollies here.'[93]

Forde and his party had been blind-sided by a new force of young activists radicalised by the Easter Rising. While Forde lashed out at an absent constitutional enemy, more lethal opponents were dealing his party a mortal wound. Republicans Dermot O'Brien and Tadhg Barry (a sports reporter employed by William O'Brien's *Cork Free Press*) stormed the stage and seized control of the meeting. Waving a tricolour, Dermot O'Brien read a Sinn Féin counter-resolution calling partition an 'intolerable outrage against the unity and happiness of the Irish nation', carried out through Martial Law and 'unscrupulous Party corruption'.

As fistfights broke out on stage, the chairman abruptly passed the resolution and closed the meeting. Triumphant republicans paraded from the hall through the city's thoroughfares, hissing the Unionist City Club and cheering the General Post Office (the former workplace of rising prisoner J.J. Walsh). Outside the *Cork Examiner* offices, the crowd booed Redmondite publisher George Crosbie, destroyed the newspaper headline board, and pulled up flagstones.[94] 'It is rather hard to do more to the *Examiner* office as the windows are so high up,' explained a disappointed Muriel Murphy (the future Mrs Terence MacSwiney). 'Of course if Redmond dares to show his nose here he will be torn to pieces.'[95]

William O'Brien never again mounted a platform in Cork city, and within a year he retired from politics. With characteristic hubris and questionable veracity, O'Brien claimed the republican leaders . . .

> . . . came out on the platform to announce that their refusal of a hearing was not through any personal disrespect or failure of affection for me, but to express their dissent from my attitude in the War, and that solely because I was the only man who had the power of winning honest Nationalists back to a Parliamentary movement which was otherwise dead and rotten.[96]

Newspapers attributed the hostile reception to O'Brien's and Healy's recruiting speeches and refusal to denounce the Easter executions. The RIC likewise explained the scenes as 'due to their advocacy of recruiting for the Army'.[97] Writing to the American consulate, republican leader Liam de Róiste described O'Brien's position: 'He appealed for recruits for the English Army, basing his attitude on the statement that "England will win and England will be grateful" for Irish help. Sinn Féiners query that England will win and are absolutely convinced that England will not be grateful no matter what help Ireland gives.'[98]

The following month, partition prompted the fledgling republicans to hold their first meeting in Cork since the rising, to be headlined by the new separatist spokesman Laurence Ginnell, MP. Posters read:

> Rebel Cork. Mr Laurence Ginnell, MP will address a public meeting in the City Hall on Friday evening 21st July 1916 to denounce the proposed partition of Ireland and the partitionists. Councillor Lane will preside and will be supported by other prominent speakers. Assemble in your thousands and show your fidelity to the Martyrs' cause. Ireland a Nation.[99]

Despite government concern and Ginnell's unexplained absence, supporters packed City Hall to denounce the settlement. The crowd of roughly 1,500 young people sang 'Remember '98' and 'A Nation Once Again', while Councillor Jerry Lane defied police threats to ban the meeting.[100] The volatile audience heeded labour leader John Good's appeal to disperse peacefully.[101] In the *Southern Star*, Tadhg Barry pointed out the remarkable new political environment: 'There we have a few men holding the largest meeting ever held in City Hall, and getting a hearing where Messrs O'Brien and Healy were refused.'[102]

Within days, the British government abandoned the Home Rule partition settlement, which only fuelled the Redmondites' sense of betrayal. Humiliated for seeming to surrender Irish unity to intransigent Ulster unionists, the Irish Party received nothing in return. The Cork City UIL Executive condemned the British government's 'dishonest and treacherous conduct' and warned that 'Dublin Castle Rule' was now impossible.[103] As historian J.J. Lee wrote, 'The failure of the negotiations ripped aside the veil of illusion in which the constitutional nationalists had garbed the 1914 Home Rule Act.'[104] In Cork, the political ground was shifting beneath the Irish Party.

'Mind the Defence of the Realm Act, Man'

On 12 July 1916, about 100 republicans gathered at the city rail station after it was rumoured the Easter Rising internees had been released. When the prisoners failed to appear, the crowd proceeded through the streets shouting 'Up Dublin' and 'Up the rebels'. While passing the army recruiting office, a stone was thrown through its large front window, and someone later tossed eggs at gathering constables.[105] Police dispersed the crowd, prompting the *Cork Free Press* to complain of 'Bobbies – who should be batoning Germans in France instead of batoning the singers of "Easter Week" in Patrick's Street'.[106] At Westminster, Major John Pretyman Newman, MP, demanded, 'Is there any place in the British Empire outside Ireland where such a procession would be allowed?'[107] The police noted the presence of 'a good deal of disloyalty and seditious feelings prevalent, particularly in the City'.[108]

Growing anti-British sentiments were voiced in the Palace Cinema a few days later. When a newsreel showed images of the king and queen visiting wounded soldiers, 'hissing was very general in the gallery.'[109] Police arrested a young man and considered the charge 'fully proved', but local magistrates acquitted the defendant.[110] Resident Magistrate (RM) R.F. Starkie complained, 'there is no hope of obtaining a conviction' for such cases in Cork.[111] A retrial produced a conviction and a fine, despite crown prosecutor Jasper Wolfe's remark that in another country the defendant 'would be taken out and shot'.[112] At Westminster, Major Newman suggested banning cinema showings of images of the king or British troops, to prevent clashes between pro- and anti-war film goers.[113] RIC District Inspector Swanzy opposed such a move, considering 'it would be most injudicious and show weakness'.[114] Instead, a military police guard was stationed inside the theatre nightly, 'to detect hissing'. A few weeks later the military arrested former Royal Navy sailor Thomas Doherty, for joining 'hundreds' in the audience jeering newsreel footage of General Douglas Haig.[115] After initially deadlocking, magistrates convicted Doherty in a retrial and fined him twenty shillings.[116]

The RIC continued to prosecute Cork citizens for seditious expressions, though local justices showed little enthusiasm for such cases. In August 1916, a petty session court cautioned a 'young lad', charged with ripping down recruiting posters after his father was killed on the Western Front.[117] The same month, magistrates fined a drunken woman for shouting 'Up the Kaiser', and cautioned two Fianna Éireann officers for marching boy scouts through the city without a permit.[118] In September 1916, justices acquitted newsagent Mary O'Mahony after police raided her shop and seized anti-recruiting leaflets and the booklet *Songs of Freedom*.[119] In December, magistrates disregarded overwhelming evidence against a local man for sheltering his son, an army deserter.[120] The Southern Command British Army intelligence officer complained, 'The local Justices, as a whole, have convicted when necessary, but the penalties imposed are practically always inadequate.'[121] The following year military intelligence reported, 'Local benches of magistrates, with one or two rare exceptions, will not convict in a case brought under the D.R.R. [Defence of the Realm Regulations], or else impose a trifling penalty.'[122] As a result, the authorities were forced to introduce 'Special Court' sittings in Cork city under the jurisdiction of two resident magistrates.[123] This suggests eroding popular support for state suppression of anti-government sentiments.

The annual Manchester Martyrs commemoration in November offered a snapshot of the city's evolving politics. Before the war, the Manchester Martyrs procession drew political leaders from across the party spectrum.[124] The 1916 version attracted 1,100 persons and nine marching bands, but police reported, 'It was a rather poor turnout and no public bodies or public men took part in it.'[125] The military authorities added insult to injury by banning Dublin IRB leader Seán Ó Muirthile from entering Cork to deliver commemoration keynote.[126] Tadhg Barry spoke in his place, and called for support of Irish industry, language and sports. Barry then read Ó Muirthile's speech, and was quoted as saying, 'The Irish people delivered the best oration they could give to the Manchester Martyrs on Easter Week . . . You should make up your minds that your duty is to serve Ireland. No man can serve two masters.'[127] During Barry's speech, members of the audience swarmed a police detective in mufti taking shorthand, and grabbed his notebook. Linking arms, Barry and meeting stewards formed a protective circle around the constable, who bravely demanded the return of his notebook. Barry retrieved and returned the officer's notebook, which proved costly. The notebook was the central evidence when the British Army court-martialled Barry on a DORA sedition charge. Barry pleaded not guilty (he recognised the military court), offering the creative defence that he had been misquoted, because the police note-taker (an Ulsterman) could not decipher Barry's thick Cork city accent. The court was not swayed and sentenced him to two years' hard labour.[128]

The night of the Manchester Martyrs procession, a fundraiser concert was held in City Hall on behalf of the Fianna Éireann boy scouts. A capacity crowd of 2,000 listened to patriotic songs and recitations, while hundreds more were turned away.[129] Police detectives entered the hall, but had to withdraw after the performers stopped and the booing crowd 'kicked up such a row'.[130] The detectives missed some spectacularly seditious stagecraft. Cumann na mBan leader Birdie Conway closed the concert by singing 'The Wearing of the Green'.[131] A participant recalled the dramatic stage cue for the Fianna boy scouts:

When she came to the line, 'High above their shining weapons hung their own beloved green,' she turned to the wings and Liam Óg O'Callaghan marched onto the stage carrying a green flag with harp, escorted by a Guard of Honour composed of Dick Murphy and Jerome Mullane, with rifles and bayonets at the sloop, and in full uniform. The people went absolutely mad with enthusiasm.[132]

The *Cork Constitution* questioned whether local magistrates would jail anyone for this 'public display of sedition'. The newspaper re-published a letter by a disgusted reader in England: 'It is monstrous! This vast and mighty Empire, with hundreds of millions in every continent, and in each hemisphere, all panting to devote their sons to our historic name – is today in the hands of a nest of crazy rebels in one corner of one island.'[133] Such provocative displays drove the military and police into action.[134] A few weeks later in December 1916, military authorities prohibited the annual Gaelic League Christmas concert, arguing it would 'give rise to grave disorder'.[135] The ban stood despite protests from Bishop Cohalan, the Cork Gaelic League, and Cork Corporation.[136]

On 2 January 1917, the same week as Tadhg Barry's court-martial, police seized Patrick Corcoran's printing press.[137] A British Army court-martial convicted Corcoran of publishing seditious material, including the musical booklet *Songs of the Rebels* and a Cork Sinn Féin pamphlet that advocated passive resistance to British rule in Ireland.[138] The 64-year-old Corcoran (a veteran of the 1867 Fenian Rising) served four months. His business was 'destroyed' by the seizure, and his health damaged by the prison term, which was partially blamed for his death in 1920.[139]

Cork's next political speech prosecution entered the realm of the absurd. John Dorgan, a seventy-year-old Poor Law Guardian, was a familiar presence in Cork's public bodies. An outspoken O'Brienite, he often engaged in fierce exchanges, gummed up meetings with parliamentary procedure, and occasionally ventured into crank territory.[140] Dorgan had recently assisted some separation women with their pension applications.[141] Trouble occurred in the unlikely venue of a Cork Workhouse classroom, while Dorgan distributed presents to child inmates.[142] While Church of Ireland Canon A.J. Nicholson (St Nicholas Church) and Catholic chaplain Fr Thomas O'Toole watched, Dorgan told the children, 'I knew cases where all people get was the King's sympathy, but the King's sympathy would not get a half penny bun in Cork.'[143] Dorgan's next remark was either, 'I hope no boy here will enter the British Army', or the more innocuous, 'I hope this cruel war would soon be over, and I hope they would not have the necessity of joining the British Army.'[144] Either way, it was too much for the loyal Canon Nicholson, who stormed out of the workhouse and notified the British authorities. While Dorgan made his comments, Fr O'Toole was heard to whisper, 'John, mind the Defence of the Realm Act, man.'[145]

The British Army prosecuted Dorgan under DORA for making statements likely to prejudice recruiting.[146] At his court-martial Dorgan denounced Canon Nicholson. 'There were some people in Cork who thought because they were Protestants that they were the only loyal people to the Empire in the city and that because a man was a Catholic like himself that he was a traitor.'[147] Dorgan desperately protested his loyalty: 'No man could say that either by hand, act, or word that he ever did anything against the Empire.'[148] His appeal fell on deaf ears, and the military judges gave Dorgan a one-month jail term.[149]

Prosecutions continued during the following weeks. In March 1917, city magistrates acquitted William O'Callaghan when he was arrested for singing 'Who's afraid of Easter Week?' while walking down a road.[150] The next month, domestic servant Bridget MacManus was charged under DORA for shouting 'Up the Rebels' while passing an RIC constable. The magistrates fined MacManus a nominal two shillings, six pence, plus costs.[151] However, MacManus refused to pay the fine and chose to spend four days in jail, sparking applause as she was led from the court. Two months later, city magistrates acquitted publican David Donovan for flying a tricolour from his upstairs window, despite his obvious guilt.[152]

Cork City did not experience a comprehensive crackdown of public anti-government expression. The city's Sinn Féin organisation rapidly expanded during this period with little overt RIC interference, while the Irish Volunteers likewise escaped vigorous persecution. Cork was hardly a police state, but its citizens could not freely express sentiments against the First World War. People had to watch their words and actions, which undermined the British government's claims of fighting the war on behalf of democracy. John Horne has persuasively argued that 'political legitimacy remained central to the process of national mobilisation'.[153] These prosecutions undermined state legitimacy which had already been seriously damaged by the Home Rule crisis and pending partition of the island. A protest from the Cork Poor Law Guardians explained:

> We direct the attention of the world to the fact that when British statesmen boast of their defence of small nationalities they are speaking with their tongues in their cheeks; we believe that their

oppressive and repressive action in this country expose them in all their naked hypocrisy to the judgments of other nations.[154]

Recruiting, Conscription and Street Violence

Rising anti-government feeling in Cork could also be seen in decreasing enlistment rates for the British Army. Though Irish recruiting had declined prior to the Easter Rising, it fell off precipitously in the second half of 1916. The Cork RIC characterised city recruitment as 'poor' or 'very poor' from July to November 1916, and 'at a standstill' by December.[155] Writing from Cork, the Southern District military intelligence officer stated in September 1916, 'practically no recruits are being obtained'; in October that recruiting was 'dull'; and in December, 'little interest is taken in it by anyone'.[156] Between 1915 and 1916, enlistments of Irish Catholics dropped by 71 per cent. The less dramatic decline of Protestant enlistments suggests the presence of a political factor in the decrease.

TABLE 3.1
Catholics as % of Irish Enlistments, 1915–17

Year	Total	Catholics	Percent
1915	51,144	31,412	61.4%
1916	18,819	10,053	53.4%
1917	12,644	5,057	39.9%

Source: John Redmond Papers, MS 15,259, NLI

During the same period, a 'conscription scare' struck Cork city. In September 1916, Liam de Róiste wrote that conscription 'is the matter most discussed', while Tadhg Barry wryly hoped it would be implemented, 'if only to make the slackers fight on some side'.[157] A few weeks later the corporation warned that forced military service 'would result in turmoil and bloodshed', while the Irish Party appealed for support to strengthen their hand in 'a tussle about conscription in Ireland'.[158] Military intelligence reported conscription 'will meet with considerable opposition', including physical resistance in County Cork.[159] The panic subsided at the end of the year, but remained in the public's mind as the war dragged on.[160]

In November 1916, the RIC county inspector reported, 'a bad disloyal feeling is prevalent . . . principally among young men eligible for military service in the city of Cork.'[161] New combativeness was revealed at the end of December. About forty British soldiers returning from a Christmas night concert at the Cork Methodist Hall exchanged words with 'nearly 50 hooligans'. Each party sang rival political songs, while the civilians reportedly shouted 'Up the rebels' and 'Down with recruiting'. As the soldiers returned to their Ballincollig barracks, civilians stoned them at Gaol's Cross.[162] Three nights later, soldiers from the same unit brawled with city residents in Patrick Street.[163]

That week, the RIC county inspector warned Dublin Castle of 'a seditious, disloyal feeling' in the city.[164] Despite the best efforts of the police and military, 'disloyal feeling' only increased in 1917, manifesting itself in a series of violent public disorders. Like a virus, sedition spread well beyond military-aged young men, and soon infected the larger city population.

IV. 'Thoughtless Young People'
and the Cork City Riots
of 1917

In some cases rows are deliberately provoked by anti-Irish elements and in most other cases by the behaviour of thoughtless young people, who imagine the striking of a policeman is a blow to the British Government.

Liam de Róiste, July 1917[1]

In the months following the 1916 Easter Rising, anti-government unrest grew. Throughout 1916 Cork citizens assertively raised funds for the INAVDF, while recruits joined the Irish Volunteers.[2] Authorities repressed republican demonstrations during the first half of 1917, which increased tensions between Sinn Féin supporters and police. The second half of the year saw a grassroots explosion of anti-government sentiment and a loss of social deference, which were manifested in a series of spontaneous riots targeting local police.

Cork city had a long tradition of street rioting dating from the nineteenth century. Mob disturbances accompanied the elections of 1832, 1835, 1841 and 1852.[3] During a bitter week-long tailors' strike in 1870, residents battled with hundreds of police and soldiers until crushed by repeated cavalry charges down Patrick Street.[4] Police advised Dublin Castle, 'Perhaps in no other part of the country is there so formidable and so disaffected a mob as that in Cork.'[5] Historian Fintan Lane explored Cork's 'Band Riots' of 1879–82, a series of violent clashes between followers of the city's numerous marching bands. These disturbances can be characterised as musically scored neighbourhood faction fights, which produced scores of injuries and at least two fatalities.[6] The Parnell split of 1891 saw frequent combat between pro- and anti-Parnell parties, which was echoed by acrimonious O'Brienite–Redmondite rivalry of the early teens.[7] During the 1910 general election, AFIL and UIL supporters collided virtually every night for two weeks, producing at least 122 injuries.[8] The more peaceful 1914 municipal election saw two nights of clashes between followers of politically affiliated marching bands.[9] Fierce mob attacks were a staple of the 1909 Cork dock strike.[10] Street fighting certainly remained a key strand of Cork's political DNA. However, the republican disturbances of 1917 were unique because the crowds focused their violence almost exclusively on police, rather than members of rival neighbourhoods or political camps. Similar outbreaks were visible in Limerick and large towns across County Cork.[11]

Prohibited Protests in Early 1917

Notable clashes between police and Cork separatists occurred on the first anniversary of the Easter Rising. Following Dublin's lead, city republicans held memorial masses for the executed rising leaders. These church gatherings provided safe venues for mainly young and politically unaffiliated residents to voice their support for the Dublin rebellion. On Easter Monday, 9 April 1917, hundreds attended a memorial mass at Cork's North Cathedral, and afterwards processed to the National Monument on the Grand Parade.[12] Wearing republican badges and ribbons, the young demonstrators sang patriotic songs until police ordered them to disperse. The crowd booed the police but eventually went home peacefully. Foreshadowing future events, separation women heckled the demonstrators.

The following weekend, police scattered two more peaceful demonstrations. The night of printer Patrick Corcoran's release from prison (see Chapter III), his Sullivan Quay neighbours celebrated his return.[13] Outside his home, they sang rebel songs beside burning tar barrels, until police charged with batons. The crowd dispersed without offering any resistance.[14] The next morning, a second Easter Rising memorial mass was held at the North Cathedral. To mark the occasion, some enterprising Republicans ran up a banned tricolour flag atop City Hall.[15] After mass, 'a crowd of young men, boys, and girls' marched to the National Monument singing 'Easter Week' in Irish.[16] Between 500 and 600 attempted to hold a demonstration at the monument, but were ordered to disperse by 40 police.[17] This time, the crowd did not go quietly. They booed and hissed the constables, and engaged in some pushing when a number of young women confronted the police. As the RIC formed for a baton charge, stone-throwing erupted. The crowd 'tried to make a stand', but scattered after the police waded into them with their batons.[18]

During the melee, the police arrested Teresa Donovan, a member of Cumann na mBan. She struck Constable Farrell with her umbrella, which 'broke off the rim of his hat and raised a lump on his head'. Though Donovan claimed she was protecting a deaf boy from

Constable Farrell's baton, local magistrates found her guilty, fining her twenty shillings or fourteen days in jail. 'I won't pay the fine,' announced Donovan, 'I'll go to jail.' The court spectators applauded as she was led away.[19] After serving her prison term, Donovan's Cumann na mBan colleagues presented her with a commemorative gold umbrella.[20]

Police attacks on demonstrators earned a pulpit denunciation from Fr Peter Sheehan, an inner-city Franciscan priest. Pointing to Cork's 'heated and highly charged state', District Inspector Walsh sought Sheehan's transfer.[21] Dublin Castle officials also debated bringing charges against Sheehan, but instead chose to privately complain to Cardinal Logue.[22] A police detective in the congregation quoted Sheehan as calling the Cork RIC 'a lot of brutes':

> He also said they were placed here, by the way, as preservers of the peace, but they were the only disturbers of the peace themselves in Ireland. He called on the people to beware of them and to be patient, and that with the help of God the day was not far distant when the Irish people could shake off the foreign yoke and would be in a position to protect their heads from the batons of a brutal police force.[23]

Republicans planned another demonstration the following Sunday. However, Bishop Cohalan intervened via a pastoral letter read in parish churches around the city. Cohalan sympathised with the protesters and pointed out the government's inconsistencies. 'If a procession started from a Church,' wrote Cohalan, 'and cheers were called and hurrahs given for Irish soldiers at the front, or the disposition of the Tsar, or the coming of America into the war, the procession or demonstration would not be considered unlawful or disorderly.' However, to prevent further clashes, the bishop ordered mass attendees to refrain from processing or demonstrating.[24] The relieved RIC inspector general reported, 'The Bishop's action, though resented by the Sinn Féiners, is expected to achieve the desired result.'[25] There seem to have been no further post-mass demonstrations during the remainder of the year.

In May 1917, the Cork city police warned that Sinn Féin 'appears to be growing in strength'.[26] Illegal tricolour flags appeared in unexpected locations around Cork, including one fastened so tightly to a telegraph pole that police had to cut the wire to remove it.[27] On the night of Sinn Féin's Longford by-election victory, 1,500 republicans processed through city streets, followed by 40 policemen. Passing the Cork men's prison, they cheered republican prisoners, who responded by waving towels from their cell windows.[28] The only trouble occurred when the RIC threatened a baton charge after a young man climbed the National Monument to attach a tricolour.[29] When he saw constables preparing to attack, 'he thought discretion the better part of valour and got down again'.[30] Separation women counter-demonstrators abused the Sinn Féin supporters, briefly following them and cheering for the Munster Fusiliers.

June 1917 proceeded quietly enough, despite an apparently spontaneous republican street demonstration on 22 June 1917. About 200 people sang and waved republican flags while marching from the Western Road to Patrick Street. 'What gave rise to the demonstration,' reported the *Cork Constitution*, 'could not be ascertained – even those who participated were ignorant of its object.'[31] The crowd menaced the British Army recruiting office at the foot of Patrick Street, until police reinforcements arrived. They later booed and hissed the Cork City Club, the Leeside counterpart to Dublin's Kildare Street Club. Again, the RIC did not attempt to disperse the marchers.

Reception for the Released Prisoners

The British government's release of the sentenced Easter Rising prisoners in June 1917 sparked jubilant demonstrations across Ireland, including delirious scenes in Dublin. The Cork City Sinn Féin Executive organised an elaborate reception for the city's returning prisoners, which would be Cork's largest pro-independence demonstration to date. The civic welcome was not unanimous, however, as the corporation refused to erect a platform on the Grand Parade.[32]

On the evening of 23 June 1917, 10,000 citizens gathered at Glanmire rail station to greet Cork's released prisoners.[33] The freed Irish Volunteers included former city residents J.J. Walsh and Diarmuid Lynch (both veterans of the Dublin fighting), and David Kent, who lost two brothers during a police siege of his Fermoy home.[34] Four recently deported Cork city Volunteer leaders were likewise present – Tomás MacCurtain, Terence MacSwiney, Seán Nolan and Seán O'Hegarty.

Some 2,000 people escorted the prisoners from the train station to the city centre in a colourful procession 'of enormous dimensions'.[35] Marching bands led the parade, followed by wagons carrying the released prisoners. Behind them were civic bodies, social organisations, Sinn Féin clubs, Volunteer units, and republican boy and girl scouts from the city and county. GAA teams cut an attractive appearance: 'The men wore their brightly coloured jerseys and bore their hurls on their shoulders, while the female hurlers wore green blouses and carried their sports sticks', with many attaching photos of executed Dublin leaders to the ends of their hurls.[36] However, trouble broke out in front of the Soldiers' Home on Lower Glanmire Street, when about thirty soldiers and their relations jeered the procession. Separation women attacked camogie players, and shots rang out from an upstairs window. Fortunately, no one was hit by the gunfire. After police broke up the fight, the parade continued.

Thousands lined the streets and gathered on the Grand Parade. Prisoner speeches could not be heard over the wild cheering, even by reporters seated a few metres from the platform.[37] Diarmuid Lynch shouted that as a Corkman he was glad to return to his native city, and to find that it was a 'Rebel Cork, a Republican Cork, and an Irish Cork.' 'For a long time the Gael had been hounded down,' J.J. Walsh exclaimed, 'but his name was now honoured and resounded in every part of the world on account of the rifles of Easter week.'[38] Cork Volunteer commander Tomás MacCurtain blasted the corporation for failing to provide a civic reception, and called for the release of recently imprisoned republicans Tadhg Barry and Peter O'Keefe.[39] (Barry was serving a two-year sentence for his Manchester Martyrs commemoration address, while O'Keefe received five years for buying rifles from a local British soldier.)

Police had withdrawn from city streets, apparently to avoid provoking the massive gathering. Most of the crowd dispersed after the meeting ended, but two separate bodies of demonstrators marched off through different parts of the city. One headed to the foot of Patrick Street and stoned the army recruiting office, breaking its two large plate-glass windows. They then set their eyes on the City Club on the Grand Parade. As the mob shouted encouragement, two young men climbed onto the club balcony and hoisted a tricolour from its flagpole. Inside, besieged members tactfully drew the window blinds, though they could have been forgiven for believing they were witnessing the start of a popular uprising.[40]

A second crowd of about 500 proceeded to the men's prison on the Western Road, perhaps inspired by Tomás MacCurtain's concern for the two republican prisoners inside. Demonstrators shouted encouragement to the inmates, and then stoned the structure, breaking most windows. It is unclear how the imprisoned Tadhg Barry and Peter O'Keefe felt about this display of solidarity.

The throng returned to the city centre via the county courthouse on Great George Street (now Washington Street). There they halted to hoist a tricolour from atop the building. They pushed out a city fire escape – a large, wheeled hook-and-ladder used by the Fire Brigade to access high buildings.[41] An unidentified demonstrator scurried up the ladder to the courthouse roof. He then hauled himself atop the building's dome to its flagpole, and ran up a tricolour amid cheers. Retreating to the roof, he approached the statue of Lady Justice holding a life-size replica of the scales of justice. The *Cork Constitution* reported, 'A very disgraceful act was then perpetrated.'[42] It is unclear whether the young man was motivated by political symbolism or imaginative vandalism. Regardless, he removed the bronze scales and tossed them onto the street. They were broken into pieces, and triumphantly carried home as souvenirs.[43] The mob also broke the fire escape while lowering the ladder, so they smashed its sections and hurled pieces through the courthouse windows.[44] About midnight the exhausted demonstrators finally dispersed. Police were determined to regain control of the streets the following day.

The Battle of Patrick Street

Sunday 24 June 1917 began peacefully, though wood planks now covered the shattered windows of the army recruiting office on Patrick Street. Following an afternoon camogie match at the O'Neill Crowley grounds, a piper band led spectators back towards the city centre. Waving tricolours and drawing in passing pedestrians, the procession stopped outside the men's prison to cheer republican prisoners. Stone throwing then broke out, though few windows were left undamaged from the night before. 'Having satisfied themselves that there was nothing left to break',[45] the crowd continued its circuitous route to the city centre. On working-class Gillabbey Street, the procession was confronted by families with relatives in the British Army. The two sides exchanged insults and stones before separating.

The next stop was the Irish Volunteer Hall on Sheares Street. The previous month military authorities had closed the building and barricaded its doors to prevent a re-entry.[46] These obstacles received the crowd's wrath, as sealed doors were forced open. Amid more cheering, still another tricolour was raised on the roof. The disturbance was ended by the start of a republican 'monster meeting' on the Grand Parade of 5,000 to denounce the upcoming Irish Convention.[47] (See Chapter VI for details.) Following its conclusion, spectators milled about the city centre until events took a violent turn.

At 9 pm, a counter-demonstration by separation women sparked trouble. After republicans insulted some of these women on the street, they responded by throwing stones.[48] Summoning reinforcements, fifty defiant separation women soon paraded along Patrick Street behind a Union Jack. According to a newspaper reporter, the vocal women 'incensed the Sinn Féiners by attacking them and trying to remove favours they wore'.[49] Brawls drew a crowd that eventually reached 5,000.[50] 'The Union Jack was captured,' wrote a reporter, 'and the crowd, excited by the occurrence, turned their attention to the Recruiting Office.'[51]

Converging at the recruiting office, young men pried off planks covering broken windows, climbed into the building, and demolished the interior. They smashed furniture and stripped the walls of moulding and woodwork. Outside, two boys scaled the building and ripped down various Allied flags hanging from the upper floor (including the American 'stars and stripes'). Another young man climbed the flagpole and cut down a large Union Jack that had flown since the outbreak of the war. He tossed it to the cheering crowd, which threw it into the River Lee. A portrait of Lord Kitchener likewise took the plunge.[52] An Irish tricolour fastened to the top of the flagpole proved difficult to remove. (The following day soldiers used another civic fire escape to take down the flag. Like the courthouse mob, the soldiers had difficulty handling the fire escape and broke it.)[53]

At this stage, a small party of police armed with rifles arrived to the chaotic scene. Head Constable John Brown recalled, 'I saw that a very hostile crowd of about 5,000 persons were assembled in front of the Recruiting Office, and instantly a fierce fusillade of stones came down on us.'[54] Pushing the crowd towards Patrick's Bridge, the police came under intense attack. With fixed bayonets, the RIC charged into the throng, braving stones launched from everywhere, including shop windows above them. One witness recalled seeing a policeman barely break stride as he was smashed over the head with an ash plant.[55] Crowds soon surrounded the police, and Head Constable Brown believed 'there appeared no other remedy for us to save our lives only to resort to firing.'[56] In the nick of time, a large police party headed by District Inspector Swanzy smashed into the rear of the multitude on Patrick's Bridge, sending them flying. The move also sealed off the city's northside from the mobs in the city centre. Isolated revolver shots rang out at police, though the culprits were never identified.[57] It was a close call; as District Inspector Swanzy later testified, 'the police were fighting for their lives.'[58] The constables slowly pushed the crowds into the city centre, where they stubbornly maintained their stone barrage.

The clashes were intense. As police formations drew up for bayonet charges, rioters melted away and reconvened in side streets to renew rock throwing. Repeated bayonet charges continued for an hour, with constables freely using their rifle butts when given the chance. The police rushes often stampeded the crowds, which trampled numerous onlookers. 'It was a rather terrorising sight,' reported the *Cork Examiner*, 'to see them [police] to the number of 20 or 30 on the double with carbines lowered and bayonets fixed, while revolver shots cracked now and again.'[59]

Onlookers were difficult to disperse. Many simply jeered police, while the newspaper reported that bystanders, 'with a disregard for the dangers in front of them remained in groups, looking on with idle curiosity'. Catholic priests walked through the streets urging residents to return home, as did town councillor Jerry Lane and recently released prisoner J.J. Walsh. However, 'the disturbance raged with great violence.'[60] 'I have considerable experience of stone throwing in Cork,' remarked Head Constable Brown, 'but the ferocity of onslaught made upon the police that evening surpasses anything I have ever witnessed, and I had some experience in Belfast during the 1886 riots there.'[61]

Events took a fatal turn on Kyrl's Quay when police chased fleeing stone-throwers. An unidentified constable caught up with dock labourer Abraham Allen and bayoneted his thigh, severing the femoral artery. The thirty-year-old father of two bled to death in a few minutes.[62]

Strong military reinforcements arrived from Victoria Barracks. The soldiers set up a machine gun at the foot of Patrick Street, and brought stretchers, chaplains and an ambulance. A reporter observed, 'The presence of the soldiers immediately overawed the mob, as the news spread like wild fire that machine guns were trained on the principal streets and the preparations on an extensive scale had been made for dealing with casualties.'[63] Police and soldiers methodically cleared the side streets, and by midnight, three hours after it began, the Battle of Patrick Street had ended.

At least a dozen civilians were hospitalised, mainly with bayonet and scalp wounds, including a thirteen-year-old girl bayoneted in the head and a young man shot in the leg, both presumably by police.[64] Many others were treated and released without giving their names.[65] One pro-British demonstrator suffered a serious eye injury when someone ripped the red, white and blue ribbons from her dress.[66] Two members of the police received minor gunshot wounds (District Inspector Swanzy was hit in the leg), and other constables were injured by stones.[67] Authorities estimated the damage at £400, mainly from the two broken fire escapes, the wrecked recruiting office, and smashed windows suffered by thirty-four local businesses.[68]

With the city braced for additional violence, Lord Mayor Butterfield appealed for calm, as did the Irish Volunteer leaders, albeit with their own spin on the disturbances. Their letter appeared in all three local newspapers:

> Owing to the disorders in the city last night, the under-mentioned, on behalf of the Irish Volunteers, Sinn Féin and other national organisations, order their members and sympathisers to keep off the streets tonight, and prevent the appearance of disturbances which are being fermented to discredit the national organisation.
> [signed]
> Tomás MacCurtain
> Terence MacSwiney
> Diarmuid Lynch
> J.J. Walsh
> Seán Murphy[69]

The next day, authorities regained the streets with a strong show of force. Some 118 RIC constables arrived from surrounding areas, while 400 soldiers from Victoria Barracks patrolled city streets and set up machine guns at key intersections.[70] Police and military commanders toured the area, as did the lord mayor and city high sheriff.

Crowds lined the boulevards in anticipation of more violence on Monday night but were disappointed. Apparently under orders from their commanders, the Irish Volunteers did not renew the battle. A thousand young men briefly paraded the streets, singing and waving flags, but the police did not intervene and the protesters dispersed peacefully.[71] There were occasional clashes between Cumann na mBan members and separation women, with at least one exchange of stones. 'On the whole,' wrote the *Cork Examiner*, 'the displays by these parties were regarded more in the light of diversion by the general public, who, getting tired of the senseless demonstration, retired from the streets about half past ten.'[72] Soldiers remained at city intersections on Tuesday evening, though police had resumed control.[73] Normality returned on Wednesday.[74]

Reactions

The *Cork Constitution* denounced the riot as 'unrestrained savagery'.[75] The *Cork Examiner* took a more conciliatory line.

> We trust . . . that the good sense of the people will make them sternly set their faces against incidents in which necessarily

> many innocent and juvenile victims will pay with their blood for
> the passion aroused by the present situation.[76]

Public officials criticised police conduct, especially the killing of
Abraham Allen. His funeral was widely attended and a fund was
raised for his widow.[77] High Sheriff Willie O'Connor, an Irish Party
partisan, challenged the RIC version of Allen's death, while the Cork
Poor Law Guardians sent their condolences to Allen's widow and
denounced the police for 'the cruel manner they treated the helpless
children of our city'.[78] The RIC county inspector complained of Cork's
feckless civic leaders, 'I may point out that neither the Lord Mayor
nor any members of the Corporation gave us any assistance during
the week, nor are they likely to give us any in the future.'[79] No
policeman was charged in the case.[80] Sinn Féin leader Liam de Róiste
wrote bitterly:

> To the ordinary mind it was murder or at the very least
> manslaughter – whether under provocation or not is another
> question. But, of course, no policeman was tried for it, no action
> taken. Where is the law, where order, where justice?[81]

Both pro-British separation women and female republicans played
a prominent part in the Patrick Street riots. An anonymous letter to the
Cork Constitution complained, 'I heard "modest Irish colleens" dressed
in green and gold, use language that would shame the harlots of the
Strand. All this in Holy Ireland.'[82] During the Allen inquest, High
Sheriff O'Connor referred to 'drunk' separation women 'insulting
people', a charge echoed by an IRA witness years later.[83] A
Redmondite Poor Law Guardian placed the blame strictly along
gender lines, claiming: 'The cause of the disturbances on Sunday night
was solely due to women.'[84]

The Patrick Street riot can be attributed to different factors. Street
rowdies were a persistent problem in the city (*Evening Echo* newsboys
were notorious for street violence), and needed little encouragement
to participate.[85] The deployment of police armed with rifles also
implied the threat of lethal force against unarmed civilians, which may
have provoked residents. In the main, though, such disorder provided
an easy outlet for frustrated young people at a time of growing anti-
state sentiments. They targeted Cork police who had previously
suppressed peaceful demonstrations. By acting as agents of an increasingly unpopular government, police undermined their legitimacy and
neutrality. As a result, attacking the city police came to be seen as a
way to attack the British government. During the rest of the year,

crowds repeatedly assaulted RIC constables, often without provocation, in a manner that retained a strong anti-state component.

Within a month, a street ballad celebrated new defiance of the local police.

> *We hauled down the old rag and flew the Sinn Féin flag,*
> *And squared up our shoulders the Bobbies to meet –*
> *Pro-German, Sinn Féiners, and all the back laners*
> *Who fought for old Ireland in Patrick's Street.*
> *They stood out before us; we sang in a chorus –*
> *Just look at the bobbies as white as a sheet*
> *We stoned them and hit them, and bettered and split them*
> *And fought for old Ireland in Patrick's Street.*[86]

Continued Clashes

The Battle of Patrick Street was just the most notorious of several street disturbances in 1917. During the year's final six months, Cork civilians clashed with police on twelve separate occasions, with thousands of residents often participating.[87] Crowds typically focused on police or other symbols of the British crown, leaving unionist and Protestant institutions untouched and British soldiers largely unmolested. None of the Cork riots produced looting or assaults on private property.[88] During this period there were four separate attacks on the Cork recruiting office, and six disturbances at the Cork prison, mainly crowds stoning police stationed outside.[89] As a result, for the remainder of the war a police guard was maintained outside the recruiting office and the men's prison. The riots seem to have been spontaneous, and not directed by the republican leadership. They should be viewed as anti-government protests, though many participants likely joined for apolitical reasons.

An episode two weeks after the Battle of Patrick Street illustrated the spontaneity of anti-government violence. On Sunday evening, 8 July 1917, a group of female munitions workers from the Cork artillery shell factory returned from a picnic at nearby Crosshaven.[90] Passing through Patricks Street in three wagons, they sang 'The Red, White and Blue' and waved Union Jacks at pedestrians. As the wagons entered the Cornmarket Square, a jeering crowd of between 300 and 500 gathered, and stoned the vehicles. One woman fell out of the wagon and had her dress partially torn off, another was punched, and others were stoned at close range, before they found sanctuary at a nearby police station. RIC baton charges subsequently cleared the area. At the urging of the Irish chief secretary, four 'Patrick's Street Huns'

were prosecuted for the brutal assault.[91] During their trial, crown solicitor Jasper Wolfe claimed such actions would bring 'the blush of shame
to the darkest Negroes in the wilds of Africa'.[92] However, the victims'
wagon drivers testified that the munitions workers took a circuitous
route through the city's main thoroughfares, in order to shout
'slackers' at male pedestrians not in military uniform.[93] The convicted
men had fairly convincing alibis, though one, Michael Meyers,
admitted to being in the crowd and hearing one of the victims shout,
'You knock-kneed bastard Meyers, do not think we don't know you.'[94]

A large crowd attended an appeal hearing for the four prisoners in
September 1917.[95] The victims had to testify again, and were escorted
from the courthouse by armed police, followed by a booing mob that
included women. Soon a crowd marched to the National Monument
behind an *Evening Echo* newsboy carrying a tricolour. There, the
'unwashed and bare-legged juvenile' climbed a lamppost and
addressed the crowd, 'with a fluency which betokened considerable
practice'. He then led them to the nearby British Army recruiting office.
Climbing the Fr Matthew statue, the pocket Spartacus gave another
rousing speech, shouting, 'Let the police come here with their rifles and
helmets. The helmets, spikes and all, won't be much good to them if we
got stones.'[96] The newsboy incited the crowd to start stoning constables
guarding the recruiting office. RIC reinforcements with rifles and fixed
bayonets were met by hisses and a 'regular fusillade' of stones.[97]
Constables beat the crowd back with rifle butts and bayonets.
'Spreading out across the road, they ran at a terrific pace,' wrote a *Cork
Constitution* reporter, 'their bayonets glittering in the semi-darkness and
striking terror to the evildoers whom they were overhauling.'[98] For an
hour, crowds kept reforming in side streets, with whistles signalling
when to emerge and shower the police with stones. At 11.30 pm, 15
constables passing the courthouse encountered up to 200 stone-
throwers.[99] As the police lined up for a bayonet charge, a teenage
Fianna boy scout opened fire with a revolver, hitting Head Constable
John Brown in the thigh.[100] Miraculously, the police did not return fire,
and only a few rioters and police were wounded in the encounter.

The crowd was likely stirred by the recent visit of the Irish
Convention and the death of Thomas Ashe two days earlier.[101] The following night, the RIC warned 'all respectable citizens' to stay off the
streets after 8 pm.[102] In the early morning hours, civilians and police
clashed in various locations, exchanging stones and baton charges.[103]
Calm returned the next evening, as Bishop Cohalan walked city streets
urging young people to go home, while 100 police reinforcements took
up positions at key intersections.[104]

Throughout the year violent clashes were absent from official republican processions and meetings, though tension was palpable. On at least two occasions, republican leaders denounced mob violence and beseeched volatile crowds to disperse quietly.[105] During both episodes, police did not intervene, which helped keep the situation under control.

Still another street riot foreshadowed Tomás MacCurtain's 1920 assassination. In November 1917, a couple of thousand residents greeted J.J. Walsh after he was released from prison following a hunger strike.[106] After a public meeting, the Brian Boru Pipers Band led an estimated 1,500 people back to its rooms on Hardwick Street. Outside the band rooms the crowd turned on an RIC contingent. A *Cork Constitution* headline read: 'The Usual Sequel – Police stoned'.[107] The RIC had to rescue two passing British Army officers and their female companion, after they were assaulted by a crowd composed of men, women, and a few uniformed Irish soldiers.[108] Police eventually broke up the throng with batons and rifle butts, injuring sixteen men and boys.

A few hours later, angry police constables sought to pay the pipers, who enjoyed a reputation for rowdiness reminiscent of the 'band menace' of the 1870s.[109] A small group of police led by senior officers (including District Inspector Swanzy) broke into the Brian Boru band rooms on Hardwick Street and smashed band instruments and furniture. They turned their attention to the building's other occupant, the Northeast Ward Sinn Féin Club, which was holding an Irish class upstairs.[110] According to the victims, 'They then commenced to belabour us with the butt ends of their carbines, jumping on and brutally kicking us.'[111] The beating was severe enough that one student escaped by jumping from a second-floor window.[112] Five republicans were hospitalised with broken bones and scalp wounds, including club vice-president Patrick Brady (the son of an RIC constable), who was knocked unconscious and received a near-fatal bayonet wound in his thigh. Two of the victims spent seven weeks in hospital, while another was bed-ridden for three weeks.[113]

Fearing further police violence against its supporters, the Cork City Sinn Féin Executive publicised the Hardwick Street incident, submitting a joint deposition from the victims to newspapers and the corporation.[114] When Dublin Castle suppressed the statement, Sinn Féin published it as a pamphlet entitled, *English Law and Order in Ireland*, which was distributed around Cork.[115] Two of the victims sued Constable Daniel Harrington and won £35 in damages, but the verdict was reversed upon appeal.[116] Commenting on the civil case, the crown solicitor advised it was 'in the interests of the morale of the Police Force that the defendant's conduct on the occasion in question should be suitably rewarded'.[117] Though the decision raised police morale, it set a poor precedent for police discipline. Three of the raid's police participants were shot in 1920 by the IRA for suspected involvement in the reprisal assassination of Tomás MacCurtain. They included the head of the piper band expedition, District Inspector Oswald Swanzy.[118]

Police Retreat

In October 1917, Lord Mayor Butterfield asked Sinn Féin officials to help form a citizen's street patrol, 'to keep "the irresponsible young people quiet"'.[119] He hoped it would reduce the public expense of maintaining high numbers of police on the street.[120] The Cork City Sinn Féin Executive refused to participate, blaming street disorder on 'the presence of armed police and the repeated ill-treatment which peaceable citizens have suffered at their hands'. Pointing out the peaceful nature of Sinn Féin meetings, the republicans offered another solution:

> We have no doubt whatever but that if the police forces are withdrawn, and if the Police provocations, and the provocative actions of the authorities cease, the city will return to normal conditions . . .[121]

Though Tomás MacCurtain considered using the Irish Volunteers for street patrols, he also appeared to be forgiving of republicans involved in the clashes. Fifteen-year-old Fianna boy scout commander P.J. Murphy shot and wounded Head Constable Brown during the 27 September riot. For this unauthorised shooting, a Fianna court-martial stripped Murphy of his rank. However, MacCurtain requested Murphy be restored to his commmand. According to Murphy, MacCurtain 'gave me a clap on the back saying, "I wish we could get the same spirit into the Volunteers"'.[122]

As the situation continued to deteriorate in late 1917, the city police pulled back from possible provocation. In October and November, the RIC failed to intervene in the Irish Volunteer public defiance marches.[123] (See Chapter V for details). By December, the RIC county inspector offered an unofficial truce. Using Bishop Cohalan as an intermediary, County Inspector Clayton suggested withdrawing police from the city streets during republican rallies and parades, leaving 'de Valera's friends' to keep order. The bishop explained that the county inspector was reluctant to withdraw his armed constables in the evenings.

He has no fear from Volunteer or Sinn Féin men. The source of
trouble, he says, are the irresponsible boys and girls. How can I,
he asks, protect my police from these?[124]

During 1918, the city RIC largely turned a blind eye to demonstrations, only intervening when assisted by armed soldiers, which further
militarised the environment. Occasional riots still broke out in 1918,
including a remarkable episode during a factory fire in the city centre,
when 'irresponsible young people' started stoning soldiers and police
battling the blaze.[125] During that year, there were also four separate
crowd attacks on crown forces attempting to arrest civilians or army
deserters.[126] Though continued anti-government hostility remained
visible, none of these later clashes matched the size, frequency or
ferocity of the riots experienced in the second half of 1917.

It would appear the reorganisation of Cork's Irish Volunteers contributed to the decline of street rioting. The Volunteers provided an
outlet for many frustrated youths previously involved in clashes with
police. Amid the reconstitution of city units and return of strong leadership, rank-and-file Volunteers acted with increasing discipline in
1918. Eager to distance the independence movement from chaos, vandalism and crime, republicans used the Volunteers to maintain order
in Cork. While street violence still occurred, Volunteers frequently
quelled disturbances before they got out of hand. Beyond mobilising
young republicans, the Irish Volunteer organisation simultaneously
acted as a brake on its supporters, channelling their energies from
unfocused street violence to disciplined paramilitary activity.

The local environment improved once Cork police adopted a less
confrontational attitude. However, this was no longer enough to
ensure order, as young people in Cork increasingly lost their deference
to civil authority. The public likewise became conditioned to accept
violent attacks upon police constables who were symbols of an unpopular government. City residents throwing stones at police in 1917–18
were the forebearers of urban guerrillas who preferred revolvers and
grenades in 1920–21.[127]

The June 1917 riots marked a rapid decline of state power in Cork.
From this point until the truce of 1921, the Cork city RIC could not hold
its own against determined republican demonstrations of strength. The
police only intervened when directly assisted by armed British soldiers.
As the Cork RIC withdrew from city streets, the Irish Volunteers filled
the policing vacuum. They maintained that position until the Black and
Tans arrived in Cork during the bloody summer of 1920.

V. The Republican Front: Sinn Féin, the IRB, and the Irish Volunteers in 1917

Sinn Féin – now the accepted name – is sweeping the country like a whirlwind, like a tornado, like a rushing tide, like anything that rushes onward and changes the face of nature.

Liam de Róiste, January 1917

Energised by the Easter Rising, Cork's republican community developed a mass movement in 1917 that ultimately seized control of city politics in 1918. Organising, as one veteran recalled, 'in a loose but effective way', republicans experienced a rapid and almost organic growth of the Irish Volunteers, IRB and Sinn Féin.[1] (Cumann na mBan and the Irish Transport and General Workers' Union should be considered part of this 'republican front', but will be dealt with separately later.) Initially there was little outward indication of the change afoot, as separatists struggled to recover from the Cork disaster known as the Easter Rising.

The INAVDF

In the unsteady weeks following the surrender of the Dublin insurgents, Cork republicans focused on fundraising for rebel dependents. The Irish National Aid and Volunteer Dependent's Fund (INAVDF) proved very successful in Cork, raising over £2,500 in the city by July 1917 and totalling £4,000 for the county by year's end, which surpassed Red Cross donations.[2]

From 1916 to 1917, the INAVDF offered an effective organising device for Cork separatists. Sanctioned by constitutional politicians and the Catholic hierarchy, the fund expressed anti-government sentiments at a time when demonstrations and 'seditious' language were essentially illegal. Activists held monthly church-door collections, and organised benefit fundraisers, including Gaelic League céilís, GAA matches and theatrical productions, usually organised and staffed by Cumann na mBan and Irish Volunteer members.[3] Each event served as a public relations exercise that flew the subversive republican flag before thousands of Cork citizens. New recruits found outlets for their separatist allegiance, while working committees built activist networks across County Cork. With top Irish Volunteer leaders imprisoned and drilling proclaimed, the INAVDF offered demoralised Volunteers simple and legal tasks. Within the Cork INAVDF one can see coalescing elements of the republican front that would dominate the city for the next four years.

Republicans used the Cork INAVDF as a platform to protest against the treatment of Irish political prisoners. In December 1916, the Cork branch published its own pamphlet, *Official Report of the Ill-Treatment of the Irish Prisoners of War at Frongoch Internment Camp*.[4] The Cork Poor Law Guardians in August 1917 adopted an INAVDF resolution condemning the 'inhuman treatment' of republicans held in Cork's Victoria Barracks.[5] A few months later the corporation passed another strident INAVDF motion supporting republican hunger strikers in Cork men's prison.[6]

Constitutionalists opposed such partisanship, wanting the INAVDF to remain a humanitarian and non-political organisation. At the end of February 1917, the crown deported to England three senior Irish Volunteer leaders (Tomás MacCurtain, Terence MacSwiney and Seán Nolan).[7] The INAVDF asked Lord Mayor Butterfield to demand their return at an upcoming meeting of Cork magistrates.[8] Butterfield refused, arguing that the INAVDF 'was started on the understanding that the fund would not enter party politics'. Other constitutionalists distanced themselves from the INAVDF. When the fund executive was re-elected in June 1917, five of seven officers and the chairman were now active republicans.[9]

The INAVDF was mandated to provide funds to the families of those killed, injured and imprisoned during the Easter Rising. However, the Cork INAVDF wanted to subsidise new republican prisoners and victims of crown violence.[10] Following the Patrick Street riots of June 1917, the Cork INAVDF distributed £7 to the families of two civilian casualties of police violence. INAVDF National Executive secretary Michael Collins approved the specific donations but opposed establishing a precedent, because 'strictly speaking the cases do not come within our constitution'.[11] As more activists entered jail, the Cork branch argued, 'a great necessity now exists to keep the fund going.'[12] Collins rejected further assistance to new prisoners, including a subsistence grant for jailed printer Patrick Corcoran.[13] The INAVDF was ultimately replaced in 1918 by the Irish Republican Prisoners' Dependents' Fund, which dominated separatist fundraising for the next three years.[14]

The Cork INAVDF was a transitional republican organisation in the demoralising months following the Easter Rising. It provided an effective organising opportunity to separatist supporters. Amid the government's post-rising crackdown, even seemingly innocuous fundraising activities required moral courage by participants. Cork separatists moved onto bigger and better things later in 1917.

'Half-a-Dozen Absurd Nobodies' and the Re-Birth of Sinn Féin

Despite growing public support following the Easter Rising, no formal republican party structure existed in Cork until December 1916. The political vacuum was especially acute in Cork, because William O'Brien's AFIL offered disillusioned nationalists an alternative to John Redmond. The All-Fors' threat to republicans became evident during a December by-election to fill a parliamentary vacancy in west Cork.[15]

After the rising, Queenstown solicitor Frank Healy had been briefly interned because of his association with the Gaelic League. In December, he stood for the vacant Bantry (west Cork) seat on behalf of the AFIL, while claiming to represent Irish political prisoners.[16] Healy denounced partition, conscription and the detention of republicans, but refused to abstain from the House of Commons.[17] Writing on behalf of fellow republican prisoners in Reading jail, Tomás MacCurtain repudiated Healy's candidacy. Volunteer leaders in Cork also charged Healy with attempting to co-opt their movement.[18] In the *Cork Free Press*, William O'Brien disparaged Cork's 'so-called leaders . . . inactive during the rising', calling them 'half-a-dozen absurd nobodies, whose only importance is their being unknown to any one Irishman in a thousand in Cork'.[19] Despite O'Brien's intervention, Healy lost the Bantry by-election to a Redmondite (a second AFIL candidate split the All-For vote). The defeat convinced O'Brien to wind down the AFIL and shut the doors of his money-losing *Cork Free Press*.[20] Republican Seán Nolan wrote of O'Brien, 'We are glad that he has manly acknowledged the uselessness of constitutionalism and only await the day that all our MPs will realise the fact.'[21]

The Bantry by-election underscored the danger to republicans in the months after the Easter Rising. Harassed by authorities and led by relatively obscure figures, the independence movement was vulnerable to a hostile takeover by opportunistic politicians like Frank Healy. Nationally there was neither a formal political organisation nor a clearly defined republican policy. In this vulnerable embryonic stage, the independence movement could have split philosophically between those advocating republicanism or dual monarchy; physical force or passive resistance; abstention from Westminster or tactical engagement. Recognising the danger, Cork republicans advocated separatist unity, insisting only on a clear departure from the AFIL/UIL partisanship that had been so destructive to Cork public life.

In December 1916 (two weeks after the Bantry by-election), Cork republicans reformed the lapsed city branch of Sinn Féin. The provisional executive featured only long-time separatists, with trade unionist John Good (secretary, National Union of Railwaymen) and former town councillor Denis O'Neill enjoying the highest civic profiles.[22] Cork's first Sinn Féin branch had collapsed in 1911 owing to republican opposition to Arthur Griffith's dual-monarchy programme. Five years later, tensions were evident at the new branch's inaugural meeting. Both Liam de Róiste and Donal Óg O'Callaghan initially declined to take the chair. The acting commander of the city Volunteers, Seán O'Sullivan, advised his officers not to join the branch executive. A discouraged Liam de Róiste wrote, 'thus was Sinn Féin re-established in Cork and I would say it was not too promising a beginning.'[23]

The Cork City Sinn Féin Executive focused on 'quiet organising and recruitment of new members' and educating the public about Sinn Féin ideals.[24] Recognising stifling government restrictions that discouraged open meetings, the American consul at Queenstown expressed admiration for the strong growth of an organisation, 'mainly working without light and air'.[25] Sinn Féin printed membership cards and a pamphlet written by de Róiste entitled *Sinn Féin, Its Objectives and Means*.[26] Emphasising 'passive resistance to English law in Ireland', the pamphlet promised economic, cultural, and industrial rejuvenation, while rejecting parliamentarianism as 'un-Irish, un-manly, and disastrous to our country'. Party leaders shepherded through a Cork Corporation appeal to President Woodrow Wilson to secure for Ireland representation at any post-war peace conference.[27] By April 1917, an energetic Sinn Féin had established branches in every city ward.[28] Yet the emergence of Count Plunkett's Liberty League in March 1917 presented the budding Sinn Féin organisation with a dangerous challenge.

Sinn Féin: The Liberty League

After the rising, separatist leaders in Dublin debated whether to form a new political organisation or to fall in with Arthur Griffith's moderate, non-republican Sinn Féin party. Griffith had opposed the Easter Rising, and republicans feared a split among Griffith's Sinn Féin, the Irish Volunteers, Cumann na mBan, and the nascent Nation

League.[29] Following his Roscommon by-election victory, Count Plunkett convened a national conference of separatists and sympathetic public officials, to be held in April 1917 at the Dublin Mansion House. Plunkett's invitation received mixed responses from Cork, with the Poor Law Guardians sending a small delegation but the corporation refusing to respond.[30] Veteran Cork republicans attended, including de Róiste, John Good, and Seán Jennings (Sinn Féin), Mary MacSwiney (Cumann na mBan) and Robert Langford (Cork Volunteers); but so too did a number of recently converted constitutional politicians, like Paddy Meade, Con Buckley, John Dorgan and C.P. O'Sullivan.[31] At the meeting itself, a 'Mansion House Committee' was formed to coordinate different separatist organisations. The Cork Sinn Féin Executive promptly suggested this new committee declare national independence and establish a provisional government.[32] However, at the meeting Plunkett also announced the launch of his new Liberty League movement to challenge Sinn Féin.[33]

While setting up his Liberty League in May 1917, Plunkett sought contacts in Cork. Despite the availability of numerous hardline republicans suspicious of Arthur Griffith, Plunkett chose to work with town councillor Jerry Lane. An operator on the fringe of Cork republican circles, Lane had canvassed for Sinn Féin during the recent Longford by-election. Originally a labour councillor but now an independent, Lane was regarded as an opportunist, or 'a political prostitute' in the words of one colleague.[34] He gained notoriety in March 1916 after he was removed as a justice of the peace for remarking, 'as long as we are bound up by this cursed Empire, so long would they be on the verge of starvation.'[35] Lane passionately defended the Easter Rising at the corporation, and addressed the city's first separatist rally in late 1916.[36] Now working with a national figure in Plunkett, Lane attempted to build the Cork Liberty League at the expense of the new Sinn Féin organisation.

Lane advised Plunkett that the local Sinn Féin Executive wanted the Count in Cork to headline a monster meeting launching the Liberty League in Munster.[37] In fact, the Cork Sinn Féin Executive strongly opposed the Liberty League, believing it was sowing confusion, duplicating efforts, and under the control of questionable characters.[38] It accused opportunistic politicians of bolstering their careers 'by advancing with the wave of public opinion', while they split Sinn Féin in the city and county.[39] Though the Cork Sinn Féin Executive asked Lane to delay the Liberty League meeting, Lane reassured Plunkett that there was no need 'to conciliate this little un-influential clique'.[40]

TABLE 5.1
RIC-Report of Sinn Féin Clubs and
Membership, Cork City & East Cork, 917

Month	Clubs	Members
June	6	1,689
July	13	2,180
Aug.	NA	NA
Sept.	28	3,393
Oct.	38	4,442
Nov.	47	4,946
Dec.	56	5,360

Source: CI Reports for June–December 1917, CO 904/102–103

At the beginning of June, Plunkett cancelled his Cork meeting 'in the interest of the advanced movement', and joined unification talks with different separatist bodies.[41] Those negotiations produced a new Sinn Féin party, led by Irish Volunteer leader Éamon de Valera rather than Arthur Griffith.[42] With the republican party now united, Sinn Féin branches rapidly expanded in Cork, bolstered by the mass conversion of AFIL supporters.[43] By the end of the year, Sinn Féin counted 110 clubs in County Cork, out of a national total of 1,240, with 12 operating in the city.[44] 'The Cork Sinn Féin Committee have the whole city now ... The country is grand at present,' one jubilant republican wrote to Tomás MacCurtain in England. 'There is no truth in the rumour that Seán O'Cuill has immolated himself on the altar of liberty!'[45]

Sinn Féin: Continuity vs Departure

As the Cork Sinn Féin organisation was constructed in 1917, very few Irish Party office-holders crossed over to the republicans. Those that did were dismissed as 'cranks' by J.J. Horgan.[46] The most prominent Redmondite defectors were former lord mayor (and ex-Fenian) Alderman Paddy Meade; fellow ex-Fenian and labour leader C.P. O'Sullivan, (now a Poor Law Guardian); Marie Lynch, a Guardian and a suffragette; and Captain Jeremiah Collins, a harbour commissioner and member of the UIL Executive who smuggled Captain Robert Monteith out of Ireland in late 1916.[47] Though possessing political experience, none received significant roles in the budding Sinn Féin organisation. During the 1920 local elections, only Captain Collins was re-nominated by Sinn Féin, while the remainder stood down at republican instruction. Likewise, Sinn Féin did not absorb any of the AFIL town councillors or party leaders, despite their prior sympathy with separatism and the migration of the AFIL rank and file to the republican banner. Within labour, Sinn Féin reached out to the NUR and ITGWU (leaders John Good and Cathal O'Shannon were on the Cork Sinn Féin Executive), but the establishment AFIL-oriented Michael Egan/Patrick Lynch Cork Trades Council faction remained aloof.

Overall, when combining the 1918 Cork Sinn Féin Executive with the party's 1920 corporation candidate list (which included ITGWU candidates) a total of sixty-three republicans can be identified.[48] Of those sixty-three, only four (6 per cent of the total) previously held elected office (as town councillor, rural district councillor, or Poor Law Guardian).[49] The republican leadership sample also shows domination by artisans and members of the lower middle-class. Thus, this new generation of activists were a social step below the Irish Party elite, comprised mainly of large merchants and professionals. This Cork evidence supports Fergus Campbell's findings in Connaught, which challenges David Fitzpatrick's 'old wine decanted into new bottles' thesis of direct political continuation between the Irish Party and Sinn Féin.[50]

TABLE 5.2

Cork City Sinn Féin Leadership Occupations

Occupation	No.	Percent
Semi/Unskilled	6	10%
Artisan	16	25%
Organiser	6	10%
Clerk	5	8%
Shop Keeper	7	11%
Teacher	5	8%
Professional	13	21%
Merchant	5	8%

Sample: 63
Source: *Cork Examiner*, 14 January 1920

Table 5.3

Cork City Irish Party Leadership Occupations[51]

Occupation	No.	Percent
Semi/Unskilled	-	-
Artisan	4	14%
Organiser	-	-
Clerk	1	3%
Shop Keeper	2	7%
Teacher	1	3%
Professional	12	41%
Merchant	9	31%

Sample: 29

Sinn Féin: Relations with the Irish Volunteers

The city's twelve Sinn Féin branches secured premises in various meeting rooms and parish halls around Cork. Republicans organised elaborate demonstrations during the summer and autumn, addressed by local leaders and occasional luminaries like Arthur Griffith, Eoin MacNeill, Count Plunkett and Countess Markievicz.[52] In June 1917, 10,000 people greeted the released political prisoners and 5,000 denounced the Irish Convention; a September demonstration drew up to 8,000 to the Grand Parade (in the days before sound systems, the crowd was accommodated by holding three simultaneous meetings); and up to 8,000 heard Éamon de Valera speak in December.[53] Often local Sinn Féin leaders headlined republican fundraising concerts, or spoke at Gaelic League meetings and other outdoor picnics, further blurring the line between the Gaelic League and the independence movement.[54] Senior Irish Volunteer officers also frequently appeared on Sinn Féin platforms.[55] Tomás MacCurtain joined the Sinn Féin Executive in August, despite a rebuke from his friend Tadhg Barry over the failure to separate the Volunteers from Sinn Féin.[56] That same issue created problems prior to Sinn Féin's inaugural national convention in October 1917.

Every Sinn Féin branch was allocated a convention delegate, to be elected in early October. Though the Irish Volunteers had largely ignored Sinn Féin up to this point, the organisation intervened in these branch votes. Acting on the orders of the brigade leadership (probably initiated by the IRB), Volunteers packed the meetings to elect pre-approved candidates.[57] As a result, most of the city's convention delegates were Volunteers, reliable republicans, and probably more militant than the branch membership. Florrie O'Donoghue described the overall situation from the Volunteers' perspective:

> Party politics had dominated public opinion for so long that it was difficult for those who had been immersed in its conflicts to accept the new conception of national service; and more difficult still to accept it from a younger generation. We were in the dilemma of either keeping Volunteers out of the political organisation and thereby taking the risk that it would become a menace to our aspirations, or allow them to go in and thereby distracting them from their primary duties and responsibilities. The compromise solution was that a limited number of officers and men went into the Sinn Féin organisation, sufficient to exercise a reasonable degree of control and to ensure that the national claim was not endangered.[58]

Going forward, the Volunteers retained a strong voice within the Cork Sinn Féin Executive. Three influential Volunteer officers – Seán Nolan, Tadhg Barry and Donal Óg O'Callaghan – switched to primarily political roles.[59] Within three years, Nolan was a TD, Barry an alderman and O'Callaghan the lord mayor. MacCurtain became the Sinn Féin Executive vice-president (de Róiste was president), while his fellow Volunteer officers Seán Murphy and Seán O'Hegarty (also the head of the city IRB) served as a vice-president and treasurer respectfully.[60] Their presence ensured that physical force adherents dominated the Cork republican movement. The remaining four executive officers came from the Gaelic League, while Mary MacSwiney lost the election for executive vice-president. All members of the city executive were male and Catholic, with significant prior experience in the Irish-Ireland movement.

A few weeks later, the Cork Sinn Féin Executive established departments to mirror its National Executive, anticipating battles with Dublin Castle over food exports, conscription and the post-war peace conference. The departments were: Organisation, Finance, Elections, Propaganda, Agriculture, Labour, Industry/Trade/Commerce, Food, Local Government, Public Health, Plebiscite, and Education/Irish Language.[61] The plebiscite director gathered signatures for a petition demanding the upcoming peace conference confer Irish independence.[62]

The presence of Volunteer officers in the Cork Sinn Féin leadership improved relations between the two organisations.[63] When Éamon de Valera visited Cork in December, both Sinn Féin and the Irish Volunteers asked him to speak under their auspices. The problem was settled amicably, with the Volunteers giving way to Sinn Féin but still supplying meeting stewards. Cooperation increased over the coming months, as did closer coordination with Cumann na mBan.

Irish Volunteers: Rising from the Ashes in Cork

Following the end of the 1916 Easter Rising, thirteen Cork city Volunteer officers were arrested, including Brigade Commander Tomás MacCurtain and Vice-Commander Terence MacSwiney.[64] All but MacCurtain and MacSwiney were released within a few weeks, but the Cork city Volunteers remained effectively decapitated, as at-large officers kept a low profile.[65] During this time, rising fugitives used the port of Cork to escape from Ireland. Volunteers and Cumann na mBan activists smuggled out Jim Riordan, a County Kerry Volunteer wanted for shooting two constables in Firies, and Captain Robert Monteith who had been hiding since he disembarked with

Roger Casement from a German submarine in Kerry.[66] More dramatically, a priest and three nuns arrived at the Capuchin monastery at Rochestown, in the city suburbs. Two of the nuns were actually disguised Cumann na mBan members, while the third was fugitive Volunteer leader Liam Mellowes.[67] He was subsequently smuggled aboard a ship to the United States by the monastery provincial general and a sympathetic unionist shipmaster.

Cork Brigade adjutant Pat Higgins believed that during these months, 'the movement had practically collapsed in Cork City and County', while another Volunteer officer recalled 'a state of chaos in Cork City'.[68] For the remainder of the summer and well into the autumn, the city Volunteers stayed underground. By August 1916 the Cork Brigade had reformed itself informally, and joined a new national executive with the remnants of Volunteer headquarters in Dublin.[69] By late September Tadhgh Barry reported to the imprisoned Tomás MacCurtain, 'Individually, the boys are all in good health and if sick at heart yet hopeful.'[70] City Volunteers collected funds for the INAVDF, reopened the Volunteer Hall during October, and in late November marched as individuals in the annual Manchester Martyrs commemoration. [71]

Detainees were released during Christmas 1916, including Cork Brigade leaders Tomás MacCurtain and Terence MacSwiney, while Seán O'Hegarty returned from government banishment in Ballingeary. Cork veterans recognised the immediate presence of the three men, who provided 'a steadier hand on the helm' that strengthened the organisation's re-launch.[72] However, MacCurtain and MacSwiney first needed to address their inaction during the Easter Rising.[73] A dark cloud hung over the Cork Volunteers, especially those senior officers who refused to fight when it mattered most. On 13 January 1917, the Volunteer leadership gathered in the Grianán, using a Gaelic League céilidh as a cover. At the meeting, Tomás MacCurtain and Terence MacSwiney received stinging criticism from country officers, most notably Tom and Seán Hales of Ballinadee (Co. Cork), who had urged attacks on police during Easter Week.[74] 'At one point it looked as if recriminations would become too heated', so a second, more formal meeting took place on 27 January 1917.[75] Over 100 Cork delegates met at an inquiry presided over by three representatives from Volunteer headquarters in Dublin – Cathal Brugha, Diarmuid Lynch and Con Collins.[76]

During the hearing, the Hales brothers again tore into MacCurtain and MacSwiney, 'amounting to an imputation that they refused to fight'.[77] Tom Hales later recalled, 'I felt that the same situation could arise again', but a MacCurtain loyalist felt the Hales wanted 'to advertise the fact that they (the Ballinadee men) wanted to fight and others did not'.[78] The inquiry ultimately vindicated MacSwiney and MacCurtain, who maintained the support of their fellow officers.[79]

However, indicative of lingering discomfort, brigade leaders distributed 500 pamphlets justifying their inaction during the rising.[80] MacCurtain and MacSwiney's retention of power is a testament to their high personal standing within the brigade, though each had some unfinished business. MacCurtain promised Tom Hales, 'If I live I will redeem 1916.'[81] MacSwiney reassured west Cork officers, 'we are all young men yet, there is plenty of time to fight.'[82] A friend later recalled, 'In my mind there are two Terry MacSwineys – the one I knew prior to 1916 and the tragic figure that finally gave his life for Ireland . . . He was a changed man from the time of the Rising.'[83] Desperate to regain their credibility and possessing an intact paramilitary organisation, the Cork Volunteers moved into the vanguard of the Irish Volunteer movement, where they remained for the next five years.

Irish Volunteers: Expansion

In County Cork, individual Volunteer companies were structured into different battalion areas, forming a single county brigade commanded by city officers. (At the end of 1918, the county was divided into three brigades: No. 1, Cork city and Mid-Cork; No. 2, North Cork; and No. 3, West Cork.) With a strong foundation of pre-rising officers and units, the Volunteer organisation rapidly expanded in Cork city and county. Throughout 1917, city officers travelled about the county reconstituting old Volunteer companies (see Millstreet, Mourne Abbey, Midleton and Skibbereen) and starting up units in virgin territory (see Ballincollig, Inniscarra, Newmarket and Kiskeam).[84] Every Sunday, organisers cycled wide distances to train new members, primarily using as primers British Army manuals (in abundance, owing to the war). Companies took root in 1917, and by 1918 the Volunteers enjoyed a presence in almost every county parish. Parish companies belonged to regional battalions, built around large towns such as Mallow, Fermoy, Bantry, Macroom, Bandon, Midleton and Charleville, which ranged across the Cork Brigade's satellite structure. The new areas paid rich dividends during the guerrilla war of 1920–21, as locales first visited in 1917 becoming IRA strongholds, sometimes providing sanctuary to the officers who first organised them.[85]

In late 1916, new recruits flooded into the movement. By the end of the year, one officer estimated the city strength at close to 1,000, up from 300 at the time of the Easter Rising.[86] One leader recalled, 'After the release of the prisoners (Christmas 1916), new Volunteers began to pour in, and from that period onwards every officer was engaged in some way or other in organising or training the new Volunteers.'[87] Among the novices was draper's assistant Florrie O'Donoghue, who enlisted at the end of the year with his co-worker Leo Murphy (killed in 1921 while commanding 3rd Battalion, Cork No. 1 Brigade). Though neither O'Donoghue nor Murphy knew any republicans, they were determined to join the movement and offered their services at the Volunteer Hall:

> We were accepted without question or formality. At first I was not impressed by what I saw – rather the reverse. My recent reading had included much that idealised and gave a romantic glamour to the national struggle for freedom. I found it hard – impossible in fact – to relate these poetic misconceptions to the stark reality represented by groups of shabby youngsters gossiping in the Volunteer Hall or muddling through some clumsy drill.[88]

During the first half of 1917 Cork city Volunteers drilled in Sheares Street, undertook secret night training, and occasionally paraded publicly as a recruiting tool.[89] New companies were created to keep up with the influx of recruits that continued throughout the year. Prior to Easter 1916, the city Volunteers had formed a single battalion composed of four geographically structured companies.[90] By the end of 1917, the city boasted sixteen companies covering the breadth of the city, organised into two battalions and numbering about 2,000 men.[91]

Irish Volunteers: The IRB

Concurrent with the reorganisation of the city Volunteers was an expansion of the Irish Republican Brotherhood (IRB). Blaming the confusion of Easter Week on parallel IRB/Volunteer chains of command, a number of top republicans resigned from the brotherhood, including Éamon de Valera, Austin Stack and Cathal Brugha. Cork leaders Terence MacSwiney and Tomás MacCurtain ('a 100% IRB man' in the words of one senior brother) also departed 'the Organisation'.[92] Despite these defections the IRB reorganised itself on a national basis in early 1917.[93] In County Cork, senior Volunteer officers reformed and expanded the IRB during 1917, led by Seán O'Hegarty, now the brigade vice-commander.[94] Florrie O'Donoghue, a new brother, reflected on the IRB:

> It was not propagandist; it sought rather to find and bind together men of good character who had themselves reached the

conviction that there was no solution to the problem of achieving national freedom except through the use of physical force. It was good to find such men. They knew their own minds; they had a clear and definite objective; and they had an intelligent and practical approach to the realities of our situation.[95]

IRB circle leaders recruited competent and reliable Volunteers, thus serving as a second vetting of potential activists. New brothers shared the organisation's physical-force ethos, and only Volunteers were admitted.[96] This reorganised Cork city IRB seems to have acted along strategic rather than tactical lines, to influence policy rather than undertake independent operations of its own.[97] At this stage it was unclear if the Volunteers and/or Sinn Féin would embrace physical force and a republican programme. The IRB, therefore, promoted physical-force republicans into influential positions within separatist organisations, members and non-members alike. Brigade adjutant Pat Higgins, who refused to join the brotherhood, recalled: 'My own experience was that I found the IRB very fair and not prejudiced against a man because he was not a member.'[98] Within the city, most senior Volunteer officers were in the IRB, while brothers were deliberately elected as company quartermasters to retain control of weapons, which would prevent a repeat of the Easter Rising arms surrender.[99] Generally, the IRB stayed in the background during this period. A crisis over dual control of the Volunteer organisation ultimately emerged in mid-1919, and was only resolved after considerable internal turmoil.[100] At the same time, the IRB retained the loyalty of most emerging leaders of the Volunteer movement, and positioned itself to strike down any divergence from the republican path.

Irish Volunteers: Motivations

Why did these young men become physical-force republicans? IRA veteran testimony usually understates the movement's initial attraction, perhaps recognising the complexity of the decision. When recalling the tough city men in his first Volunteer company, Florrie O'Donoghue noted their 'truculent, sturdy characters without a trace of subservience' but could never fully comprehend their impetus. 'It was a puzzle to me why they were Volunteers at all,' he wrote. 'And yet, when it came to the test, they proved their courage, their loyalty, and their readiness always to take the post of greatest danger.'[101] Clearly their decision was part of a personal process that may be as difficult for historians to understand as it was for the participants themselves.

Considerable attention has been paid to the high number of prominent separatists educated in Christian Brothers schools (CBS).[102] In an
impressive geographical study, Peter Hart demonstrated a correlation
between revolutionary intensity and CBS pupil rates. This suggested to
him that, 'in teaching patriotism, the brothers created gunmen'.[103]
Indeed, a good portion of Cork's Volunteer leadership came from the
Christian Brothers' North Monastery (North Mon) secondary school,
which attracted 'respectable' working-class students.[104] There they were
exposed to the Irish language, Gaelic sports, and a few separatist
teachers. On the other hand, the North Mon was also a rugby power-
house, and until 1915 was headed by a Christian Brother described by
police officials as 'a strong pro-Britisher'.[105] In addition, the North
Mon's republican output greatly surpassed Cork's upscale Christian
Brothers College, which catered to the city's Catholic middle and upper
classes.[106] Few leading republicans came out of 'Christians', a school
that rivalled the Protestant middle-class Cork Grammar School for
wartime contributions to the British Army and surpassed it for rugby
prowess.[107] Though other factors may have contributed to the different
politics of the two Christian Brothers schools, social class seemed to be
a coefficient. Similar class concerns and conceptions of 'respectability'
can also explain the absence of serious republican activity at University
College Cork and the elite Presentation Brothers College prior to 1918.
Middle and upper middle-class Catholics ultimately joined the independence movement, but they followed public opinion rather than led
it. In this context, the question 'Who was teaching?' may be less important than the query 'Who was being taught?'

With limited membership data, it is impossible to reconstruct individual motivations for those who joined the Volunteers, though some
speculation is warranted. Peter Hart has attributed participation
largely to 'collective' rather than personal decisions, made by networks of young men tied together by communal loyalty, a theme
echoed by David Fitzpatrick.[108] Joost Augusteijn also emphasised the
importance of family connections to separatist politics. While both
factors should be considered (familial connection was especially
important prior to 1916), solid conclusions cannot rest on simple associations between individuals within the republican movement.
Though Hart emphasises republican peer group, family or workplace
connections, he cannot quantify persons within the same networks
who refrained from joining the separatist movement. Without such
detail, cause and effect cannot be determined. For example, if
Volunteer X had a brother already in the Volunteers, one might
presume his family connection drove him to enlist in the Volunteers.

However, that presumption is less convincing if Volunteer X also had six brothers who refused to join the Volunteers, and even less so if those six brothers served in the British Army. Social networks are inherently complex and difficult to deconstruct, especially in an interconnected country like Ireland, where on a local level it seems most individuals are within two degrees of separation from another.

The collective nature of revolutionary enlistment also seems less appropriate to those who joined in 1916 and 1917. At that time, young men enrolling in the Volunteers were not following the crowd but leaving it. Even at the height of the movement in late 1918, city residents serving with the British forces outnumbered Irish Volunteers by a factor of three or four to one. Prior to the conscription crisis, individual republicans frequently defied the wishes of their family, friends, neighbours, teachers and (perhaps most importantly) employers. Rather than expecting a material gain, most faced poverty, imprisonment, exile or death. Despite this, they knowingly chose to participate in a dangerous anti-government movement.

A more satisfying explanation for Volunteer membership can be found within studies of Irishmen joining the British Army during this same period.[109] David Fitzpatrick considered the wartime enlistment of Irish soldiers a 'dangerous, uncomfortable, and ultimately "irrational" decision' that put the participant at risk with little material gain.[110] His description can be easily applied to young men joining the Irish Volunteers. Some enlisted out of a conscious nationalist (separatist) ideology, or from a patriotism that transcended ideology, or because they came from a family with a (separatist) service tradition, or because they were politicised by propaganda, or from a sense of adventure and entertainment, or because their family and friends did. Most members signed up for a combination of the above reasons. One clear difference between enlistment in the British Army and the Irish Volunteers was that no one joined the latter from economic need.[111] The Volunteers paid weekly membership dues, which poses an intriguing question of those Irishmen who joined the British Army: How many would have served His Majesty if they had to pay for the privilege?

Though political motivations have been downplayed by some scholars, republican physical-force and separatist ideology obviously appealed to new adherents. That attraction grew after the Easter Rising when Ireland was being 'remobilised' for a costly war that Britain seemed to be losing. Both the republican message and its timing seem relevant to its success. The presence of a healthy separatist community in Cork prior to 1916 also appears germane. The movement was organised well enough to attract and retain new Volunteers, which would support Marie Coleman's and John O'Callaghan's findings about the importance of strong local leadership in the revolution.[112]

One missing ingredient has been previously identified by David Fitzpatrick. His exploration of Irish martial culture before the First World War, with local boy scouts, rifle clubs and military drilling (by both the UVF and Irish Volunteers), provides a precedent for later paramilitary activity.[113] However, Fitzpatrick's observations must be extended into the First World War years, when Irish popular society experienced even greater militarisation. The conflict saturated newspapers, magazines, literature, advertisements and newsreels, championing the patriotic sacrifice, personal fulfilment, and glory of wartime service.[114] Recruiting posters tied military service to masculinity, advising young men to join up, if only so they could say, 'Thank God I too was a man.'[115] Conscientious objectors and 'slackers' were often stigmatised, and Cork republicans sometimes received such hostility.[116] In this environment, one can see the appeal of a part-time, distinctly Irish paramilitary organisation.

The Great War itself seems to have made republican ideals even more attractive. Physical force was being practised by every combatant of the Great War. Republican promises of a fresh Gaelic society echoed the Allies' millennial rhetoric, which guaranteed a new world order after the 'war to end all wars'. Amid an unprecedented global conflict and the collapse of Tsarist Russia, this mentality likely appealed to prospective Irish Volunteers. Was this a once-in-a-century opportunity to drive Britain from Ireland? Were they joining the rebellion to end all rebellions?

Wartime celebration of young men willing to kill and be killed in defence of their country resonated unexpectedly in Ireland.[117] Contemporary documents show British military terms seeping into the republicans' slang of sedition, heavily dosed with irony. After 'the Big Push' (Easter Rising), Volunteers went on 'active service', fought in 'the scrap', 'did their bit', signed up in 'Pal's Battalions' (local companies), criticised 'slackers', joined 'the flying corps' (going on the run), fought 'the Huns' (English), issued statements from the 'Competent Military Authority', took orders from their 'O/C', and often ignored their own 'brass-hats' at 'GHQ'[118] Ironically, Britain's effective wartime propaganda machine blew back on itself, creating a generation of enthusiastic fighters. Unfortunately for the government, these new recruits were of the Irish rebel persuasion.

Irish Volunteers: Securing Arms

Authorities nervously watched the rebirth of the Cork Volunteers, and periodically struck at its leaders. In late February 1917, brigade officers Tomás MacCurtain, Terence MacSwiney and Seán Nolan were deported and held under open arrest in England for four months.[119] A few weeks later, police raided the Volunteer Hall on Sheares Street, and took the names of seventy men drilling inside, though many Volunteers remained silent or only responded in Irish.[120] Brigade adjutant Pat Higgins and two teenage Fianna Éireann officers, Seamus Courtney and Seán Healy, were convicted of illegal drilling and sentenced to six months and three months respectfully.[121] Two months later (May 1917), the military authorities closed the Volunteer Hall.[122] Individual Volunteer companies found drilling space in various meeting halls around the city, including the Sinn Féin headquarters on the Grand Parade.[123] In June, police arrested five Volunteers who refused to vacate the Sheares Street hall.[124]

Throughout 1917, the Cork Volunteers quietly secured weaponry. These illegal efforts were non-violent, in contrast to later seizures in 1918. Volunteers working on the Cork docks searched luggage shipped to British officers at Victoria Barracks, which occasionally produced small arms and ammunition.[125] At the port some 'odd weapons' and ammunition were brought in by merchant sailors.[126] Mercenary soldiers at the Ballincollig and Victoria barracks sold guns to Volunteers.[127] In January 1917, Peter O'Keefe, a Volunteer and bread van driver, received a five-year sentence for purchasing five rifles from a shady soldier at Victoria Barracks.[128] Florrie O'Donoghue described buying three rifles from three deserting Connaught Rangers, who demanded £6 and a change of civilian clothes. 'I remember thinking at the time,' wrote O'Donoghue, 'that if the average British soldier was of the same standard as these Connaught Rangers they were not such formidable opponents as we thought.'[129] Tomás MacCurtain employed P.J. Murphy to approach soldiers about procuring their weapons. Murphy recalled, 'Being a youth of 15 years, I did not come under suspicion and was able to move around more freely than an adult.'[130] Volunteer officer 'Pa' Murray considered soldiers on leave 'an easy mark for the purchase of arms'.[131] Weapon thefts and illegal sales became so common in late 1917 that the British Army prohibited furloughed Irish soldiers from carrying their rifles home.[132]

The Cork Volunteers made their most successful procurement during a well-planned burglary of the Church of Ireland's Cork Grammar School.[133] The school maintained a small arsenal of rifles for its Officers Training Corp, a class for secondary students prior to entering the British Army officer corps. An Irish Volunteer workman painting the school noted the rifles and made an impression of the school's door lock, from which a key was made. Showing a separatist continuity, the twenty-five raiders were briefed inside An Dún, the O'Growney branch Gaelic League branch hall. In the early hours of 3 September 1917, the Volunteers broke into the school and took at least forty-seven rifles.[134] The seizure raised republican morale; as raid leader Robert Langford later claimed, 'it once and for all wiped out whatever stigma was there on the arms surrender of 1916.'[135]

Irish Volunteers: Public Defiance

During this period city Volunteers publicly defied government DORA restrictions on drilling, wearing of uniforms, and public assemblies. Following the Sinn Féin by-election victories in Longford (May 1917) and East Clare (July 1917), the Volunteers paraded the city streets behind their colourful piper band.[136] An imprisoned republican fondly recalled one march, when a crowd, 'came up around the jail shouting and cheering for our benefit. We in turn waved the small white towel each prisoner had out through the bars.'[137] Foreshadowing the paramilitary spectacles of 1920–21, Cork Brigade officers used the funeral of Volunteer Denis Murphy (who died of natural causes) as a demonstration, with 500 Volunteers and the piper band marching behind the tricolour-shrouded coffin.[138]

Historian Joost Augusteijn has explored similar public defiance in the Irish Volunteer movement during 1917, with a watershed occurring after Thomas Ashe's death by force-feeding in September.[139] Yet in Cork city there were additional reasons for the public mobilisations besides Ashe's death. During the summer and autumn of 1917, anti-government street violence had grown intense and frequent, with September proving an especially bad month. As previously mentioned, Cork experienced five separate nights of street rioting in September, during three unrelated episodes. The last two disturbances included civilian revolver shots and police bayonet charges.[140]

When Tomás MacCurtain addressed young republicans the night after Thomas Ashe's funeral, he condemned the repeated street clashes, and 'strongly counselled his audience to help in maintaining order'.[141] His Cork Brigade then approached Volunteer headquarters in Dublin and asked for a public parade of all units.[142] These illegal demonstrations were scheduled for Sunday 21 October, with fifty occurring in County Clare and forty in County Cork, along with major mobilisations in Tralee, Limerick and Cork city.[143] Seemingly brigade commander Tomás MacCurtain sought a constructive outlet for his young Volunteers, while seeking to boldly defy government prohibitions on the movement. MacCurtain wrote, 'We knew we would be arrested but something new was needed to stir the people up', a sentiment also expressed by 1st Battalion commander Fred Murray: 'When we went out, we went out to be arrested.'[144]

The Cork mobilisation was a dramatic piece of street theatre. Outside their shuttered headquarters, at least 700 Cork city Volunteers gathered, along with the Volunteer Piper Band, Cumann na mBan members, republican girl guides, and Fianna boy scouts.[145] The *Cork Constitution* wrote of the Fianna, 'Young boys wearing uniforms could be seen at almost every street corner – and where half a dozen of them got together one of the number took it upon himself to put the others through military movements.'[146] Florrie O'Donoghue recalled, 'Only a minority had full uniform, but all made the best show possible, with Volunteer caps, bandoliers, belts, and puttees. No arms were carried.'[147] The entire body followed the pipers down the Western Road and through the surrounding countryside, periodically rendezvousing with other Volunteer companies. After a few hours, 1,500 Volunteers returned to the National Monument, and drilled for a few minutes before dispersing.[148]

A few days later the police arrested virtually the entire Cork city Volunteer leadership, including Tomás MacCurtain and Terence MacSwiney.[149] However, this did not prevent the Volunteers from marching two weeks later to a Gaelic League aerideacht (gathering) in Blarney. Between 1,500 and 2,000 Volunteers again assembled at Sheares Street on 4 November 1917.[150] The Volunteers marched outside the city for eight hours, and the *Cork Constitution* wrote, 'There was much anxiety as to what the outcome of their persistence in defying the Realm Act would be, and crowds thronged the streets during the afternoon awaiting their return.'[151] The Volunteers quietly arrived in the city, once again without provoking a government response to their civil disobedience.

The city Volunteers gathered yet again two weeks later, on 18 November 1917, with 1,200 marching and drilling in the city centre and suburbs. A correspondent reported:

> A crowd gathered while the drilling was in progress, and they watched with interest and not a little anxiety this audacious defiance of the Realm Regulations . . . Their familiarity with the various military movements through which they were put rather

suggests that constant drilling is going on, though where all but the revolutionists are ignorant.[152]

Inside Dublin Castle the chief secretary observed, 'the massed drills in County Cork are a new departure', and asked RIC Inspector General Byrne if they should be broken up with police and soldiers. Byrne advised against dispersing Volunteer parades, since it could 'stir up more trouble than the local police could cope with', and instead suggested they arrest local Volunteer leaders.[153] Fortunately for the authorities, the Volunteers felt they had made their point and ended their public defiance campaign. Hereafter they trained quietly, usually during the evenings in the privacy of meeting halls, or secluded fields and crossroads.[154]

Irish Volunteers: Militarised Prison Culture

Arrested for illegal drilling in October 1917, MacCurtain and MacSwiney used their stay at Cork men's prison to replicate the politicised prison environment they experienced in Frongoch and Reading jail during 1916. They installed a military regime for 'IRA Prisoners of War' (now numbering about fifty), organising a chain of command, work details, signalling practice and military drills.[155]

Facing DORA military court-martials, the republicans created a spectacle out of their refusal to recognise the court (a relatively new concept in Cork).[156] Former Irish teachers MacCurtain and George Clancy (of Limerick) came up with the phrase, 'Níl meas madra agam ar an gCúirt seo', which translated roughly to 'I haven't a dog's respect for this court'. They then taught inmates the proper Irish pronunciation.[157] On the first day of hearings, prisoners answered the judge only with this Irish phrase, much to the latter's consternation.[158] A few prisoners with Gaelic League backgrounds defended themselves passionately in Irish, which sparked prolonged laughter from spectators. The next day, another batch of prisoners entered the court, including teenage Fianna officers Seamus Courtney and Seán Healy (facing their second jail term). Courtney's Irish response triggered audience laughter, which caused the irate court president Major Bowen to clear the court. He explained, 'I am not going to sit here and be insulted by any man.' Seán Healy was next, and his identical answer caused Bowen to explode, 'I'm top dog here anyway . . . I won't have this Hottentot language.'[159] Bowen's insult of the Irish language sparked denunciations from the corporation and the Poor Law Guardians, a protest meeting by the Cork Gaelic League, and a hostile question in the House of Commons.[160] Republicans subsequently embraced the term 'Hottentot' as a nickname for themselves.[161] After the November court-martials, Cork Volunteer prisoners continued to refuse to recognise the courts, albeit with considerably less flair.

The prisoners were not finished rattling their cage. In the wake of an epic Mountjoy jail strike, Cork inmates demanded the same political treatment granted to prisoners in Dublin.[162] On 19 November 1917, thirty-seven Cork men's prison inmates hunger struck for political treatment, along with a further sixteen detainees who were transferred to Dundalk.[163] For two days concerned crowds gathered outside the prison, singing and signalling to prisoners until dispersed by a police baton charge.[164] Spooked by Thomas Ashe's controversial death, the General Prison Board promptly released all thirty-seven Cork prisoners under the Cat and Mouse Act.[165] They emerged from the prison gates with a propaganda triumph, and left behind a militarised jail culture. Recognising the new confrontational attitude, the Cork prison governor sought to segregate political prisoners from ordinary criminals, 'owing to the dangers of contamination'.[166] Over the next three years, there would be a further eighteen hunger strikes in Cork men's prison, resulting in the release of fifty-nine prisoners.[167] The tactic was only abandoned after the globally famous strike of August – November 1920 that saw the death of Terence MacSwiney and two other Cork Volunteers.

Days after their prison victory, the Volunteers made another impressive display at the annual Manchester Martyrs commemoration. Up to 15,000 residents watched the massive paramilitary spectacle.[168] An estimated 3,000 Volunteers from the city and county marched in the procession, alongside 500 Fianna boy scouts, 200 Clan na Gael girl guides, and 3,000 members of the ITGWU. Appreciating the parade's magnitude, republican pioneer Tadhg Barry reminded listeners of the humble founding meeting of Cork's Irish Volunteers four years previously, when they were assaulted by their Hibernian opponents: 'It was not so long ago when they in Cork broke J.J. Walsh's head and hunted Casement, but that would not happen again.'[169]

The year 1917 opened with hidden groups of republicans covertly contacting each other, but closed with a resounding victory for the new national front. Éamon de Valera, leader of both the Irish Volunteers and Sinn Féin, visited Cork on 8 and 9 December 1917. The British authorities debated banning a scheduled Volunteer parade, but commanders on the ground argued that repression 'would be very much worse than the review itself'.[170] (A reluctant Dublin Castle instructed the military to disarm any Volunteers carrying weapons.)[171]

De Valera was met at the train station by 1,200 Volunteers and escorted to his hotel. The following day he reviewed 2,000 Volunteers in the city centre prior to a mass meeting of 6,000 to 8,000 city residents.[172] The Redmondite *Cork Examiner* applauded the Volunteers' discipline: 'The demonstration was as orderly as any ever held in the city.' Pointing out the implied threat by a public parade of a paramilitary body, the *Examiner* also argued, 'No doubt many Sinn Féiners and Irish Volunteers still cling to the idea of an independent Irish Republic, but men of common sense can scarcely hope to see this won by force of arms.'[173] Common sense would come under a more determined threat in 1918.

VI. Twilight of the Mollies: The Decline of the Irish Party in 1917

I have been warning them for two years that they did not understand the new mind of Ireland and that disaster would come.
Colonel Maurice Moore to Henry Donegan, May 1917[1]

The Irish Party in Cork city remained a strong and multifaceted organisation in 1916. The United Irish League served as its political apparatus, with five branches operating in the city. Redmondite officials ran Cork Corporation and other public bodies, pursuing an Irish Party agenda whenever possible. The Ancient Order of Hibernians buttressed the party, while the Irish National Volunteers militia (NV) acted as a paramilitary counterweight to the Irish Volunteers. Though Cork Redmondites lost significant ground between 1914 and 1916, they still monopolised power at the beginning of 1917. However, over the next twelve months Irish Party support collapsed outside its narrow activist base. Popularity of the Irish Party fell in Cork as anger rose against government coercion, possible conscription, pending partition, and John Redmond's continued inability to deliver Home Rule.

Public Bodies: The Cork Poor Law Guardians

Among the city's elected officials, the Cork Poor Law Guardians showed the clearest transformation from Redmondism to republicanism. Though nominally composed of seventy members, Board of Guardian meetings rarely mustered more than a dozen attendees, except for votes filling employment vacancies. Responsible for managing outdoor relief, the Cork Workhouse, and healthcare for impoverished city residents, the board relied on a small band of devoted Guardians, disproportionately composed of progressive activists, trade unionists and advanced nationalists.[2] After Easter 1916, these members coalesced around republicans on the board, countering the Irish Party's strong numeric majority.[3] They frequently passed motions intended to embarrass the British government, which constitutionalists proved reluctant to oppose. Similar denunciations of Dublin Castle continued over the coming months.

In late May 1916, the Guardians called for the release of interned Irish political prisoners, for the imaginative reason that they were needed as labourers for the coming harvest.[4] The following month, the board denounced martial law, and characterised partition as 'the creation of another Pale in Ireland'.[5] In July, it protested the 'murder' of Sir Roger Casement, the 'hatred and perfidy of the English Government towards Irishmen', and the absence of constitutional government in the country.[6] During 1917, the Guardians condemned police brutality, food profiteering, and the British Army's killing of civilians during the Easter Rising.[7] Indicative of their republican trajectory, the Guardians in April 1917 sent delegates to Count Plunkett's separatist convention in Dublin (albeit by taking the vote at the end of a meeting after most members left), and endorsed Sinn Féin in the South Longford and East Clare by-elections.[8] The Guardians' most common concern was the detention and treatment of Irish political prisoners, an issue addressed on seven separate occasions in 1917.[9] Violent anti-government language became more evident in Guardian motions, such as protests against 'the insidious poison of English deceit, hypocrisy and cant';[10] and 'the militarists who . . . hypocritically masquerade before the nations of the world as the "champions of small nationalities"'.[11]

In September 1917, the Guardians fired their workhouse store-keeper for graft, replacing him with Irish Volunteer and IRB leader Seán O'Hegarty.[12] They overcame vigorous protests from Irish Party officials, whose claims of IRB intimidation in the hiring prompted a Local Government Board (LGB) inquiry.[13] The LGB ultimately cleared O'Hegarty and his supporters, amid counter-charges by O'Hegarty's attorney Maurice Healy (MP) that the inquiry had been arranged by the AOH.[14] Over the next three years, O'Hegarty's strident campaign against workhouse corruption earned unlikely applause from the unionist *Cork Constitution*.[15]

In November 1917, the Poor Law Guardians became Cork's first public body to elect a republican chairman, Denis Hayes of Blarney. He attributed his selection to 'the noble and patriotic policy of Sinn Féin and Volunteers'.[16] The Guardians remained Cork's most audible republican public body through the truce of 11 July 1921.

Public Bodies: Cork Corporation

Recognising changing public opinion after the Easter Rising, the Redmondite-controlled corporation sharpened its anti-government rhetoric, but stayed loyal to the Irish Party. Only one of thirty-seven Redmondite town councillors defected to Sinn Féin. A number of AFIL councillors, many formerly affiliated to the Cork Labour Party, also expressed sympathy with Sinn Féin. The leading Sinn Féin convert on the corporation was independent councillor Jerry Lane, another former Labour Party representative.[17] Republicans mustered no more than seven reliable votes on the corporation, thus remaining hopelessly outnumbered by Redmondites.

The corporation loudly trumpeted its nationalist credentials in the months following the rising. As the American consul at Queenstown explained, Irish Party leaders 'have chosen to weather the popular tempest by driving full sail before it; and by pandering to the violent Anglophobe sentiment'.[18] In the summer and autumn of 1916, strident motions celebrated Bishop Dwyer's criticisms of General Maxwell, condemned partition, and threatened 'turmoil and bloodshed' if the government introduced military conscription.[19] In September 1916, the corporation six times refused to provide a quorum for a resolution congratulating the Royal Navy on its victory at Jutland.[20] After finally passing the motion (tendering 'our grateful appreciation for the magnificent service rendered by them to the cause of humanity') disapproving Redmondites played a cruel hoax on the motion's persistent advocate, their UIL colleague and loyal British Army recruiter, councillor M.J. O'Riordan.[21]

Following a corporation meeting, Lord Mayor Butterfield invited the councillors into his chambers for a special ceremony. Calling forward councillor O'Riordan, Butterfield presented him with a garish eighteen-inch ribbon attached to a medal inscribed with the words 'Imperial Service.' O'Riordan asked Butterfield to pin the medal 'next to my heart', and sang 'A Soldier and a Man' before the giggling councillors.[22] Buttterfield then read a letter to O'Riordan, supposedly from Sir John Jellicoe, admiral of the North Seas Fleet:

> . . . The document began with some flattering expressions towards himself for carrying his resolution about the battle of Jutland so successfully in the Corporation, but towards the end of it were expressions reviling him for bringing on the resolution and for his attendance at recruiting meetings.[23]

Understandably, the practical joke infuriated O'Riordan. 'My name is Riordan. I come of the old Milesian line, and my ancestors were here thousands of years before the Christian era, but you,' he sputtered at Butterfield, 'you are the son of a shipwrecked mariner.'[24] O'Riordan reluctantly accepted Butterfield's apology, but leaked the episode to the press, to the corporation's embarrassment. The councillors also readied a fake decoration for High Sheriff William Hart (another pro-war Redmondite), supposedly from Admiral Beatty thanking Hart for helping to strip the freedom of the city from German scholar Kuno Meyer in 1915. A kind-hearted councillor directed Hart away from the satirical ceremony.[25]

The corporation mocked pro-war councillors even as it passed a pro-war resolution. Denouncing partition during the Lloyd George negotiations in 1916, the corporation also declared 'full and complete confidence in the honesty, wisdom, and statesmanship of Mr John Redmond and the Irish Parliamentary', despite Redmond's acceptance of partition.[26] Weeks after congratulating Limerick Bishop Dwyer for criticising the British military regime, the corporation refused to grant him the freedom of the city. The *Southern Star*'s Cork correspondent (republican Tadhg Barry)[27] underlined clumsy Redmondite efforts to remain on both sides of the fence:

> The actions of the Cork Corporation are beautifully inconsistent. Votes of thanks to Bishop Dwyer are passed as readily as votes of confidence in Mr Redmond; while it is considered again a Nationalist principle, to congratulate Jellicoe on his North Sea victory . . . Members make violent speeches expressing their willingness to be shot with their backs against the wall and the next minute express the opinion that those who did this spoiled Home Rule. So the jumble goes on with the man in the street growing more disgusted hourly with all representatives, denying that any of them represent public opinion.[28]

Strong anti-government rhetoric flowed from the corporation in late 1917. Angry protests were lodged over British Army killings of civilians at Portobello barracks during the Easter Rising, the force-feeding death of Thomas Ashe, 'so foully murdered in a British Prison', and Britain's 'reign of terror' intended to deny Irish self-determination.[29] Reflecting rising Irish expectations caused by America's recent entry into the war and Woodrow Wilson's self-determination rhetoric, the corporation sent six separate appeals to the United States calling for Irish self-determination and democracy for small nations.[30] Like the Poor Law Guardians, the corporation paid particular attention to political prisoners, passing eight different protests concerning their treatment and detention in 1917.[31] Yet a series of public controversies in 1917 showed Redmondite councillors trapped between their loyalty to the Irish Party and increasing public hostility to the British government.

Public Controversy: The Irish-Canadian Rangers Visit Cork

A visiting Canadian Army battalion marked the Irish Party's last major celebration of the war in Cork. The Duchess of Connaught's Canadian Rangers (more commonly known as the Irish-Canadian Rangers) began as a Territorial Army unit drawn from Montreal's Irish Catholic and Protestant communities.[32] During 1916, it produced a battalion of Irish-Canadians for overseas service in France, which was also intended to improve recruiting in Ireland.[33] Battalion officers retained strong ties with the Irish Party, and claimed the unit's mixed Catholic/Protestant heritage reflected the new Home Rule Ireland.[34] After some difficulty securing enlistments (a problem experienced across Canada in 1916), the Rangers trained and shipped out to England at the end of 1916. Upon its arrival on 3 January 1917, the War Office informed commanding officer Colonel Harry J. Trihey that his battalion would be broken up (like other newly raised units) and his officers and men distributed as individual replacements to Canadian Corps in France. Colonel Trihey and his executive officer resigned and returned to Canada in protest at the decision. However, before the battalion's disbandment became public knowledge, Colonial Secretary Andrew Bonar Law arranged for the Rangers to tour Irish cities to bolster recruiting.[35] The visit included parades, civic receptions, and footage taken for a propaganda film later shown in Britain, Canada and the United States.[36]

John Redmond activated his Irish Party apparatus to facilitate the Canadian Rangers in Cork. 'I am extremely anxious that it should be well received,' he told Cork UIL leader J.J. Horgan, asking for assistance in 'every way in your power'.[37] Joseph Devlin worked with J.J. Horgan to mobilise supporters.[38] They formed a reception committee that included the city's AFIL MPs, Bishop Cohalan, and representatives from public bodies, the chamber of commerce, IDA, and Cork Trades Council.[39] Scheduled for 30 and 31 January 1917, the Ranger itinerary featured a civic reception, entertainment for the troops, and a battalion parade. The Rangers received similar welcomes during their stops in Armagh, Belfast, Dublin and Limerick.

The corporation hosted an elaborate hotel luncheon for the Ranger officers. The city's political and commercial elite gave patriotic speeches and drank to the king's health. The Rangers' new (and final) commanding officer, Colonel James Patrick Vincent O'Donahoe, briefly spoke, apparently referring to local suspicion about the Rangers' mission: 'I had also been asked, in a sort of mysterious way, what we were doing in Ireland, and I answered, we were having the best time we ever had in our lives.'[40] The following year, the *Cork Examiner* recalled O'Donahoe's charm and striking six foot four frame, after he was killed in Flanders.[41]

The highlight of the Rangers' visit was a parade through Cork city centre. Many homes and shops flew Union Jacks, and thousands lined the route to catch a glimpse of the 800 Canadians.[42] *Cork Examiner* editorials described the city's 'cordiality and hospitality' for the Rangers, and boasted 'nowhere was a more hearty welcome to these sons of Ireland'.[43] The reception was not unanimous, however. Though Bishop Cohalan was a member of the reception committee, he did not attend any of the Rangers' festivities, explaining to the authorities, 'he would thus have more influence over Sinn Féin'.[44] Republicans likewise boycotted the proceedings, and later posted notices outside fourteen city shops:

> From this shop the Union Jack was displayed on the occasion of the visit of some Canadian soldiers . . . Will you support a firm which displays this cheap and mercenary loyalty?[45]

The Ranger tour was the Irish Party's last concerted embrace of the war effort in Cork. Considering its prior reluctance to engage in recruiting, Cork's Irish Party could hardly have welcomed Redmond's enthusiasm for the Rangers visit, which seemed more appropriate for January 1915 than January 1917. The tour reflected Redmond's faith that his vision for Ireland could still prevail against unionist and republican opposition. Emphasising the Irish-Canadian Rangers' fealty to the crown, their Canadian nationalism, and their dual Catholic and Protestant identity, Redmondites claimed the battalion symbolised a new imperial Ireland unified under Home Rule. Yet the realities of the Great War had already overtaken both Redmond and the Rangers. The Canadians' tour ultimately proved no more than a cynical government public relations ploy. While Dublin Castle and the Irish Party portrayed the battalion as Irish Protestants and Catholics fighting shoulder to shoulder for Home Rule, the War Office had already secretly broken up and scattered the Rangers across the four corners of the Canadian Army in France. The battalion's motto 'Quis Separabit', or 'Who Shall Separate Us?' proved as illusory as Redmond's Home Rule dream for Ireland.

Public Controversy: The *Daily Mail* Visits 'A Modern Baghdad'

Local Redmondites revealed striking sensitivity over the city's association with political disturbances during a row with the conservative English newspaper, the *Daily Mail*. In February 1917, *Daily Mail* Ireland correspondent Harold Ashton wrote a sensational article about a particularly rowdy evening in Cork city:

> Dublin may be the capital of Ireland, but Cork is the chief city of Sinn Féin and its many ramifications. It is a modern Baghdad for romance and astonishing happenings. Tonight the people streamed throughout the streets like pilgrims arriving at Mecca ... Sinn Féiners were out in platoons, roving the streets in a spirit of high bravado. Most of them were young men, upon whom the drilling preliminary to the adventures of last Easter Week had left its mark. And for an hour or so, the warm night was very lively with detonations, excursions, and alarms, but the tall, quiet-eyed men of the Royal Irish Constabulary, moving always in couples among the press, armed with revolvers and handy little staves cleverly broke up the demonstrators and never allowed any mass formation. Meanwhile, an intelligent eye was kept on the rebel headquarters in Sheares Street and in certain other districts, and everything was completely, though invisibly, in hand.[46]

The article raised cackles in Cork, especially since the writer entirely misread his Saturday-night excursion. Rather than a parade of seditious republicans, Ashton stumbled into unruly Cork schoolboys, celebrating a rugby match result by blowing horns and throwing firecrackers at pedestrians on Patrick Street. (Bitter city rivals Presentation College and Christian Brothers College had just played to a draw in the Munster's School Cup semi-final.)[47] 'Things had come to a strange pass if the fact of boys going around rejoicing after a cup tie,' argued Lord Mayor Butterfield, 'could be turned into a political business to injure the city of Cork in the eyes of the world.' Butterfield denied that any political demonstration had occurred, explaining that 'the usual horseplay ... was done in Cork from time immemorial'.[48] The RIC district inspector agreed, reporting, 'it was an absolutely normal night', which satisfied the Irish chief secretary when the matter was raised in the House of Commons.[49] The *Daily Mail* claimed their correspondent had not 'ever before mistaken a football crowd for a demonstration', but added sullenly, 'the distinction is, however, not always very marked in Ireland.'[50]

Public officials rushed to undermine what they claimed to be a deliberate campaign to sully the city's good name. High Sheriff Willie O'Connor complained, 'It was a cowardly and mean and contemptible thing to try to turn a football match into a political disturbance', while former Redmondite Lord Mayor Sir Henry O'Shea asserted, 'There was not a more law-abiding city than Cork.' Magistrate P.H. Curtis believed the article came from jealous commercial interests, 'trying to frighten away English investors from Cork'.[51] City magistrates held a special meeting to protest against the article that 'deliberately intended to create disunion and ill-feeling in the community'.[52] Three separate *Cork Examiner* editorials criticised the *Daily Mail*, and the corporation passed a motion applauding Butterfield's vigorous handling of the episode.[53]

Though accurate about the events in question, Irish Party partisans incorrectly claimed all was peaceful in Cork. They either deliberately downplayed or failed to see emerging republican opposition to British rule in the city, which manifested itself in numerous street riots later in 1917. As the change in public opinion became increasingly clear, Cork Redmondites expressed ambivalence towards the British administration and the war effort, though not without a rallying call to a final attempt to solve the Home Rule impasse.

Public Controversy: Partition and the Irish Convention

In March 1917, the British government re-opened the Home Rule debate by announcing it would not force Ulster into submitting to an Irish parliament. Outraged, John Redmond led the Irish Party out of the House of Commons, warning, 'If the constitutional movement disappears the Prime Minister will find himself face to face with the revolutionary movement.'[54] The *Cork Examiner* raged over this 'breach of faith', and wrote six straight editorials denouncing the government.[55] Local Redmondites felt aggrieved by the pending partition of the country and the government's failure to implement the Home Rule Act on the statute books, especially after Redmond's firm support for the war.

On 12 March 1917, the UIL Cork City Executive held a special meeting to denounce the government's decision.[56] 'Ireland was not alone disappointed, but horrified,' remarked coroner William Murphy, 'particularly Irishmen who believed Great Britain open to reason, and that the English Government was honourable and trustworthy.'[57] He further argued that the British government received the support of nationalist Ireland in the war, 'under false pretences, apparently', a theme expanded on by other Redmondites. 'At the outbreak of the war the people of Ireland were promised Home Rule,' continued Willie O'Connor, 'and in accordance with that pledge plenty of Irishmen took up arms and joined the colours on behalf of the Empire.' Lord Mayor Butterfield agreed: 'they knew that the promises that had been made to them were never intended to be fulfilled.' The UIL Executive passed a motion protesting against 'the treacherous and dishonourable conduct of Mr Lloyd George's Government', and explained that the principle of self-determination 'cannot be applied with justice to Belgium, Poland, and Serbia, unless it is also applied to Ireland'.

Local observers disagreed about the impact of partition on the political fortunes of Cork Redmondites. 'The Nationalist Party have recovered a good deal of their former prestige by the truculent attitude they have assumed in the House of Commons,' reported local British military intelligence officers. 'As a result, many "wobblers" are again supporters of the Constitutional policy as distinct from that of Sinn Féin.'[58] However, the *Cork Constitution* claimed local Redmondites were in 'the deepest depression and despair', believing 'their movement had received a deadly blow, from which it will hardly recover'.[59] The Cork city police thought the continued Home Rule impasse was increasing public impatience. 'I have noticed that a great change has come over the City and Riding in regards to Home Rule,' wrote the RIC county inspector. 'The desire for self-government has become intensified in the Nationalist community, and what is more remarkable is that some who were militant Unionists a year ago, now desire a settlement and peace.'[60]

Trying to end the stalemate, the British government organised the 'Irish Convention' composed of moderate-opinion leaders within Ireland's political establishment. It was hoped they could reach a Home Rule settlement amenable to unionists and constitutionalists.[61] Yet nationalist expectations for the convention seem to have been dashed by the Government's unwillingness to prevent partition. The convention's lack of a democratic mandate also damaged its credibility, as Dublin Castle arbitrarily determined the delegation strengths. The AFIL's William O'Brien argued that selected representatives '. . . would quite certainly be defeated if they were obliged to face their constituents at the polls'.[62] J.J. Horgan likewise considered the Irish Convention 'utterly undemocratic and unjust', and later wrote that Sinn Féin, 'even at that time, probably represented the majority of the Irish electorate'.[63]

Sinn Féin never contemplated entering the conference, with the deported Tomás MacCurtain summarising the republican attitude:

'Now they invite us to fix the Irish while they pack the convention and make it impossible to agree,' he wrote to his wife. 'The dirty pack of thieves, do they think to guile us this way?'[64] More disappointing to the government was the AFIL's refusal to join, despite Lloyd George's personal appeals to William O'Brien.[65] Beyond his concern about the convention's democratic mandate and strong opposition to partition, O'Brien believed a resolution could only be achieved by a small gathering like the 1902 Wyndham land conference. The Cork Trades Council also rejected participating in the convention, thinking the government would use its attendance to excuse the exclusion of the Irish Labour Party.[66] Overall, three of the city's five political parties boycotted the convention.

University College Cork president Sir Bertram Windle and Lord Mayor T.C. Butterfield acted as the Cork UIL delegates. Other Cork Redmondites endorsed the convention with little enthusiasm. The corporation cited the government's 'apparent insincerity of trying to "tackle" the Irish Question whilst the blessings of Martial Law and Defence of the Realm regulations are lavished on the Irish people'.[67] Bishop Cohalan counselled patience: 'though the constitution of the convention may not be perfect, they should give that body a fair chance, and reserve criticism until they see its recommendations.'[68]

In June 1917, the city's commercial and political elite gathered to publicly endorse the convention and its presumed settlement.[69] Through this 'most representative and far-seeing and practical body of the citizens', the *Cork Examiner* promised, 'the seed of unity which is to be planted in Cork today will grow into a flourishing tree.'[70] Sinn Féin pre-empted with its own rally of 5,000 republicans to denounce the convention and its Cork supporters. Speakers emphasised the convention's undemocratic nature, characterising nationalist delegates 'as representative of the people as the history of 100 years ago'. Liam de Róiste promised, 'Sinn Féin was prepared to abide the voice of the people if their voice was taken.'[71] Resentment was expressed at the city's commercial elite approving the convention on behalf of Cork residents. The Sinn Féin motion repudiated 'the right of any body of men in Cork to speak for the people of this city', and demanded an election under universal suffrage to determine 'the future form of Government we are to live under'.[72] More would be heard from republicans the following day.

Sir Bertram Windle chaired the pro-convention meeting of about 500 male unionist and Irish Party adherents.[73] The gathering attracted leading city merchants, bankers, railway directors, medical professionals, solicitors, magistrates, university professors, and Church of

Ireland clergy, including Bishop Dowse. The meeting's cross-religious support was undermined by the absence of Bishop Cohalan and other Catholic clergy. Less understandable was the non-attendance of most of the city's UIL leadership, including twenty-seven of thirty-three town councillors and the triumvirate of coroners McCabe, Murphy, and Horgan.[74]

The list of speakers reflected the commercial makeup of the assembly, which heard from, among others, Sharman Crawford and Richard Beamish (the brewers), Braham Sutton (Sutton's Drapers), T.B. Lillis (director, Munster and Leinster Bank), S.D. Budd (director, Provincial Bank), and Sir Stanley Harrington (chairman, Cork, Blackrock, and Passage Railway). They advocated a Home Rule settlement on the grounds of pragmatism and anticipated economic benefits. However, fifty to a hundred republican hecklers soon stopped the proceedings.[75] Amid their singing and booing, the republicans scattered pamphlets titled 'Trust the People', demanded Windle read a Sinn Féin resolution, and shouted down Bishop Dowse, despite cries of 'shame' from the assembly.[76] Though the republicans chanted familiar slogans like 'Up the Rebels' and 'Up the Sinn Féiners', they also expressed class resentment with cries of 'Down with Capitalism' and 'This is a meeting of sweaters' (i.e. owners of sweat shops).[77] The republicans brought the meeting to a halt, sabotaging Cork's moneyed classes' endorsement of the Irish Convention.

Three months later, the Irish Convention arrived for a three-day sitting in Cork on 25–27 September 1917. The visit to 'the Southern capital' prompted a massive civic reception, with luncheons, excursions, and presentations on Cork's economic viability. The corporation issued a commemorative booklet titled *Cork: Past and Present*, and the *Cork Constitution* included a commercial supplement highlighting investment opportunities to visiting press and dignitaries.[78] Cork Harbour Board chairman Daniel Lucy compared the sitting to the 'historic Dungarvan Convention', while the *Cork Examiner* warned, 'we cannot perceive of a greater tragedy or one more fraught with dire results for our beloved country than its failure.'[79] The Irish Convention reception committee included bishops Dowse and Cohalan, prominent unionists, and the local Redmondite leadership.[80] Illustrating convention delegates' class composition, they enjoyed temporary membership at the County Club, City Club, and the Royal Cork Yacht Club.[81]

The preceding Sunday, Sinn Féin held a mass protest against the convention that drew 7,000–8,000 spectators to the Grand Parade. John Good promised that republicans would ensure 'no gang of capitalist thieves deprived the poor of the right to live'.[82] Despite their

protests, the republican leaders had already decided against inter-
fering with the convention's sittings in Cork, and advised their
followers to 'simply let it go by'.[83] Taking no chances, the RIC drafted
in police reinforcements.[84]

The convention delegates arrived in Cork by special train, but John
Redmond and Joe Devlin slipped into the city unannounced by automobile.[85] A small crowd of Redmondites met delegates at Glanmire
station; Church of Ireland Bishop Dowse attended, but not Catholic
Bishop Cohalan. The next day, 200 Irish Party supporters cheered the
delegates' arrival to their sitting at the Crawford Technical Institute,
though Redmond and Devlin heard hissing while entering the
building.[86] The convention sat for just two hours before breaking for
the day, indicative of its glacial workrate in Cork. (In three days of sittings, the convention sessions totalled seven hours, roughly a third of
the time delegates spent at entertainment functions.)[87] Delegates proceeded to a luncheon hosted by the Cork Harbour Commission at the
Imperial Hotel, where they drank toasts to the king and the success of
the Irish Convention. A deputation of female Irish Party supporters
handed a bouquet to John Redmond, inscribed with lines that likely
resonated with the fading Irish Party leader :

> *Tho' friends may turn against you.*
> *And forces say what they will.*
> *Our hearts are in our country,*
> *And we love our leader still.*[88]

The invitation list for the banquet illustrates the restrictive nature
of Cork's political and commercial establishment in 1917. Among the
guests were the chairs of Cork's public bodies, Catholic and
Protestant bishops, bank managers, merchant princes, newspaper
publishers, judges, police officials, army and navy officers, members
of parliament, and shipping line agents. However, the 296 invitees
included just two representatives of organised labour, one republican,
and no women.[89]

A more exotic civic reception occurred on the Irish Convention's
second day, when the lord mayor hosted the 'Throwing the Dart' ceremony in Cork Harbour.[90] The 400-year-old annual excursion consisted
of the lord mayor throwing a small spear into the water off Roche's
Point, to demark the city's maritime boundary. Convention delegates
and city officials boarded the City of Cork Steampacket SS *Inniscarra*
(sunk by a German u-boat in 1918).[91] The itinerary included a cruise
past the Ford factory to view construction progress, a tour of Cork
Harbour, and an elaborate luncheon while anchored off Roche's

point.[92] However, the outing seemed ill-fated from the start. As the *Inniscarra* pulled away from Custom House Quay, one of her crewmen (an Irish Volunteer) covertly unfurled a tricolour from the ship's stern.[93] Though unnoticed by those aboard, the flag drew derisive cheers from the Ford workmen, and the waving of more tricolours from various points ashore.

After the 'throwing the dart' luncheon, John Redmond disembarked at Queenstown, perhaps because he was aware of potential trouble in Cork. The *Inniscarra* later eased into Penrose Quay (Cork), where a crowd of republican men and women waited. Proceeding down the gangplank, the delegates passed through a gauntlet of hisses and jeers.[94] Roars greeted Joe Devlin, forcing Redmondites to form a protective ring around the Belfast leader. As the Hibernians moved towards their cars, the republicans made a rush at Devlin, throwing mud and stones and engaging in 'a rough and tumble scuffle'.[95] According to the *Constitution*, Devlin 'seemed to resent the humility of having to be protected by his supporters, and waving his hands cried, "Let me Go"'.[96] Police with batons kept the crowd at bay, until *Examiner* publisher George Crosbie's car pulled alongside for a quick getaway. 'Excited and warlike',[97] Devlin first clambered to the car roof, apparently to defy the crowd, before he recognised the danger and climbed inside for his escape. 'The driver,' continued the *Constitution*, 'alive to the exigencies of the moment, did not wait for any signal to drive off.'[98] The crowd departed the dock behind a tricolour, singing 'The Soldier's Song'. The *Cork Examiner* failed to report the entire humiliating episode.

The final day of the convention's sitting, a farewell luncheon was held at the Imperial Hotel, hosted by Southern unionist Lord Middleton. After the meal, Redmond exited the hotel to the cheers of local Hibernians. However, as his motorcade departed Cork via Great George's (now Washington) Street, young republicans ran alongside the vehicles shouting insults at the Irish Party chief.[99] That evening, a street riot broke out near the Cork Courthouse and spread to the British Army recruiting office, though the disturbance was probably attributed to the recent death of Thomas Ashe. Thus ended the Irish Convention's visit to Cork.

A strange addendum to the Irish Convention's Cork visit concerned 'the comic relief' provided by whiskey-soaked English millionaire Malcolm Lyon.[100] Patriotic and adventurous, Lyon also showed (in the opinion of Scotland Yard) 'signs of mental derangement'. At the war's outset Lyon transformed his mansion into a military hospital and bought and personally delivered several ambulances to the Western Front.[101] In September 1917, Lyon arrived in

Dublin's Shelbourne Hotel. His exotic entourage included 'a distinguished Japanese friend', *English Review* editor Austin Harrison, and Major Hugh Stewart Stephens, 'a journalist of rather doubtful character' who police reported was 'sponging' Lyon.[102] Malcolm came to trumpet an exciting solution to the Irish Home Rule impasse, via the 'International Magna Carta', a half-baked precursor to the League of Nations.[103] Lyon proposed 'an International League of Justice', composed of 'wise men and elders of the people and the greatest intellects in humanities and science'. Under the League of Justice, Britain and Ireland would enter into binding arbitration, mediated and guaranteed by the Japanese government. A Home Rule solution would follow.

Despite the impracticality of Lyon's plan, in Dublin he met with Sinn Féin leaders Liam Cosgrave, Eoin MacNeill and Darrell Figgis, along with labour officials.[104] Trying to secure a mouthpiece, Lyon covertly provided the ITGWU with £5,000 to start its new newspaper *The Voice of Labour*. He also attempted to 'bribe' the *New Ireland* weekly into assuming an anti-Sinn Féin editorial policy.[105] International Magna Carta advertisements ran in Cork newspapers, and Lyon's colleague Austin Harrison travelled to Cork to meet with Irish Party officials and labour mediator Fr Thomas Dowling (apparently to influence the Cork Trades Council).[106] Lyon harried Fr Thomas with dramatic telegrams, such as 'The delay in your arrival here will be measured in terms of death and pain to others', and 'Ireland in saving herself can save the world'.[107] Sinn Féin publicist Frank Gallagher believed Lyon was attempting 'to split Sinn Féin and Labour in the interest of the Empire', while Liam de Róiste thought the Magna Carta movement was intended to 'counter Sinn Féin or get Sinn Féin to lay its cards on the table'.[108] However, Lyon appears to have been merely a well-intentioned and well-financed freelancer, though he was also, in the opinion of Irish Command O/C Lieutenant General Shaw, 'evidently partly insane, and is greatly addicted to drink'.[109]

The war's slaughter seemed to unhinge Lyon, feeding his mania to the point that he believed his actions alone could stop the global conflict. Resolving the Irish impasse through arbitration would demonstrate the viability of his messianic proposal to end the world war. Preparing to countenance the collapse of the Irish Convention, Irish Party leaders coroner William Murphy and George Crosbie considered Lyon's harebrained Magna Carta solution.[110] 'Should the convention now assembled in Ireland fail to arrive at a decision, which I do not for a moment anticipate,' wrote Crosbie, 'I can see no better way in finding a solution for Ireland's ills.'[111] Indicative of their desperation, two of Cork's most senior UIL figures followed the unbalanced Malcolm Lyon rather than their previously unquestioned party leader, John Redmond. This reflected the unhappy state of the Irish Party during the bleak autumn of 1917.

Public Controversy: The Siege of Blackrock Castle

The following month, an unexpected controversy produced wild scenes in the corporation chamber. In October 1917, the new Blackrock Sinn Féin Club petitioned to lease Blackrock Castle, a faux Elizabethan fortress on the bank of the Lee River owned by the corporation.[112] At a hearing of the corporation Law and Finance Committee, Sinn Féin representatives promised to maintain the structure and keep it open for public use. By a vote of four to one, the committee approved a one-year lease for £5, with only Redmondite High Sheriff Willie O'Connor dissenting, claiming he was 'opposed to their Irish Ireland movement'.[113] The lease required confirmation from the corporation, which was usually a formality.

The unionist *Cork Constitution* immediately jumped on the issue, publishing a series of dubious anonymous letters from 'Ratepayer', 'Indignant', 'Northeast Ward Resident', 'Civis', 'Man on the Street', and 'Jaques'.[114] The correspondents referred to 'the universal storm of indignation aroused', over the 'the shameful and insidious deal', that 'would be an ever-lasting disgrace to our city'.[115] The paper objected to giving a pro-German body (Sinn Féin) control of a strategic strongpoint in Cork Harbour. An editorial half-joked that the republicans would next request the city engineer to 'strengthen the battlements to provide suitable emplacements for a gun of sufficient calibre to command not only the river traffic but railway communication to Queenstown'.[116] There seemed little evidence of public consternation beyond the *Constitution*'s vivid paranoia.

On 9 November, a Blackrock Sinn Féin Club deputation submitted its application to the corporation. Anticipating quick approval, they were shocked when councillors rejected the castle rental by a vote of nineteen to nine.[117] Unionist councillor Dan Williams opposed the lease, even though he had supported it on the Law and Finance Committee. The Blackrock Sinn Féin Club spokesmen Stephen O'Riordan and Michael Mehigan protested that 'three fourths' of their club members were former National Volunteers, to whom the corporation had rented the castle in 1915. They offered to raise the rental fee from £5 to £20, which was submitted as a compromise resolution. But the meeting chairman, High Sheriff Willie O'Connor, refused to table the motion, prompting Mehigan to warn: 'The Sinn Féiners would have the Castle, and we will pay the Corporation no rent for it. It will take the Corporation and the British Army to put us out of it.'[118] Amid roars from the gallery, O'Riordan promised, 'you have men up against you who are ready to give up their lives in this matter.'[119] Furious Sinn Féin supporters jumped onto the chamber floor, and Willie O'Connor had to be saved from assault by a member of the fire brigade (acting as a chamber guard).[120] 'Considerable disorder prevailed in the Chamber,' recorded the meeting minutes.[121] O'Connor ultimately resumed the sitting, vowing, 'We will not be terrorised.'[122] After the meeting concluded, O'Connor navigated a crowd of shouting republicans, angered by his dismissal of the petition by parliamentary sleight of hand.

The republicans dug in, refusing to yield to public grandstanding or patronage politics. At the ensuing Law and Finance Committee meeting on 14 November, republican councillor Jerry Lane claimed, incorrectly, that the RIC had occupied Blackrock Castle, further fuelling the controversy.[123] The Cork City Sinn Féin Executive distributed leaflets denouncing the corporation's action and naming the individual councillors who voted against the lease.[124] Republican pressure was apparent at the next corporation meeting.

Before a packed gallery, the corporation allowed the Blackrock Sinn Féin Club to resubmit its application on a parliamentary technicality. Spokesman Michael Mehigan again offered to pay £20 annual rent, and blamed Lord Mayor Butterfield and Sheriff Willie O'Connor for the alleged police seizure of Blackrock Castle.[125] Butterfield and O'Connor hotly denied the charge, as did the RIC county inspector in a letter.[126] During the hearing, a republican shouted at military-aged Redmondite councillors, 'Why are ye not in khaki like men? Ye are cowards.'[127] Amid the uproar, numerous Irish Party councillors switched their votes, approving the castle lease by twenty to seven. British Army military intelligence attributed the change to 'a week's energetic intimidation having been applied to the members' by republicans.[128] Speaking for the Blackrock Sinn Féiners, Stephen O'Riordan thanked the councillors for their support, but caustically warned opponents, '. . . They made themselves ridiculous. The time would come when he and his friends would remember it for them.'[129]

The Sinn Féin triumph proved short-lived. The following afternoon, General Beauchamp Doran of the Southern Command notified the corporation that he was seizing Blackrock Castle for 'the public safety and the defence of the realm'.[130] He demanded the castle keys, but the town clerk refused to deliver them without a written order.[131] Undeterred, thirty soldiers in full battle kit knocked down the castle doors and took possession of the structure. Rumours of republican resistance ran through the city, including one that put J.J. Walsh at the head of a Sinn Féin mob marching on the castle, like 'Don Quixote and Sancho Panza in their tilt against a windmill'.[132] Nervous British sentries atop the Blackrock Castle battlements spied no republican hordes, except 'a dozen young fellows who beguiled the guard with feeble efforts to play "The Soldier's Song" on tin whistles'. Despite the garrison's vigilance, during the night stealthy Republicans crept to the flagpole in front of the castle and hoisted and tied off a tricolour.[133] The next morning, curious crowds watched soldiers struggling to remove the flag. 'All Cork is laughing,' crowed Liam de Róiste. 'No wonder. If this action represents the state of mind of the military authorities in Ireland, they are to be pitied or ridiculed.'[134]

Two days later, the corporation Law and Finance Committee denounced the military's occupation of city property, which was legal under DORA. 'They [the British Army] had now made history for the Castle,' fumed Jerry Lane, 'and it would be known universally in the future, for by taking it over they had extended the war from Flanders to Blackrock.'[135] The committee denounced the seizure 'by force of arms and frontal assault', and demanded General Doran pay the corporation £20 rent for the castle.[136] Reluctantly, Jerry Lane withdrew a sarcastic amendment asking the military to swap Blackrock Castle with Cat Fort, an abandoned post in Cork city. The British Army's Irish Command later proposed a lease for Blackrock Castle, though the staff officer dryly added, 'said Department cannot agree to let Cat Fort to the Blackrock Sinn Féin Club.'[137] The Law and Finance Committee rejected the lease, but took no further action.[138]

A platoon of British soldiers occupied Blackrock Castle for the remainder of the war.[139] In January 1919, the garrison withdrew and returned the keys to the corporation. Hours after they departed, republicans entered the castle and hoisted a tricolour flag, which flew for three days until removed by police.[140] The following week, the corporation leased the castle to the Blackrock Sinn Féin Club on the 1917 rental terms.[141] Days later, a large crowd marched from the city to the castle to celebrate Sinn Féin's takeover.[142] Thus ended the siege of Blackrock Castle, with the forces of the Irish Republic in firm, if belated, possession.

Irish Party: The National Volunteers

The Irish Party's core structures in Cork took a beating during 1917, continuing a downward trajectory from 1914 to the final collapse in

1919. The National Volunteers militia was the first to go, having degraded significantly in 1915. Between 1914 and 1915, police estimates of NV membership in Cork city and east Cork declined by 55 per cent, from 3,804 to 1,709.[143] By mid-1915, the organisation rarely drilled, and most branches outside the city collapsed.[144] The City Regiment fell to 200 reliable at the end of the year, with J.J. Horgan explaining to John Redmond that it 'has almost ceased to exist', having lost members to the British Army and the despised AFIL.[145] During the Easter Rising, the British military did not bother to accept assistance offered from the Cork NV.

After the rising, NV chief of staff Colonel Maurice Moore attempted to reinvigorate the organisation, but Redmond vetoed plans to drill in defiance of the government ban.[146] The Cork NV changed its tone, recruiting new members with promises to 'resist Conscription by force'.[147] Privately, NV leaders debated their response if conscription arrived.[148] Pondering 'some talk of revival and fighting', J.J. Horgan pointedly asked Colonel Moore, 'Who are we going to fight?'[149] Despite the National Volunteers' new belligerence, the British Army in Cork judged the militia's Cork reorganisation 'a complete failure'.[150]

Little more was heard until May 1917, when Moore called for a meeting of the NV National Committee. Cork NV commander Henry Donegan grumbled that he was 'completely in the dark' as to Moore's intentions, but was informed that the organisation required drastic action to catch up with the new national sentiment.[151] 'What really ruined the Volunteers and in my belief damaged the Parliamentary Party,' Moore complained, 'is holding aloof from the people and consulting only a narrow clique of political partisans and camp followers, who have neither honour nor brains.'[152] In July 1917, Moore and his followers took control of the NV headquarters and armoury in Dublin, and attempted to merge with the Irish Volunteers.[153] Claiming the NV Executive had 'ceased to exist', Moore convened a convention of dissident NV companies in early August, that drew 176 delegates, including one unidentified (and probably unauthorised) representative from Cork.[154]

Moore's amalgamation efforts convinced Dublin Castle to disarm the National Volunteers the following week. The militia held an estimated 8,300 rifles throughout Ireland (half in Ulster), and the RIC Special Branch believed 'in certain eventualities these might be passed over to the Sinn Féiners'.[155] Two weeks later police and soldiers raided NV armouries across the country.[156] In Cork, the authorities secured the NV's 100 obsolete single-shot Italian rifles stored in the Corn Market. The seizure only received a small paragraph in the *Cork Examiner*, despite local rumours of troops and machine guns on the streets during the operation.[157] Most of Cork's Irish Party apparatus remained silent, seemingly embarrassed over its failure to prevent the weapons seizure.[158]

Redmondites called a new NV convention on 28 September 1917 to repudiate Colonel Moore's faction. The Cork NV County Board selected a convention delegate at a well-attended meeting at City Hall, which drew top figures from the AOH and UIL.[159] Cork NV leaders blamed Moore for the government's seizure of their arms and swore allegiance to John Redmond.[160] The ensuing NV national convention attracted just sixty delegates, who formed a new executive.[161] However, Moore's rebellion effectively finished the National Volunteers. In Cork, it seems that after the convention the organisation effectively dissolved.[162] Its only brief sign of life was during the 1918 general election, when ex-soldiers marched behind an old NV banner in support of Irish Party candidate and former NV commander, Major Maurice Talbot-Crosbie.[163]

Irish Party: The UIL

The five city branches of the United Irish League (UIL) served as the constituency arm of the Irish Party in Cork.[164] Like the wider Redmondite political machine, the UIL sharply declined between 1914 and 1916, as seen in rough police estimates of party strength in the city and east Cork. Membership dropped 25 per cent between 1914 and the first quarter of 1916, prior to the Easter Rising.

TABLE 6.1
RIC Report of UIL Organisation Cork City
and East Riding, 1914–20

Quarter	Branches	Members	£ Raised
Q1 1914	61	3,794	374
Q1 1915	55	3,692	105
Q1 1916	52	2,832	14
Q1 1917	44	2,456	7
Q1 1918	43	2,422	7
Q1 1919	28	1,297	–
Q1 1920	9	554	–

Source: RIC Crime Special Branch Reports, PRO 904/20, TNA

During 1917 UIL branches continued to meet regularly and frequently attacked Sinn Féin.[165] J.J. Horgan called the republican programme 'political suicide for the nation';[166] Willie O'Connor argued the public 'could see the hopelessness of overthrowing the millions of trained soldiers of the British Empire'.[167] UIL officials loudly criticised partition, government coercion, and the denial of Home Rule during a war ostensibly fought to secure self-determination for small nations, an irony repeatedly emphasised by public bodies throughout 1917–18.[168] Counselling patience, first with the implementation of Home Rule and later with the Irish Convention, the UIL failed to inspire the populace. For George Crosbie, the situation could have been avoided had the government answered the Ulster unionists in 1914.[169]

> Up to then the authority of Parliament had never been questioned. A breach of faith was committed against the Irish people that is unprecedented in constitutional history . . . no faith can be put on promises made by English statesmen.[170]

With growing alarm, party loyalists monitored depressing returns from the Longford and East Clare by-elections.[171] Hearing of de Valera's victory in East Clare, a Redmondite stalwart moaned, 'God help us now, The Party is done.'[172] UIL drifted in Cork, seldom offering a compelling message.[173] In May 1917, the UIL City Executive called for a reorganisation of city and county branches, and in October conducted a speaking tour of branches throughout Cork.[174] Though its leaders scrambled to match Sinn Féin, the UIL drew little of the political energy coursing through the city in 1917.

The UIL functioned until the 1918 general election. Police estimated the UIL shed almost half its remaining members from June 1918 and 1919. By the end of 1918, the RIC characterised the UIL in Cork city and east Cork as 'quite inactive and possess no influence'. The party effectively ceased operating by mid-1919.[175] During the January 1920 municipal elections, Cork Redmondites ran either as independents or members of 'The Commercial Party' (a coalition of merchants and unionists), thereby ending the UIL as a political entity.[176]

Irish Party: The Ancient Order of Hibernians

The Cork Ancient Order of Hibernians steadily declined from its apex during the Home Rule crisis. It experienced a precipice drop in membership between 1914 and 1916, prior to the Easter Rising.[177] In the summer of 1916 the dire situation warranted the dispatch of AOH organisers across County Cork to revitalise dormant branches.

Though the reorganisation 'succeeded in modifying any irregular views on the political situation which were very rampant at the time',[178] one Cork leader reckoned that 'a great drawback to the organising work was the want of a lead by Mr Redmond and the Party'.[179] Another brother attributed 'the apathy creeping in all over the county' to the Irish Party's failure to keep in touch with local constituencies.[180]

AOH county membership dropped by 22 per cent in 1917, while AOH County Board revenue declined nearly 35 per cent from 1916 to 1918.[181] By 1918, Northeast (county) Cork remained well-organised, but Southeast Cork lost 180 members and South Cork showed an even worse decline.[182] Hibernian organisers tried to bolster sagging branches, but found that 'where Divisions were visited a great spirit grew up for a few days, and then died down again'.[183] The anxious Cork County Board appealed to the AOH National Executive for organising funds at the beginning of both 1918 and 1919.[184] Like an unsteady boxer taking too many punches, Cork's AOH finally hit the canvas in 1919. Troubled divisions fell away in towns such as Ballyvourney, Queenstown, Castletownbere, Ballydehob, Skibbereen, Ballinspittle, Kinsale, Blarney, Leap and Bandon.[185] While thirty-four divisions attended the Annual Cork County Convention in February 1916, just eleven attended the 1920 convention. The county secretary explained the legacy of years of faction fighting with the AFIL: 'When it was dead, they turned and joined the Sinn Féiners so that bitterness – now thoroughly envenomed – always remained with us.'[186]

The Order's decline was more gradual in Cork city. Membership dues from the city's six strongest divisions declined by 40 per cent between 1914 and 1916, but stabilised in 1917 and 1918. At the end of 1916, the city organisation was considered 'robust', but 'not as flourishing' as the previous year.[187] The AOH introduced the Second Degree Order for committed Hibernians, as 'a source of influence over the ordinary members of the Order in Cork'.[188] During 1917 the Cork city Hibernians initiated 150 brothers into the Second Degree, who focused on providing electoral assistance to the UIL, government patronage jobs to worthy brothers, and commercial support for Hibernian business interests.[189] But the new organisation gained little traction, attracting only twenty-eight new members in the city during two years, despite recruiting ex-servicemen and introducing Irish-language classes.[190] The Second Degree Council failed to meet throughout 1919; membership dues fell into arrears; and most divisions ignored attempts to revive the Division Council.[191]

TABLE 6.2
County and City Divisions Attending AOH Annual County
Convention, 1913–20

Year	County DV	City DV	Year	County DV	City DV
1913	35	7	1917	24	8
1914	35	8	1918	22	9
1915	31	8	1919	24	8
1916	34	8	1920	11	5

Source: AOH Cork County Convention Reports, U389a/25, CCCA

TABLE 6.3
Six AOH City Divisions Paid Membership Dues,
912–18 in Shillings

Year	1912	1913	1914	1915	1916	1917	1918
Shillings	345	368	342	265	204	207	211

Source: AOH Cork Dues, U389a/5, CCCA

Overall, Cork city AOH membership fell off 'slightly' in 1917, and during 1918 'the city divisions were practically as healthy as they were a year ago'.[192] The endurance of city Hibernians can be attributed to a determined core of activists, who diligently worked to revitalise the Order amid a deteriorating political situation.[193] Despite their efforts, while some AOH divisions remained strong, others disintegrated. City Division #126's attendance book shows a steep drop in paid membership.[194] The division counted thirty-one members in good standing for January 1917; the number fell to twenty in January 1918; was down to five by January 1919; and the division ceasing to exist in August 1919. The 'Irish Club', a promising new AOH division formed in 1917 to attract young members, collapsed the following year.[195]

TABLE 6.4
The Death of AOH City Division #126:
Monthly Paid Membership Dues

Year	Jan.	Feb.	March	April	May	June	July	Aug.	Sept.	Oct.	Nov.	Dec.
1917	31	32	33	33	29	28	28	27	23	15	13	9
1918	20	20	20	20	20	15	15	14	10	9	8	7
1919	5	5	4	3	3	1	2	–	–	–	–	–

Source: AOH Division #126 Book of Attendance, U389a/4, CCCA

The decline of the city AOH continued in 1919, after the Irish Party's destruction in the 1918 general election. City divisions actually gained members in 1919, almost certainly from ex-servicemen returned from the war, but more troubled chapters collapsed.[196] During the year, the city AOH lost divisions #122 and #1164 (the University College Cork branch), and Ladies' Auxiliary #2226, dropping from nine divisions to five in just two years.[197] Though city leaders promised the Order had 'passed through the crucible', they admitted 'never was the moment so dark than at present'.[198] In the summer of 1919, none of the city's five remaining divisions could afford travelling expenses for the National Convention in Dublin.[199] The county secretary also lamented the intimidation brothers suffered from young republicans.

> If in some districts our Divisions came out in open propaganda, the members would be attacked to and from the meeting, and the meeting itself broken up. In fact even here in the city we must always be on the alert. [200]

Though city Hibernians lost much political power and rank-and-file support during the troubled times of 1920–1, a devoted nucleus kept the organisation alive.[201] In January 1922, the county's remaining seven divisions agreed to continue as a Catholic social organisation supporting the fledgling Free State Government.[202] By 1926, three city divisions encompassed the remnants of the AOH movement in County Cork, retaining a modest though relatively significant 530 members.[203]

The Decline of Cork Redmondism in 1917

Cork's Irish Party did not collapse overnight. The movement's steepest decline occurred between 1914 and 1916, prior to the Easter Rising. The party functioned in 1917 and 1918, until its meltdown following the cataclysmic general election. Public officials and an activist core remained loyal to John Redmond and constitutionalism, despite the considerable change in public opinion. Aware of the new national mood, loyalists tried to adjust as best they could. The party's failure was not due to its machine, but rather its message. Acquiescence with Dublin Castle, appeals to the House of Commons for Home Rule, and continued support of the war effort no longer commanded strong public support. When the Allies declared their war aims as securing democracy and self-determination for small nations, expectations for both rose in Ireland, especially after American entry into the war.

Citizens who gave their political allegiance to Sinn Féin clearly expressed a desire for self-determination and opposition to the war effort. In 1918, such expressions grew in volume, popularity and intensity. They resulted in a civil uprising against conscription, and Sinn Féin's sweep of the general election.

VII. Cork Women, American Sailors and Catholic Vigilantes, 1917–18

The attacks at Cork on American sailors were in part the result
of a determination of the Irish manhood to protect Irish women.
Éamon de Valera, November 1919[1]

The streets of Cork experienced waves of protests and disturbances in 1917 and 1918. Police blamed young independence activists, labour radicals, and ordinary street rowdies for Cork's numerous riots, brawls and assaults. However, the most surprising culprits for a separate round of Cork's street violence were residents concerned about sexual immorality, who between 1917 and 1918 attacked local women consorting with American sailors.

'The Irish Lead'

During the first two years of the war, Cork Catholic clergy largely stayed aloof from political controversy. This changed in December 1916, during the staging of a pro-recruiting play in Cork city, which was disrupted by a combination of Catholic activists and advanced nationalists. The abandonment of 'The Irish Lead' at the Palace Theatre provoked wild scenes and a subsequent public controversy.[2]

Capitalising on the celebrity of County Cork's Victoria Cross winner Michael O'Leary, 'The Irish Lead' was a ham-fisted drama intended to encourage Catholics to join the British Army. It depicted a doomed west Cork love affair between Sergeant O'Leary of the Munster Fusiliers and his neighbour Norah MacCarthy. The upstanding O'Leary proposes marriage, but Norah's family forbids the match due to their prejudice against Irishmen like O'Leary taking the king's shilling. At the end of the second act, a distraught Norah escapes to a convent in France.

> Molly: In Hivin's name where are ye going to? At this hour of
> night?

Norah: I'm going away to the Convent, Molly. I'm going there
            now, for my heart is broken.
Molly: To the Convent! To be a nun!
Norah: Yes, there is nothing else left me now.[3]

The third act opens years later in wartime France, where Norah is now the mother superior of her convent refuge. Rampaging German troops descend on the convent, desecrate its church, kill the parish priest, and shoot the mother superior (Norah). They are interrupted and routed by Sergeant Michael O'Leary and his hearty band of Munster Fusiliers, but the Irish have arrived too late to save Norah. Cradled by her beloved Michael, she uses her dying breaths to beseech Ireland: send more soldiers to protect the convents of Belgium and France.

The play was staged in Cork on 9 December 1916 for the 'Tipperary Club', a benevolent organisation raising funds for dependents of British servicemen. A 'large and fashionable audience' attended, along with wounded soldiers and the Leinster Regimental Band. However, after the curtain was raised a section of 200 young men and women in the balcony broke into boos. By the opening of the third act, 'there was bedlam', despite the best efforts of director Mrs Nellie Standish Barry (a member of the Catholic gentry), who also played the part of Norah MacCarthy. As the crowd sang 'Faith of our Fathers' and 'God Bless our Pope', Standish Barry gamely continued with her lines, even when the rest of the cast fled the stage. Ultimately, Standish Barry recognised defeat and abandoned the play. The *Cork Examiner* wrote of the demonstrators: 'They kept on singing until the screen was lowered and the people in the stalls got up to leave . . . The protest finished with "cheers for our Bishop" and "cheers for the Children of Mary", and "cheers for the Mollies".'[4] The protesters concluded by marching out of the theatre and parading through the city streets until peacefully dispersing.

The *Cork Constitution* denounced 'the gratuitous blackguardism' as the work of 'a gang of pro-German Sinn Féiners', who shouted 'Up Dublin' and 'Up the Rebellion' during the disruption.[5] However, the *Cork Examiner* claimed, 'The young men in the gallery were determined to stop a travestied presentation of the significance of religious communities for women.'[6] AOH provincial chaplain Fr John Russell (Cork Cathedral) denied the *Constitution*'s charges, and exclaimed, 'A good stroke has been struck for faith and religion.'[7] An anonymous city priest wrote to the *Examiner* to protest at the play's treatment of convent life as 'grotesquely wrong from a Catholic point of view', and claimed the protesters enjoyed 'the support and countenance of the whole Catholic community of Cork'.[8] Military authorities advised

Standish Barry to abandon any further stagings of 'The Irish Lead', and she was subsequently 'jeered at, and abused and received numbers of insulting and threatening letters'.[9] A showing of 'The Irish Lead' was abandoned in Youghal, after the Rural District Council complimented Cork's 'plucky young men who asserted their right to defend the one heritage handed down from their forefathers'.[10]

'The Irish Lead' offended clerics by depicting Norah MacCarthy's vocation as a romantic escape rather than a spiritual calling. Angry Cork priests apparently organised the theatre protests, and the Royal Irish Constabulary reported, 'The resentment of the audience seemed to have arisen rather from religious than political reasons.'[11] However, the demonstrators clearly voiced anti-government sentiments. Letters to the *Cork Constitution* claimed protesters sang 'Who's Afraid of Easter Week?' shouted 'Down with Enlistment', and remained seated with their hats on during the playing of the national anthem.[12] It seems that city clerics called for protests of the play and a republican element used the opportunity to voice their opposition to the government. This volatile fusion of Catholic and republican direct action reappeared in Cork during the summer of 1917, after America declared war on the Central Powers.

American Sailors in Cork

In May 1917, a few weeks after the United States entered the First World War, a vanguard of six US Navy destroyers docked at Queenstown before scores of curious onlookers. Amid heavy German submarine activity on the western approaches to Europe, an American fleet was stationed at Queenstown to protect troop transports that ultimately carried two million doughboys to France.[13] The new American naval base eventually hosted a fleet of 36 destroyers and up to 7,000 sailors.[14] Within weeks, hundreds of American 'blue jackets' were taking shore leave in Cork and Queenstown. As might be expected, many of the tourists spent their liberty pursuing the opposite sex, and some of their efforts were commercial in nature. Their activity created significant problems.

Cash-rich and assertive, the Americans proved popular among the ladies of Cork. Dublin Castle explained, 'American seamen who come ashore in very high spirits and with an abundance of cash prove very attractive.'[15] According to a British naval officer, 'In the early days you would find US sailors walking along the streets of Cork with a girl on each arm, and perhaps a third bringing up the rear hopefully.'[16] An IRA veteran recalled, 'Their pay and allowances were then huge, by British standards, and they spent money like water on all kinds of luxuries throughout the city.'[17] The American naval commander in Europe, Rear Admiral William S. Sims, put a chaste spin on the situation.

> Our men had much more money than the native Irish boys, and could entertain the girls more lavishly at the movies and ice cream stands. The men of our fleet and the Irish girls became excellent friends: the association, from our point of view, was a very wholesome one . . .[18]

Some of the Americans' relations with the opposite sex were undoubtedly innocent and many were romantic, but despite Sims' spin, the American sailors also seemed responsible for an upsurge of prostitution.[19] The lack of documentation makes it impossible to determine how far the protagonists were driven by their own patriarchal and class constructs; and to recognise the precise boundaries of contemporary social standards and female sexual freedom. While an increase in recreational, consensual sexual relations was clearly apparent in Cork, the scarcity of records makes it very difficult to disentangle these from different forms of prostitution. Evidence does indicate that something was amiss in Cork during 1917. The previous year, Cork councillors boasted that 'the fame of the city of late was second to none for the virtue of its young girls'.[20] Yet Cork's political elite grew so agitated by the new situation that they deliberately subjected the city's reputation to unflattering scrutiny.

Protests Against 'Unseemly Conduct'

Historians Maria Luddy and Diarmaid Ferriter have persuasively argued that Irish prostitution in this period was popularly associated with both venereal disease and military personnel.[21] Prostitution had long been evident in Cork, which possessed a busy port, three nearby British military bases, and a large population living in extreme poverty.[22] The Contagious Diseases Acts (enforced from 1864 to 1883) reflected Cork's position in regards to prostitution and venereal disease. The laws empowered local authorities in 'subjected districts' to: certify women as prostitutes; order their compulsory medical inspections for venereal disease; and detain infected women in 'Lock Hospitals' for up to nine months.[23] Just three subjected districts were created in Ireland: the Curragh, Queenstown and Cork. Between 1872 and 1881, authorities registered 664 Cork women as prostitutes. Scholarship has shown that prostitution continued in Cork during the early twentieth century.[24]

Wartime concern over prostitution and other sexual activity became apparent in Cork during 1915 and 1916. In May 1915, dissident Poor Law Guardian John Dorgan (jailed in 1917) and a colleague claimed the workhouse was 'managing a brothel for Kitchener's Army', and demanded Dublin Castle pay for the maintenance of unwed mothers rather than Cork ratepayers.[25] They were promptly shouted down by other Guardians for 'showing us up in every part of Ireland'.[26] Following a complaint in 1916 from Fr John Russell, Cork Corporation appointed a taxi inspector to stop 'outrageous and scandalous behaviour'.[27] Apparently, 'a foul pest was going around at night', hiring hackney taxis solely to use their back seat. When police raided a Cork brothel a few months later, Catholic Bishop Daniel Cohalan warned the young women of his flock: 'One shudders at the thought that the motor ride or excursion trip might on some occasions end for a poor girl who had been good and virtuous in a house of ill fame.'[28] Thousands of young American sailors entered this simmering environment in the summer of 1917.

Shortly after the Americans' arrival, public protests began in Cork. At the Cork Corporation meeting of 8 June 1917, former mayor Sir Edward Fitzgerald condemned scenes around the city. 'It was a scandal to allow the streets of Cork to be used as at present by soldiers and sailors and bad characters – well-dressed bad characters.'[29] The corporation asked the RIC to repress 'the unseemly conduct' carried on by servicemen and 'young girls on the streets and other thoroughfares of the city'.[30] The following week, another councillor complained about women and servicemen spending nights at the waterworks, a secluded area on the city outskirts. The corporation again referred the matter to the police.[31] Public objection may have arisen from the visibility of these activities. Writing to the *Irish Independent*, 'Corkonian' complained of 'women of the most undesirable class . . . whose doings were bringing disrepute to the city and preventing decent people from allowing their families to walk the streets after dusk'.[32]

During the Cork Diocese Synod on 9 July 1917, the city's Catholic clergy tackled the menace with pastoral vigour:

> We deplore the lack of parental control which we witness in
> the city; that we appeal to parents to exercise the closest
> vigilance over their young daughters; and that we again call
> on public authorities to safeguard public morality in the out-
> skirts of the city.[33]

Pulpit denunciations proved ineffective. The Cork Harbour Commission had recently opened public access to Carrigrennan

Woods, located on the railway line between Cork and Queenstown. Hundreds of new weekend visitors drew the ire of Carrigrennan owner Arthur Julian, who complained repeatedly to harbour commissioners.[34] In late June, Julian reported disreputable conduct by sightseers 'of an objectionable class'.[35] He held the board 'morally responsible for the fall of young girls. Young couples did not seek secluded spots for innocent purposes.'[36]

Amid rising resentment, Cork priests apparently encouraged their parishioners to form a 'vigilance committee' to police wayward young women.[37] Before the First World War, Irish vigilance groups campaigned against pornography, drunkenness and prostitution.[38] In Cork, Irish Party officials during 1911–12 led a cross-party, ecumenical campaign against 'immoral, suggestive, or irreligious' written material.[39] Cork's Catholic 'Advisory Committee' had recently fought to ban children from attending evening cinema shows.[40]

During the war, the massive increase of soldiers and sailors within Ireland created new concerns. A 'moral panic' arose over the sexual activity of working-class women separated from husbands on wartime service; the exposure of Irishmen serving in the British military to prostitution; and the spread of venereal disease beyond its normal social confines.[41] Starting in 1915, female vigilantes in Dublin and Belfast organised 'Women's patrols' in red-light districts, to prevent prostitutes plying their trade.[42] Similar wartime sexual policing occurred across urban Great Britain. Studies of anti-prostitution activists in Britain, Dublin and Belfast indicate that they displayed strong class biases, featured wealthy unionist suffragettes, coordinated efforts with police, and championed the war effort. Cork's anti-prostitution vigilantes of 1917–18, however, were seemingly composed of working-class Catholics, lacked suffragettes, attacked police, and opposed the war. In addition, while the Women's Police Service targeted women for prosecution, Cork vigilantes physically assaulted both men and women involved in these activities. Unstable political conditions in Cork produced a very different response to the same perceived prostitution problem experienced in Dublin, Belfast and Great Britain.

The Royal Navy claimed the anti-prostitution campaign in Cork was 'fomented by Sinn Féin leaders'.[43] The British Army likewise reported that the committee was composed 'entirely of Sinn Féin sympathisers', while the Royal Irish Constabulary identified the vigilantes as 'Sinn Feiners'.[44] The anti-sailor demonstrators clearly expressed anti-government sentiments, yet republican records largely omit mention of these activities. Participants seem to have acted as unorganised individuals rather than as representatives of separatist organisations, which reflected the fluid nature of Cork republicanism in this period. The Cork vigilance demonstrations attracted the same demographic as the republican movement – young members of the working class and lower middle class, losing their social deference, and drawn to direct action. Their actions in September 1917 and March 1918 seemed motivated by a mixture of sexual Puritanism, parochialism, and anti-war sentiment.

Mob Attacks

The Cork Vigilance Committee struck city streets on the weekend of 1–3 September 1917. Over three successive nights, bands of civilians assaulted American sailors and local women walking together.[45] Much of the abuse was verbal as the vigilantes followed courting couples and 'hurled insulting and sometimes disgusting epitaphs at the parties'.[46] However, many men and women were pushed and shoved, and occasionally punched and stoned. On Saturday night, a rowdy crowd of 300 cornered three couples in front of the Palace Theatre. After their American dates fled, the three women were slapped and only saved from further damage by a police baton charge.[47] One victim testified that her male assailant shouted, 'The priest of the parish has sent us out to prevent ye from going with American sailors.' Later that night, demonstrators smashed the window of the British Army Recruiting Office in Patrick Street.[48]

The attacks continued across the city centre on Sunday and Monday evenings. On Monday night, a crowd of about 300 hissed and booed different groups of Americans, including some sailors walking without female companions. They surrounded one unlucky tourist outside the Coliseum Theatre in King Street (now MacCurtain Street), but he was rescued by a police patrol. The mob then fell in behind 'a group of juveniles, bearing a Sinn Féin flag in front'.[49] The police immediately charged with their batons, receiving a scattering of stones and shouts of 'Up Dublin' and 'Up the Huns'. The crowd moved towards the British Army recruiting office, which was under police guard.[50] As demonstrators mulled their next target, they spotted and chased four American sailors.[51] Admiral Sims later wrote that 'several' of his men were seriously injured in similar collisions around the city.[52] 'The Sinn Féiners made quite a row,' US Navy Commander Joseph Taussig noted in his diary.[53] 'The Irish-American fracas is an awful mess,' fumed his comrade, Lieutenant Lucien Green of the *USS Tucker*, 'and it is a rotten shame the way our men are being treated.'[54]

Following the attacks, the naval authorities cancelled all shore liberty in Cork city.[55] Blacksmiths aboard the American flagship *USS*

Melville were detected manufacturing brass knuckles for the sailors' next visit to Cork, and it was reportedly 'common knowledge that blood would have flowed' had the city not been put out of bounds.[56] Lieutenant Green wrote of the enlisted men, 'if they could but have half a chance there would be no more of this beastly business.'[57]

Appalled by the anti-American violence, the *Cork Constitution* ran anonymous letters demanding city officials formally apologise to the US fleet. One writer denounced 'the ragamuffins of the city', while another asked, 'Is the rabble which held the streets Sunday and Monday night to express the accepted views of the citizens of Cork?'[58] On the other side of the political divide, anonymous letters to the Redmondite *Cork Examiner* attempted to ease hostility against the visitors. Correspondents assured readers of the Americans' 'respectability and good conduct, more especially where ladies were concerned';[59] and reported the Cork assaults thrilled the Germans, who, it was promised, had been historically responsible for producing the first caricatures of the Irish resembling apes.[60]

The police arrested only one man during the September disturbances, Irish Volunteer James Dunne, who was charged with punching a woman outside the Palace Theatre.[61] At his trial, Dunne's solicitor emphasised the popular outrage at perceived public immorality in Cork: 'It was a scandal. Anybody could see what was going on. If one walked down the Lower Road [near the train station] one could see bands of girls waiting for American sailors.'[62] The defence proved effective, as city magistrates acquitted Dunne.[63]

A few weeks later, a delegation of Irish Party officials and business leaders travelled to Queenstown to apologise to 'the sailors of our gallant ally'. Led by Lord Mayor Butterfield, they presented a memorial to Vice-Admiral Sir Lewis Bayly (Royal Navy) and Captain Poinsette Pringle (US Navy) on behalf of 'the respectable inhabitants of Cork', denouncing the 'unseemly and disgraceful' attacks.[64] After expressing regrets to the US Navy and the American people, the delegation essentially requested that the sailors and their wallets be allowed to return to Cork.[65] The naval officers responded by complaining of Cork's frequent anti-government riots and illegal Irish Volunteer parades.[66] When pressed, Butterfield could not promise to end seditious demonstrations, since they were beyond his control. Bayly dismissed a compromise that would have allowed daytime access to the city, because 'it would appear that the men were free to spend their money by day and then required to leave the town before dark'.[67] Instead, Admiral Bayly extended his Cork ban indefinitely, for both British and American sailors alike. After bidding farewell to the furious naval authorities,

Lord Mayor Butterfield reportedly told his colleagues, 'But by the grace of God I left through the door and not by the window.'[68]

With RIC batons unable to control republican demonstrators, Admiral Bayly requested police and military reinforcements to suppress the anti-navy demonstrations.[69] Fearing the deployment of troops would produce fatal (and politically disastrous) collisions, Dublin Castle refused.[70] With the government unable to protect his sailors, Bayly removed them from harm's way. For the rest of the war, the city of Cork remained out of bounds to naval-enlisted personnel, though naval officers and (more significantly) British soldiers retained access. Owing to the ban, Cork women were cut off from the US Navy. Scores of them now travelled by train to Queenstown, and were routinely greeted at the station by large crowds of enthusiastic Americans.[71]

Residents tended to identify presumed prostitutes as English rather than Irish. The Queenstown Urban District Council attributed 'immorality in our streets' to 'strangers'.[72] When three women were detected in flagrante at Carrigrennan Woods, the Cork Harbour Commission carefully identified the offenders as 'Liverpool ladies'.[73] In a newspaper letter, 'Corkonian' claimed of prostitutes, 'it is also known that 99%, if not all of them, are English women who have come over here within the past two years.'[74] This is consistent with Maria Luddy's work and Ben Novick's analysis of Sinn Féin's wartime propaganda which ascribed moral vice to British rather than Irish influences.[75] This was not a uniquely Irish response, though, as anti-prostitution agitators in pre-war Britain likewise blamed vice on outsiders rather than local women.[76]

Finally, it is noteworthy that the disturbances were ignored by the two leading female political organisations in Cork, the anti-war Cumann na mBan and the pro-war Munster Women's Franchise League. Nationalism in both cases (Irish and British) trumped gender issues. One exception was Marie Lynch, a Poor Law Guardian, Sinn Féin convert and prominent suffragette who tried to diffuse the moral panic later in 1917.

Bloodshed in Queenstown

Communal norms and US Navy control over its sailors should be considered when comparing Irish–American relations in Queenstown to Cork. Queenstown bore the brunt of the American shore leave, yet did not face as much turmoil as Cork. Living in a port town with a long tradition of sailors seeking recreation, Queenstown residents likely possessed a higher tolerance of boisterous sailors. In addition, US

Navy shore patrols (military police) toured Queenstown's streets, which deterred unruly excesses.[77] Despite this, Queenstown did experience disturbances in early September, two days after the Cork riots. On 5 September 1917, the Americans 'were out in great numbers', and damaged some public houses during intramural brawls between rival ship crews.[78] At one point, a large crowd of Queenstown residents faced off against a number of sailors, but an American shore patrol ushered the sailors back aboard their ships.

Two nights later, an American's flirtation with a Queenstown woman proved deadly.[79] Fred Plummer, a painter at Haulbowline shipyard, had befriended machinist Mate J.W. Parente, from the American flagship USS *Melville*. While the two men enjoyed an evening promenade, machinist Parente made a pass at Plummer's girl-friend, asking her to take a walk, so, in her words, 'he might see what kind of girl I was'. The offended Plummer announced, 'he would not have any young girl insulted by a stranger', and the two men squared off.[80] Punched by the American, Plummer fell against a kerbstone and suffered a fatal skull fracture. British Army intelligence reported that Plummer's death 'caused considerable bad feeling' among Queenstown residents, which was reciprocated by American sailors, 'who are now greatly incensed at the local attitude towards them'.[81] At Sunday mass in St Colman's Cathedral, three American naval officers stormed out after the priest labelled their comrades 'vultures . . . who were preying upon the purity of our daughters of Queenstown'.[82] Other pulpit denunciations followed, but as the *Irish Independent* reported, 'The intense feeling at Queenstown is not so much against the sailors as against the girls, who travel in hundreds from Cork to meet them.'[83] A few days later, American diplomats received a disturbing report from Queenstown:

> Late Sunday afternoon about 200 girls of flapper type who arrived by train from Cork were met by crowd of about fifty youngsters (street urchin type and eldest not over 17) armed with sticks and stones and chased back to station where they boarded next train. Some girls had hats and dresses torn off.[84]

British authorities found themselves saddled with the controversial Plummer case. Witnesses stated that when the fight began, Plummer had his hands in his pockets; Parente made to shake Plummer's hand, but then punched him unexpectedly; after onlookers separated the two men, Parente pretended to walk off but broke away and sprang back to deliver the fatal blow.[85] On 5 October 1917, the RIC charged machinist Parente with manslaughter, which seemed appropriate. US Navy authorities delivered Parente, but he was immediately released on bail.[86] Despite strong evidence for a prosecution, the attorney general advised Cork police officials, 'there is an element of accident in the case.'[87] The crown solicitor took the hint and dropped the charges at a hearing in December, apparently with the understanding that the US Navy would compensate Plummer's family.[88] Aboard USS *Melville*, Parente's shipmates had raised a fund of $300–400 for such a payment, but senior American naval authorities refused to forward the money to Plummer's parents. The family's compensation claim was later investigated by Assistant Secretary of the Navy Franklin D. Roosevelt, but both Roosevelt and his successor refused to award damages. The US Navy did not discipline Parente for the incident, though he was 'transferred to a distant port of the station in order that his further presence at Queenstown might not be the occasion of any untoward incident'.[89] The case was closed without further communal hostility or antagonism from the US Navy, which seemed to satisfy Dublin Castle and naval authorities, if not the family of Joseph Plummer.[90] Admiral Sims later added insult to injury by incorrectly describing the episode in his celebrated memoir *The Victory at Sea*. Sims' version included the false claim that the fight resulted from Parente's intervention to stop the 'hooligan' Plummer from striking his girlfriend.[91] Despite strenuous appeals from Queenstown officials, Sims never corrected his account.

Explanations

The anti-American disturbances cannot be easily attributed to xenophobia. Because of Cork's thriving port and large British military presence, generations of local women had been courted by non-Irish servicemen and merchant sailors. Cork republicans did not attempt to stop women dating British soldiers until 1920.[92] Hundreds of non-Irish soldiers in the city's two major bases were unaffected by the trouble. In July 1917, a US Navy baseball exhibition at the Mardyke Cricket Grounds drew 4,000 polite, if bewildered, spectators.[93] Considering Ireland's long and warm relationship with the United States, the question remains as to why the Americans aroused such a violent reaction from Cork residents.

The American sailors seem to have upset Cork residents in three ways: (1) They engaged with local prostitutes in a more open manner than was deemed permissible; (2) They broke social taboos by making vocal sexual advances on local women; (3) They enabled local women to transgress communal limits on physical contact with men who were not their husbands.

Maria Luddy has suggested that in Ireland prostitution was generally permitted if it occurred out of sight.[94] Tacit approval disappeared
once prostitution became visible to the general public. In the late nineteenth century, visibility frequently sparked 'moral panics' about
public health and possible contagion. Such a dynamic appeared in
Cork, especially during the second bout of disturbances in March 1918,
as will be discussed below.

American interaction with 'respectable' women was also problematic in Cork. The British Army ultimately attributed the vigilantes'
formation to 'the disrespectful attitude shown by the Americans
towards local women'.[95] Éamon de Valera claimed, 'the attacks at Cork
on American sailors were in part the result of a determination of the
Irish manhood to protect Irish women.'[96] Dublin Castle pointed out
that 'the free and easy relationships which spring up naturally cause
some disquiet and annoyance', adding that 'all the philandering that
goes on is by no means platonic'.[97] Cultural tensions seem to have
arisen over acceptable male/female interactions, as experienced by
machinist Parente, who inadvertently sparked manslaughter by asking
a woman to take a walk. In Cork, an additional catalyst for unrest may
have been provided by a report that a young local woman 'was found
drugged in a park after being in the company of a naval rating'. That
alleged episode was later investigated by the influential Irish-
American politician US Senator James Phelan of California.[98] While
there was no verification of the occurrence, the story appears to have
circulated in Cork at the time of the disturbances.

Months and years after the clashes, American commentators cited
various anti-American provocations by Cork residents, including the
spitting on sailors and insults to their flag.[99] However, such aggression does not appear in contemporary records, and was likely
conflated with earlier events and the disturbances. There was one
recorded episode at the Palace Theatre in 1917, when the cinema audience hissed newsreel footage of US troops marching through
London.[100] However, as previously mentioned, this was a general
problem with pro-war newsreels in Cork. Accusations concerning
insults to the American flag may have stemmed from the 'Battle of
Patrick Street', when the flags of the Allied nations, including the
United States, were torn from outside the army recruiting office (see
Chapter IV).

Evidence indicates that tensions in Cork were not one-sided. An
anonymous letter to the *Cork Constitution* illustrated American culture
shock.

Sir,

Your beggars are a disgrace to your city, running after our
sailors . . . Your beggars in Cork are brazen beggars: And your
females with shawls over their heads are worse again. Shocking
in the extreme. Such I never saw but in Cork.

JCB (An American Officer)

P.S. And as for Home Rule, I would prefer giving it, (after what
I have seen), to African niggers.[101]

An obvious aggravation to the Americans was the presence of
numerous healthy males in Cork who refused to serve in the armed
forces. 'There seemed to me a great many men for a country supposed
to be at war,' mused American Commander Joseph Taussig after his
first visit to Queenstown. 'I have since learned that the Irish people
have generally held aloof from any participation in the war and do not
consider themselves a party to it.'[102] Admiral Sims claimed that his
sailors 'were disgusted at the large numbers of able-bodied men
whom they saw in the streets, and did not hesitate to ask some of them
why they were not fighting on the Western Front'.[103] Two other
American naval officers reported 'open hostility' between the two
sides:

The average male Sinn Féiner was blessed with health and physical force yet he did not wear the uniform of the British military
forces. The Americans looked upon him, therefore, as a slacker
. . . We were amazed, indeed, at the large percentage of the male
population, all of military age, going about their daily existence
of loafing during the day and sneaking around in military formations in preparation for their threatened revolt by night.[104]

In addition, senior British and American naval officials incorrectly
believed local republicans were supplying Allied shipping information to Germany. Historian Paul McMahon has shown that this false
impression came from the paranoid Royal Navy director of intelligence Captain Reginald 'Blinker' Hall, rather than any serious
espionage threat from Irish separatists.[105] Owing to Hall's inaccurate
reports, Admiral Bayly assumed that in Queenstown, 'there were
spies in the dockyard, as well as everywhere else around us.'[106] To
frustrate supposed republican agents, Bayly's anti-submarine 'Q-
ships' (warships disguised as unarmed merchant vessels) undertook
elaborate security precautions after departing Cork Harbour,
including repainting themselves at sea and changing false masts and
funnels. In 1918, Bayly sought to remove shipyard workers 'of
doubtful loyalty', but found it impossible. The RIC county inspector

later remarked, 'I am afraid if action were to be taken against every disloyal man employed at Haulbowline, the yard would have to be closed.'[107] At the growing Queenstown hospital complex, American Red Cross officials excluded Irish staff, since 'the proposition of having some Sinn Feiner in close proximity to the camp does not appeal very strongly'.[108] Upper echelon suspicion of Irish republicans likely filtered down through the ranks, and contributed to mutual suspicion between sailors and local residents.

Venereal Disease Concerns

During the First World War, Sinn Féin's wartime propaganda charac-terised venereal disease as an infliction made upon pure Ireland by an immoral British Army garrison.[109] This expanded upon earlier repub-lican efforts to use fear of venereal disease to discourage Irishwomen from dating soldiers and Irishmen from joining the British army.[110] Historian Margaret Ó hÓgartaigh has also pointed out that many anti-venereal disease activists were motivated by genuine health concerns for marginalised prostitutes and working-class children.[111] Though anti-venereal disease sexual policing began in Dublin and Belfast during early 1915, it was not detected in Cork prior to 1917.

In the autumn of 1917, persistent Cork rumours blamed the Americans for infecting local women with venereal disease. Writing to the *Cork Examiner*, Poor Law Guardian Marie Lynch addressed the issue as directly, if delicately, as possible.

> Many wild stories, unproved by any specific facts, were spread throughout the city regarding the conduct of some American sailors towards girls. It was mentioned that the Cork Union could produce evidence to bear out the allegations against the sailors. Upon investigation there I found there was not the slightest proof of the scandal mentioned. I questioned many of the medical profession in our city, and learned they also regarded the charges as unfounded. I am quite aware that many good people were led by specious arguments to believe those wicked tales against the sailors, and were so deceived themselves. Now it is a well-known fact that the American Navy, composition and organisation, is one of the best in exis-tence. Strict and constant supervision is exercised over every man by the officers in charge, aided by the most perfect medical cooperation.[112]

Anxiety about venereal disease figured in Cork's next round of street disturbances in March 1918. During 1917, the British House of

Commons passed the Public Health (Prevention and Treatment of Diseases) (Ireland) Act, which financed and mandated treatment of venereal disease in Irish hospitals.[113] At the end of the year, the Irish Local Government Board instructed Cork health authorities to implement venereal disease treatment programmes.[114] Officials met in February 1918 to coordinate their response, with delegates representing Cork Corporation, Cork County Council, Poor Law Guardians, and the South Charitable Infirmary.[115] Matters came to a head in March, when the county council and the Corporation refused to comply with the treatment scheme.[116] The non-cooperation of those bodies mirrored the stance taken by the Sinn Féin Health Department in Dublin. It called for mandatory venereal disease testing of all soldiers returning from overseas service, and denounced any attempt by the British Government to foist disease treatment onto Irish public boards.[117]

Also in March 1918, the British government issued Defence of the Realm Act (DORA) Regulation 40D, requiring the arrest of women who infected members of the armed forces with venereal disease.[118] Around the same time, the government announced the opening of a military venereal disease hospital in Buttevant Camp, north Cork, but it had to be abandoned owing to local protests.[119] City residents believed that a new VD hospital was to be opened on Spike Island (in Cork Harbour) to treat British servicemen. It is unknown if the government intended to treat infected soldiers there, or whether the rumours stemmed from fears raised by the Local Government Board scheme and the introduction of Regulation 40D. It is clear that civic leaders assumed that such a clinic was to be opened.

On 15 March 1918, Bishop Cohalan called a special conference of city priests, which produced the following resolutions.

1. That we again call attention to the terrible evil of young girls going to Queenstown for the purposes of vice. We most earnestly remind parents of the duty incumbent on them of exercising a close vigilance over their daughters. We appeal to our young girls to remember and esteem the fair fame of Irish womanhood for purity; and we warn them of the terrible danger which they are running of contracting a loathsome disease by indulging in sexual vice.

2. It being rumoured that the Government contemplates the establishment of a hospital for syphilis on Spike Island, in this diocese, we most strongly protest against the establishment of such a hospital in our midst. The rare local cases of the disease which occur must be treated somewhere. Ireland has got practically nothing of the millions spent on the war, and it is nothing short of an outrage to establish in our midst a

hospital for treating English and other patients afflicted with this loathsome and most dangerous disease of syphilis, caused by sexual vice.[120]

The next day, Queenstown Urban District Council passed a motion
that opposed the opening of any VD clinics in Cork, applauded the
bishop's warning to women visitors, and protested 'against the disgraceful scenes of immorality' on public thoroughfares.[121] The Cork
Sanity Authority likewise denounced the treatment of VD patients in
Ireland.[122] The Cork Poor Law Guardians instructed the Cork
Workhouse to report the number of venereal disease cases treated, and
whether those patients were quarantined. The Guardians resolved:

> That all foreigners suffering from the disease indicated be imme-
> diately deported to their own country. That as medical treatment
> should be undergone in the country where the disease had been
> contracted, that no afflicted person be allowed to enter the Port
> of Cork, with a view to preventing miniature leper colonies
> being set up on Irish soil.[123]

Within days, Cork residents responded to clerical summons 'to take
the law into their own hands'.[124] As mentioned earlier, since the US
Navy put Cork city out of bounds in September, a 'trainload' of Cork
women embarked daily for Queenstown to meet American sailors.[125]
On 18 March 1918, hundreds of men, women and boys descended on
Cork's Glanmire (now Kent) train station and attacked the 5 pm train
departing for Queenstown. 'Many girls were roughly handled,
assaulted, and their garments torn,' reported the *Cork Examiner*, as
the crowd pulled female passengers from the carriages.[126] The mob
targeted women travelling 'for, as alleged, purposes of immorality',
but because it was a bank holiday they also attacked a number of
'quite innocent persons' (female day visitors returning to
Queenstown).[127] After some minutes, police armed with rifles made a
baton charge and chased the crowd from the platform. Regrouping
outside the station, vigilantes showered the constables with stones
and fired a few revolver shots.[128] Following hours of stone throwing,
the mob attempted to assault passengers boarding the 9.40 pm
Queenstown train, but was scattered by police using 'their rifle butts
to some effect'.[129] The following evening, a crowd attacked a woman
in King Street. When she reported the incident to the nearby RIC barracks, a 'mob' jeered and shouted insults, until dispersed by police
baton charges.[130]

Apparently to rein in the mob violence, the following week city
clerics announced the formation of a new vigilance committee, 'under
the guidance of the priests'.[131] Church officials 'requested that the

matter be now left to the Vigilance Organisation, and that persons willing to aid by advice or information, or other active cooperation, will speak to the priest of their district'. This seemed to end the trouble in Cork.

Historian John O'Callaghan has described a similar series of street clashes in Limerick city stemming from a venereal disease moral panic, during the same period of February and March 1918.[132] Limerick anti-prostitution agitators targeted British soldiers, as indicated by the title of the short-lived underground newspaper *Soldier Hunter*. Its editors vowed to use physical force to protect Limerick women from moral contamination, in the name of 'social hygiene'. Street fights between residents and soldiers (members of the Welch Fusiliers) resulted in the latter's confinement to barracks for three days. The parallels with Cork even include a local rumour of a foreign serviceman drugging a local girl. However, beyond subtle distinctions between the two rounds of street clashes, there was one significant difference with Cork. The Cork vigilantes ignored British soldiers from the sizable city garrison, even though these non-Irish troops were 'outsiders'. Here again, varied local factors produced different responses to similar social pressures.

Epilogue

Within days of the Glanmire station riot, events at Westminster over-shadowed concerns about venereal disease. Conscription in Ireland quickly dominated all political thought in Cork. During the remainder of the war, there were no further mentions of a vigilance organisation or additional clashes between Cork citizens and American sailors. An epilogue occurred in July 1918, when a local priest surreptitiously landed by row-boat onto a beach below the notorious Carrigrennan Woods. During his stealth inspection of the woods, Canon Thomas Barrett of Passage West stumbled upon three American sailors and three women, engaged in 'a revolting act'.[133] Reacting to the canon's report, the Cork Harbour Commission closed Carrigrennan Woods, despite its popularity as a picnic spot with the city's working classes. Harbour Commissioner J.J. Horgan proclaimed, 'If they only succeeded in keeping young girls and young boys out of the place and preventing them from seeing such conduct, they would be doing good work (hear, hear).'[134]

As the war drew to a close, lingering anti-American sentiment faded in Cork. Republicans looked forward to the Paris Peace Conference, with expectations raised by President Woodrow Wilson's promises of self-determination for small nations. Republicans now focused on winning American support for the Irish independence claim. On 4 July 1918, large crowds attended an elaborate American Independence Day celebration at Cork Harbour, while the city's public buildings flew the Stars and Stripes.[135] Two months later, Cork Corporation changed the name of Great George's Street to Washington Street, to honour America's first president.[136] Some weeks afterwards, the corporation awarded President Wilson the freedom of the city, to be collected on his way to Paris. (He declined.)[137] Unionists gleefully used the anti-sailor disturbances to undermine Cork's opportunistic pro-American tack. Letters to the *Cork Constitution* unfavourably compared the city's welcome to President Wilson with its treatment of his navy;[138] and suggested erecting a statue representing the allied nations, with Ireland behind them, holding a dagger in one hand and German gold in the other.[139]

Though largely unreported during the war, the Cork disturbances gained international attention in 1920 when Admiral William Sims published his Pulitzer-Prize-winning memoir *The Victory at Sea*. Sims had emerged as a popular American hero of the First World War, and his book achieved commercial and critical success.[140] The memoir also reinforced the admiral's reputation as an anglophile with a penchant for controversy. In it, Sims described mob assaults on his sailors in 'that dangerous city' of Cork, and general Irish hostility to the American naval presence. He further claimed Irish republicans had passed shipping intelligence to Germany, prolonging the war, assisting German spies, and costing American lives.[141]

Sims' book was released while Éamon de Valera and Sinn Féin toured the United States to secure recognition of the Irish Republic. De Valera himself answered Sims via a press release:

> President Éamon de Valera has stated plainly that the attacks at Cork on American sailors were in part the result of a determination of the Irish manhood to protect Irish women. President de Valera went further and said that with the same situation confronting them today the men of Cork would inflict the same punishment as before.[142]

The iconoclastic Admiral Sims was then engaged in a dispute with the US Secretary of the Navy Josephus Daniels over shortcomings in the American preparations for the First World War.[143] Battling a Democratic administration allied with Irish-America, Sims used the Cork disturbances to denounce attempts by 'hybrid Americans' (i.e. Irish-Americans) to 'stir up hatred against our allies in the war'. In Boston, Sims denounced 'the domination of the country by "hyphenated" interests', and blamed Irish republicans for 'a great many of your sons at the bottom of the sea'.[144] Speaking to the English-Speaking Union in London in June 1921, Sims called for an Anglo-American partnership to 'run this round globe' and again claimed Cork republicans had 'the blood of English and American boys on their hands'. More provocatively, he also characterised Sinn Féin's Irish-American supporters as 'asses', who were 'making war on America'.[145] The comments aroused a furore in the United States, giving Secretary Daniels grounds to recall Sims to Washington DC. However, a strong public defence of Sims allowed the admiral to escape with a written reprimand.[146] Thus closed this strange episode in Irish-American relations.

The 1917–18 anti-sailor disturbances in Cork appear to have been driven by Catholic indignation at outspoken advances on young women, and a moral panic following a visible and potentially unhealthy upsurge in prostitution. The situation was further complicated by tensions between gender, class and sexual boundaries. In other cities at other times, similar reactions have greeted sudden influxes of outsiders, including foreign servicemen.[147] However, many Cork vigilantes also expressed anti-government and anti-war sentiments, and eagerly attacked police when given the opportunity. Considering the historic ties between Ireland and the United States, the enmity shown these American visitors would appear abnormal. But these were not normal times nor normal visitors. The American sailors were uniformed combatants in a war that had become unpopular in Ireland. They arrived at a time of rising political instability, when state power was being challenged by separatists on the streets of Cork. When mixed with Irish cultural norms, these political and social ingredients produced an explosive reaction.

In the weeks following the November 1918 armistice, the American sailors recovered from earlier public hostility. The naval ban on Cork seems to have been informally relaxed; during Sinn Féin's general election triumph in December 1918, American sailors reportedly attended 'every S.F. meeting and concert'.[148] On 31 March 1919, the last American blue-jackets in Cork Harbour returned to the United States via Dublin.[149] Hundreds of Queenstown residents bid farewell to the sailors' troop train, which was decorated in red, white and blue bunting and a large banner reading, 'Au Revoir, Erin. Bound for the USA'. To avoid offending the British government, US Navy authorities reportedly prohibited their men from carrying Irish tricolours at the station. However, as the train pulled away, sailors in the final car unveiled a giant tricolour, which they waved from their window to the crowd's delight. The *Cork Examiner* reported that these last American sailors left County Cork 'to the accompaniment of tumultuous cheering'.[150]

VIII. Gender, Nationalism and Cork Cumann na mBan, 1916–18

Then here's to the women of Ireland
Who bravely faced death in the van
Old Ireland is proud of her daughters
Hurray for the Cumann na mBan
(A song for the Cumann na mBan,
circa 1919)[1]

Cork Cumann na mBan played a key role in the evolution of the independence movement from 1916 to 1918. Though it initially served as an auxiliary to the Irish Volunteers, Cumann na mBan assumed new responsibilities, primarily managing fundraising and the care of political prisoners. Though Cork's republican leadership largely excluded Cumann na mBan from decision-making in 1916 and 1917, during 1918 the assertive organisation had joined the republican front.

Gender and Political Identities

Prior to 1914, the Munster Women's Franchise League (MWFL, headquartered in the city) had been Cork's most dynamic female political organisation. At the outbreak of the First World War, many MWFL suffragettes took a pro-war stance that reflected their unionist identity. In August 1914, the MWFL organised an ambulance company for the National Volunteers; in September it trained members in home nursing, first aid and invalid cooking; and in December 1914 it purchased a military ambulance for local use.[2] Similarly, the smaller Cork branch of the Irish Women's Suffrage and Local Government Association knitted socks for Irish prisoners of war.[3] The focus on war relief disrupted the MWFL, and it became 'almost crippled' by the loss of branch officers to the war effort.[4] The leadership turnover included Cork's most prominent suffragette, Poor Law Guardian Susanne Day, who resigned her post to serve as a military nurse in France.[5] Participation in the war effort also sparked internal divisions

139

within the MWFL, as republican Mary MacSwiney quit the organisation in protest at its focus on 'war propaganda'.[6] The suffragette
newspaper the *Irish Citizen* criticised the MWFL's pro-war emphasis,
claiming it 'went to sleep at the outbreak of the war', and
subsequently retired 'from active service'.[7] In turn, the MWFL
disassociated from the newspaper because of the latter's anti-war
rhetoric.[8] Divided and diverted by the war, the MWFL faded from rel-
evance after early 1915.[9] Other feminists beyond Cork joined the war
effort in urban Ireland, Britain and the United States. More could be
found in the Ulster Volunteer Force.[10] Cumann na mBan should be
contextualised as one of many political mobilisations of women
during this period.

A limited number of Cork Cumann na mBan leaders were suffragettes active in the MWFL.[11] Both Mary MacSwiney and Alice Cashel
served on the MWFL executive until late 1914, along with Poor Law
Guardian Marie Lynch who defected to Sinn Féin in 1917.[12] Though
supportive of women's suffrage, Cork Cumann na mBan focused primarily on the independence question. It displayed little interest in
local gender issues, such as alleged drunkenness among separation
women, sexual immorality, and the venereal disease scare (discussed
in the preceding chapter).

The Cork Cumann na mBan leadership came from the city's vibrant
separatist community, active since the turn of the century. In 1905,
Maude Gonne formed a Cork branch of the women's separatist organisation, Inghinidhe na hÉireann (Daughters of Erin), whose members
included future Cumann na mBan leaders Nora O'Brien, Margaret
(Madge) O'Leary, and Annie and Susan Walsh.[13] Indicating the close
cooperation between male and female separatists, Cork Inghinidhe na
hÉireann shared rooms with the Celtic Literary Society, and later combined with it to form the city's first Sinn Féin branch.[14] A number of
Cumann na mBan leaders also played camogie, and many joined the
Gaelic League's republican O'Growney Branch.[15] Some women were
connected with prominent male republicans, such as Mary MacSwiney
(sister of Terence), Madeleine O'Hegarty (wife of Seán), and May and
Lil Conlon (sisters of Sinn Féin's Seán). Others also joined the separatist circle on their own initiative.

Sinead McCoole's *No Ordinary Women: Irish Female Activists in the
Revolutionary Years, 1900–1923* offers the most detailed Cumann na
mBan leadership profiles yet produced. Unfortunately, McCoole's list
is skewed towards Dubliners from the middle and upper classes.[16] For
a more nuanced understanding of the organisation, systematic studies
of its provincial leadership are needed.

In Cork, a lack of thorough biographical information makes it difficult to draw unqualified conclusions about the Cumann na mBan social composition. However, the known occupations of the organisation's elite indicate the predominance of 'respectable' women from the Catholic lower middle class. These women achieved financial independence through their professions rather than personal wealth. Compared with the MWFL, Cumann na mBan drew few women of real means. Members holding university degrees such as Mary MacSwiney, Alice Cashel (both teachers) and Dr Alice Barry were the exception rather than the rule.[17] The University College Cork faculty and student body produced no notable leaders, and a college Cumann na mBan branch did not function until 1921.[18] More representative of the Cumann na mBan social milieu were governess Susan Walsh and her sister Annie, a shop assistant.[19] Organisation president Nora O'Brien managed a hat shop, while movement pioneer Josephine Coleman ran a boarding house.[20] Blackpool branch officials Maria Murphy and Margaret Murray were a shop assistant and an office secretary respectively.[21] The first Cork District Council president Madge O'Leary was a teacher, and her successor Sarah Duggan a seamstress. Duggan's two influential sisters Peg and Annie sold flowers, initially in a shop (closed by police in 1919) and then in an outdoor stall at Cornmarket Square.[22] Early Cumann na mBan members Sheila and Nora Wallace operated a newsagents (they later migrated to the Citizen Army and the IRA). This sample suggests Cumann na mBan drew from the same petty bourgeois demographic as the early versions of Sinn Féin and the Irish Volunteers. Like other separatist bodies, Cork Cumann na mBan was almost exclusively Catholic.

From Founding to the Rising

Nationally, Cumann na mBan formed in April 1914 to provide the Irish Volunteers nursing and fundraising assistance, a subordinate status that sparked criticism from Irish feminists.[23] Mary MacSwiney and Madeleine O'Hegarty launched Cork Cumann na mBan at Cork City Hall on 8 June 1914, an initiative supported by the Irish Volunteers.[24] Recognising the city's bitter O'Brienite/Redmondite split, the Cork women recruited both AFIL and Irish Party leaders for their launch meeting.[25] Mary MacSwiney chaired, but mainly males spoke, including J.J. Walsh, Bulmer Hobson, J.J. Horgan, Fr John Russell and Michael O'Rahilly (The O'Rahilly).[26] Approximately 100 women pledged allegiance to the Irish Volunteers rather than Cumann na mBan, and began raising money for the Volunteers' 'Rifle Fund'.[27]

Initially, Cumann na mBan functioned less like the Ladies Land League and more like a voluntary war work group. Despite this conventional beginning, Cork Cumann na mBan soon struck its own distinctive and subversive path. New members learned first aid, Morse code, and how to shoot a .22 rifle.[28]

At the start of the First World War, Cumann na mBan suffered from the same inter-nationalist spilt that struck the Irish Volunteers. The organisation lost some of its Redmondite rank and file, but retained an estimated 50 to 100 members organised in a single Cork branch.[29] Cumann na mBan enjoyed a strong leadership cadre that included MacSwiney, Madeleine O'Hegarty, Nora O'Brien, Birdie Conway and Sarah Duggan, all active in the organisation from 1914 to 1922.[30] In early 1915, twelve members were certified in first aid, emergency nursing and ambulance driving, happily exploiting a British government scheme that trained female nurses for the war effort.[31] Throughout 1915 and 1916, Cumann na mBan staffed Irish Volunteer social fundraisers such as dances and concerts, and marched with the Cork Volunteers during the 1916 St Patrick's Day procession.[32]

Cork Cumann na mBan was mobilised for the Easter Rising. Prior to Easter Sunday, members collected keys to homes to be converted to combat hospitals. Women also ran messages and collected information on British troop movements.[33] Branch secretary Alice Cashel was tasked with booking numerous motorcars to collect the German rifles to be landed in County Kerry.[34] Annie and Mary MacSwiney carried critical communications with Dublin, and Cumann na mBan members appeared at Volunteer headquarters.[35] At the end of Easter week, the women smuggled numerous Irish Volunteer rifles to safety, and cheered Volunteer prisoners as they departed Cork railway station.[36]

Following the rising, the military arrested branch leaders Nora O'Brien and Mary MacSwiney, the latter in her St Ursuline's College classroom.[37] The women were released shortly afterwards, though MacSwiney lost her job as a result. (She promptly launched her acclaimed Irish-language school, Scoil Íte.) MacSwiney then travelled to Reading prison and Frongoch camp, to secure better treatment for her brother Terence.[38] British prison authorities complained that MacSwiney was 'a great mischief maker' and used language that would have warranted her arrest had she not been a woman.[39]

Demonstrations and Separation Women

As previously mentioned, Cumann na mBan were prominent in Cork's first post-rising republican protests on the anniversary of the

Easter Rising.[40] Female republicans participated in a number of anti-government street clashes in 1917. At the 'Battle of Patrick Street' riots, camogie players helped initiate two separate rounds of fighting.[41] During that riot, a witness described leader Nora O'Brien: 'She wanted to be in the thick of it ... That girl didn't know what fear was.'[42] Cumann na mBan marched in 1917 republican demonstrations, the Irish Volunteer public defiance assemblies, Manchester Martyrs processions, and the first (of many) IRA paramilitary funeral spectacles in 1918.[43]

Female republicans clashed several times with pro-war separation women counter-protesters.[44] Separation women lived in the city's working class neighbourhoods, and received a government Separation Allowance while their husbands or fathers served in the British military.[45] Separation women were the most vocal war supporters in Cork, especially during 1917 and 1918. When republicans celebrated Sinn Féin's Longford by-election victory, 'a number of women and young girls hissed the Sinn Féiners, and patriotic songs, and followed the demonstrators cheering for the Munster Fusiliers.'[46] During the Battle of Patrick Street, a group of separation women sparked the worst round of rioting, and engaged in at least three different physical clashes with female republicans.[47] Separation women later fought with Cork republicans during the armistice celebrations of 11 November 1918, and brawled with Cumann na mBan members on polling day 1918.[48]

Similar aggressive pro-war protests were visible across urban Ireland, as working-class women banded together to defend the war service of their loved ones, creating a distinct loyal identity in the process. Separation women jeered and attacked republicans from 1915 to 1918, including episodes at Limerick, Offaly, Waterford and Dublin throughout the Easter Rising.[49] It is worth considering if other parts of Ireland would have yielded similar pro-government sentiment had enlistments reached the saturation levels of certain urban neighbourhoods.

Ben Novick's work on Sinn Féin propaganda argued that republicans linked separation women to 'alcoholic and moral/sexual depravity', a theme expanded on by Maria Luddy.[50] Such negative stereotypes were not constructed by Sinn Féin propagandists, but rather exploited by them for political advantage. From the outset of the war, Cork's political establishment expressed moral concerns about these working-class women. In August 1914, the *Cork Examiner* called for a coalition of priests, police and vintners 'to put down the drinking habit amongst the women', arguing later that they spent government maintenance money 'on liquor instead of their children'.[51] Similar charges provoked a special inquiry by Dublin Castle, which found no basis for charges of drunkenness.[52] In April 1915, Cork police reported the women consumed 'too much' alcohol, a complaint echoed by local magistrates.[53] Six months later, Cork magistrates held a special meeting to address the women's alleged excessive drinking.[54] In Dublin, pro-war female unionists established the 'Irishwomen's League of Honour' in late 1914, to encourage 'prayer, purity, and temperance' among at-risk separation women, which echoed the 'Women Police' movement in Britain (see Chapter VI).[55] Class and gender biases affected attitudes towards separation women, but additional research is required to determine if problematic drinking behaviour existed. It is clear that separation women in Cork persistently scourged republicans, and were not afraid to use violence when the opportunity arose.

Concerts, Collections and Public Defiance

Following the Easter Rising, Cork Cumann na mBan focused on relief funds for Dublin.[56] When the Irish National Aid Association launched its Cork branch in June 1916, Birdie Conway served on its Provisional Committee, while numerous women attended its founding meeting.[57] Despite a heavy Cumann na mBan presence, women were excluded from the Irish National Aid Association executive committee, composed of twenty-six male members from across Cork's political spectrum.[58] When the INAVDF elected officers in the summer of 1917, it likewise omitted female representation.[59] Disregarding the slight, Cumann na mBan proved reliable fundraisers for the INAVDF, and Mary MacSwiney attended branch meetings.[60]

Republican fundraising was probably Cumann na mBan's most important contribution to the independence movement in Cork. Despite the hostility of the city's three daily newspapers and its commercial and upper classes, republicans successfully competed financially with the well-funded Irish Party. During this period, charities and other philanthropic bodies raised money primarily through top-down donations from the middle and upper classes, whose donations were listed in local newspapers.[61] Republican funds, however, were raised from the bottom up, mainly through contributions from working-class, grassroot supporters. For example, the largest individual donation in the 1918 General Election Fund was £26, with most of the balance raised in much smaller donations.[62] Republican funds arrived in pence and shillings, generated through dances, drawings, concerts, plays, flag days and church-gate collections. Cumann na mBan staffed these efforts, which paid rich dividends. In Cork city, the

INAVDF raised £2,500;[63] the 1918 General Election Fund £1,600;[64] the Anti-Conscription Fund over £5,000;[65] and the Dáil Loan £11,145.[66] These totals were in addition to financial assistance to individual branches (Sinn Féin, Cumann na mBan, Irish Volunteers, etc.), or the long-running Prisoners' Fund.

Probably the most effective republican fundraising came from dances and concerts. The success of these events should not be attributed solely to patriotic sentiment, especially in a society that limited social interaction between young men and women. Concerts and dances were held under the auspices of different republican funds and organisations. Regardless of where the money went, Cumann na mBan members staffed the events. With a capacity of 2,000, Cork City Hall provided an excellent venue. Republicans used other sites, including an AOH hall near Holy Trinity Church. The outraged AOH county secretary later complained that the Ladies Auxiliary Division rented this hall 'to Jews and Sinn Féiners, altogether contrary to the letting agreement'.[67]

Concert talent was primarily home-grown, but occasionally attracted Dublin performers.[68] Christina Connolly, widow of the actor Seán Connolly (slain during the Easter Rising), fronted the 'Lewes-Frongoch' touring party, composed of released 1916 veterans and their female relations.[69] Their repertoire included: 'The Dublin Brigade'; 'Resurrection of Ireland (written and composed in Lewes Gaol)'; 'Dead Who Died for Ireland'; 'Cork Volunteers March'; and closing with (as always) 'The Soldier's Song'.[70] A 1918 Cumann na mBan concert programme reveals a commercial aspect to the blossoming republican movement.[71] Small shops (booksellers, newsagents, drapers) purchased adverts instead of major retailers and employers. Ad copy emphasised Irish-Ireland products: 'Irish-Made Gentleman's Outfitting Goods'; 'Volunteer outfits provided'; 'Buy Irish produce'; 'All Ireland Papers Stocked'; 'Lives and Times of Illustrious Irishmen'; 'Economic Rebirth of Munster'; and 'All Irish-Ireland and Labour Papers Stocked'. In a symbiotic relationship, republican customers patronised shops supporting the republican movement.[72] Republicans created a distinct culture, community and even commerce, open to anyone dedicated to the cause.

During the summer months, Cumann na mBan branches held outdoor picnics featuring singing, recitations, music and dancing.[73] Céilís (traditional dances) also proved popular, with many held outside during summer months.[74] For example, in June 1918 branches organised six such outdoor events.[75] Amateur theatrics also featured in Cumann na mBan fundraising.[76] Such titles as 'The Story of the

Immortal Pearse', 'Ireland First' or 'O'Donoghue, Insurgent' reflected the patriotic mood of the times, as did local productions of works by republican authors like Patrick Pearse and Piaras Beaslaí.[77]

Cumann na mBan street collections sparked public defiance in 1917. Under Irish statutes, flag-selling or box collections required police permits, though the RIC seldom enforced these regulations on legitimate charitable organisations.[78] After 1916, republicans stopped requesting police permits, which they considered an acknowledgement of Dublin Castle's governing authority. In response, on successive weekends in March 1917 Cork police cited Gaelic League members for collecting without a permit.[79] Later in the year, police likewise charged sixteen-year-old Rita Twomey and fourteen-year-old Esther McGugin with collecting for the INAVDF without a permit.[80] Reading from a prepared statement, Twomey explained her and McGugin's refusal to recognise a court 'established by English authority'. The unimpressed magistrate cut her off mid-sentence and fined the teenagers a penny each, which Twomey refused to pay.

More embarrassing for the government was the incarceration of Madeleine O'Hegarty, a top figure in Cumann na mBan and the wife of IRB/IRA leader Seán O'Hegarty. In late 1917, magistrates in Ballingeary (west Cork) convicted O'Hegarty of collecting for the INAVDF without a permit. When O'Hegarty refused to pay her five-shilling fine, the RIC lodged her in Cork women's prison to serve a seven-day sentence.[81] Demanding the right to receive meals from outside jail, O'Hegarty immediately commenced a hunger strike. Lord Mayor Butterfield appealed to the chief secretary to give in, fearing for her health.[82] Facing a mounting crisis, Dublin Castle learned that the attorney general wrongly categorised O'Hegarty as a DORA prisoner, when she was actually convicted under an ordinary criminal statute.[83] Since Irish prison regulations allowed criminal inmates to receive outside meals, relieved prison authorities acceded to O'Hegarty's request. She then ended her hunger strike, completing her sentence with a moral victory over her jailers.[84]

A similar controversy occurred in November 1918 when Cork police charged four Cumann na mBan members with an unauthorised collection for the Irish Prisoners' Fund. Mary Flynn, Josephine O'Sullivan, Susan Walsh and Nora Murphy proved problematic for their captors. While collecting outside a church, Mary Flynn spotted the approaching constables, and promptly passed her collection box to a man, who escaped. She and other prisoners either remained silent or answered questions in Irish.[85] Cork magistrates refused to convict the defendants, even after acknowledging the women's guilt and debating the legality of a permit issued by the Irish Republic.[86] Alarming Dublin Castle, they dismissed the charges 'in the interests of peace of the city and county'.[87]

An infuriated solicitor general regarded the Cork magistrates as 'very corrupt', and questioned the sanity of one 'who behaves in a very unaccountable manner'.[88] The attorney general appealed the acquittals, but not before the Cork police took another public relations hit. A few weeks later, the Cork Poor School Children Meals Fund (providing lunches to impoverished students) held a street collection.[89] Flag day chairman Willie O'Connor (the Redmondite lord mayor) neglected to obtain the necessary police permit.[90] As a result, police targeted 300 collectors on the city streets, citing 21 of them for collecting without a permit and effectively shutting down the charity flag day. Outraged Cork magistrates considered adjourning the petty sessions for six months as a protest.

By this time, a high court had ordered the retrial of the four Cumann na mBan defendants, and instructed the Cork magistrates to adhere strictly to the rules of evidence.[91] The four women were duly convicted, though they refused to attend the hearing or pay their nominal two-pence fines. Adding insult to injury, the republicans demanded the return of the money inside the INAVDF collection boxes, confiscated during the women's arrest. The magistrates returned the money, minus the prisoners' two-pence fines.[92] They thus scored a double victory by poking a finger in Dublin Castle's eye, while resolving the women's refusal to pay their penalty.

Similar courtroom defiance reappeared two months later. In April 1919, Cumann na mBan wrote and distributed 15,000 leaflets concerning inmate conditions inside Cork men's prison.[93] Police declared the leaflets seditious and arrested six Cumann na mBan members, including some senior officers. The ensuing court scenes at the Cork Bridewell were a farce. Since local magistrates boycotted the proceedings, royal magistrate Robert Starkie heard the case alone before a gallery jammed with female spectators. Prior to entering the court, the prisoners could be heard singing rebel ballads in their cells; and throughout the hearing two of them kept their backs turned to Starkie. The six defendants (Sarah Duggan, Nora Murphy, Nora O'Brien, May Conlon, Katherine Hayes and Nellie Murphy) refused to recognise the court or pay their fines, and instead served one-month jail terms.[94] Outside the courthouse, a large crowd of sympathisers cheered the women. 'We had a great time the day we were coming in the caravan,' wrote defendant Katherine Hayes 'We were singing The Soldier's Song the whole way up. Such a crowd were at the prison gate.'[95]

After a brief hunger strike over the wearing of prison uniforms, the women settled into their jail routine.[96] 'Nearly three weeks gone and then out march the heroines,' Maire Conlon wrote to her sister May. 'Well to be ye – we can't all say in days to come when will come the query – "what did you do in the Great War"? – that we did time for our poor neglected small nation.'[97] Every evening, a group of Cumann na mBan members serenaded the prisoners from Strawberry Hill, just above Cork women's prison. Following her release from the jail, Hannah Doody of Limerick Cumann na mBan wrote her Cork colleagues:

> I expect if I were in prison now at seven o'clock I would be in my high dreams listening to all you singing outside on the hill. Keep up their courage by singing on that hill . . . The Saxons will come down yet and with God's help Ireland will be free, and their prison will be filled with the Saxons, by the Irish Republican Army. And we will then shout from Strawberry Hill.[98]

Expansion, Power and Militarisation

In early 1918, Cork Cumann na mBan rapidly expanded from two branches at the end of 1917 to fourteen (city and suburbs) by February 1918.[99] These branches remained relatively stable over the next three years, with a total estimated membership running to between 250 and 500 women.[100] Their locations were deliberately aligned with Irish Volunteer company areas, to ensure clear and close cooperation between the two organisations.[101]

Shandon branch meeting minutes show normal branch activities. In addition to fund-raising duties, members prepared for a combat support role with the Irish Volunteers. They trained in first aid, signalling, and field cooking (for Volunteers on the march).[102] Other activities were designed to attract recruits, such as traditional singing instruction and route marches outside the city.[103] Cultural pursuits included Irish classes and amateur theatrics, which were a special passion of branch president Birdie Conway.[104] Occasionally the branch also engaged in humanitarian work, such as caring for victims of the 1918 influenza epidemic or raising funds for the School Meal Committee.[105] During the 1918 general election, the Shandon branch registered new women voters, sold badges at campaign rallies, and tallied votes at three separate polling places.[106]

A girl youth wing was started in 1917. Dublin organiser May Kelly established the Cork Clann na Gael (more popularly known as the Girl Guides), which was commanded by Annie Duggan, sister of Peg and

Sarah.[107] The guides drilled under the instruction of a Fianna Éireann officer and learned first aid. They wore uniforms of green blouses, green wool skirts and Tara brooches.[108] During an October 1917 demonstration, Clann na Gael marched with Fianna Éireann, with the *Constitution* reporting that the guides 'seem to have been drilled as methodically as the scouts'.[109] By December 1917 Clann na Gael mustered fifty guides, and Peg Duggan reported their strength to be in the low hundreds by 1921.[110]

With increased Cumann na mBan membership, organisational structure followed. The Cork District Council (CDC) formed in February 1918, to coordinate activities and communications among different branches. Each branch sent a representative to the CDC, which decided policy collectively. The CDC did not interfere with the internal running of branches, but sanctioned new groups, arbitrated problems between branches, and forwarded policies and directions from the National Executive and cooperating republican bodies.[111]

As Cumann na mBan expanded in 1918, it became more militarised, a development also seen in the Irish Volunteers. Military ranks were added to the Cumann na mBan organisation table, with branches appointing captains, lieutenants, quartermasters, adjutants and section leaders.[112] Members frequently wore uniforms. During May 1918, the Cumann na mBan National Executive (Dublin) ordered each branch to align and subordinate itself to the nearest Irish Volunteer company, instructing, 'All military orders should be given by the Vol. Captain to the Captain of the C.n.Mb Branch.'[113] Deference to the Irish Volunteers continued even during the 1918 general election, as the CDC promised to assist the campaign, but 'of course, work for the Volunteers comes first'.[114]

Individual branches coordinated their efforts informally with their corresponding Volunteer company (or, more frequently, companies). However, larger mobilisations generated structural problems for Cumann na mBan. The organisation maintained itself as a separate, self-governing body. However, its work responsibilities frequently came from Sinn Féin and Irish Volunteer initiatives, which created a dysfunctional republican workflow. The CDC asked that all cooperation requests be funnelled through that council, which slowed turnaround time. As a result, Cumann na mBan moved outside its organisational structure as needed. From 1918 to 1921, Cork republicans created ad hoc working committees to tackle important events or crises, often built around a dispersal fund, such as the National Defence Committee (anti-conscription),[115] the Munitions Strike Committee,[116] or the Cork Distress Fund (following the 'burning of

Cork'.)[117] These committees typically featured representatives from Sinn Féin, the Irish Volunteers, the Cork Trades Council and Cumann na mBan to coordinate their group's participation. When help was needed from Cumann na mBan (usually for fundraising or administration), the CDC asked branches to supply volunteers who were seconded to the fundraising committee for as long as needed.[118] One such committee, the Irish Republican Prisoners' Fund, relied almost exclusively on Cumann na mBan, and was largely administered by Republican women (it provided prisoners with care packages, meals, and payments to their dependents).[119] However, Cumann na mBan did not obtain such responsibility immediately or easily.

Throughout 1917, Cumann na mBan was not represented at republican demonstrations or within ad hoc committees. Newspaper reports of eight republican rallies in Cork show no addresses by a woman, nor the platform presence of Cumann na mBan representatives.[120] During Countess Markievicz's first post-rising visit to the city, Cumann na mBan officials met her train and presented a bouquet after her evening speech, but only male republicans addressed the gathering at City Hall.[121] Women were excluded from the leadership of different republican organisations, such as the INAVDF Executive and the Abraham Allen Fund.[122] During December 1917, the Cork City Sinn Féin Executive elected seven officers and thirteen department heads, none of whom were women.[123]

As republican bodies became more dependent on Cumann na mBan for fundraising, the organisation demanded better representation. After it was excluded from the (anti-conscription) National Defence Fund Committee, Cork Cumann na mBan requested and received two committee places.[124] Before Sinn Féin kicked off its 1918 general election campaign, Cumann na mBan asked for its own section of reserved seats at the official launch. 'This act of courtesy ought to be shown to CnamB,' wrote the exasperated CDC secretary, 'as they had proved themselves of such valuable assistance to the S.F. organisation.'[125] In 1918, republican women were increasingly visible within the city's independence movement. During the conscription crisis, Cumann na mBan organised a special women's protest meeting, reportedly 'the largest of its kind probably ever seen in Cork'.[126] Mary MacSwiney addressed a separate labour-themed rally for 'women workers' the same week.[127] In the general election campaign, Mary MacSwiney spoke at two campaign rallies, and Sinn Féin held a special women's meeting devoted to female voters.[128] The latter rally featured exclusively women speakers (except the parliamentary candidate, Liam de Róiste).[129] This contrasted sharply with Cumann na mBan's founding meeting four years previously, when women were seen but not heard. By the spring of 1921, when Cork Sinn Féin selected four candidates to contest the May general election, the Cumann na mBan CDC confidently requested the allocation of one seat to a woman.[130] Sinn Féin acquiesced and selected Mary MacSwiney, whereby she was elected to the Second Dáil. (Her brother Seán filled Terence MacSwiney's parliamentary vacancy in mid-Cork.) Mary MacSwiney's victory reflected the prominence of Cumann na mBan within Cork republicanism, though not her controversial standing inside the women's organisation.

The Split

Despite its success, a self-inflicted wound hindered Cork Cumann na mBan from 1917 to 1921, as the organisation suffered from what Liam de Róiste termed 'the inevitable "split"'.[131] While every republican organisation in Cork experienced similar intramural clashes, the Cumann na mBan leadership dispute was noteworthy for its length and absence of substantive issues.[132]

The leading figure within Cork Cumann na mBann was its founder and first president, Mary MacSwiney ('Minnie Mac' as she was affectionately called). Able, intelligent and charismatic, the university-educated MacSwiney was a leader in her own right before her brother Terry's death. Afterwards, Mary served as one of the movement's most electric public speakers.[133] MacSwiney could be polarizing: Sinn Féin leader Barry Egan called her 'a dangerous menace, a mad woman, and a damned nuisance'.[134] While MacSwiney's gender and hardline republicanism provoked much of this hostility, her uncompromising personality was a problem. She possessed all the skills needed for political greatness, yet MacSwiney retained the fatal flaw of inflexibility that made her difficult to work with.

According to Peg Duggan, the Cork trouble began in early 1917 when Cumann na mBan still functioned as a single Cork branch (MacSwiney served on the branch executive, but was no longer its president).[135] At MacSwiney's urging, the branch scheduled a céilí on St Patrick's Day, which fell on Palm Sunday eve. Out of religious sensitivity, the branch executive changed the dance date without first checking with MacSwiney. Duggan claimed MacSwiney was 'very annoyed at her wishes being questioned', and called a special meeting to remove the offending executive officers. She dramatically misread the feelings of the rank and file, as they instead voted MacSwiney and two of her allies off the executive. With her rival Madge O'Leary now heading the Cork branch, MacSwiney and her supporters started a new branch they called Poblacht na hÉireann. Since MacSwiney represented Cork on the Cumann na mBan National Executive, she claimed Poblacht na hÉireann was the only sanctioned Cumann na mBan organisation in Cork. For months confusion reigned as to which branch represented Cumann na mBan, with each branch demanding sole recognition from cooperating republican bodies.[136]

The establishment of multiple city branches offered a way out of the impasse, but trouble resumed with the creation of the Cork District Council in early 1918. MacSwiney's Poblacht na hÉireann candidates were easily defeated for council offices by Madge O'Leary's faction. Poblacht na hÉireann did not take the defeat well, and boycotted the CDC for the next seven months.[137]

The dispute seeped into the city's republican movement at the height of the conscription crisis in April 1918. Liam de Róiste believed the quarrel 'almost split' the Volunteers, while Tomás MacCurtain thought it might divide the movement 'in two'.[138] Florrie O'Donoghue reported trouble on the Irish Volunteers Cork Brigade Council, over what the newcomer called 'a stupid row by two groups of jealous women, relatives of almost everyone on the Council except myself'.[139] Attempts to arbitrate the split produced vitriolic attacks from MacSwiney on republican leaders.[140] MacCurtain complained to his close friend Mary MacSwiney, 'The two Branches of Cumann na mBan have given more time and energy to fighting each other than to developing the object for which they were formed.'[141]

In September 1918, the Cumann na mBan National Executive attempted to resolve the impasse, but the only agreement found was mutual resentment at Dublin interference.[142] The situation escalated when the National Executive allied itself with Mary MacSwiney. Rancorous letters were exchanged between the National Executive's Jennie Wyse-Power and CDC president Madge O'Leary, with each woman threatening the other with legal action. A visit to Cork by two senior national leaders only stoked anger within the O'Leary group.[143] At the Cumann na mBan national convention the following month, Madge O'Leary and five followers were suspended from the organisation for factionalism, which caused outrage in Cork.[144] No more was heard from the suspended women until March 1920, when they sued Mary MacSwiney, Jenny Wyse-Power and Countess Markievicz for 'slander and victimisation' in a Dail Éireann court.[145] Though a hearing was scheduled, unfortunately there are no further records of that remarkable legal action.[146] Reconciliation attempts failed in 1920, and the Cork organisation split a second time over the Anglo-Irish Treaty in 1922.[147] A majority of branches accepted the treaty and again repudiated Mary MacSwiney. Pro- and anti-treaty Cumann na mBan organisations operated in Cork throughout the Civil War.[148]

Each faction of Cumann na mBan in Cork was comprised of talented and experienced activists. The organisation's pursuit of a destructive feud shows the inherent tensions present in similar separatist groups in Ireland. Expansions, pressures and tactical disagreements could easily spiral out of control, which the republican movement demonstrated on a much larger scale during the Irish Civil War.

The Cork Cumann na mBan split should not overshadow the organisation's contributions during 1917 and 1918. Individual branches ably administered republican fundraising during this period, and mobilised critical women voters in the 1918 election. Despite its often-dysfunctional leadership, Cumann na Ban provided strong assistance to both Sinn Féin and the Irish Volunteers. Though a womens' organisation, Cork Cumann na mBan devoted itself exclusively to the independence movement and rarely outwardly engaged with gender politics. However, the act of political mobilisation itself seemed to have raised a gender consciousness within members. They successfully created a distinct role within the independence movement, for which they demanded, and ultimately received, recognition.

IX. Cork Labour, Economy and the ITGWU

*. . . It would be the workers who would decide the form of government
we will have, and I believe the Irish people will have in the future a
worker's republic.*

John Good, November 1918

After years of internal discord, the Cork labour movement reunited in
late 1916. Its new driving force was the militant ITGWU (Irish
Transport and General Workers' Union), which advanced rapidly in
1917 and 1918. The ITGWU made little headway during the first year
and a half of the world war, as it attempted to weld skilled and
unskilled labourers into a single industrial union.[1] The outlook
improved during 1916, and by early 1917 *Southern Star* correspondent
Tadhg Barry boasted the union was 'growing stronger daily'.[2] It introduced a level of muscular militancy previously unseen in Cork. It was
a remarkable recovery for a union that disappeared in Cork for three
years after its disastrous 1909 dock strike.

Wartime Economy and Inflation

Severe inflation prompted Cork trade unionism during these years.
Consumer prices more than doubled in Britain and Ireland during the
war.[3] Historian Liam Kennedy attributes wartime inflation to the government's suspension of the gold standard, massive deficit financing,
and delayed introduction of price controls.[4] Irish transportation costs
jumped owing to loss of merchant shipping, rail rolling stock, and
draught animals (the latter two serving the British armies in France).
As Germany unleashed unrestricted submarine warfare at the beginning of 1917, Cork city's shipping-dependent economy suffered.[5] By
mid-1918, the entire six-ship City of Cork Steam Packet fleet had been
sunk, costing Cork its primary import/export mechanism, as well as
the lives of ninety-six city sailors.[6] Transportation was further affected
by the diversion of Allied shipping in 1917 to carry two million

154

American soldiers to France.[7] Livestock feed, meal, and transport price increases drove up the cost of food production, creating a knock-on effect that struck consumers. Lucrative military contracts that provided well-paid jobs in Britain did not fully materialise in Cork city.[8] While prices doubled across both the United Kingdom and Ireland, wages were unequal. Cork workers were paid roughly two thirds that of their counterparts in England's industrial north.[9] British buyers could outbid Irish retailers for food stocks, which produced alarming shortages in Ireland. As the US consul explained: '. . . the question with Cork importers was not at what price goods might be secured but whether they might be secured at any price.'[10]

Food prices jumped at the outset of the war, and continued to climb over the next two years. In mid-1916, the Cork Coopers Society reported that, owing to inflation, 'we find it at present very difficult to keep our homes together'.[11] In the same period, labour activists and social progressives formed the Cork Consumers' League to raise public awareness of spiking retail prices.[12] By the middle of 1917, Cork police reported, 'the abnormal prices of food stuffs make it difficult for workers and their families to maintain themselves on their wages.'[13] Sharp costs for meat and butter coincided with fears that milk prices would rise, 'til the children of the poor would perish for want of it in the winter'.[14] The Cork Asylum for the Blind, the Cork Lunatic Asylum, and the Cork Workhouse all complained of exploding expenditures owing to inflated provisions costs.[15] (Budget estimates were submitted at the beginning of the year.)

TABLE 9.1

Proposed Budgets, Cork/Youghal Asylums

Year	Amount
1916–17	£14,753
1918–19	£23,612

Source: Cork Corporation Law & Finance Committee Meeting Minutes, 31 March 1918, CCCA

TABLE 9.2

Cork Workhouse Estimated Annual Budget

Year	Amount
1917	£60,030
1918	£87,100

Source: Cork Poor Law Guardians Meeting Minutes, 14 January 1918

TABLE 9.3

Cork Workhouse Weekly Provisions
Expenditure

Period	Milk	Tea
Dec. 1916	£ 67.16.01	£25.13.03
Dec. 1917	£140.14.11	£40.08.00

Source: Cork Poor Law Guardians Meeting Minutes,
14 January 1918

TABLE 9.4

Cork Workhouse Weekly Cost of Maintenance Per
Inmate (in shillings), and Weekly Cost of Overall
Provisions Consumed (in £)

Month/Yr	Per Inmate	Provisions
August '13	3.5	£305.08.01
August '14	NA	NA
August '15	4.1	£389.10.05
August '16	5.1	£449.10.07
August '17	8.8	£616.14.06

Source: Cork Union Statistical Minutes, Cork Poor Law Guardian
Meeting Minutes, 1913–1917

David Fitzpatrick recently emphasised the war's economic benefits
for the Irish public, especially those employed in the lucrative munitions sector.[16] While Ulster reaped a fair share of war production, little
munitions revenue reached Cork. Irish trade advocate E.J. Riordan
reported Irish businesses securing just £25 million of the £934 million
War Office domestic orders placed during the war. Of the 252 Irish
firms to receive British military contracts, Riordan identified 160 from
Ulster (not surprising, considering its industrial base), 64 from
Leinster, and the remaining 28 divided between Munster and
Connaught.[17] Cork commercial and political leaders frequently
denounced the lack of war production allotted to the city.[18] A Ministry
of Munitions report supported some Cork complaints, pointing out
that the government 'purchased from English contractors goods that
had been made in Ireland and which could have been purchased more
cheaply directly from the Irish producer'.[19]

While acknowledging the difficulties facing urban wage-earners,
Fitzpatrick points to wartime nutrition improvements as people consumed more vegetables and less meat and butter. However,
contemporary health consciousness was not shared by the public in

1914–18. Local unease could be perceived in the 1918 query by the Cork Poor Law Guardians, who asked medical staff to study if the Spanish influenza epidemic was being worsened by 'un-nutritious food, the want of meat or any fatty food, milk shortage, and bad bread'.[20]

TABLE 9.5

Munster Livestock Feed Costs, 1916–17, in Shillings

Date	W. Maize	Red Bran	Barley	Dom. Cake
Jan. 1916	11.4	11.8	11.8	14.9
Oct. 1917	22.3	17.1	20.0	25.1

Source: Dept. Agriculture & Tech. Instr. Comm. Journal, 1916–17

TABLE 9.6

Cork Commodity Retail Prices, 1914 vs. 1919, in Pence

Commodity	1914	1919
Cotton Pants	36	108
Flannel Shirt	30	90
Cap	30	84
Blouse	23	35
Tweed Shirt	71	210
Cotton Petticoat	23	42

Source: Cork Profiteering Committee Report, *Cork Constitution*, 28 January 1920

TABLE 9.7

CORK BULK FOOD PRICES, 1914 VS. 1918, IN £

Item	Size	1914	1918	Item	Size	1914	1918
Flour	ton	9.08.06	17.14.00	Tea	lb	0.01.03	0.02.06
Oatmeal	ton	11.00.00	36.00.00	Coal	ton	1.01.03	3.03.09
Bacon	cwt	4.06.05	9.18.00	Butter	cwt	5.03.00	12.16.00
Beef	cwt	2.11.04	6.02.06	Eggs	dz	0.01.02	0.04.05
Beans	cwt	0.15.09	2.16.00	Potatoes	ton	3.12.06	7.05.00
Mutton	cwt	3.03.00	7.07.00	Whiskey	gal	0.19.09	3.07.00
Sugar	cwt	0.14.03	3.05.05	Milk	gal	0.00.09	0.02.02

Source: Cork Poor Law Guardians Minute Books, 13 January 1919

Cork farmers did very well during the war, though Cormac Ó Gráda reports an overall decline in exports in real terms, when accounting for inflation.[21] Undoubtedly, city businesses profited during the war's early years, as the RIC reported in 1916, 'there are not many industries in the city or Riding but those that are doing well.'[22]

Local ship-building and repairs saw higher demand, with Rushbrook and Passage dockyard employment doubling to 800.[23] The busy Queenstown Naval Command required provisions and entertainment, some of which was supplied by city businesses. Munitions box saw milling employed an undetermined number of city workers, though the Cork Industrial Development Association expressed 'considerable dissatisfaction' with the War Office preference for English firms over Irish firms.[24] The Cork Spinning and Weaving Company employed 700 women to produce aeroplane cloth, and the Douglas Woolen Mills secured military blanket contracts.[25] Cork's share of the munitions industry was a single artillery shell factory opened in 1917.[26] It employed 150 mainly women hands, and ultimately produced almost 30,000 4.5 inch shells valued at £44,000.[27] Thousands of impoverished city residents also enlisted in the British forces, and their weekly separation allowances gave families a cushion from normal desperation. The Cork Workhouse showed a small but significant decline of inmates, though outdoor relief remained relatively level.[28] Overall, evidence indicates that the war in Cork produced neither extraordinary prosperity nor extraordinary poverty.

TABLE 9.8

Cork Workhouse Inmates & Outdoor Relief Recipients, 1914–18

Year	Month	Workhouse	Outdoor	Year	Month	Workhouse	Outdoor
1914	October	1602	2193	1916	October	NA	NA
1915	February	1645	2193	1917	February	NA	NA
1915	June	1495	2216	1917	June	1401	1976
1915	October	1443	2166	1917	October	1268	2038
1916	February	1562	2151	1918	February	1331	2064
1916	June	1456	2043	1918	June	1267	1982

Source: Cork Poor Law Guardian Minute Books, 1914–1918, BG/69/A142–148, CCCA

In 1917 Cork experienced economic dislocation from the German submarine blockade and the structural changes required to fuel Britain's war machine. Diverted for war production, raw materials became expensive and scarce, affecting numerous Cork industries.[29] The Cork IDA reported of the city's industrial firms, 'the difficulty of procuring raw materials crippled some and killed others.'[30] A lack of imported leather damaged shoe-making; the loss of dye chemicals hurt linen manufacturing.[31] Facing barley shortages and increased tax duties, spirits distilling and beer brewing dropped sharply in 1917–18, with Murphy's brewery discharging a third of its Cork staff in May 1917.[32] Coal shortages and price increases punished both businesses and consumers, especially during the winter of 1917/18. Struggling with a massive increase in material costs and a scarcity of timber and cement, Cork's building trades were especially hard hit, with building labourers experiencing 'distress' by the summer of 1917.[33] Diverted shipping also hurt Cork's important harbour income.[34] The Port of Cork opened an operating deficit of over £6,000 in the second half of 1917. Compared to 1915 revenue figures, harbour totals declined by £8,000 in 1916 and £10,000 in 1917.[35] By early 1918, the port reported a 25 per cent loss of income, compounded by 75 per cent higher operating costs. These mainly came from inflated material prices, such as increases of coal by 65 per cent; bricks, 80 per cent; cement, 107 per cent; iron, 137 per cent; steel, 187 per cent; oil, 200 per cent; and timber, 240 per cent.[36] While such shortages and price spikes did not wreck the Cork economy, they increased anxiety at the beginning of 1918, rolling back the war's earlier economic benefits.[37]

TABLE 9.9
Irish Beer Output & Irish Porter Output,
1913 vs 1917

Year	Barrels	Year	Hogsheads
1913	1,335,000	1913	859,056
1917	362,000	1917	508,987

Source: E.J. Riordan, p. 157

TABLE 9.10
Irish Cement Imports, 1913 vs 1917

Year	Tons
1913	125,491
1917	48,935

Source: E.J. Riordan, p. 144

TABLE 9.11
Cork Timber Prices, 1914 vs 1916,
Per 165 Cubic Feet

Year	Price
1914	£ 10.13.00
1916	£ 24.10.03

Source: Cork Chamber of Commerce, *Cork: Its Trade and Commerce, 1919*, p. 175

By 1917, wages significantly lagged behind inflation, producing persistent industrial unrest by Cork workers seeking pay rises.[38] Local wage patterns are reflected in the payroll records of Murphy's brewery. Murphy's non-unionised staff wages did not keep up with inflation, which had run at roughly 100 per cent of pre-war prices by 1917. That only changed after industrial unrest at the brewery in 1918.

TABLE 9.12

Murphy's Brewery, Non-Union Staff Weekly Wages, 1914–18, in Shillings

Year	Washer	Watchmen	Enginemen
1914*	20	26	30
1915	21	27	31
1916	24	30	34
1917	30	36	40
1918	40	41	50

*Pre-War

Source: Murphy's Brewery Workmen's Pay Register, 1913–1924, BL/BC/MB/494, Boole Library, UCC

Murphy's unionised tradesmen were paid on a city-wide wage rate that differed from non-unionised brewery workers. The tradesmen enjoyed similar wage increases as non-unionised brewery staff, though they secured a reduction in their work week. This resulted from a ten-day city-wide tradesmen strike in 1917 that yielded a significant pay raise (the city carpenters stayed out for three additional weeks before settling).[39] Indicative of a domino effect among wage demands, the Cork Cooper Society then sought a pay rise to keep pace with their colleagues' pay rise, which they duly received three months later.[40] Non-union staff members were granted a wage increase following the tradesmen strike, as seen in the 1918 figures in Table 9.12.

TABLE 9.13

Murphy's Brewery, Unionised Staff Weekly Wages, 1914–21, In Shillings/Pence

Year	Plumber	Plasterer	Carpenter	Fitter	Cooper
1914*	38.3	36.18	36.0	37.4	39.0
1915	38.3	36.18	37.6	40.0	39.0
1916	41.5	36.18	39.6½	44.0	51.0
1917	45.0	42.01	43.9	57.0	57.0
1918**	62.4	54.02	54.2	62.4	60.6

Source: Murphy's Brewery Workmen's Pay Register, 1913–1924, BL/BC/MB/494, Boole Library, UCC

* Pre-War **Work Week reduced from 54 hours to 50, Carpenters, Plumbers & Plasterers

Similar wage stagnation and reactions were visible with corporation labourers and carters. A weekly pre-war rate of twenty shillings had risen only to thirty-one shillings by the end of 1917, an increase of 35 per cent. The corporation carters' wages, however, doubled during the same period, from a pre-war thirty-nine shillings to seventy-eight. The carters' higher pay rise followed their successful organisation by the ITGWU. A strike notice submitted in October 1917 yielded a significant jump in pay.[41] Similar industrial agitation became commonplace throughout the city during this period.

TABLE 9.14
Cork Corporation Labourers' Weekly
Wages, 1914–17, in Shillings

Date	Wage
Apr-14	20
Apr-16	22
Apr-17	28
Sep-17	31

Source: City Engineer's Report, 9 April 1918, Corporation Public Health Committee Minutes, CP/C/CM/PH/A27, CCCA

TABLE 9.15
Cork Corporation Carters' Weekly
Wages, 1917, in Shillings

Date	Wage
Apr-14	39
Mar-17	54
Apr-17	66
Oct-17	78

Source: City Engineer's Report, 9 April 1918, Corporation Public Health Committee Minutes, CP/C/CM/PH/A27, CCCA

The ITGWU and Labour Militancy

The war created favourable organising conditions for Irish trade unionists, especially the ITGWU.[42] Army enlistments drained excess unskilled labour, which had previously impaired industrial organisation. The spiralling cost of living motivated workers to organise themselves to secure wage increases.[43] New British government legislation reduced debilitating industrial strife. The 1915 Munitions Act (and amendments) required workers and employers in war-related industries to submit three-week notices before downing tools or locking out staff.[44] The workers could submit a strike notice and initiate Board of Trade arbitration, which prevented an employer lockout and almost guaranteed a pay adjustment.[45] Government intervention thus incentivised Irish workers to organise and threaten strike action. Each victory increased wage disparities between sectors, which only motivated workers to unionise. The Cork ITGWU seized the new situation by pressing for pay rises and organising new employment areas.

In 1917, Cork ITGWU branches submitted strike notices or downed tools in the following sectors: building labourers in January;[46] tramway staff in both March and June;[47] bread van drivers during August;[48] wool mill hands and gas plant staff in October;[49] and dock labourers and paper factory workers during December.[50] Along the way, the union won pay raises for workers in the coal trade, gristmills, and two shipping lines.[51] By the end of the year, the revitalised Cork city ITGWU boasted six separate branches, secured a spacious new headquarters on Camden Quay, and claimed an impressive 4,000 members.[52]

The ITGWU bolstered its Cork membership by recruiting two previously ignored sectors. Through its Irish Women Workers' Union affiliate, the ITGWU mobilised female factory workers involved in paper manufacturing, woollen milling, jam-making, and laundries.[53] During late 1917, the ITGWU conducted a remarkable cross-sector that shut four paper manufacturers for five days. Over 120 female assembly line workers picketed, along with 20 male clerks, packers, and messengers, who all secured desired pay increases.[54] During the summer of 1918, 700 ITGWU women mill workers won a pay hike after downing tools for three days.[55] In the same period, the British-based National Federation of Women Workers successfully organised female factory workers in Cork, including those at the Douglas Woolen Mills and the new artillery shell factory.[56]

Cork's most bitter strike of the period followed from ITGWU organisation of teenage women staff at Alfred Dobbin's jam factory.[57] When the workers asked for a wage increase in late 1917, Dobbin discharged their spokesperson and four successive workers who refused to perform her duties. In January 1918, fifty-five women struck the factory, inciting a sympathy action by ITGWU staff at Dobbin's Palace Theatre, including the unionised orchestra.[58] The strike continued for the next year and a half, generating police prosecutions of picketers, mob attacks on replacement workers, and expensive police escorts of company lorries.[59] Dobbin ultimately replaced his workers and crushed the strike, though not without considerable cost and residual communal anger. An unidentified gunman took a shot at Dobbin during 1920, and his mansion was burned as an IRA counter-reprisal in 1921.[60]

Outreach to agricultural labourers proved even more successful for the ITGWU. Like government intervention in industrial relations, the 1917 Corn Production Act mandated binding arbitration for agricultural workers, establishing the Agricultural Wages Board for Ireland to determine minimum wages and working hours.[61] The act also placed an extra 10 per cent of Irish acreage under the plough during 1917, and a further 5 per cent in 1918. This excess supply compounded the agriculture labourer shortage created by military enlistments. The ITGWU gratefully exploited these conditions in 1917, overtaking the duelling land and labour associations (D.D. Sheehan's and P.J. Bradley's) to emerge as agricultural labourers' primary representative body.[62] By early 1918, the ITGWU had organised 400 farm labourers in the city suburbs alone, and soon fielded healthy branches in the Cork 'Liberties' of Bishopstown, Whitechurch, Douglas, Lehenagh and St Mary's.[63] By late 1918, the ITGWU had nine agriculture labourer branches in the city suburbs, which later produced some of the most radical strikes of revolutionary Ireland.[64]

Industrial Unrest

Amid lagging local wages, labour militancy expanded beyond the ITGWU during 1917. Cork police reported 'a good deal of discontent' among artisans and labourers in March 1917;[65] 'unrest' with railways staff in April;[66] and trouble with tramway and mill workers in May.[67] In April, 900 building tradesmen struck for a week; 400 dock labourers downed tools in July and narrowly averted a strike in August.[68] Similar industrial disturbances broke out in Great Britain during the same month, and in Australia over the summer.[69] In October the Cork drapers' assistants and grocery and vintners assistants formed their own unions, and the National Teachers Organisation affiliated with the Cork Trades Council.[70]

Strike notices became more frequent during the summer of 1917, and by the middle of 1918 strikes and work stoppages were a regular occurrence in the city.[71] Inflationary pressures undoubtedly drove many of these actions, but slumping wartime morale may have affected the situation.[72] Hugues Lagrange's study of a surge of French industrial unrest in June 1917 connects it to the public's loss of confidence in the government following the collapse of the Nivelle Offensive on the Western Front.[73] His description of 'the dissolution of social consensus, political polarisation, and the loss of legitimacy suffered by military and political authority' could easily apply to Ireland. The public was aware of continued coercion following the 1916 rebellion, Russia's recent withdrawal from the war, and the British Army's disastrous Passchendaele offensive of the autumn of 1917.[74] The worsening battlefield situation likely contributed to local destabilisation in Cork.

TABLE 9.16
Cork City Strike Actions, 1917–18

Year	Month	Strikes
1917	Jan-June	3
1917	July-Dec	3
1918	Jan-June	19
1918	July-Dec	11

Source: *Cork Constitution* & *Cork Examiner* 1916–1919; RIC County Inspector Reports for Cork City & East Riding, 1916–1919

The organising of 1917 paid dividends at the beginning of 1918. A quick reading of the January 1918 *Voice of Labour* newspaper indicates intense industrial unrest in the city. The Munster Laundry workers won their second pay rise since Christmas; after the successful bag-makers strike, the ITGWU paper printing branch now represented all factory labourers, printers and clerks in the city.[75] Child labourers at Ryan's Soap Factory successfully struck for a wage increase, as did city painter apprentices and the storeroom staff at Green & Co. Grain Merchants.[76] Harness makers at Day & Company demanded to be paid hourly instead of by piece; the Dobbin jam factory strike kicked off; and city chemist assistants threatened a walkout if two of their discharged members were not reinstated. All this activity occurred in a single month in Cork city. The newfound militancy even leapt the gates of University College Cork. In March 1918, young boys paid to weed the college grounds struck for a wage increase. Unfortunately, college authorities simply replaced them with non-unionised young girls.[77]

Political and Republican Engagement

Emmet O'Connor wrote that in 1917 the Irish labour movement 'began to take on a dynamic connotation, ceasing to be a merely collective description for the trade unions'.[78] A new public role was apparent in Cork, as labour activists intervened to protect working-class welfare. Union members were encouraged to join the Cork Cooperative Society, which opened its own premises the following year.[79] Trades Council representatives demanded increased public relief for workers and price controls for milk and potatoes.[80] Union representatives also protested against food profiteering and prepared industrial action to retain food supplies.[81] On the Cork Trades Council, republicans overtook the dominant AFIL leadership faction of Michael Egan and Patrick Lynch. At the end of 1918, republican Éamonn O'Mahoney of the Railway Clerks Association took charge of the Trades Council, with the support of fellow republicans John Good, Henry Marsh and George Nason. Under their leadership the previously disorganised and de-centralised Cork Labour Party built itself into a practical political force. While Cork Labour was not overtly republican, its membership and leadership significantly overlapped with the independence movement. The Cork Trades Council eagerly cooperated with republicans when the two movements' interests intersected, most notably in February and April 1918 (see Chapters X and XI).

The Cork ITGWU leadership was dominated by two full-time organisers, Denis Houston and Cathal O'Shannon. Houston was a Donegal native who cut his teeth with the Belfast Trades Council.[82] He was dispatched to Cork in October 1916, and proved productive during his two-year stay. Local branch leaders also emerged during this period, including William Kenneally (a mill worker), Richard Hawkins (of the Cork Tramways), Bob Day (a laundry cart driver), J.J. McGrath and Michael Hill. However, Cathal O'Shannon became the key figure upon his arrival in Cork in July 1917. A product of the Belfast Irish-Ireland community, O'Shannon was an IRB member, an officer in the Belfast Irish Volunteers, and a recent Reading jail colleague of Tomás MacCurtain and Terence MacSwiney.[83] O'Shannon straddled the militant wings of both republicanism and trade unionism (he was vocally pro-Bolshevik), and served as a conduit between the two movements.[84]

In late 1917, O'Shannon restarted the Cork company of the Irish Citizen Army (ICA), which had collapsed in 1914. Florrie O'Donoghue believed the new ICA 'didn't amount to much', owing to lingering, if misplaced, anger over its role in the confused Easter Rising mobilisation.[85] The Cork ICA was later absorbed by the Irish Volunteers during the 1918 conscription crisis. More successful was the formation of the 'Women's Citizen Army' and the ICA boy scouts and girl guides. The key figures in these endeavours were Nora and Sheila Wallace, long-time separatists who ran a small newspaper shop that sold republican and left-wing periodicals.[86]

The Wallace sisters organised a single Cork branch of the Women's Citizen Army, more commonly known as 'Connolly's Own', which functioned like Cumann na mBan but with little cooperation from that body.[87] The Cork Women's ICA existed until the truce of 1921, hosted socials and fundraisers, and organised another branch in nearby Passage West.[88] Nora Wallace also formed a city branch of the ICA girl scouts, which often led ITGWU processions.[89] The ICA boy scouts appear to have made some inroads within the republican Fianna boy scouts, causing, in the words of one Fianna veteran, 'a split in our ranks'.[90] The ICA scouts numbered up to forty in 1919, but became extinct in 1920.[91] There is little record of the activities of Cork's various Citizen Army branches, beyond appearances at public processions, Irish Volunteer marches, and funerals of IRA trade unionists later in the conflict.[92]

The ITGWU and the republican movement often intersected in Cork. British military intelligence in early 1917 reported the union to be 'in close touch with the Irish Volunteers'. The RIC inspector general later described the ITGWU as 'the Socialist and Labouring wing of the Irish revolutionary movement', and pointed out that it was strongest in republican areas.[93] Tadhg Barry, a prominent Volunteer and Sinn Féin leader, maintained strong ties with the ITGWU. He brought James Connolly to Cork in 1911 to discuss socialism, and months before the Easter Rising to lecture on street fighting.[94] Barry became a full-time ITGWU organiser in 1919, taking charge of agricultural labourers. Cathal O'Shannon served as labour director on both the Cork City Sinn Féin Executive and the Sinn Féin National Executive.[95] He lodged above the shop owned by Nora and Sheila Wallace, which had recently become the Irish Volunteers' brigade headquarters.[96] During the 1920–1 conflict, the Wallace sisters were among Cork's most trusted guerrilla activists.[97] Sheila Wallace served as the Cork No. 1 Brigade's communications officer, which made her (apparently) the highest-ranking woman in the IRA, while Nora acted as an IRA intelligence agent.[98] In the 1920 local elections, Sinn Féin and the ITGWU ran a joint ticket that won a corporation majority. The IRA leadership of that period included some devoted ITGWU members.[99]

In November 1917, the Cork ITGWU displayed its separatist pedigree at the annual Manchester Martyrs commemoration. Led by the Connolly Memorial Marching Band and Citizen Army boy scouts and girl guides, some 3,000 ITGWU workers joined the republican procession.[100] That evening, workers packed City Hall to hear Cathal O'Shannon's lecture, 'James Connnolly, Socialist and Revolutionist'. Recitations and singing followed in both Irish and English, along with dancing to the musical accompaniment of the James Connolly Band. 'Cork, of course, claims that "God's own town" is marching away from the rest of the country,' boasted the *Voice of Labour*, 'and with some reason, because it would seem that the vast majority of Cork workers are now organised.'[101]

The Cork Labour Party emerged from the First World War unified and strengthened, and took its place as a junior partner in the city's ruling republican coalition.[102] Driven by the ITGWU, militant trade unions played an active role in the city's extraordinary political turbulence of 1918. As will be seen in the next two chapters, labour stood at the forefront of the struggles to retain food supplies and to stop military conscription.

X. Preventing Another Black '47: The Cork People's Food Committee 1917–18

Food grown by the farmers of Ireland was the property of the Irish nation, and the Irish people had the first claim upon it.
Diarmuid Fawsitt, People's Food Committee, January 1918[1]

Reflecting on his First World War leadership, David Lloyd George wrote, 'The food question ultimately decided the issue of this war.'[2] Though wartime Great Britain escaped the bread riots experienced by other combatants, a food shortage crisis emerged in Ireland during late 1917.

Food scarcity stemmed largely from the German submarine blockade of Britain, the diversion of merchant shipping to transport American troops to France, North America's poor 1916 harvest, and the British government's ideological reluctance to intervene in the free market.[3] In early 1917 Lloyd George's new coalition ended government laissez-faire policy, introducing price regulations and a Food Controller. Rationing followed at the beginning of 1918. However, amid deteriorating food supplies in late 1917, fear grew that the shortages rocking continental Europe would reach Britain. Ultimately, the 1918 food deficits were made up by the introduction of the convoy system that helped defeat the submarine menace, increased domestic agriculture production, and (especially) economy measures in the production of flour and other grains that improved yields. Before Britain's food crisis passed, it created near revolutionary conditions in Ireland just weeks prior to the conscription crisis.

Cork residents had expressed concern about food supplies and prices since late 1915.[4] In September 1915, the Cork Poor Law Guardians asked the Local Government Board to intervene to control local bread prices. The LGB refused, naively suggesting that Cork bakers would not 'take advantage of the present crisis to make an exorbitant profit'.[5] In January 1916, the Guardians requested an inquiry into inflated milk prices, but once again the LGB baulked.[6] Two months later, the Guardians condemned excessive oat exports from Ireland, reminding government officials of the 'cruel famine' of 1846–8 and their duty 'to protect the food of their subjects'.[7] In November 1916, the Consumers' League asked the corporation for price controls over milk, potato and coal supplies.[8] The corporation declined, but requested government price regulations, 'to keep want, if not actual starvation, from the homes of the poor this winter'.[9] Complaining again of high prices at the beginning of 1917, the *Cork Examiner* wrote, 'Acute distress does, in fact, exist in the city, and that distress can be attributed to the war', while Poor Law Guardian Marie Lynch demanded action to prevent the urban poor, 'slowly starving to sickness or to death'.[10]

During 1917 and 1918, numerous Cork public officials made pointed references to the possibility of a new famine striking Ireland. Seventy years after Black '47, the Potato Famine remained a living memory that cast a shadow over Irish public life. Most of the population seemed to have accepted the orthodox nationalist interpretation of the calamity: that Ireland starved because the government allowed farmers to ship food out of the country. During three years of war, the Irish public experienced unsettling food shortages and read persistent newspaper accounts of wartime starvation in places like Russia, Germany and Austria-Hungary.[11] This seems to have raised anxiety among the population. Across the political spectrum, Irish leaders expressed concern about possible mass starvation. Though such warnings might be dismissed as panic or political opportunism, they were understandable in a country with a collective memory of catastrophic famine. While the Irish people quietly abided with poverty, illness, emigration and political violence, the threat of starvation could not be ignored. As the food situation worsened, Sinn Féin cries of 'Never Again' resounded across the country.

'The Food Crisis'

Throughout 1917 Cork Corporation repeatedly debated measures to alleviate food shortages.[12] A sense of crisis mounted during February 1917 after food price controls were introduced in Britain and Ireland, which led city grocers to immediately spike their prices. 'This is unnecessary,' wrote the RIC county inspector, 'and an unjustifiable increase of price of the necessities of life will press very hard on the poor who already have a hard struggle due to the high price of food.'[13] The failure of local authorities to prevent food profiteering remained a potent political issue in Cork during 1917 and 1918.[14]

Facing what he called 'The Food Crisis', Lord Mayor T.C. Butterfield called a public meeting the same month (February 1917), attended by town councillors, business leaders, and the Catholic and

Church of Ireland bishops.[15] 'Since the war began they were aware that prices of food stuffs were increasing day by day and week by week,' stated Butterfield. He complained of profiteering farmers 'out for graft', and asked civic leaders to curtail food prices. Church of Ireland Bishop Dowse reported local anxiety 'as to the possibility of famine before next harvest', while Catholic Bishop Cohalan advocated a separate Irish Food Controller to limit prices on basic staples. 'If there was danger of starvation, then they should all starve together,' argued Redmondite councillor John Horgan. '. . . The first duty of a Government was to govern so that the people should live and not die.' The meeting established a new public fund to help poor residents purchase food, and sent an appeal to Dublin Castle for an Irish Food Controller.[16] Before breaking up, the gathering heard from Irish Party supporter and labour mediator Fr Thomas Dowling:

> The word 'famine' had a sinister meaning for every Irish heart (applause). They recollected the times in the past when their people died by the roadside, and when crops grown in Ireland were allowed to be exported to foreign lands (hear, hear). They wanted to safeguard themselves from such a bitter tragedy in the future, and they wanted everything that was produced in Ireland to remain in Ireland.

During the same period (February–March 1917), the city suffered a month-long 'Potato Crisis'.[17] Potato supplies disappeared from the Corporation Market, and on some days no potatoes could be found in the city, causing distress among those dependent on this dietary staple.[18] With concern rising, city authorities embraced the Local Government Board's urban tillage campaign. Residents were encouraged to plant produce in public gardens established on the city outskirts, with the government providing allotments, tools, and seeds for potato, leek, spring onion, cabbage, parsnip and turnip.[19] Bishop Cohalan urged his flock to raise their own food, while Lord Mayor Butterfield ploughed a field before delighted city residents.[20] 'The poor in urban districts in Ireland are feeling acutely the privations that the war has imposed,' wrote the *Cork Examiner*. '. . . Duty and necessity both point to increased tillage.'[21] Cork residents welcomed urban tillage, as seen in the city's Northwest ward (one of nine wards in Cork), which had 170 allotments working within the month.[22] However, despite ample farmland surrounding the city, the corporation did not secure enough land for the programme's success. By February 1918, the Northwest ward reported 181 working allotments but a waiting list of 300 applicants, while South Ward officials claimed they could accommodate 500 more residents if its gardens were increased from three to ten acres.[23] The land shortage seems to have resulted from poor management by the corporation and the Irish Department of Agriculture. The latter was slow to approve compulsory land acquisitions, set unnecessarily high rents for the plots, and ultimately made it unaffordable for the corporation to obtain more allotments from local farmers.[24]

TABLE 10.1
Cork Potato Prices, in Pence

Month	Year	Price
Nov.	1916	9d
January	1918	18d

Source: *Cork Constitution*, 4 November 1916, 4 January 1918

'On the Verge of Starvation'

After much nationalist grumbling, the British government finally established the Irish Food Control Committee in early September 1917.[2] 'Were a Home Rule Parliament in existence,' complained the *Cork Examiner*, 'there cannot be the slightest doubt that it would look after the interests of the Irish consumer.'[26] The Irish Food Control Committee omitted representatives from organised labour and Sinn Féin, which infuriated the former and gave the latter an excuse to boycott the organisation.[27] Despite new price controls, Cork retailers continued to mark up food supplies. As the city's working classes struggled to keep up with inflation, Cork's labour movement forcibly intervened.

On 17 September 1917, 140 delegates representing every Cork labour body gathered to secure 'the necessary commodities of living to the working people of this city'.[28] Demanding 'strong virile action', the representatives urged a national convention to address 'the alarming increase in the prices of foodstuffs'. A Cork trade union committee was formed to prepare direct action if the situation did not improve. At a public meeting six weeks later, Cork Trades Council representatives called for the establishment of food depots in the city. ITGWU organiser Cathal O'Shannon also blamed Cork's high infant mortality rate on the diminishing milk supply. He blasted dairy farmers for selling poor-quality milk, foisted on the city's underclass already squeezed by high rent and increased fuel costs.[29]

With the approach of winter, social activists expressed concern for the survival of Cork's impoverished population. At a Consumers' League meeting, Mrs Warren declared, 'Poor people and little children were famishing for want of meat.'[30] Lord Mayor Butterfield convened a meeting of the city's charitable bodies to address food and fuel supplies for at-risk residents.[31] Bishop Cohalan likewise gathered the city's wealthy citizens to initiate the 'Cork Poor Children's Milk Fund' to subsidise milk supplies for the city's poor.[32] During that meeting, the president of the Cork Trades Council demanded they pressure the government 'to retain the milk supply of Ireland for Ireland'.[33] Fr O'Sullivan also claimed, 'This was not a matter of charity but justice . . . These families must be on the verge of starvation.'

Cork's milk situation demonstrated the strange dance between wartime market forces, government intervention and commercial accountability. The Cork Consumers' League had long complained of a dairy supplier 'milk ring' rigging city prices.[34] (Similar 'rings' were alleged against politically connected bakers, and potato and other vegetable suppliers[35]). When the Irish Food Controller set wholesale milk prices at one shilling, four pence per gallon in early December 1917, Cork dairy farmers claimed they could not produce milk at the new prices owing to a tripling of cattle feed costs.[36] They threatened to halt production and create a 'milk famine' if the price control was enforced in Cork.[37] Negotiations between farmers, the lord mayor and the Irish Food Committee resulted in the raising of Cork's milk price limit to one shilling, eight pence, the pre-regulation price.[38] Dublin Castle's inability to effectively control prices aroused disgust in Cork. The *Cork Examiner* complained, 'The experience of the past twelve months has been that Irish prices tend to approach the English maximum, and in one notorious instance is now higher [milk] . . . It is a curious anomaly too, that Irish bacon can be bought in England cheaper than in some Irish cities.'[39]

In November 1917 the corporation formed the twelve-man Cork Food Control Committee to monitor shortages and merchant profiteering.[40] However, the Irish Party controlled the committee, and allotted no seats to Sinn Féin and only a single seat to the Cork Trades Council, which prompted the latter to boycott the organisation.[41] The *Voice of Labour* newspaper agreed with the stand and argued:

> Sugar, tea, butter, margarine and milk are now practically unprocurable at any price. Bread, potatoes, and meat are so high in price as to be almost beyond the reach of the average worker . . . We think it is only necessary to point out the conditions of '48

> to stir our people into action. We must make it very clear that we
> in Ireland think Irish produce is primarily for Irish needs.[42]

It should be emphasised that though there was widespread anxiety about hunger, the city did not suffer from famine. Throughout these months, there were no mob attacks on food retailers, which was not the case during the Great Famine.[43] The Cork petty sessions indicate no uptick in food theft and assaults on food suppliers. Death and illness levels seemed steady in the public healthcare sector. However, residents appear to have been alarmed by shortages and price increases. Fear of hunger, rather than hunger itself, lay at the centre of this agitation. Such anxiety was not unreasonable considering the hunger experienced in continental Europe, the aggressive food rationing instituted by the British government, and the ominous submarine toll on Allied merchant shipping, which featured prominently in Cork's newspapers during these months.

'Exceptionally high prices mean practical starvation for the poor,' warned the *Cork Examiner*, '. . . self-reliance is the most useful as well as the most practical motto.'[44] This sentiment reflected the entire ethos of Cork Sinn Féin, which titled its educational pamphlet *Watchword Self-Reliance*.[45] Recognising a potential humanitarian crisis, a weapon against British rule in Ireland, and an opportunity to put its ideals into practice, Cork republicans entered the fray. Sinn Féin speakers mentioned the food question at a meeting of 15,000 in the Grand Parade on 23 September 1917. Fr Seamus O'Flynn argued that if food supplies were found wanting, farmers should stop selling to British markets and the Cork Harbour Board should prohibit food exports.[46] The meeting resolution included a call on civic bodies to 'avert the danger of the famine of the tragic period of '47'.[47] At the end of October 1917, the Cork Sinn Féin Executive asked Catholic priests to conduct food surveys within their parishes.[48] In mid-November, the new Sinn Féin National Executive Food Committee instructed local branches to ascertain current food supplies, which seemed to have occupied Cork city Sinn Féin clubs.[49] As winter approached, republicans considered practical steps to prevent starvation in the country.

Republican and Labour Counter-Measures

Citing the Potato Famine, Sinn Féin's message of 'never again' synchronised with its broader anti-government and anti-war themes. Éamon de Valera told a Kanturk (County Cork) crowd in December 1917:

> Did you not hear of famine – the year 1847? At that time there
> was sufficient food in this country to support its then large pop-
> ulation. But what was the result? The English soldiers took it
> away and left three million of our people either fall victim to
> famine or emigrate to a foreign shore.[50]

Meeting in December 1917, the Sinn Féin National Executive
appointed IRB leader Diarmuid Lynch as the Sinn Féin Director of
Food.[51] The executive also encouraged better coordination between
farmers and retailers, the creation of food depots, and joint action with
trade unions.[52] Activists perceived 'the chief danger' coming from
rapidly increasing livestock exports to Britain. Tomás MacCurtain
attended the meeting, and quickly organised a special conference in
Cork on 28 December to tackle the crisis.

The attendees reflected a coalescing republican coalition and
included Sinn Féin activists Liam de Róiste, Patrick Brady, Seán
Twomey and John Good; Irish Volunteer leaders Tomás MacCurtain
and Seán O'Hegarty; and ITGWU organisers Cathal O'Shannon and
Denis Houston. They prepared to establish a food preservation committee, representing different political parties and public boards. To
head off possible famine, MacCurtain also suggested the Sinn Féin
Executive declare itself a provisional government.[53] 'There is a big task,
a very big task, before us,' mulled Liam de Róiste, 'nothing less than
taking over the administration of the country.' Cork Sinn Féin
appointed Tomás MacCurtain Director of Food to spearhead an anti-
export campaign.[54] While MacCurtain was vice-president of the Cork
City Sinn Féin Executive, his command of Cork's Irish Volunteers provided muscle to enforce an export ban.[55] De Róiste believed
prohibition of food exports would receive widespread support, 'even
from some of the pro-English'.[56]

In the first week of the New Year, republican emissaries visited
public bodies to mobilise support to protect local food supplies. The
delegations typically included representatives of Sinn Féin, the Irish
Volunteers, and organised labour. Liam de Róiste outlined their task
as: (1) arouse public awareness of possible famine, (2) convince the
public to 'depend on themselves' for action, instead of Dublin Castle
or London, and (3) prepare the public for 'extreme measures, such as
picketing docks, railways, and roads to prevent exports'. The delegates' first stop was the Cork Trades Council, where they 'were met in
an exceptionally friendly fashion'.[57] Labour promised close cooperation and assigned two council members to Sinn Féin's working
group.[58] The Cork Poor Law Guardians listened to a delegate demand
the suspension of exports to prevent 'what happened in '47 and '48'.[59]

The Cork Harbour Commission declined to interfere with exports, but agreed to provide any food shipping data needed.[60] 'Political opponents of ours on the Board slavered us with praise,' remarked Liam de Róiste, though they hesitated to take action.[61] Facing public anxiety, Cork Corporation adopted the forceful Sinn Féin resolution:

> . . . To ensure that there shall be no shortage, nor anything approaching a famine, [we] hereby call upon all producers and dealers in commodities, such as oats, bacon, fish and cattle, more especially cows, the slaughter of which interfere with the output of milk and the production of butter, to sell only to buyers for exclusive Irish use, as otherwise the people may be forced in self-defence to adopt the rigorous measures to prevent exportation of the necessary food supplies, upon which they are solely dependent, between now and the next harvest.[62]

'The crisis is not pending in Ireland, it is upon us'[63]

In January 1918, famine anxiety grew throughout Ireland. The fear seems to have been sparked by the introduction of government food rationing that month; continued supply shortages and price inflation; and the need for tillage land as the planting season approached. That month Sinn Féin formed the 'All-Ireland Food Conference', comprised of labour and grocer association representatives;[64] the Carlow Urban Council and Navan Poor Law Guardians warned of starvation;[65] the Gorey Poor Law Guardians planned to purchase oats, flour and potato supplies for the general public;[66] and the Waterford Trades Council called for a suspension of food exports.[67] The Irish Plotholders' Union demanded the free transfer of tillage plots to the unemployed, arguing, 'The allotments of 1918 must replace the soup kitchens of '46 and '47.'[68] Concerned about 'threatened famine', Clare's Bishop Fogarty called on the government to break up grazing ranches to provide small tillage plots for the landless.[69]

Land agitation broke out in counties Kilkenny, King's, Queen's, Meath, Galway, Roscommon, Clare, Sligo and Tipperary.[70] Under pressure to provide tillage land, grazers suffered from cattle drives, boycotts, and the ploughing of pastures by crowds of landless neighbours.[71] Sinn Féin food depots were opened in Kilkenny, Wexford, Mayo, Tipperary, Cavan, Athlone, Nenagh and County Dublin.[72] Facing persistent meat shortages, Belfast's Catholic bishop permitted meat to be taken on fast days. Wexford foundry workers demanded a change in their payday, as meat supplies were always sold out before they received their weekly wages.[73] Flour shortages affected bread supplies in Athlone, Derry and surrounding counties, and became so acute on Achill Island that residents were compelled to eat their next season's potato seed.[74] The *Irish Independent* warned: 'It is absolutely essential that sufficient food supplies should be retained in the country to ensure that there should be no undue shortages, and that anything approaching a famine shall be averted.'[75] In an article titled 'There Must Be No Second '47', poet and Irish cooperative activist George Russell (AE) wrote, 'A country with that tragic lesson of the past, that produces enough food and allows itself to starve at the same time, has no purpose or excuse for remaining on the face of the earth.'[76]

Catholic Lenten pastorals read in dioceses across Ireland vocalised famine anxiety. Describing the war as 'the Divine wrath', Cardinal Logue warned, 'Want of necessaries of life, if continued much longer, must end in famine.'[77] Some of the hierarchy offered practical advice: Bishop Bernard Coyne (Elphin) called on farmers to patriotically increase tillage production, while Bishop Patrick O'Donnell (Raphoe) asked for the storage of food to prevent panic. Other bishops were not so circumspect. Bishop Charles McHugh (Derry) considered the food shortage 'little short of famine', and asked his flock to retain food supplies in Ireland, cooperate with each other to prevent hunger, and end profiteering. Cavan's Bishop Patrick Finegan echoed Sinn Féin self-reliance: 'The remedy against famine is in our own hands for the country can produce more than enough food to support ourselves.' Members of the hierarchy also called for an end to the war in clear and uncompromising terms.

In Cork, the new year brought new shortages. At the Corporation Market, potato transactions dropped to their lowest rate on record as farmers withheld their supply, driving prices to the highest in Ireland.[78] City consumers could not buy bacon for a month, which local curers blamed on British buyers outbidding the Irish market.[79] Butter supplies largely disappeared throughout Ireland, which was compounded by the halt of British margarine imports into the country.[80] Cork residents faced a severe coal shortage from Christmas, while the bishop's Poor Children's Milk Fund now provided two pints of milk a day to 800 impoverished families.[81] Despite new price controls, profiteering retailers escaped with light fines from local magistrates.[82] The St Vincent de Paul Society successfully lobbied the Cork Poor Law Guardians to increase outdoor relief payments by 100 per cent, 'to meet the present high cost of food'.[83] At the end of the month, the corporation appealed for government funds to improve flour milling.[84] Even the city's wealthiest citizens did not escape the shortages, as the Cork

County Club stopped serving toast, biscuits and barmbrack, and with-held meat on Wednesdays and Saturdays.[85] The *Voice of Labour* demanded trade unionists halt the continued food and fuel shortages, arguing, 'The crisis is not pending in Ireland, it is upon us.'[86]

Reviewing export data from the Cork Harbour Commission, Tomás MacCurtain warned of unsustainable livestock exports. This was not entirely accurate, as cattle, pork and sheep exports in 1917 were higher than previous years, but remained within historic norms. Export figures were also not conclusive without knowing the size and health of the Irish livestock population, which were affected by dislocated animal feed supplies that reduced animal weights and milk yields.[87]

TABLE 10.2
Cork Harbour Livestock Exports, 1913–17

Date	Pigs	Sheep	Cattle	Totals
1911	16,555	55,372	54,136	125,389
1912	17,025	68,317	51,698	137,380
1913	17,675	67,685	133,992	219,443
1914	9,028	33,877	94,968	137,653
1915	13,119	29,453	57,502	120,975
1916	32,730	47,751	70,878	155,503
1917	18,985	67,291	77,252	164,623

Source: *Dept. of Agriculture & Technical Instruction Committee Journal,* 1911–1918

MacCurtain was on more solid ground in his concerns about high exports of calves and dairy cattle, which threatened the sustainability of Irish herds.[88] Exports of Cork dairy cattle in 1917 almost doubled from previous years, while calf exports also jumped significantly (sur-passed only by the 1913 outlier). The Irish Department of Agriculture recognised a milk famine 'at their door', and on 1 December 1917 limited calf and dairy cow exports to a quarter of the previous year's level.[89] Livestock continued to leave the Cork docks, amid Agriculture Department investigations into the illegal slaughter of calves and dairy cattle around the city.[90] However, about a dozen prosecutions resulted in only light fines for the offenders.[91]

TABLE 10.3
Cork Calf & Dairy Cattle Exports, 1911–17

Year	Dairy	Calves
1911	2,456	8,777
1912	1,013	3,716
1913	3,124	15,065
1914	1,642	9,549
1915	3,340	7,434
1916	4,310	3,952
1917	6,406	12,284

Source: *Dept. of Agriculture & Technical Instruction Committee Journal*, 1911–1918

TABLE 10.4
Cork Calf Exports,
January/February Total,
1917 vs 1918

Year	Total
1917	1,368
1918	5,490

Source: *Cork Examiner* Weekly Food Export Reports, February to May 1918

TABLE 10.5
Cork Calf Exports as % of Irish Total, 1913–17

Year	Cork	Ireland	% Total
1913	15,065	53,045	28%
1914	9,549	34,271	28%
1915	7,434	27,009	28%
1916	3,952	13,200	30%
1917	12,284	25,992	47%

Source: *Dept. of Agriculture & Technical Instruction Committee Journal*, 1911–1918

The city's dead meat trade (livestock butchered locally, rather than exported and slaughtered across the Channel), remained unaffected by Department of Agriculture controls. Unfortunately, there are no definite figures for dead meat exports from the Port of Cork, though a February newspaper report pegged daily totals at between ten and twenty tons.[92] In late 1917, local meat suppliers agreed to pay their staff overtime, indicating an increased output for the overseas markets.[93] The Cork People's Food Committee subsequently focused on the city's dead meat trade, along with the illegal slaughter of calves and dairy cows.

The People's Food Committee

Facing republican and labour pressure, Lord Mayor Butterfield called a public meeting on 18 January 1918 to create a 'People's Food Committee'.[94] Though Bishop Cohalan acted as chairman, most of the city's elected officials and commercial leaders boycotted the gathering. A committee was formed to survey local food supplies, prepare for conservation, and emphasise 'the duty of merchants to retain for the use of the people the existing supplies'. Members included commercial figures such as Jerermiah Lucey (Southern Ireland Cattle Association) and T.P. Dowdall (Cork IDA), but retained strong progressive elements, including Cathal O'Shannon (ITGWU), Patrick Lynch (Cork Trades Council), Tomás MacCurtain (Cork Sinn Féin and Irish Volunteers), and Edward Sheehan (Cork Consumers' League and Sinn Féin). Tomás MacCurtain referred to the 'alarming' rate of food exports, while other speakers advocated ending the cross-channel meat trade. 'The workers had "their gore up",' announced ITGWU organiser Denis Houston, 'and they intended to take decisive action.' The People's Food Committee was a departure from previous public nutrition efforts in Cork, which were voluntary, philanthropic, and initiated by the city's middle and upper classes. This new group acted in the name of the people, sought no legal sanction, implicitly threatened violence to compel obedience, and was willing to defy government authority. With some justification, the *Voice of Labour* would later call the Cork's People's Food Committee 'a local soviet in embryo'.[95]

Two weeks later, the People's Food Committee held a second public meeting, which was again boycotted by the city's political and commercial elite, as well as 'establishment' members of the committee.[96] The tenor of this gathering was more strident, from the singing of rebel songs by Fianna boy scouts to the booing that greeted the announcement of Lord Mayor Butterfield's absence. Sinn Féin's Seán Nolan 'attributed the war and the resultant food crisis to capitalism following on bad Government', and said they would 'defend the foodstuffs of their country'. Speaking for the Irish Volunteers, Seán O'Hegarty proposed ending meat and oats exports, and appealed for the public to support 'drastic action' that might be needed. Warning of a repetition of the Great Famine, republican Tadhg Barry added ominously, 'if they were going to die, they would not die starving.'

The People's Food Committee prepared for direct action. Under Sinn Féin's auspices, a potato depot was established at the Corporation Corn Market, intended for emergency distribution to the city's poor.[97] Critical to severing exports, city railway workers (John Good's National Union of Railwaymen) agreed to 'support any action taken by the local Food Committee to conserve the food supply and prevent famine'.[98] To build its case, the People's Food Committee requested thirty-two separate weekly livestock export reports from the Harbour Commissioners.[99] However, the South of Ireland Cattle Trade Association refused the committee's request to curtail live and dead meat exports, claiming there was enough meat on hand to feed Cork.[100]

At the beginning of February, the People's Food Committee dropped the hammer, issuing a notice to all Cork meat traders and exporters. It was signed by representatives of the Cork Sinn Féin Executive, the Irish Volunteers, the Cork Trades Council; the ITGWU, and the Cork #3 branch, National Union of Railwaymen:

> A cara – On behalf of the above committee empowered by the citizens of Cork, in a public meeting assembled on Monday January 28th, we hereby warn you and all whom it may concern that in consequence of the present scarcity and likelihood of famine, the exportation of fresh meat, beef, mutton, pork, and meat offal must cease as from February 3rd.[101]

People's Food Committee delegates called on individual butchers and cattle exporters to either comply with the order or negotiate with the committee during its nightly sittings. On one day, no livestock was shipped to Britain, but this seemed to have been a demonstration, as exports re-started without interference.[102] Within a week, dead meat exports in Cork virtually disappeared, dropping from the estimated ten to twenty tons per day, to less than half a ton.[103]

Food traders downplayed the threat of hunger and warned of damage to the city's dead meat trade. However, many city butchers began to dispose of surplus stock.[104] The People's Food Committee raised a strike fund and deployed Irish Volunteers and union members to observe the railways and docks, though picketing proved unnecessary.[105] The Irish Volunteers kept close watch for any destruction of calves and dairy cows, inspecting butcher shops and slaughterhouses throughout the city.[106] When faced with resistance from reluctant traders, the committee used other tactics. On 6 February, unidentified parties destroyed six mutton carcasses prepared for export in a Pouladuff Road slaughter house. Other meat traders were visited in Cork, 'with pressure to bear on these men to discontinue the export of dead meat'.[107] In Whitechurch, about twelve miles from Cork, activists drove and scattered forty-five head of cattle before they could be exported to Britain.[108]

The committee spurred more robust action from government authorities. On 12 February, the Cork Rural District Council asked Dublin Castle for public slaughtering facilities in Cork, to stop the butchering of calves and lambs in the city suburbs, beyond municipal control.[109] The RIC began to aggressively prosecute city merchants violating government food regulations. Charges were filed on three consecutive days (13–15 February) for illegal calf slaughtering and excessive retail food prices.[110] Two weeks later, the corporation established its own food depot on Barrack Street.[111]

The People's Food Committee faced considerable opposition from Cork's commercial and political establishments. The Southern Cattle Traders threatened to slow tillage output if the committee continued its 'interference with surplus cattle'.[112] The *Cork Constitution* warned of a destructive trade war with Britain, preventing the import of flour, tea and sugar into the country.[113] Amid repeated complaints about 'that autocratic decree',[114] the *Cork Examiner* argued:

> The Committee is drifting towards increasing industrial unrest on the plea of conserving the food supply . . . the food problem, complex and menacing as it is, is being exploited for purposes that may end up in the holding up of trade and industry in the city of Cork, thus intensifying poverty and bringing want and privation into many homes.[115]

Unfortunately there is no record of public reactions to the People's Food Committee, though it should be noted that the organisation was a product of Sinn Féin and organised labour, which represented a strong majority of working-class residents. Liam de Róiste privately raged at the attitude of local commercial leaders:

> You see famine seldom touches the moneyed people. It is a concern of the poor. It is the poor who first suffer from the scarcity of food. 'Don't interfere with trade, don't upset the principles of exchange, don't anger the English' – such are the yelpings, exactly as they were in the great famine of '47, '48, and '49. But today there are many in Ireland who would harken to the advice of John Mitchell. There are men who will neither be bluffed nor frightened, neither angered nor stampeded. There will be no famine in Ireland if Sinn Féin and Labour men in Cork can prevent it. But for the Óglaig [Irish Volunteers], decisions could not be put into force. They are the best argument in this as in other matters.[116]

National Food Agitation

Food agitation broke out across Ireland during February, most commonly in the form of republican-sanctioned land seizures. This agrarian upheaval occurred during the weeks when rural Ireland readied to sow crops for the next harvest. Anticipating food shortages, many landless farm labourers and at-risk townspeople demanded small tillage plots to raise vegetables for the coming year. Land was sought from large farmers who used their holdings for pasture (to raise livestock) instead of tillage (to grow crops). The long-standing 'cow vs plough' tension exploded in February 1918, with land disturbances reported in eighteen separate counties.[117] The RIC inspector general painted an unsettling picture for Dublin Castle: 'In Sligo, Roscommon, Leitrim, Galway, Clare, Mayo, Limerick, Kings, Queens, and Westmeath, large bodies of men with ploughs and often with bands and Sinn Féin flags marched to grazing farmers, and if the owner did not submit to their demands under this intimidation, they took forcible possession of as much as they required.'[118] Following 140 separate cattle drives (some led by the Irish Volunteers), British troops were deployed to Sligo, Mayo, Roscommon, Galway, Tipperary and Clare.[119] In Roscommon, land was confiscated 'by order of the Irish Republic', while a Sligo Sinn Féin leader announced to 200 people preparing to plough a seized field, 'this land is let for ten years at £4 per acre, in the name of God and the Irish Republic.'[120] The RIC county inspector for Galway East Riding warned, 'Sinn Féin is now being worked in this Riding as an agrarian movement for the forcible possession of lands.'[121] Clare police shot dead a 23-year-old cattle driver, and by late February the disturbed county was declared a Special Military Area.[122]

Rural agitation fused popular anxiety about the coming harvest with old-fashioned land hunger. It mainly struck areas similarly affected during the Ranch War, and was compounded further by the wartime suspension of land purchases and the Congested Districts Board's leasing of untenanted land to grazers. Though republican leaders apparently did not plan the outbreak, they were willing to 'cash in', to quote one Volunteer leader.[123] Laurence Ginnell toured the country, advocating cattle driving and breaking up ranches for the landless.[124] (He was subsequently prosecuted for one such speech in Meath.)[125] Count Plunkett called on the Irish Volunteers and ITGWU to stop food exports, while Éamon de Valera suggested the Volunteers might be needed to divide land fairly.[126] Sinn Féin-inspired food protection committees and depots sprung up in Tyrone, Kilkenny, Mayo, Kerry, west Cork, Meath, Westmeath, and Wexford. The Drogheda Sinn

Féin branch prohibited food exports until it completed a food census,[127] while the Kanturk Food Committee confiscated potatoes readied for export, and sold them to the town's impoverished residents at market price (returning the proceeds to the owner).[128] On 21 February 1918, amid a national bacon shortage, Sinn Féin Food Controller Diarmuid Lynch and a group of Irish Volunteers seized thirty-four pigs being driven along the Circular Road to Dublin's docks for export to Britain.[129] As a crowd of delighted Dubliners looked on, the pigs were butchered in a nearby yard and then sold to a local retailer for home consumption, with the proceeds returned to the original owners. Lynch received two months for 'conspiracy to seize pigs'.[130]

Fearing unrest and political division between the landed and the landless, republican leaders stepped back from food and agrarian agitation. On 23 February 1918, the Sinn Féin Standing Committee discouraged branches from participating in land seizures and cattle driving.[131] The following week, the Irish Volunteers headquarters prohibited members from joining agrarian disturbances. Agrarianism subsequently subsided in March, and almost entirely disappeared by April 1918.[132] The decline was also affected by the passing of planting season, the approach of the conscription crisis, and the arrest of many activists, who often seized land publicly as a form of civil disobedience.[133]

Returning from a meeting of the Sinn Féin Executive in early March 1918, Liam de Róiste related Éamon de Valera's instructions about the coming conscription crisis, which indicates Sinn Féin's cooling towards food preservation agitation.

> Don't go on a line of action unless you know you can see it through. Pick our steps carefully. Don't be led into conflagration. Don't be driven by England into action. Let us bide our time. Don't get us involved in side issues at present. You must get the whole country behind you if you are to win . . . avoid challenges if you can.[134]

TABLE 10.6
Cork Calf & Dairy Cattle Exports, 1916–18

Year	Dairy	Calves
1916	4,310	3,952
1917	6,406	12,284
1918	1,447	5,972

Source: *Dept. of Agriculture & Technical Instruction Committee Journal*, 1914–1918

TABLE 10.7

Cork Calf Exports as % of Irish Total, 1916–18

Year	Cork	Ireland	Cork %
1916	3,952	13,200	30%
1917	12,284	25,992	47%
1918	5,972	20,752	29%

Source: *Dept. of Agriculture & Technical Instruction Committee Journal, 1914–1918*

TABLE 10.8

Cork Harbour Livestock Exports, 1916–18

Date	Pigs	Sheep	Cattle	Total
1916	32,730	47,751	70,878	155,503
1917	18,985	67,291	77,252	164,623
1918	13,980	21,211	41,668	77,553

Source: *Dept. of Agriculture & Technical Instruction Committee Journal, 1911–1918*

Following Sinn Féin's and the Irish Volunteer intervention in late February, no more was heard from the Cork People's Food Committee. The cross-channel dead meat trade that largely disappeared from Cork in early 1918 had not recovered by 1919.[135] Government restrictions on calf and dairy cow exports undoubtedly reduced cross-channel livestock sales.[136] However, the People's Food Committee likely contributed as well, by bringing heavy pressure on farmers, sellers and exporters to retain food stocks in the country. Overall, Cork livestock exports sharply dropped in 1918, numbering less than half of the 1916 and 1917 totals. That decline was roughly three times the national rate. The most likely explanation for the difference was the food preservation campaign waged by the Cork People's Food Committee.

TABLE 10.9

Livestock Exports % Decline from 1917 Total to 1918 Total

Place	Pigs	Sheep	Cattle	Total
Ireland	–19%	–20%	–14%	–17%
Cork	–26%	–68%	–46%	–53%

Source: *Dept. of Agriculture & Technical Instruction Committee Journal, 1917–1918*

Cork food supplies and prices ultimately stabilised through the defeat of the German submarine menace, a healthy 1918 harvest, and effective price and production controls in Britain. Newspaper reports indicate an easing of public anxiety as prices stabilised and more food became available at a local level.[137] The disappearance of the People's Food Committee in March was probably also linked to the political mobilisation surrounding the conscription crisis in April and the republican movement's retreat from socio-economic agitation.

TABLE 10.10
Cork Standard Food Commodities, 1918, in Pence

Date	Eggs	Butter	Bacon	Bld Beef	Tea	Milk	Potato	Bread
2 Jan. 1918	50	26	24	14	44	3	18	9
6 Nov. 1918	75	31	34	16	32	3	20	9

Note: 12 eggs, lb butter, lb cut rasher, lb boiled beef, lb tea, pint milk, weight potato, 4lb loaf bread.

Source: *Cork Constitution,* 2 January, 6 November 1918

The Cork People's Food Committee reflected local anxiety about mass hunger, which carried special resonance in Ireland. While Cork did not starve, the threat of famine aroused local civic leaders across the political spectrum. Food rationing, local shortages, and reports of famine in Europe made the situation very real to Cork residents. The British government's effective response to the food situation forestalled destabilising activities by anti-state actors in Cork and elsewhere. They showed an unwillingness to endure significant privations to achieve victory in a war that no longer enjoyed popular support. Fearful of hunger, some Cork residents prepared to confiscate food from local suppliers, while their rural counterparts marched along scores of rural laneways to seize tillage land. One can envision even more radical responses had Ireland's fear of starvation evolved into the real thing, as experienced in parts of Europe during the last year of the First World War.

XI. Insurrection: The 1918 Conscription Crisis

Oh, would when Kings quarrel
Their own blood would be shed,
And not like cowards snarl
Whilst slaves must fight instead
Tadhg Barry, 1917[1]

Separate strands of wartime unrest fused following the passage of the Military Service Bill in April 1918. The conscription threat in Ireland produced an unequivocal challenge to British authority, the eclipse of constitutional nationalism, and the triumph of the radical republican movement. Changing public opinion evident since Easter 1916, crossed the threshold into open rebellion in the spring of 1918.

Military Recruiting in Cork

British Army enlistments in Cork had steadily declined prior to the Easter Rising, but fell sharply afterwards. Writing from Cork in September 1916, the Southern District military intelligence officer offered this analysis:

a. The labouring class, which has supplied all the recruits up to the present, is now exhausted and very few more may be expected from this quarter.

b. Political reasons. There is an inherited distrust and dislike of the Army which is difficult to overcome, and the Sinn Féiners make great efforts to keep this feeling alive.

c. The fact that the Roman Catholic Clergy, as a whole, have either discouraged recruiting or taken no part in assisting the movement.

d. Social reasons. It is an undoubted fact that practically all the recruits so far obtained have been those of the labouring classes. The farmers' sons, both those engaged on the farms and in commercial life, the clerks, and the shop assistants will not enlist in the same regiments as men they consider socially far beneath them . . .

e. The attitude of the Press, which is lukewarm. They write as a rule to the effect that sufficient has been done by Ireland . . .

f. 'Soreness' caused by matters arising out of the Rebellion. This feeling is dying out rapidly.

g. No material advantage gained by enlisting. The available men are mostly unmarried, so the separation allowance is no inducement . . .[2]

Enlistments continued to drop in 1917, with the police characterising city recruitment as 'poor' or 'very poor' in March, May, June, September, October, November and December.[3] (In January it was 'fair'; February, 'practically dead'; April, 'slightly better'; and July, 'bad'.)[4] Republicans did not openly disrupt recruitment, but the county inspector explained, 'This is no doubt owing to the present power to suppress such movements.'[5] Military intelligence connected enlistments to economic necessity: 'Only boys and a few of the labouring class join up; the latter being attracted by the separation allowances.'[6] There was also a large drop in enlistments following the Sinn Féin victory in the East Clare by-election;[7] and a tendency for recruits to join non-combat military units 'where no risk is incurred' instead of infantry regiments.[8] The situation remained dire in November 1917, with the military intelligence officer warning, 'no improvement need be looked for.'[9]

Nationally, recruiting fell to low levels in 1917. The decline was more marked among Catholics than Protestants, as Catholic enlistments dropped roughly 20 per cent between 1915 and 1917. Overall, Catholic enlistments declined by 84 per cent in two years, from 31,412 in 1915 to 5,057 in 1917. In the last four months of 1917, a total of 1,140 Catholic recruits enlisted in the army throughout the entire country, providing a paltry average of 9.3 men per day.[10]

TABLE 11.1
Catholics as % of Irish Enlistments

Year	Catholics	Total	Percent
1915	31,412	51,144	61.4%
1916	10,053	18,819	53.4%
1917	5,057	12,644	39.9%

Source: John Redmond Papers, MS 15,259, NLI

TABLE 11.2

Catholic Recruiting Monthly Comparison, 1915–17

Month	1915	1916	1917
January	2,256	1,779	458
February	2,607	1,281	455
March	2,250	771	447
April	3,915	827	460
May	3,598	543	513
June	3,260	653	542
July	2,011	494	310
August	2,448	487	388
September	2,145	598	615
October	1,413	680	329
November	3,436	517	306
December	2,073	423	234

Source: John Redmond Papers, MS 15,259, NLI

Perceptions of the War

City residents maintained no illusions about the cost of the grim industrial warfare practised on the Western Front. Day after day, month after month, the *Cork Examiner* reported the death of local men, often accompanied with photographs of proud uniformed soldiers and sailors. Many prominent city residents became fatalities. Martin Lillis, the son of the Munster-Leinster bank director, was shot down while flying with the RAF;[11] Percy Dale, son of UIL Alderman Henry Dale, was killed in France.[12] John Dinan, a Cork Poor Law Guardian and director of Eustace & Company, had lost all three of his sons by the end of 1918.[13] Two of University College Cork's pre-eminent athletes fell: Irish rugby international scrumhalf Vincent MacNamara was killed at Gallipoli in 1915, and former Olympic sprinter and British Isles champion P.J. Royce died of fever in Iraq during 1917.[14]

Munster Fusilier Lieutenant Francis Biggane, of Presentation College and UCC, was the city's most celebrated war hero. Shortly after the Easter Rising, German soldiers placed a placard in front of the Munster Fusiliers' trenches that read, 'Irishmen, why will you fight for England when they are shooting your wives and sisters in Dublin?'[15] That night, Biggane and another soldier retrieved the sign, and later presented it to King George at Buckingham Palace.[16] Biggane was wounded at Passchendaele a year later, and while he was carried to the rear, a shell hit his stretcher and literally blew him to bits.[17] Killed during the same battle was the popular Palace Theatre bandmaster

W.G. Swanson and former National Volunteer officer John O'Brien.[18] Professor Edward H. Harper, head of UCC's Mathematics Department, died in France in 1916, one of thirty-nine UCC students or graduates to die during the war.[19] More frequently, it was obscure members of the working class who suffered. During two weeks in July 1916 (during the Somme Battle), seventy-four Cork city men were listed as casualties.[20] Dan and Christopher Kelly were killed in France and Salonika in 1915 and 1916 respectively.[21] Pope's Quay mourned the three Hogan brothers lost on the Western Front, John (1914), David (1916) and Patrick (1917).[22] Patrick Hurley, James Sullivan and Maurice Murphy went down with the HMS *Indefatigable* during the Battle of Jutland, while Patrick Higgins of Vicar Street was killed aboard HMS *Tiger*.[23] Shandon Street's Sergeant-Major Henry Doherty, a Boer War veteran, died in 1915; Jack Coughlan, already wounded four times, was killed the following year.[24] Each tragedy created its own tiny ripple in Cork city, which grew to waves by early 1918. At the time of the conscription crisis, few city residents would have been unaffected by war losses.

The Military Service Bill

The German spring offensive caused massive casualties among the British Army, including the disintegration of the 16th Irish Division.[25] In response, the British government introduced conscription to Ireland, to boost manpower and to justify raising Britain's mandatory military service age to fifty.[26] In Ireland, the War Office began to replace Irish garrison troops with English ones and the cabinet debated conscripting priests.[27]

Public scepticism of Allied victory should be factored into the conscription crisis. In April 1918, the Italians seemed on the verge of total collapse following their disastrous retreat from the Battle of Caporetto. Russia dropped out of the war entirely, signing a separate peace on 3 March 1918. The Americans had not yet fully deployed their army, and it was unclear how it would perform. The French Nivelle and the British Passchendaele offensives both failed spectacularly in late 1917. The u-boat blockade brought food shortages to Britain. The March 1918 German spring offensive ripped through the Allied lines with rapidity unseen since the war's opening weeks. In such circumstances, the Irish public could be forgiven for anticipating massive British casualties and an ultimate German victory.

As the House of Commons voted on the Military Service Bill, tensions rose in Cork. Throngs crowded outside newspaper office message boards to monitor the latest updates from London.[28] The

Constitution recorded, 'wherever one went knots of people were to be found excitedly discussing the measure', with many expressing 'pronounced hostility' towards the measure.[29] Around Cork, buttons appeared reading, 'Conscription? Not damn likely'.[30]

Public Response

The public response to conscription was swift and virtually unanimous. Cork Corporation denounced the act in striking terms that deserve lengthy quotation:

> It is against the Constitutional rights of the Irish nation and excludes us from the right to self determine our own destiny . . . In Ireland a remnant today is only left of our Ancient Race in the land of their fathers . . . Therefore bearing in mind the disaster which is bound to ensue by conscription, we appeal to foreign governments . . . to our countrymen abroad and their kin who are forced from Ireland by Alien rule, to all our race in foreign lands, to those we appeal for support . . .[31]

The Cork City Sinn Féin Executive immediately repudiated Britain's 'right to rule this country', and advised 'the unarmed portions of our people to adopt the policy of passive resistance, to all English legislation in the country'.[32] The Poor Law Guardians attested, 'the Irish people are not Irish swine, and therefore protest against their treachery in being . . . sent to the slaughter on any front.'[33] The Cork Harbour Commission rejected the House of Commons' 'moral or legal right to conscript the people of Ireland'.[34] Protests poured in from diverse organisations like the Cork District Trades Council, the Railway Clerks' Association, the University College Cork Students' Club, the Southern Ireland Cattle Traders, the Munster Vintners, the Cork Evicted Tenants' Association, the Cork Technical Education Committee, and the Barrack Street Band.[35]

City High Sheriff Willie O'Connor wired his resignation to the Lord Lieutenant, owing to the bill passing 'without the consent of her people and heedless of the warnings of the Irish Party'.[36] The Cork Crown Prosecutor also offered his resignation if conscription proceeded.[37] On 16 April, a meeting of twenty-seven nationalist and Labour city magistrates declared conscription 'unjust and tyrannical'.[38] The RIC remained loyal for the moment, but in the opinion of Lieutenant General Bryan Mahon, 'the Police cannot be relied upon to assist effectively in carrying out conscription and the military alone must do it.'[39] Cork's unionist High Sheriff Philip Harold Barry promised unprecedented national unity that reflected 'a fearfully quiet, earnest determination to die rather than accept conscription'.[40]

All members of Cork's public bodies denounced conscription, with the exception of four prominent unionists. Cork Harbour Commissioner Benjamin Haughton challenged Irish Party officials over their prior support for the war, and argued, 'Ireland would stand or fall with England.'[41] Charles Furlong also spoke against the resolution: 'Numbers of people in Ireland had sent their best to help England in the war, and why should not other people do the same?'[42] At a meeting of the Cork Technical Education Committee, Church of Ireland Canon A.J. Nicholson and brewer Sharman Crawford would not condemn the Military Service Bill. Nicholson claimed to be 'exceedingly glad' conscription had come to Ireland, and asked, 'Was it not a disgrace when one entered the Cork shops to see fine young men behind the counters selling pieces of tape and ladies stockings?'[43] The more circumspect Sharman Crawford celebrated the bravery of local soldiers in the Irish regiments, and believed the public should support 'their men at the front'.[44]

Their courageous, if unpopular stand was received with hostility. A chaplain at the Cork Workhouse, Canon Nicholson drew fire from the Poor Law Guardians. The Guardians volunteered to continue to pay Nicholson's salary if he joined the British Army, and hoped 'his four sons, who are all of military age, will follow his example'.[45] The corporation received a Cork Trades Council delegation demanding the expulsion of the four dissenters from all public boards.[46] 'Repugnant as it was to them to pillory men for their political opinions and actions,' remarked the spokesmen, 'the times they lived in permitted no questions.' The councillors hesitated, largely out of respect for Sharman Crawford, a highly regarded philanthropist. Labour Alderman Jeremiah Kelleher, though, would have none of it: 'If these gentlemen had built the city from stem to stern, it still wouldn't pay for this demand for conscription in Ireland.' Redmondite councillors rallied to Crawford's aid, with Willie O'Connor asking, 'Were they in Cork . . . to be as intolerant and as big bigots as they were in Belfast?' Ultimately councillors repudiated the four men's statements but retained their services on the public boards.

Cork Sinn Féin Executive emissaries met with Éamon de Valera and other Sinn Féin leaders in Dublin, who apparently believed conscription was a deliberate 'proposal for the extermination of the Irish people'.[47] Cork constitutionalists expressed similar fears of genocide. The corporation protested against 'the final effort of the English Government to blot out of existence a race'.[48] 'It is an outcome of an infamous conspiracy to exterminate the scanty remnant of the Irish race,' alleged Cork nationalist and labour magistrates.[49] From his Catholic pulpit, Fr Brendan O'Leary vowed, 'Where Cromwell failed and Elizabeth before him failed[,] in this age of enlightenment and progress Lloyd George and his accomplices would fail also.' His colleague Fr Murphy characterised Lloyd George's government as the successors of those 'who in days gone by, by every means that human malice could devise, tried to extirpate the Irish race'.[50]

Other constitutional nationalists employed apocalyptic language. Harbour Commissioner P.D. O'Brien explained, 'after the famine years their population dwindled from 9½ million to 4½ million, and it was contemplated to take that little remnant to the slaughter house.' Canon Sexton stated, 'No Government has the right of forcing on a nation the supreme sacrifice of death against the free will of the people.'[51] J.J. Horgan believed the government was 'driving the young men of Ireland to the slaughter', while Fr Thomas Dowling sought to 'prevent a holocaust of blood'.[52] Citing his two brothers wounded on the Western Front, Willie O'Connor added, 'the treatment of the country was enough to make the corpses of Irishmen in Flanders to appear.'[53] He later warned Prime Minister Lloyd George, 'Not alone are the men determined to die rather than submit to conscription, but also their mothers, wives, and sisters are prepared to do likewise.'[54]

For nationalists of all stripes, conscription without the assent of the Irish public was fundamentally undemocratic and underlined Ireland's failure to achieve the self-determination promised by Woodrow Wilson's Fourteen Points. Nationalist magistrates believed 'it is a flagrant defiance of . . . the rights of small nationalities and the self-determination of her peoples.'[55] Coroner William Murphy told the UIL Executive, 'as a nation they were entitled to self-determination . . . they would not be coerced, driven, or forced by threats.'[56] Bishop Cohalan issued a pastoral letter denouncing conscription 'against the will of our nation'.[57] The Cork Harbour Board believed that 'with the principle of self-determination and liberty for small Nationalities which England is alleged to be waging this war, the Irish nation can only be conscripted by a freely elected Irish Parliament'.[58]

In retrospect, Cork Redmondites considered conscription a political disaster. 'Now all trust in constitutional methods vanished,' wrote J.J. Horgan. He argued, 'conscription placed constitutional Nationalists in an impossible position.'[59] For the AOH, the Military Service Bill was 'the last straw breaking the camel's back', as voters 'exasperated at the Government's failure and blundering' moved to Sinn Féin in the ensuing general election.[60] Military intelligence stated that Sinn Féin clubs in Cork city 'probably swelled from about 1,500 members to 4,000 and 5,000 in a single week', while the local Irish Volunteers absorbed a flood of new recruits.[61]

Demonstrations and Non-Violent Resistance

For the moment, civil disobedience was the preferred mode of opposition. Former AFIL leader William O'Brien promised, 'Against such a form of moral resistance no armed force can prevail.'[62] Bishop Cohalan asked the city's young men 'to avoid playing into the hands of their enemies by a formal military rising', but he added a provocative caveat: 'I am putting the matter, so far, solely on the grounds of utility and expediency.'[63] Sinn Féin distributed leaflets calling for passive resistance to all government legislation, but left the door open to armed conflict.[64] At a mass meeting of city workers, the Cork Trades Council promised resistance, but for now urged people 'to keep clam, and give no provocation for any attack being made upon them'.[65]

Initially, the Irish Volunteers refused to meet the City Sinn Féin Executive, apparently reluctant to risk interference with their intended physical resistance. Within a few days the discord was sorted out and a joint plan agreed to. On 14 April republicans huddled with Cork labour leaders, who 'were for resisting conscription at all costs'. However, trade unionists still deferred to their Dublin leadership and would not reject all British legislation in the country. Two days later, Redmondites called a meeting of all city political parties, chaired by Fr Thomas. 'They all were very desirous of knowing what Sinn Féin intended,' recorded Liam de Róiste.[66] He subsequently received republican criticism for agreeing to share a platform with Irish Party officials, despite the emergency.

An impromptu public demonstration on 15 April drew thousands to the National Monument.[67] Bands processed to the city centre, while Northwest Ward residents marched behind their parish priests and a banner reading 'Cork's Resolve – Death before Conscription'. Redmondites, O'Brienites, trade unionists and republicans shared the platform. Bishop Cohalan explained, 'The young men of Ireland did not see that the present war was Ireland's war, and they protested against being asked to join the British Army against their will.' The meeting passed off peacefully, though that evening youths once again stoned the army recruiting office, shattering its windows for the sixth time in two years.[68]

All Cork's Catholic churches held masses of intercession the next Sunday, praying to halt 'the scourge of conscription'.[69] The *Examiner*

reported enormous congregations, in scenes that were 'at once edi-
fying and inspiring', and reminiscent of the Ulster Covenant signings
four years earlier.[70] Following mass, parishioners took the anti-conscription pledge from their priests, promising 'to resist conscription
by the most effective means at our disposal'.[71] The *Examiner* described
one city church, when the priest 'removed his vestments and came
outside the church wearing his alb and stole, stood on a pedestal, and
bidding the thousands of men to remove their hats and lift their right
hand, the priest with his hand so uplifted read the pledge, the words
repeated by the vast crowds echoing through the streets or dying
away over space and hills'.[72]

The following day, 23 April 1918, Cork's trade unions moved into
the vanguard. Ireland experienced a one-day general strike called by
the Irish Trades Union Congress and Labour Party. Across Cork, shops
and factories closed, trains and trams were idle, pubs shut their doors,
and the harbour fell silent.[73] That afternoon, the Cork Trades Council
hosted a massive protest meeting at the National Monument drawing
up to 30,000, in what was likely the largest protest in city history.[74] The
platform speakers were confined to labour leaders, with meeting
chairman Fr Thomas proclaiming, 'In their name, in the name of peace,
he raised his voice in all vehemence against the suicidal policy of the
Government.'[75] The crowd shouted their defiance at a military aeroplane that buzzed the gathering.[76] Afterwards, participants signed the
anti-conscription pledge at tables staffed by Cumann na mBan
members.[77] The U.S. consul-general at Queenstown was impressed by
the 'perfect order' during this 'very successful demonstration of Irish
unity [,] determination and discipline'.[78]

Later that afternoon, City Hall hosted a special 'Women's Meeting'
to denounce the Military Service Bill. 'Principally girls and young
women' packed the hall, with so many turned away that speakers
addressed overflow crowds in the vestibule and streets in front of the
building.[79] The *Examiner* believed the meeting 'was the largest of its
kind probably ever seen in Cork'.[80] The gathering heard from women
only, such as the lady mayoress Helen Butterfield, Poor Law Guardian
Marie Lynch, and republican Mary MacSwiney. The *Examiner*
reported, 'Feminine enthusiasm proved even more voluble and spir-
ited than that at the National Monument.' Liam de Róiste was pleased
to observe separation women 'walking in large numbers through St
Patrick's Street, singing Sinn Féin songs'.[81] The Cork Trades Council
organised a second women's meeting, which was addressed by
Alderman Kelleher, republican John Good, the ITGWU's Denis
Houston, and Mary MacSwiney and Margaret O'Leary representing

two feuding wings of Cumann na mBan.[82] Women took their own pledge, refusing to assume the job of any conscripted man.

The ITGWU instructed its branches to 'resist any attempt to slaughter its members whether in Ireland in the interests of the British Empire, or in France in the interests of international capitalism'. Workers would not sign government documents, obey orders, answer questions or 'contribute by any word or act to help another to murder him'.[83] The newspaper *Watchword of Labour* called conscription the greatest crisis 'in living memory'.[84] Its editor, Cork ITGWU organiser Cathal O'Shannon, also saw opportunity, as he suggested that 'Russia may yet have a sister Soviet'.[85] During this period, the small Cork Citizen Army company was mobilised, before it merged with the Irish Volunteers in an arrangement brokered by O'Shannon and Tomás MacCurtain.[86]

Five days after the Cork general strike, mass civil opposition was visible during church-gate collections for the 'National Defence Fund'.[87] Donations were taken after every mass at seventeen churches, with collections totalling between £5,000 and £6,000.[88] For the *Cork Examiner*, 'the scenes outside the churches were unparalleled in the history even of this country.'[89] Further contributions flowed from wealthy merchants, though they carefully put holds on their cheques until after the military draft had actually begun. The aggressive anti-conscription stance taken by Catholic clerics struck the local military intelligence officer: 'Led by the Roman Catholic hierarchy, all sections of Nationalists, Constitutional and Sinn Féin, have coalesced for the moment for this object.'[90]

In Dublin, the new Mansion House Committee represented the Irish Party, Sinn Féin, the Irish Labour Party and the AFIL. It included a strong Cork contingent, with MP William O'Brien representing the AFIL, and Michael Egan of the Cork Coachbuilders Society serving on behalf of the Irish Labour Party, with Cathal O'Shannon acting as a secretary.[91] The committee became a ruling body for the national campaign of resistance, with both Cathal O'Shannon and Tim Healy suggesting it should declare itself a provisional government if the situation deteriorated further.[92]

The Mansion House Committee ordered every parish to form a 'Local Defence Committee' to implement civil disobedience on a massive scale.[93] Parishes also organised local branches of the National Defence Fund, to finance the campaign.[94] If the government began to enforce conscription, the country would undergo a one-week general strike, in concert with 'united passive resistance'. Essential workers in the railways, docks and civil service would periodically down tools to disrupt civic administration. No one would replace conscripted men or striking workers; food exports would be stopped; and all bank deposits were to be simultaneously withdrawn to create runs on the banks.[95] If arrested, conscripted men were to demand a civil trial; when handed over to the military, they would obey no orders. Solicitors were organised for mass court-martials and advised to read *'The Manual of Military Law'* and *'The King's Regulations.'*[96] The plan intended to disrupt and eventually paralyse Ireland's economic and legal frameworks.

During May, the Cork City Defence Committee and Defence Fund Committee raised money and prepared for civil resistance.[97] With the exception of unionists, all major political parties were represented on the committees, with Bishop Cohalan serving as the Fund Committee president and J.J. Horgan as its secretary.[98] The Cork Trades Council instructed union members to donate one shilling to the Defence Fund.[99]

After the war, the Cork Defence Fund caused a controversy when Bishop Cohalan unilaterally appropriated it for the building of the North Cathedral, despite vocal opposition from republicans and trade unionists.[100] Tim Healy vocalised common disbelief, when he privately laughed at the bishop's 'cranky position'.[101] This contributed to a schism between Cohalan and Cork separatists, which would culminate in his excommunication of IRA activists in both 1920 and 1922.

The Volunteers Prepare to Resist

Beyond civil disobedience, the Irish Volunteers prepared for physical resistance, which they organised furiously, albeit underground. 'There is no doubt a good deal going on quietly in an underhanded way,' reported the RIC county inspector.[102] Just prior to the conscription crisis, Tomás MacCurtain and his brigade adjutant went on the run, visiting rural units to tighten the Cork Brigade structure. Additional battalions were organised throughout the county, including two in the city, the 1st Battalion (north side of the River Lee) and the 2nd Battalion (south side).[103] Newly-appointed brigade communications officer Florrie O'Donoghue built up a sophisticated dispatch system across the county, which would well serve the IRA during 1920–1. A signalling corps was also established.[104] The brigade ordered important officers to accept bail if arrested, and local units to remain in close contact with headquarters.[105] Despite the improved organisation, Volunteer units were virtually unarmed except for a few shotguns and pistols.

The Volunteers bolstered their scanty arsenal in numerous ways. Local Soldiers occasionally sold their rifles to discreet civilians.

Novelist Robert Graves wrote that during his brief posting to Cork in 1918, 'Irish troops at the depots were now giving away their rifles to the Sinn Féiners.'[106] Despite a recent order from IRA general headquarters forbidding arms raids on private homes, there were at least eight of these in the city and suburbs from May to July.[107] Shotguns were easier to procure, and Volunteer workmen produced their own heavy slug ammunition for them.[108] Weapon manufacturing proved dangerous. One Volunteer described filing down rifle ammunition to fit an exotic pistol, but during a test-firing the gun barrel exploded, destroying both the pistol and the tree to which it had been tied.[109] The city Volunteers dispatched an officer to London to buy as many arms as possible. On the boat over, he ran into Cathal Brugha, who intended to assassinate the British cabinet upon the start of conscription.[110] Illustrating the desperate weapons shortage, city blacksmiths produced 'croppy pikes', while a Volunteer burgled University College Cork's natural history museum to retrieve a dusty Boer War Mauser Rifle mounted as a war trophy.[111] More pragmatically, the Volunteers attempted to fashion their own hand grenades.

The Volunteers seized gelignite from county council quarries, secured chemicals, and stole scrap metal from local shipyards and machine shops.[112] Officers attended explosives classes taught by Ray Kennedy, a UCC chemistry postgraduate, while blacksmiths, carpenters and shipyard fitters produced explosives.[113] Volunteer companies held a city-wide contest to design a grenade for mass production.[114] Individual companies manufactured 'canister bombs', tin cans filled with scrap metal, sealed with cement, and inserted with a stick of gelignite.[115] Bomb-making went on in homes around Green Lane, Grattan Street and Shandon Street; a business premises on Cook Street; a farm in Ballinlough; and the Maylor Street University Student Club.[116] 'We had several close escapes from serious injury, or even worse, from the premature explosions of these crude weapons,' recalled apprentice blacksmith Robert Ahern.[117] In April 1919, one such bomb factory blew up on Grattan Street, destroying a house, killing one Volunteer, and wounding four more along with a Cumann na mBan member.[118]

Florrie O'Donoghue dryly summarised the Volunteer military strategy: 'A plan of resistance had been worked out, the main feature of which was (in the best tradition) that we should take to the hills.'[119] MacCurtain established a base in the mountainous Ballingeary area, intending to seal off the military inside the city. He tasked one officer with blowing up the Blackpool railway tunnel to sever the main Dublin/Cork line.[120] A young civil engineer, Denis Kennedy (brother of bomb-maker Ray), surveyed the county's roadways, railways and bridges to plan the disabling of British communications and movements. 'Tomás,' marvelled Kennedy years later, 'saw far ahead of us at that time.'[121] MacCurtain told the Blarney Volunteers that once conscription began they should immediately destroy all the liquor in their area and attack police posts.[122] Virtually unarmed, the brigade intended to raid the arsenal at Ballincollig Barracks and distribute captured rifles to Volunteer units.[123] Ever the realist, Florrie O'Donoghue later remarked, 'It is certain resistance would have been determined and sustained; whether it would have been successful is another question.'[124]

The conscription crisis produced a new generation of leaders in the city Volunteers. Younger men replaced senior officers who expressed reservations about pending violence, left Cork as fugitives, or suffered burnout after years of service. Early Volunteer leaders came from the Gaelic League, had long experience in Cork's republican community, and were respectable members of the lower middle class. For example, brigade adjutant Pat Higgins and quartermaster Seán Murphy were office clerks; battalion commanders Seán O'Sullivan and Fred Murray worked as an insurance agent and master mason respectively; Donal Óg O'Callaghan was a teacher and Tadhg Barry a journalist. When Florrie O'Donoghue was promoted to brigade adjutant in early 1918, he felt inadequate owing to his lack of secondary education and Irish fluency compared with other officers.[125] He was the first of a new circle of IRA leaders that dominated the city in 1919–21. They were largely working class and only tangentially connected to the cultural movement, mainly as GAA players. O'Donoghue was a drapers' assistant, as were Joe O'Connor and Seán Culhane; battalion commanders Sandow O'Donovan and Mick Murphy were carpenters; Jerh Keating and Matt Ryan were shop assistants; Dominic O'Sullivan a lorry driver, Jim Grey a mechanic, Connie Neenan a printer, and Denis MacNeilus an electrician. Over the next three years, these intelligent and tenacious officers turned Cork city into one of the most violent areas of Ireland. After 1919, only Seán O'Hegarty, Tomás MacCurtain and Terence MacSwiney remained from the pre-rising Volunteer leadership. The latter two did not survive 1920.

The conscription crisis was a useful exercise for the Cork city Volunteers. Like a shakedown cruise, it allowed the organisation to judge the performance of leaders, structures and units under real conditions. The Volunteers improved their training, secured premises for secret activities, and established special services like signalling, communications and engineering. They collected information on crown force positions and personnel. The organisation that emerged from the conscription crisis differed fundamentally from the pre-rising conventional warfare model. It closely resembled the organic guerrilla machine that effectively waged war on the British Empire in 1920 and 1921.

British Plans

As envisioned by the new lord lieutenant, Field Marshal Sir John French, British contingency plans were no less ambitious than the Volunteers'. Concerned that the police were over-matched and unreliable, the military intended to assist the RIC secure unwilling conscripts and crush any armed resistance from the Irish Volunteers. Senior officials believed their most dangerous opponents were clerical. Warning of a possible insurrection, Lieutenant General Bryan Mahon, O/C of the Irish Command, believed, 'Against us will be a combination of practically united Ireland with the support of the Roman Catholic Church which is likely to have an effect on the loyalty of the R.I.C.'[126] Colonial Secretary Walter Long explained, '. . . with a population as superstitious and subservient to the priests as are the class of Irish people[,] this state of things means that it's impossible for the moment to attempt conscription without most certainly meeting violent resistance.'[127] General French complained to Lloyd George about clerics and constitutional nationalists 'preaching open and absolute rebellion', and added wistfully, 'The Army in France would simply murder them to a man, and I only wish it were possible to have a few regiments direct from the trenches to help me in restoring order here.'[128] Writing to King George, General French saw the bright side to the Military Service Bill. Because conscription would remove 'useless and idle men between the ages of 18 and 24 or 26', this would put into uniform 'the turbulent element of the population' and thus remove, 'the canker which now poisons the political atmosphere'.[129]

The War Office increased British troop strength in Ireland from 25,000 to 37,000 soldiers, and deployed artillery, armoured cars and aeroplane squadrons. Royal Defence Corps units were also dispatched to guard railways and bridges in the Cork suburbs.[130] French set up four 'air camps' of fighter planes (one in Buttevant, north Cork), hoping the aircraft would 'put the fear of God into these playful young Sinn Féiners'.[131] When conscription was implemented, Cork and other Irish cities would be 'placed in a state of siege at an hour's notice'. A contingent of infantry, artillery and armoured cars would concentrate in the city, while police arrested all separatist leaders.[132] If the Volunteers resisted, French advised the government to use troops 'without any kind of doubt, hesitation, or interference'.[133]

The German Plot

On 18 May 1918, Dublin Castle announced a 'German Plot' – collusion between Sinn Féin leaders and Germany – and immediately seized republican leaders around the country. At the same time, Lord French outlined a voluntary recruitment scheme, giving the Irish public an ultimatum to deliver 50,000 recruits in exchange for postponing the start of conscription. The day of the announcement, police raided homes across the country, arresting much of the Sinn Féin elite. 'The whole affair has met with quite unexpected success,' French boasted to Lloyd George.[134] The Cork police reported the arrests had 'an excellent effect', while British Army military intelligence believed 'the cutting off of the heads of the conspiracy which has weighted on the country for the past year has been an enormous relief to all decent citizens.'[135] British officials frequently attributed their troubles to a few ringleaders leading the masses astray. This was an understandable, if often repeated, misappraisal of a mass movement by a class-bound British government elite.

Police raids across the city caused 'a great sensation', but succeeded in netting only the unfortunate Tadhg Barry, missing the city's four senior Volunteer officers in the process.[136] Referring to Barry's supposed involvement in the 'plot', Liam de Róiste wrote, 'The very writing of it makes me laugh at the absurdity.'[137] At Cork railway station, a large crowd met republican prisoners arriving from counties Cork and Kerry, who were cheered while being driven to Cork Gaol.[138]

The arrests aroused vocal opposition in Cork. J.J. Horgan complained, 'such arbitrary action used to be branded as peculiarly characteristic of Prussian militarism.'[139] William O'Brien believed, 'Since the popish plot of some centuries ago, there has been nothing more disgraceful to English states craft', and called on the public to vote Sinn Féin in the upcoming East Cavan by-election.[140] The US consul thought the deportations only helped republicans make the case 'that Ireland is a conquered province ruled by a foreign power from outside'.[141] The Poor Law Guardians decried the arrests and 'the unparalleled slaughter of thousands of innocent men on the slaughter field of Flanders'.[142] The corporation called on the country to declare 'they are no longer willing to be slaves in an English province'.[143] The *Cork Examiner* issued three separate condemnations, including a pessimistic review of the government's approach to the crisis:[144]

> Arrests continue to be made, Home Rule shows no immediate prospect of materialising, the Irish Administration is in the hands of Unionists, unrest prevails in the country, unbelief in the

intentions of the Government to fulfil its pledges exists, and the drastic methods which 'firm and resolute government' connotes must strike impartial observers as being unlikely to produce an atmosphere of confidence which would alloy the unrest and bring about a happier and more desirable state of affairs.[145]

The military banned a Sinn Féin protest against the arrests, with 100 armed police surrounding the meeting place. A large crowd gathered, despite republican cancellation of the demonstration.[146] More pronounced defiance would be seen the following month.

Growing Public Anxiety

Public unrest became visible in Cork during May and June. Two weeks after passage of the Military Service Bill, a silver shortage hit the country.[147] The scarcity resulted largely from hoarding by civilians, seemingly because of 'the disturbance of public confidence' brought on by the conscription crisis.[148] The silver panic struck Cork banks on a Monday, the normal day for shop and business deposits. Silver lodgements only reached 5 per cent of their normal level.[149] Alderman Simcox told officials that his bakery usually held between £80 and £100 in silver, but the preceding Saturday possessed a total of five shillings. The manager of Cork's Provincial Bank announced silver supplies would be exhausted in days.[150] Employers could not pay wages in cash; shops could not supply change to customers; and public relief and pension payments were suspended.[151] The city's economy ground to a halt.

The lord mayor organised an emergency meeting of bank officials, merchants and Bishop Cohalan. They instructed commercial establishments to issue and accept postal orders as legal tender, and appealed to the British Exchequer for the dispatch of silver supplies to Cork.[152] Despite assurances from Dublin Castle and London, the shortage continued for two weeks, until large amounts of silver finally arrived from the Exchequer.[153] This intervention did not end the crisis. In late May, the Cork Harbour Commissioners was unable to pay its staff wages in silver, while the Cork Poor Law Guardians used postal orders for outdoor relief payments through June.[154] The silver run indicates high local anxiety, and concern about the long-term viability of British paper currency.

During the same period, rumours ran through Cork that the feared Gurkha Regiment had landed in Ireland to repress conscription resistance.[155] This story snow-balled into an anticipated Nepalese invasion of Clare. When the rumour reached Australia, its governor general asked the Colonial Office for an explanation.[156] Upon further investigation, an embarrassed Dublin Castle informed London that 'though it was believed all over Dublin today . . . The rumour started from the fact that a sentry, belonging to an English Regiment, who was on duty at Broadstone Station is of somewhat dusky hue.'[157]

Since 1916, young men of military age had settled in Ireland to avoid military service in their native places.[158] Writing to the *Cork Constitution* in 1916, 'A Granduncle' condemned young Englishmen in the local billiard halls, noting there were 'a few too many "eligibles" handling a cue who might be equally good with a rifle'.[159] The same year, the Poor Law Guardians complained that Victoria Barracks had replaced Irish clerks with English conscription refugees. They resented conscientious objectors, 'who pay attention to the Seventh Commandment "Thou Shall Not Kill" but have no objection to ejecting Irishmen out of their jobs'.[160] The following year (1917), the *Pall Mall Gazette* claimed there were 'some hundreds' of conscription fugitives residing in Cork, along with 4,600 in Dublin and 1,500 in Belfast.[161]

In July 1918, the police moved against so-called British 'skulkers' in Cork and elsewhere, with Lord French confidently believing 'they can be got up and sent back very quickly'.[162] On 19 July 1918, the *Cork Examiner* reported police intended to round up all military-aged British residents, who were supposed to register with the RIC.[163] Many of the Cork refugees relocated to Dublin to escape arrest. In an unintentional reciprocation, police claimed that a large number of Dublin 'shirkers' had fled to Cork, thus keeping the refugee population constant.[164] A few days later, the Cork RIC arrested four young men from England, who were all Jewish.[165]

Hostility towards Jewish conscription refugees deserves mention. An Englishman in Cork complained to the chief secretary about Jewish 'flyaway boys'. 'Most of these young English Jews believe they will be ruthlessly taken,' wrote Joseph Hurry. 'Why disappoint them?'[166] The Northern Command military intelligence officer likewise claimed a large number of young Jewish Britons had relocated to Belfast.[167] Stepping carefully beyond the issue's clear anti-Semitism, of the 129 aliens incarcerated in Ireland during 1918, 75 were Russian citizens, including 30 deserters from the British armed forces. Of these 75, 16 had the first names of Abraham, Israel, Jacob and Solomon, though it is impossible to discern the religion of the remainder. The 1918 alien prisoner list hints at (but does not prove) the presence of Jewish conscription refugees in Ireland, most likely from Britain. Alternatively, the arrest list may also indicate selective persecution and harassment of Jewish conscription refugees by the Irish police. This would be consistent with labour historian Manus O'Riordan's suggestion that anti-Semitism was embedded within broader pro-war, anti-German sentiment in Ireland during the war.[168] No further conclusions can be reached without additional research.

Cork's most colourful British conscription refugee was a young Scotsman, Ian MacKenzie-Kennedy, fondly remembered as 'Scottie' in republican folklore.[169] A supposed linear descendent of Robert the Bruce, MacKenzie-Kennedy's parents sent him to Cork in 1917, but he moved to the Irish-speaking district near Ballingeary to study the Irish language. 'Scottie' was devoted to his kilt and his bagpipes, with which he frequently regaled his new neighbours. He joined the Irish Volunteers and became a celebrated member of the 8th Battalion, Cork No. 1 Brigade, albeit a source of frequent amusement for his comrades (among MacKenzie-Kennedy's eccentricities was attaching a sail onto his bicycle, and attempting to build a massive spring device to destroy police barracks doors.) In a sad irony, MacKenzie-Kennedy survived the First World War but was killed in the Irish Civil War while serving with the anti-treaty IRA at Rochestown in August 1922.

'Sheer Obstinacy': The GAA, Gaelic League and Public Assembly Ban

Amid a deteriorating security situation, Dublin Castle aggressively moved against 'seditious' organisations and gatherings. On 3 July 1918, Dublin Castle proscribed Sinn Féin, the Irish Volunteers, Cumann na mBan, and the Gaelic League. It also banned all public meetings held without a police permit, including sporting and cultural gatherings.

Privately, Irish undersecretary Sir William Byrne recognised merits in a public assembly ban, since any such meeting 'encourages people to join Sinn Féin and discourages the police and the loyal population'. However, he also foresaw difficulties enforcing the ban consistently, and warned it would be perceived 'as a fresh instance of "oppression" unless good grounds could be shown for the restriction'.[170] The ban's timing also added problems, as it came at the height of summer, which was the busiest time of year for Gaelic League and GAA gatherings.

The public assembly proclamation aroused strong criticism, especially over its inclusion of the Gaelic League. The corporation argued the ban was 'a negation of the principles of Democracy and self-determination'.[171] The *Examiner* ran five editorials condemning the 'provocative policy', proclaiming that 'Ireland is being provoked as well as coerced'.[172]

On the weekend of 6 and 7 July, meetings were suppressed around County Cork. At Cork's Victoria Cross grounds, a force of police ordered two camogie teams to stop their game. The players refused, and finished the match under the scrutiny of annoyed constables.[173] Defiant camogie players in Dunmanway were not so lucky. Many of them were injured by a police baton charge.[174] The same day at Ballymacoda in east Cork, police and military appeared at a Gaelic League árd-fheis. The RIC district inspector allowed the athletic events to continue, but tactlessly told organisers, 'I will not allow any addresses in Irish.'[175]

Republican propagandists exploited this indiscretion to ridicule the government's attack on the Irish culture movement. One wag wrote to the *Cork Examiner*:

> Sir, As a loyal citizen of this great Empire I am very anxious to do what is right but I must say that the recent incidents regarding the Irish language leave me somewhat mystified. I see that according to what took place at Ballymacoda we are not allowed to speak Irish in public, but I am quite in the dark as to whether it is lawful to use the language in private. Now my poor old mother has a habit when she sneezes of saying 'Dia linn,' and when she takes snuff of piously remarking, 'Beannact De le hananah na marbh,' and I would like to know if I ought to stop her. If I thought for a moment that her foolishness would unduly prolong the war I certainly would not hesitate a moment . . . Of course I am aware that I cannot any more say 'Dia dhuit' or 'Slan leat' to a friend in the street, but must adopt the harmless 'how do' and 'ta ta' or 'na pu' of my acquaintances. If the authorities would kindly write a little note in your columns telling us what we ought not to do and what we may do with safety to the cause he would much oblige many others besides yours truly.[176]

Initially, there was confusion whether GAA fixtures fell under the public assembly ban. The Cork County Board initially failed to address the matter, focusing instead on the expulsion of the city's St Nicholas Football Club for rough play (outraged club supporters subsequently stoned the county board office in the city centre).[177] Three days later Dublin Castle clarified the policy, informing Irish newspapers, 'football and hurling matches, Feiseanna and Aerideachta, public meetings, and all similar gatherings are in future to be regarded as coming under the recent order.'[178]

The following weekend, police and soldiers dispersed Gaelic League meetings in Skibbereen and Bandon. Armed guards were posted inside the Grianán, the city Gaelic League headquarters, to prevent the holding of Irish classes.[179] The same week, the Cork city Gaelic League announced an aerideacht in the city suburbs and erected a platform, which was then occupied by armed police. Unbeknownst to the constables, the organisers secretly moved the gathering to a nearby glen, which according to the *Examiner*, 'lent an air of romance to the whole affair . . . As an aerdheacht it was one of the most enjoyable held for a considerable time in Cork.'[180] GAA matches received inconsistent official treatment on Sunday, 14 July. Hurling, football and athletics meetings were broken up in Dunmanway, Fermoy and nearby Coachford, but hurling finals were played without interference at Ballinhassig and the Cork City Athletic Grounds. However, police officials informed the Cork GAA that future matches held without a permit would be considered illegal assemblies.[181]

The Cork County Board debated the growing crisis, as a permit application by one club and the non-interference of police at other fixtures had created confusion. The board scheduled seven fixtures for the following Sunday, and instructed clubs to abandon matches if police inquired about permits. County chairman Seán MacCarthy declared no club should contact police authorities, and thundered, 'the authorities might well try to exterminate the Irish race as to try and stop these traditions that had survived much greater antagonism from the authorities in the past.'[182] The following week, the county board changed tack again, by following the Cork Gaelic League example and encouraging matches to be played secretly rather than abandoned. The GAA Central Committee in Dublin prepared for a national day of protest in two weeks.[183]

The same day as the first county board meeting, thirty constables armed with rifles occupied Cork's Fitzgerald Park to prevent a marching band promenade organised by the South ward Sinn Féin Club. The *Cork Examiner* noted that the police amused themselves by watching a cricket match in the park, 'for which, presumably, a permit was granted or the necessity for applying for such was not incumbent on the promoters'.[184] This underscored the RIC's lack of consistency in requiring permissions for different sporting events. During these weeks, non-GAA sports fixtures came off without apparent deference to the permit requirement. For example, the following weekend, three cricket matches were played in the city, a large tennis and croquet tournament was held at Rushbroke Tennis Club, and horse racing continued at Limerick Junction. Local newspapers did not mention any police permit applications or interference by the authorities.[185]

This perceived double standard drew scorn in the House of Commons. Member John Donovan asked Irish chief secretary Edward

Shortt why Dublin Castle had not banned cricket, boxing, golf, yachting and other sports.[186] Michael Flavinn wanted to know if the RIC would 'arrest people who played marbles or slashed tops or 29 or 31 at cards'.[187] An anonymous letter to the *Cork Examiner* ridiculed Dublin Castle:

> Mr Shortt owes it to the public, I think, to state definitely what games are permissible in Ireland; whether, for instance, such games as 'ring o roses' or 'blindman's buff' and so on, are held to be innocuous when played in this country. I am the mother of a large family of young children, principally girls, who are addicted to playing the above games. As a loyal citizen, it would distress me very much to have my children indulge in games which, in the opinion of the best judges, would be likely to prove prejudicial to the safety of our great Empire . . . Would Mr Shortt state whether it is necessary for me to obtain a permit each time the children desire to have a game?[188]

On 21 July, police moved against scheduled GAA fixtures near Cork city. When constables occupied the GAA grounds at Carrigaline, the football players relocated to another pitch a quarter of a mile away and played 'before a fair attendance'.[189] In the suburb of Riverstown, armed police and soldiers occupied the village to prevent the holding of two hurling matches. The club secretary refused to unlock the pitch gate, so police broke into the enclosure and patrolled the grounds for the afternoon. At the Cork Athletic Grounds, thirty armed police occupied the stadium, forcing matches to be abandoned.[190] Police records show numerous hurling, football and camogie matches dispersed across the country during this period.[191]

The same weekend the Cork Gaelic League continued its civil disobedience campaign by scheduling additional feiseanna (outdoor meetings composed of Irish dancing, music, athletics, and language contests). In the city outskirts, organisers announced gatherings at certain venues and constructed platforms. Unbeknownst to the authorities, the meetings were then diverted to alternative locations. The scale of these efforts can be seen in the 700–800 residents who reportedly attended a meeting in Upper Lota.[192] The same day in Ballinhassig, near the city, a feis was successfully held after organisers announced it would take place on a different date. An informal communications network directed thousands of city residents to events held in hidden venues. Remarkably, the crown forces failed to locate the gatherings, despite dispatching search parties assisted by military aeroplanes.[193] On different occasions the planes seemed to have deliberately buzzed the crowds, causing stampedes.[194] Author Frank

O'Connor described attending a banned Gaelic League concert in Cork during this period. When police occupied the grounds, the crowd relocated to an open field a couple of miles away and held their own concert.[195] O'Connor wrote:

> At any moment the police might appear, and this time there could be real bloodshed. It was sheer obstinacy that had driven respectable people to walk miles just to attend a concert they were not very interested in, and they paid their sixpences and went home, rightly feeling that they were the real performers.[196]

Police suppression and republican civil disobedience climaxed the following weekend. On July 28, thousands attended three Gaelic League gatherings near Cork city. These meetings all escaped police interference, as police and soldiers once again occupied 'decoy' venues, complete with false platforms, banners and tricolour bunting.[197] Near Ovens, police fell for the decoy ruse and arrived late to the feis. They attempted to arrest event organiser Tim Herlihy while he refereed a camogie match. When the constables walked onto the pitch, Herlihy ignored them. Witnesses recalled, 'He was apparently intent on the game, but really evading them. They dashed here and there after him but the players got in their way and they were being made a laugh of by onlookers.'[198] The joke ended when police fixed bayonets and scattered the players and the crowd. Despite such efforts, the authorities could not keep pace with the various social events, as indicated by the five separate céilis carried off around Cork during July by Cumann na mBan.[199] The battle of wits, according to the US consul at Queenstown, 'gives a rather comic touch to the government order suppressing public meetings'.[200]

Cork police suppression reached its nadir the same Sunday. A benevolent fund had been established for the families of ninety-six Cork merchant sailors killed in German submarine attacks.[201] Before the public assembly ban was issued, the Cork Athletic Grounds scheduled Gaelic football and hurling benefit matches for the Cork Sailors Widows and Orphans Fund. Shortly before the throw-in, thirty-five armed police entered the pitch and turned away players and spectators. The organisers defied the RIC, directing the crowd to a nearby field where the matches were played without interference.[202] Referee Michael Mehigan (of the Blackrock Sinn Féin club) boasted, 'He did not see a single bit of fear in the face of any player.'[203]

Not surprisingly, the suppression of a widows and orphans benefit match proved a public relations disaster for Dublin Castle. A *Cork Examiner* editorial called the action 'unworthy and unjust',[204] and Irish chief secretary Edward Shortt fielded hostile questions in the House of Commons.[205] Amid popular resistance to the ban and embarrassment over its implementation, British officials retreated the next day. On 29 July, Dublin Castle informed Irish newspapers that police would no longer interfere with GAA matches.[206] In the House of Commons, the Irish chief secretary publicly reversed course:

> The only meetings which are intended to require permits are those which have a political character. If you will mix up political speeches with your sports, then that particular sports meeting will require a permit; but unless that is so, the sports require no permit at all.[207]

Regardless of the change in policy, the GAA Central Council delivered a clear statement the following weekend. The council declared 'Gaelic Sunday' as a national day of protest, with 1,500 hurling, football and camogie matches to be played simultaneously across the country, starting at '3 o'clock Irish Time'.[208] The Cork County Board announced forty fixtures throughout the county, involving almost 1,200 male and female players. On Sunday, 4 August, an estimated 54,000 association members joined the protest in Ireland, which came off peacefully and without police interference.[209] In County Cork, heavy summer showers caused the abandonment of some matches, though the county board reported that teams appeared in almost every case. A large crowd attended the Cork Athletic Grounds, and despite the poor weather 'favourable interest in the fixtures was undiminished'.[210] A county board official boasted, 'their action proved that they would not be deterred from playing their games by any threats from the English Government.'[211]

Dublin Castle continued to ban political meetings, which provoked more republican civil disobedience. Sinn Féin national headquarters instructed all its branches to hold 'patriotic public meetings' on 15 August, less than two weeks after Gaelic Sunday.[212] Rather than risk police dispersal of a centralised gathering, Cork republicans organised simultaneous meetings around the city and suburbs.[213] Residents could be seen moving to these 'hole and corner' assemblies throughout the evening. While police and soldiers surrounded the advertised meeting venues, crowds gathered elsewhere. Once again, it appears Cork residents learned of meeting arrangements by word of mouth, and police failed to locate and disrupt any of the gatherings.[214] During the remainder of the year, police interfered with few republican demonstrations, seemingly bowing to the ban's unpopularity and enforcement difficulty.

Heavy attendance at proscribed gatherings indicates republican mobilisation of residents who resented government coercion. Overshadowed by the violence of ensuing years, the meeting ban sparked one of the most successful civil disobedience campaigns in twentieth-century Ireland. It also conditioned large segments of the Cork public to defy state authority. Lessons learned in the summer of 1918 would be applied two years later by the underground Dáil Éireann government in Cork city.

'Worse than Useless': The Autumn Recruiting Campaign

When Dublin Castle passed the public assembly ban, Lord French simultaneously announced that Ireland could escape conscription if it provided 50,000 recruits for the British Army. The government created enlistment quotas for every recruiting district, and promised to exclude areas that surpassed their goal. 'If a district knew that it could save itself by coming forward and would not suffer for the shortcomings of other districts,' reasoned Chief Secretary Shortt, 'many districts would come forward.'[215] Over the ensuing months, the government issued daily recruiting tallies for each district, to pressure communities into supplying enough young men to avert mandatory military service. 'Ireland was asked for 50,000, but if they had conscription three times that number would be taken,' one army recruiter explained to a Cork audience. 'The result would be a sorrowful country.'[216] Outside the Cork General Post Office, the Recruiting Council placed a giant enlistment 'clock'. It tracked city and county recruiting totals against the district quota and deadline.[217]

The recruiting campaign's coercive nature was clarified in a leaflet mailed to military-aged men in the city during October 1918:

> TO CORK MEN
> Do you realise how you stand? Have you considered:
> 1. The advantage to yourself of voluntary service over conscription.
> 2. Have you thought of the consequences to Ireland of failure to supply the quota called for?
> 3. Have you noticed the clock at the GPO shows that about 3500 more men are needed from the City and County of Cork, and that time is running short?
> It is better to let a comparatively small number of men go, and select their own service and unit, than to have practically every male adult rendered liable for service.

THINK THIS OUT FOR YOURSELF AND CONSIDER HOW
YOU ARE LIKELY TO BE AFFECTED.
Think also of the fate of Ireland if the sympathy of American
and the other Allies is withdrawn from us.
REMEMBER that this is your last opportunity to serve as a
Volunteer, and should you respond in time your name will be
registered as one who came forward at a crucial time to redeem
the fair name of the City and County of Cork.
Help stave off Conscription at all costs.[218]

Such explicit blackmail did not endear the Irish Recruiting
Council to the community. A new public attitude could be seen in the
complaints of Daniel Delaney, who conducted the Greenmount
Industrial School band at recruiting meetings in 1914 and 1915. 'I am
paying the penalty now,' wrote Delaney, 'as I am completely
ostracised.'[219] In July and August, Cork County Council, the Poor
Law Guardians and the corporation refused a hearing to recruiting
representatives seeking assistance.[220] J.J. Horgan embodied this new
constitutionalist rejection of the war, writing that he no longer considered the conflict worthy enough 'to imperil my life and ask my
fellow countrymen to imperil theirs'.[221]

Despite the threatened introduction of conscription, Cork provided
only a modest level of recruits who seemed to have enlisted tactically.
During the last three months of the war, 56 per cent of new Irish
recruits joined the Royal Air Force, though it comprised only 6.4 per
cent of Britain's total military forces.[222] City police reported that 350
men enlisted during August, but 'practically all of these have joined
the Navy or Air Force', which mirrored a national trend.[223] Since the
Royal Navy and (especially) RAF were immeasurably safer services
than the British Army, many likely joined as an alternative to possible
conscription into the dreaded infantry.

In September and October 1918, the recruiting campaign intensified in Cork, featuring newspaper advertisements, military parades,
leaflet airdrops, war trophy displays, public meetings, and shows of
'thrilling lantern slides from the front'.[224] The well-financed effort was
unsuccessful. By 1 October, the embarrassed Irish Recruiting Council
downscaled its national enlistment goal from 50,000 to 10,000. Even
under that reduced figure, Cork only achieved 60 per cent of its
adjusted quota, or a mere 12 per cent of its original goal.[225] By the 11
November armistice, Cork city and county produced a grand total of
840 recruits from its original quota of 5,250, reaching just 16 per cent
of its target.[226] While the 1918 recruiting campaign has been called a
'striking success', it would be more accurately termed a conspicuous

failure, especially when considering its coercive nature.[227]

Two elaborate recruiting meetings were held in the city during October. A few hundred gathered to hear a member of the Recruiting Council denounce 'the disgrace' of Cork's small enlistment totals, while Hibernian Bank director H.A. Pelly appealed for recruits to 'avoid the terrible catastrophe of conscription'.[228] A second meeting at the National Monument proved more explosive. When a military band played martial airs on a street corner, the Volunteer piper band stood nearby and answered with rebel tunes.[229] About a thousand people attended the meeting, including a couple of hundred young republicans.[230] They shouted down one speaker after another, with cries of 'Sasanach' and 'Go down man'. RAF Captain Irvine protested, 'It was not sporting like'; Sergeant Redmond Connolly yelled, 'you will not listen because some of you have been bribed by German gold.'[231] 'The noise was terrible,' reported the *Constitution*, 'and the sergeant, after further effort, was howled down.' When the meeting was abandoned, the speakers retired to the City Club for liquid refreshments, but were pursued by hundreds of republicans and had to be rescued by repeated police baton charges.[232] 'For all practical purposes, these recruiting meetings are absolutely futile,' judged the RIC county inspector, 'and in the City of Cork worse than useless.'[233]

End of the War

As the Allied armies closed on the German frontier, Cork residents were distracted by a two-week milk strike by dairy farmers (protesting against price controls), that produced long lines, milk shortages, and ITGWU threats of 'drastic action' against the farmers.[234] The first wave of the dreaded Spanish influenza epidemic also struck Cork.[235] During four weeks, over 2,000 residents were struck down, causing forty-nine deaths and the closure of schools, theatres, libraries and other public areas.[236]

At 10 am on 11 November 1918, the armistice was announced in Cork. Crowds filled Marlborough Street, and at 11 am Protestant church bells rang out in celebration. City workers and soldiers were given a day's holiday, and military bands played an impromptu concert at Victoria Barracks. Union Jacks flew from a few large businesses. Tactfully, City Hall raised the municipal flag while other business premises hoisted the French tricolour. Working-class neighbourhoods rejoiced most heartedly, reported the *Constitution*, 'for it was these districts contributed most liberally when recruits were called for'.[237]

In another part of the city, a small group of Irish Volunteers celebrated for an entirely different reason. A week earlier, Volunteer officer and gunsmith Denis MacNeilus had shot a policeman during a raid on his lodging house on Leitrim Street. (MacNeilus and his 57-year-old landlord brawled with the arresting constables for twenty minutes, and were applauded by 300 neighbours when they were finally dragged outside).[238] As his police victim hovered between life and death, Irish Volunteers prepared to save MacNeilus from a possible death sentence. While city residents waved Union Jacks in Patrick Street, six armed Volunteers entered Cork men's prison disguised as visitors (one was dressed as a Christian Brother). They knocked warders unconscious with sandbags, led MacNeilus out of the visiting room, unlocked two prison gates, and ran to freedom.[239] About twenty Volunteers participated as raiders and assistants, and their boldness and precision impressed observers.[240] The MacNeilus escape was perhaps the most spectacular Volunteer operation in the country since Easter 1916, and foreshadowed the guerrilla tactics of the following three years.

That evening fist fights broke out between republicans and separation women and British soldiers. The latter used their belts to beat 'shirkers', while youths on Patrick's Hill stoned police and soldiers.[241] In familiar scenes, baton charges dispersed the republicans, who suffered about a dozen casualties.[242]

In his home listening to the celebratory church bells, Liam de Róiste wrote:

> The war is over . . . I too am glad that the phase is finished. Now for the newer phases. Now for the 'new world'. Now for the things that matter – the rise of the small nations, the overthrowing of old autocracies, the coming to power of the people . . . In its war with English military autocracy during the past four years, Ireland has won too and won magnificently. Rejoice you people of Ireland. Let there be no doubts in your hearts. You too, in very essential things, have won gloriously in this period. You have found your national soul. You faced an Empire's power and won out. Lift up your hearts then in joy for the victories won thus far and the hopes of greater victories to come.[243]

XII. The Victory of Sinn Féin:
The 1918 General Election[1]

. . . She [Ireland] has thrown discretion to the wind, and at a very
critical moment has trusted her affairs to men of little experience.
                                  Cork Examiner, 30 December 1918

During the final months of the war, it became increasingly clear that
Prime Minister Lloyd George intended to call a general election
shortly after the Armistice. In Cork, the timing of the campaign generated optimism among republicans, fear in Redmondites, and
indecision among unionists and trade unionists.[2]

The Opponents

As previously described, the Irish Party shed support during 1918. Yet
the endemic organisational atrophy attributed to the Irish Party during
this period was not apparent in Cork city.[3] The Redmondites retained
political patronage networks in the city and county government,
enjoyed the support of the commercial elite, and controlled two of the
city's three daily newspapers (with the other being unionist). The
party possessed sufficient organisational strength to win a campaign,
assuming it could find support among voters.

Facing the Irish Party was Cork's neophyte Sinn Féin organisation, now possessing 12 branches and 5,000 members.[4] It was
supported by 2,000 Irish Volunteers in 16 city companies, along with
an estimated 250 members of Cumann na mBan, in 14 branches. The
Irish Party failed to contest any County Cork constituencies outside
the city, focusing republican attention on Cork. (The RIC county
inspector believed Sinn Féin would have won any of these non-con-
tested seats by a four to one margin.)[5] Despite its strength, Sinn Féin
was less than two years old and possessed little institutional knowledge of electioneering, which makes its success in 1918 even more
remarkable.

Preparing the Registry

The electoral registry update required early political mobilisation, which was especially vital in 1918. The Representation of the People Act (passed earlier in the year) expanded the franchise to all males over the age of twenty-one and women over thirty.[6] Both parties had to painstakingly review voting rolls to ensure the registration of all their supporters, especially new voters. Sinn Féin began its registry update in March 1918, but efforts really took off in June.[7] The Irish Party followed suit in July, indicating the activation of its Cork electoral machine.[8] Both sides had their work cut out for them, as the new franchise rules tripled the Cork city electorate from 12,298 voters to 45,017.[9]

Rate collectors distributed voting claim forms to new voters during April 1918, at the height of the conscription crisis.[10] According to Sinn Féin's elections director, Redmondite rate collectors 'dropped hints that the claim forms, when filled up would be likely to be utilised for the enforcement of conscription', resulting in thousands of voters leaving their forms blank.[11] As the registration deadline approached, the crown clerk would issue blank voter registration forms only to individuals appearing in person at City Hall, creating a hurdle for new voters with normal working hours. An exception was made for military commanders, whose Irish servicemen voters presumably would not be supporting Sinn Féin.[12] Fortunately for Sinn Féin, a republican clerk in City Hall stole thousands of blank registration forms, which were distributed during Sinn Féin canvasses.[13]

Additional vote suppression was apparent during the revision court hearings, which allowed the public to challenge individual voter registrations. Sinn Féin and Irish Party representatives objected to scores of voters, which required attendance in person to prove eligibility.[14] Some voters had been registered without their knowledge, indicating preparations for polling day impersonation. The exasperated crown clerk condemned 'the philanthropist who is going around putting in claims on the part of people who don't exist or are children'.[15] Evidence indicates the involvement of both Sinn Féin and the Irish Party in this fraud, along with individual unionists and police constables.[16] In Cork, all parties engaged in electoral chicanery.[17]

The Incumbents

The AFIL's two parliamentary incumbents, William O'Brien and Maurice Healy, stood down prior to the election. At the beginning of 1918, O'Brien graciously, if reluctantly, passed the baton to Sinn Féin.[18]

O'Brien and his fellow AFIL MPs were prepared to resign in early 1918, but decided to wait until the franchise expansion came into effect. This maximised damage to the Irish Party since it was assumed most new voters would support the republicans.[19] Redmondite J.J. Horgan echoed this belief when he complained to Dublin, '. . . The Register has increased from 18,000 to 45,000, and it is full of irresponsible young males and females.'[20]

In late October, William O'Brien announced his retirement, endorsed Sinn Féin, and published his new pamphlet, '*The Failure of Parliamentarianism*'.[21] He told former protégé Frank Gallagher, 'The Sinn Féiners have saved the country from partition, conscription, and parliamentary corruption, and they were the only force in Ireland who could have done it.'[22] J.J. Horgan informed John Dillon that the AFIL rank and file had gone over to the republicans, and 'O'Brien will strain every nerve to get all his poisoned followers to vote S.F.'[23] The Cork All-For-Ireland Club applauded O'Brien's deferral to 'the younger minds', and offered their chief a traditional AFIL farewell: 'We pray God may spare you to see the serpent of Molly Maguirism finally crushed.'[24] Tim Healy tried to cheer up his brother Maurice about the demise of the AFIL. 'In the end they have come round to our opinions, and I don't care by what road or reasoning!'[25] Maurice Healy stood down a month later, denouncing the 'treason' of the Irish Party but failing to endorse Sinn Féin. 'I can see no grounds for believing that unconstitutional methods are likely to bring better results,' he wrote, 'nor is it obvious to me how this poor country, no matter how grossly provoked, can at this juncture benefit from turbulence, disorder, and abortive rebellion.'[26]

Nominating Candidates

Cork Sinn Féin sought a complete electoral departure, looking within its separatist community for parliamentary nominees. The easiest choice was J.J. Walsh, who received a death sentence for his participation in the Easter Rising.[27] Walsh was a national leader of the GAA, and the president of its Cork County Board. He co-founded the Irish Volunteers in 1914, and already held office as a town councillor, though he rarely attended corporation meetings. A vocal proponent of physical force, Walsh exploited his multiple prison terms by wearing his convict uniform at a Cork demonstration.[28]

A second Sinn Féin candidate proved more difficult to secure. Sinn Féin initially approached ITGWU organiser Cathal O'Shannon. The socialist O'Shannon ticked a number of boxes for Sinn Féin. He was a member of the IRB, the Gaelic League and (until recently) the Cork

City Sinn Féin Executive and the Sinn Féin National Executive.[29] O'Shannon also served on the Irish Trades Union Congress and Labour Party executive (hereafter the Irish Labour Party), and led 7,000 ITGWU members in Cork.[30] However, O'Shannon refused to stand for Sinn Féin, citing his primary allegiance to the Irish Labour Party, whose election stance was still undetermined. O'Shannon assured republicans, 'holding all the views I do, my best service to the national cause is in Labour rather than as a Sinn Féin MP.'[31]

In his stead, the Cork Sinn Féin Executive chose Liam de Róiste for the second city seat. A commercial teacher employed by the County Technical Education Committee, de Róiste was a safe choice. He was a national leader of the Gaelic League, a pre-war Sinn Féin pioneer, and the secretary of the Cork Industrial Development Association. De Róiste faced some opposition from trade unionists, who regarded him as an Arthur 'Griffithite' and probable opponent of socialism.[32] Republican trade unionists also feared de Róiste would be challenged by an 'old labour' craft union leader, who could combine moderate trade unionists with Redmondites to create a single anti-Sinn Féin block. The UIL and the *Cork Examiner* encouraged an independent labour candidacy, which would also exploit lingering tension between craft unions and pro-republican industrial unions.[33]

To field a candidate, 'old labour' needed the approval of the Cork Labour Party, now dominated by the ITGWU and other republicans. Cork Trades Council secretary Éamon O'Mahoney (a republican) reassured de Róiste that 'the bulk of the workingmen will be for S.F. even against a labour non-S.F. man'. However, ITGWU leaders wanted to run a socialist candidate, despite Sinn Féin offers to replace de Róiste with O'Shannon or another republican trade unionist. The Irish Labour Party was willing to campaign on a republican platform, but opposed unconditional abstention from the House of Commons, which was a non-negotiable Sinn Féin condition. Labour leaders appear to have wanted the option of taking their seats in Westminster, should their votes be needed by the British Labour Party to form a new government.[34] By October, ITGWU officials seemingly convinced Cathal O'Shannon to stand against Sinn Féin, a decision that would be ratified by a convention of Cork trade unionists.

Republicans prepared to mobilise their labour supporters to block a labour candidacy, but a nominating convention proved unnecessary.[35] By this time, it had become clear to ITGWU and Cork Trades Council officials that their union rank and file opposed entering the race against Sinn Féin.[36] After weeks of internal debate, the Cork Labour Party announced it would follow whatever decision was made by the Irish

Labour Party Annual Congress. That gathering promptly chose to abstain from the election.[37] The indecision of Cork labour leaders cost them a golden opportunity to leverage their electoral abstention. Having spurned a seat offered by Sinn Féin, the Labour Party received nothing in return.[38]

The Irish Party faced even deeper internal divisions. Recognising likely defeat and the implications of the post-war peace conference, Cork Redmondites sought an electoral pact with Sinn Féin. Catholic Bishop Daniel Cohalan and the *Cork Examiner* floated the idea under the guise of national unity prior to the Paris Peace Conference.[39] The bishop contacted Liam de Róiste, explaining that the Irish Party desired to 'approach the Peace Conference with one vote'.[40] Sinn Féin and the Irish Party would divvy up seats, with all candidates agreeing to: temporarily abstain from Westminster; support Irish self-determination at the Paris Peace Conference; and if that was rejected, to take a referendum to decide whether to resume their seats in London. The republicans baulked, with de Róiste telling Bishop Cohalan that the pact smacked of the very 'bossism' and 'machine methods' Sinn Féin sought to destroy. Regardless, on 10 November, the Cork UIL Executive called on John Dillon to secure an agreement with Sinn Féin along the terms outlined by Cohalan.[41]

Cork UIL election agent Henry Donegan reported the Cork pact enjoyed little support beyond the city's three senior party leaders, coroners J.J. Horgan, William Murphy and James McCabe, who pushed it through the city executive.[42] National Party chief John Dillon dismissed the Cork compromise, claiming Sinn Féin had already rejected his overtures, 'with insult and abuse'.[43] Without a pact, J.J. Horgan believed they had no 'earthly chance of winning in Cork', and he, Murphy and McCabe urged Cork's UIL Executive to withdraw from the election.[44] When they were outvoted, the three coroners resigned from the party.[45] During these weeks, city Redmondites could not persuade anyone to stand on their ticket, as republican Margaret O'Leary wrote:[46]

> The Irish Party found great difficulty in finding candidates. George Crosby was asked to stand and refused – so was TC Butterfield – so was JJ Horgan – so was Sir Henry O'Shea – so was Coroner Murphy – so was [Coroner] McCabe – so was Jerh Lucy [chairman, Southern Ireland Cattle Trade Association], who said he couldn't really speak for the Cattle Trade Association as ¾ of its members were Sinn Féiners . . .[47]

The UIL Executive held a nominating meeting that wrangled over three successive evenings before securing High Sheriff Willie

O'Connor and town councillor Henry Tilson.[48] Their selection hardly signalled a strong challenge to Sinn Féin. Both the 32-year-old O'Connor and the Protestant Tilson were low in the party pecking order and both had previously supported the British war effort. This prompted imprisoned republican Tadhg Barry to observe, 'they'd shed all others' blood but not their own. The Parliamentary Party has gone very low when these be their Gods.'[49] However, a week later, O'Connor stepped down as a candidate, citing Dublin Castle's failure to release him from the office of city high sheriff, which prohibited attendance in Westminster.[50] For unspecified reasons Henry Tilson also withdrew from the race, thereby leaving the Irish Party empty-handed once again.[51] 'The actions of the Dillonite supporters have been amusing, in fact grotesque,' laughed Liam de Róiste 'They are caught in a fix and a very bad one.'[52]

The Irish Party found two replacement candidates, Maurice Talbot-Crosbie and Richard O'Sullivan, both apparently selected to appeal to the city's ex-serviceman population. Talbot-Crosbie owned a large asphalt company in Cork, and was the son of a prominent Protestant Home Rule landlord in Kerry. In 1914 he commanded the city's Irish Volunteers and the National Volunteers, before joining the British Army and seeing action in France and Palestine, where he was wounded multiple times. Talbot-Crosbie's running mate was Cork native Lieutenant Richard O'Sullivan, a London-based barrister and journalist, returned from British Army service in Flanders.[53] Having lived abroad for almost a decade, O'Sullivan was relatively unknown in Cork city, though he was raised and educated locally.[54] A delighted Tadhg Barry wrote from jail, 'I laughed when I read of Talbot Crosbie turning up . . . he is as big an ass as ever . . . What are all the Mollie TCs [town councillors] and coroners doing. Have they deserted?'[55] The inability to attract strong candidates reflected Irish Party disarray prior to the election.

Cork unionists also suffered from internal discord. In prior elections, unionists endorsed the AFIL rather than run their own slate, but in 1918 they could not agree whether to vote tactically for the Irish Party or put up unionist candidates.[56] The militant *Cork Constitution* argued: 'The view of the immense majority of the better classes in Cork seems to be that under the present circumstances it is a waste of prestige and money to bring a Unionist into the field at all.'[57] The *Cork Examiner* noted division between hardline unionists opposing any change to the Act of Union, and moderates willing to consider Home Rule. The moderates included prominent commercial figures like Richard Beamish, Sharman Crawford, and Sir Stanley Harrington who had recently backed the Irish

Convention's Home Rule settlement.[58] These moderate unionists ultimately sat out the 1918 election, and later migrated from the Irish Unionist Alliance to the Irish Dominion League.[59]

Left to their own devices, hardline unionists proposed Daniel Williams and Thomas Farrington.[60] Williams was a marginalised town councillor, noted for his vocal loyalty to the king and recent endorsement of Irish conscription.[61] Farrington was a chemical engineer and a minor figure in the Cork Ratepayers Association.[62] Many unionists reluctantly supported their campaign, but Church of Ireland clergy and most commercial figures ignored the candidacy.[63] The Cork UIL trawled for Protestant votes, first by nominating Protestant Home Ruler Henry Tilson and (after his withdrawal) another Protestant nationalist, Talbot-Crosbie. Despite this outreach, the candidacy of Williams and Farrington split the Protestant vote.

There was little sectarianism during the campaign, with Sinn Féin largely refraining from using anti-Protestant language against Talbot-Crosbie or the unionist candidates. The city's Catholic clergy essentially sat out the election, with few priests attending the Irish Party and Sinn Féin campaign launch meetings. Though Bishop Cohalan was 'glad that the old party is ended', he refused to endorse Sinn Féin, largely on pragmatic lines.[64] Cohalan reflected clerical ambivalence towards the election in Cork. Scarred by years of violent O'Brienite/Redmond rivalry, clerics patiently waited for the people to make their decision.

Talking Republicanism

Sinn Féin launched its campaign at Cork City Hall on 18 November. Speakers placed the election in the context of democratic liberty and the popular upheaval sweeping Europe. Professor Alfred O'Rahilly heralded 'a wave of democracy in the world, and it could not be sunk with cruisers in the Irish Sea'.[65] Candidate Liam de Róiste claimed republicans wanted 'to assert the right of free speech in the country, and also to assert the right of individual liberty in the country'. But J.J. Walsh's speech caused the greatest sensation within the republican leadership. According to Liam de Róiste, prior to the City Hall rally, certain Sinn Féin leaders asked Walsh 'not to talk "wildly" as he sometimes does'.[66] Like de Róiste, Walsh made vague allusions to securing 'sovereign independence', but failed to use the term 'Irish republic', a significant omission noted by republican militants. Though Walsh applauded the Volunteers' recent rescue of Denis MacNeilus from Cork gaol, he also downplayed physical-force resistance.[67]

The issue erupted the following week at the first meeting of Sinn Féin's Cork City Election Committee. Walsh 'asked permission to talk "republicanism"', explaining that other party leaders prohibited him from doing so at the rally.[68] This prompted a heated debate between those wanting Sinn Féin to clearly articulate republicanism, and those preferring to obfuscate the issue to avoid alienating moderate voters. Representing the Irish Volunteers, Florrie O'Donoghue disliked this 'general tendency to slur over the suggestion of J.J. Walsh to keep the Republican programme well in the foreground'.[69] Closing the meeting, Liam de Róiste added fuel to the fire by remarking, 'what we wanted to do now was to win the election, to get votes: not lay down principles.'[70] De Róiste privately mused about his opponents, 'How queer some of us are and how clung to words.' This only aroused the taciturn Florrie O'Donoghue, who promptly urged the Volunteers to stand over republicanism. 'It must not be confused by any talk of influencing timid and doubtful voters, or anything else,' he wrote. 'The issue must be kept clear and definite.'[71]

The fight continued at the committee's next meeting. Seán O'Hegarty represented the Volunteers (and the IRB), and threatened to boycott the election if the candidates failed to publicly enunciate a republican position. According to de Róiste, 'He [O'Hegarty] raised the question again of the words "Irish Republic" in his own truculent fashion . . . They did not know if J.J. or myself (principally myself I suppose) were Republican candidates or not! We were dishonest if we did not say the words "Irish Republic".'[72] De Róiste had already written his next election address that specifically referred to an Irish republic, but he refused to share it with the committee. Instead, de Róiste announced: 'I state definitely I will put the issue of the election in my own way, and will not be dictated to about it.' The meeting broke up with O'Hegarty promising a Volunteer boycott if the republic issue was not clearly placed before voters.

The following evening, the Irish Volunteer leadership gathered to debate their continued involvement in the campaign.[73] Knowing the content of de Róiste's upcoming election address, one senior officer appealed to de Róiste to release the details, as 'it would sooth everybody immensely'.[74] An offended de Róiste declined, refusing 'to be forced to put the election issues in any way but in accord with Sinn Féin principles and my own ideas'.[75] Ultimately, Sinn Féin platform speakers explicitly called for a republic, apparently in terms acceptable to the Irish Volunteers, who resumed their participation in the campaign.[76]

The controversy revealed differing concepts of mandates, candidacies and parties. Physical-force republicans on the election committee advocated the clearest and most direct approach to the Cork electorate, while moderates proposed a less open and ideological campaign strategy. This reflected an almost millennial approach to electoral politics by hardline republicans. Tom Garvin has cited parallels throughout post-war Europe, as young people tempered by the Great War cast aside seemingly corrupt societies.[77] Cork republicans expressed similar attitudes that were anti-political rather than anti-democratic. They also reacted against long-time demagoguery from local UIL and AFIL political machines. Warning of 'political tricks', Tomás MacCurtain told his followers, 'once the bad influence gets hold it eats its way to the core to our entire destruction.'[78] Éamon de Valera declared to a Cork audience in 1917 that 'Sinn Féin was out to purify politics', while republican labour leader John Good (National Union of Railwaymen) claimed, 'Sinn Féin was not a political party but a national party.'[79] To many republicans, Sinn Féin expressed a patriotic nationality that transcended personalities and party politics. There was an inherent tension when putting such high-minded ideals into practice, as seen by the response of Liam de Róiste, who resented subordinating himself to the collective will of the city's Republican leadership.

Ex-Soldiers and the War

Both parties targeted the five and a half thousand Cork residents serving as soldiers and sailors overseas, who could cast their ballots by mail. The Irish Party aggressively pursued these votes by nominating two ex-soldiers as candidates. Advertisements exhorted, 'Vote for the men who fought in the war'.[80] Speaking to ex-servicemen, Major Talbot-Crosbie exclaimed, 'They as soldiers, absolutely denied the Sinn Féiners had got a monopoly on patriotism, and that they alone represented Ireland.' The Redmondites secured the endorsement of the Cork branch of the Demobilised and Discharged Soldiers and Sailors Federation (DDSSF) and its 600 members, considered 'one of the strongest organised bodies of voters in the city at the present'.[81] DDSSF leaders spoke on Irish Party campaign platforms, and members marched en masse to meetings.[82] 'The soul of Ireland was in Flanders where Irish National soldiers fought in the name of Ireland a nation,' remarked DDSSF branch chairman Maurice Donovan. 'They certainly did not fight for an Irish-American republic under the tyrannical leadership of a hybrid Portugee.'[83]

The Irish Party largely refrained from attacking Sinn Féin's anti-war stance. *Cork Examiner* publisher George Crosbie seemed to sum up the sentiment: 'They did not want war with anybody. There had been,

God knows, enough of war in the world.'[84] The lack of engagement on what should have been the most pressing issue of the day illustrates the altered political landscape in 1918. Sinn Féin speakers, on the other hand, celebrated their opposition to the war. 'Had it ever dawned on the Parliamentarians,' J.J. Walsh asked, 'that by the sacrifice of 60,000 of their Gaelic brothers in the damnable war just terminated, more suffering had been caused to the Irish race in four years than twenty rebellions for the freedom of Ireland?'[85] 'Were it not for British Imperialism,' suggested Cumann na mBan leader Annie Scott, 'the women of Ireland would not be today mourning the loss of husbands, sons, and brothers lost in the war.'[86] J.J. Walsh memorably told a Blackpool meeting, 'The Irish people were not in the sense alleged Pro-German, but if the devil himself and all the devils in hell were up against the British Government, the Irish people would be pro devil and pro hell (cheers).'[87]

Sinn Féin's anti-war rhetoric did not translate into hostility towards ex-servicemen. Cork republicans lobbied for ex-soldier votes, revealing a more nuanced attitude than is often appreciated.[88] John Good told a rally, 'They had been told that they were out to penalise the soldiers and sailors, and the relatives of those who fell in the war – the Irish Republic was out to see that every man, woman, and child earning their living in Ireland would get the same chance and the same rights.' At a large Sinn Féin meeting, ex-sailor Patrick Healy denounced job discrimination against ex-servicemen. Professor Alfred O'Rahilly followed him, explaining, 'Whether it be a sailor or soldier or even a policeman, his vote was welcome provided he believed in Ireland's claim to nationhood.' At its final campaign rally, Sinn Féin invited a disabled soldier named Walsh to speak before an audience of 10,000. Calling for national independence, Walsh asked voters to join the independence struggle, quoting a wounded comrade from France: 'They were called broken men now, but though broken in limb they were not broken in spirit.'[89]

Labour and Women

Besides ex-servicemen, both sides aggressively pursued the labour vote, which was roughly three-quarters of the new Cork city electorate. The Irish Party ran on an economic platform, arguing that Sinn Féin abstention from Westminster would damage commercial development and employment opportunities. The Redmondites also emphasised the protection of pensions and government-financed housing assistance, which was a pressing issue in a city with high slum density. Despite this effort, the Cork Labour Party remained aloof from the Redmondites, with no union leaders appearing on an Irish Party platform during the campaign.

Sinn Féin promised that Irish independence would end British economic exploitation, thereby generating jobs and industrial development. As opposed to the Irish Party, organised labour played a prominent role in the republican campaign, with union leaders speaking at fifteen of eighteen Sinn Féin election meetings.[90] John Good of the NUR promised a 'workers' republic', and believed 'Labour and Sinn Féin were one in the same thing'.[91'] He subsequently claimed Sinn Féin would 'make short work of autocracy, vested interests, and industrial and commercial thieves'.[92] Sinn Féin candidates echoed pro-labour rhetoric, with Liam de Róiste promising, 'The day had come when the working classes would have the power in the government of the country.'[93]

A final swing vote was women, first-time voters who comprised a third of the electorate. The Irish Party was wanting in this regard, making little attempt to reach women voters. This contrasts sharply with Sinn Féin, which aggressively sought female support, primarily through the work of Cumann na mBan. It began registering women voters in June 1918, as its District Council president declared, 'women will be the deciding vote at the next election.'[94] Sinn Féin also held a women's election meeting addressed by de Róiste and female republicans, including suffragette Marie Lynch, and Annie Scott and Mary MacSwiney of Cumann na mBan.[95] Speaking to this meeting, Liam de Róiste claimed suffragettes had used 'Sinn Féin methods' during their campaign for the vote. Rather than promising gender equality, Sinn Féin candidates focused on what they considered 'women's issues', such as improved pay for teachers, and better housing and working conditions. Women played a prominent role in the republican campaign, as canvassers, poll watchers, and collectors of the Sinn Féin election fund. On polling day, Cumann na mBan even offered child-minding duties to enable women supporters to get to the polls. It would be surprising if this activity did not translate into a significant advantage with women voters.

Platforms

Considering the implications of the 1918 election, much was left unsaid by both campaigns. The Irish Party rarely mentioned anti-government street riots and arms raids by republicans during the previous year. Though the Irish Volunteers were a constant presence in the Sinn Féin campaign, Redmondites failed to question physical force. This omission is even more remarkable considering that the Volunteers broke Denis MacNeilus out of prison just a few weeks before the election. Redmondites did vaguely warn that Sinn Féin represented 'chaos', while claiming the Irish Party stood for 'moderation and reason, when striving against passion and prejudice'.[96] The party's muted approach failed to raise voter anxiety about a Sinn Féin victory, which was probably the Irish Party's only chance of success. This likely reflected recognition of deep public hostility to the government following the anti-conscription campaign.

The Irish Party primarily ran on the pragmatic argument that Westminster abstention would leave nationalists unrepresented in an unsympathetic parliament.[97] To the *Cork Examiner*, Irish interests would be defended by 'Sir Edward Carson and his followers'.[98] Major Talbot-Crosbie warned, 'The people of the South of Ireland would therefore be in the extraordinary position of merely having to take the crumbs that fell to them by the grace of Ulster.'[99] Redmondites repeatedly emphasised the need for parliamentary representation to defend the city's railways, shipping and industrial concerns. Election literature asked voters to support the candidates 'who will protect your interests during demobilisation and reconstruction'.[100]

Redmondites also used violent rhetoric against the British administration. After the military authorities banned the annual Manchester Martyrs commemoration, Talbot-Crosbie warned, 'the feelings of the people revolted at such a miserable and wretched sight.'[101] Councillor William Hart suggested Irish Party MPs in Westminster were 'the only weapon to fight Imperialism', while candidate Richard O'Sullivan told an audience, 'they would go to Parliament to demand the rights of Ireland, and if they were denied them there would be war.'[102]

Foreshadowing the 1921 Anglo-Irish Treaty, the Irish Party demanded Dominion Home Rule in 1918, rather than implementation of the 1914 Home Rule statute.[103] Writing to John Dillon, Coroner William Murphy urged the Irish Party 'to adopt as its battle cry "Colonial Home Rule"'.[104] George Crosbie advised voters, 'the world war had changed everything, and undoubtedly there was nothing left to them now but to demand Colonial Home Rule.'[105] Richard O'Sullivan vowed to work for 'full Colonial Home Rule with Irish control of the Customs and Excise', and added that if the public demanded independence, 'then he would take his mandate from the people and reiterate their demand.'[106] Campaign advertisements promised 'Colonial Home Rule' along the basis of the Irish Convention proposal.[107] However, Sinn Féin ridiculed the Redmondites' Dominion

Home Rule position. Liam de Róiste wanted to know how 'the gallant English officers' would win Dominion status, 'if for over forty years the whole Irish Party could not get Home Rule with partition thrown in'. Asking his supporters if they wanted Home Rule, J.J. Walsh thundered, 'They did not and he said to hell with it.'[108]

Sinn Féin framed the election debate as a referendum on Irish independence prior to the Paris Peace Conference. Their aims fed off a popular democracy prairie fire raging across Europe. Liam De Róiste explained to voters, 'The people who had not yet won the war were the people who had not overthrown their militarists, Imperialists, and autocrats. . . . They were trying to put Ireland in the forefront of the fight for democracy and nationality.'[109] 'A greater result of the war from their own standpoint,' thought J.J. Walsh, 'was the awakening of the small nations, including Ireland, that they, like the empires, were entitled to a separate existence.'[110] Despite earlier platform division, Sinn Féin speakers repeatedly called for sovereign independence in the form of an Irish republic.[111] De Róiste frequently utilised Britain's wartime rhetoric against the Irish Party candidates. 'These two gallant men joined the army to gain independence for Belgium, Serbia and Poland, and what objection had they to Ireland getting the same independence.'[112] He emphasised that Sinn Féin 'demands' the same 'sovereign independence' as other small European nations, and should be represented at the peace conference 'as a right'.[113]

Though republicans clearly emphasised their appeal to the Paris Peace Conference, they failed to explain their fallback plan. Speakers outlined tax boycotts and the establishment of Dáil Éireann, but downplayed physical-force alternatives. Election chairman Denis Tobin claimed 'they were all pacifists', while J.J. Walsh told supporters 'Physical force had no particular fascination for him'.[114] Republican speakers did not advocate a violent overthrow of the British administration, or suggest armed resistance to government repression of Dáil Éireann. At the same time, the Irish Volunteers were very much in the forefront of the campaign, acting as stewards and canvassers and marching en masse to meetings. Both candidates encouraged young men to join the Volunteers, and Cork Brigade commander Tomás MacCurtain addressed four Sinn Féin election meetings. The Irish Party never successfully exploited the tension between the two wings of the republican party, allowing Sinn Féin to effectively have its cake and eat it too. Sinn Féin also did not explain how it intended to defeat partition, which was widely anticipated at this stage. On this front the Irish Party was also wanting, which indicated the absence of obvious solutions for such a profound problem.

Organisation

Cork republicans created a superior campaign organisation that operated independently of Dublin. Months before the election, Sinn Féin
had completed the critical and painstaking update of the electoral registry. Republicans also made vigorous house-to-house canvases for
votes, utilising Sinn Féin's great numeric advantage in enthusiastic
election workers. With geographically structured Sinn Féin clubs,
Cumann na mBan branches and Irish Volunteer companies, the republicans were perfectly positioned for localised get-out-the-vote efforts.

Since all three Cork newspapers were decidedly anti-republican,
Cork Sinn Féin produced its own election literature and posters. The
printing costs were covered by an election fund of £1,600, raised
almost entirely through small donations.[115] The campaign held orderly
and well-planned meetings in every part of the Cork constituency.
Volunteers typically acted as stewards, while Cumann na mBan
members took voter details or donations.

Election day preparations enjoyed a military-like precision. Some
300 Irish Volunteers from County Cork were drafted into the city as
'peace patrols', to prevent street violence or disorder at the polling
stations. This freed city Volunteers for canvassing and poll-tallying.[116]
Cumann na mBan members monitored polling places, canvassed, and
catered thousands of meals for election workers across the city.
Automobiles ferried workers and voters across town. The *Constitution*
noted an unusually large number of 'old and decrepit' residents at the
polls, which indicated an effort to get them there.[117] After polls closed,
shifts of Irish Volunteers guarded the ballot boxes for twelve days
until the votes were counted. Overall, Sinn Féin displayed a thorough
organisation, which was all the more impressive considering its electoral inexperience.

While the Irish Party was ultimately out-organised, its political
machine was not inactive. In August, Irish Party activists attended all
the sittings of the revision court, challenging scores of Sinn Féin voters.
During the race, UIL organising committees met virtually every night,
and undertook a vigorous canvas. On polling day, Redmondite election workers were stationed outside every polling place, and twenty
supporters monitored the ensuing ballot count. The Irish Party also
enjoyed an institutional advantage in its administration of election
machinery. Redmondite officials registered voters, ran polling booths,
and counted the votes. Since each process was vulnerable to abuse,
Cork republicans attended the registry court, observed polling places,
guarded ballot boxes, and monitored the vote count.

Evidence indicates both sides engaged in voting fraud. Redmondites were accused of suppressing republican voter registration and adding phantom soldier voters to the registry.[118] In turn, UIL election agent Henry Donegan complained of a registry, 'hopelessly stuffed with bogus names'.[119] Activists from each party registered voters without their knowledge, indicating preparations for polling-day impersonation. Newspapers reported the detection of impersonators at various polling places, such as an old lady wearing fashionable and 'dainty shoes', who beneath a shawl was found to be 'a rather good looking young girl'.[120] When Liam de Róiste and his family arrived to cast their ballots, he discovered his elderly mother-in-law had been personated.[121] De Róiste claimed the Irish Party personated throughout the morning, but Sinn Féin did so in the afternoon: 'I am sorry to say . . . It is looked upon in the light of a good joke.' Unfortunately, it is impossible to quantify and identify the various frauds perpetrated during the contest. However, it is safe to say that the voting irregularities were unexceptional by the standards of the day, that both parties employed these tactics, and that no irregularities can explain Sinn Féin's victory margin.

Perhaps the most remarkable aspect of the 1918 contest in Cork was its lack of violence, especially compared to the elections of 1910 and 1914. The four-week campaign saw only three minor faction fights: including an attempt to steal the DDSSF Band's instruments (seemingly an homage to Cork campaign tradition); and a republican invasion of an AOH Hall (after the RIC banned a Sinn Féin meeting), where 'chairs and much like weapons were freely used'.[122] In the latter episode, republicans were roused by 'a small young fellow' mimicking a polished political speech. His description sounded suspiciously like the pocket Spartacus who led an assault on the army recruiting office in 1917.[123] Tension remained, as Henry Donegan informed John Dillon, 'Intimidation by Sinn Féin made it almost criminal for us to bring rival crowds into conflict.'[124] The UIL held most of its meetings in the safety of its AOH Hall, and took steps to discourage mob violence, which departed from prior campaign tactics used against the AFIL.[125]

Polling

Polling day was largely incident-free, as Irish Volunteer 'peace patrols' maintained order seemingly without intimidating voters.[126] The election's harmonious conduct was apparent across Cork's political spectrum. The *Cork Examiner* described the contest as 'the most quiet, orderly, interesting, and momentous in Cork during a century'.[127] Irish Party candidate Richard O'Sullivan claimed, 'It had been fought with good sense, good humour, and it was an example to their own country and to other countries also.' Unionist Dan Williams complimented 'the way in which the peace of the city had been kept during the elections, and great credit was due to the leaders of the two parties concerned'.[128] Redmondite High Sheriff Willie O'Connor added that he was glad to say that 'not a single regrettable scene occurred in connection with the whole election.'

The final results showed an unquestioned Sinn Féin triumph. Just under 31,000 ballots were cast, representing 69 per cent of registered voters, with turnout lowered by poor returns from soldiers still at the front, who only submitted 27 per cent of their ballots.[129] Sinn Féin dominated the returns, with J.J. Walsh securing 67 per cent of votes cast, and Liam de Róiste 66 per cent. The Irish Party's Talbot-Crosbie received 24 per cent, and Richard O'Sullivan 23 per cent, with the two unionists getting 8 per cent and 7 per cent respectively. Compared with 1910, the Irish Party increased its tally by almost 3,000 votes, indicating it retained its base but failed to make meaningful headway with new voters, who represented almost three-quarters of the electorate.

Republicans greeted the Cork returns with parades, fireworks and burning tar barrels. Jubilant Capuchin monks in Dublin assured Liam de Róiste, 'The country is splendid and Cork superb.'[130] Writing to the jailed Tadgh Barry, J.J. Walsh predicted a difficult path ahead, 'Get a few cells ready for the new MPs, it seems the date of our departure is already fixed.'[131] Cork's Ancient Order of Hibernians looked for a bright side to its comprehensive defeat. 'The City showed fight and although it had to give way, it took its beating manfully.'[132] A headline in the Unionist *Cork Constitution* newspaper summed up the campaign's implications, 'The Irish Party "A Thing of the Past."'[133]

In 1918 Cork voters did not provide a mandate for the IRA's violent campaign of 1920–1. However, they did clearly reject both continued citizenship within the United Kingdom and Dominion Home Rule within the British Empire. By voting for Sinn Féin in such overwhelming numbers, Cork city clearly expressed a desire for full and sovereign independence, in the form of an Irish republic.

Within a month, the newly elected Sinn Féin members formed Dáil Éireann and declared Irish independence. In the two and a half years since the Easter Rising, republicanism had clearly triumphed over constitutionalism. Cork also launched itself on a collision course with the British government. From 1919 to 1922, the city experienced thrilling scenes and bloody traumas that would have been inconceivable a few years previously. For a brief time Cork became a global symbol of resistance against the British Empire, before the city slipped again into an uneasy slumber.

Conclusion

The war had brought about a new situation and Sinn Féin was taking
advantage of that new situation.

Liam de Róiste, December 1918[1]

On behalf of the Irish people, John Redmond unofficially declared war
on the Central Powers in 1914. Had the conflict ended with a quick
British victory, Redmond's decision would have been a political
triumph. However, the war dragged on four more years, ultimately
toppling Redmond along with a Hapsburg emperor, Ottoman pasha,
German kaiser, and Russian tsar. With widespread support from the
Irish public, Sinn Féin effectively withdrew Ireland from the First
World War in 1918. An Irish Free State soon emerged from the post-
war wreckage, along with a multitude of new countries.

Like the rest of Ireland, Cork experienced a political odyssey
between Easter 1916 and the end of 1918. In two and a half years,
republicans evolved from a marginalised minority into the city's
unquestioned masters. Along the way republicans buried the AFIL,
smashed the Irish Party, and defied government suppression. By the
end of 1918, Sinn Féin readied its parallel parliament Dáil Éireann, the
Irish Volunteers prepared for armed insurrection, and the ITGWU agitated for one big union.

The First World War transformed Cork politics. The war's outset
seemed to validate John Redmond's vision of an Imperial Home Rule
Ireland, as unionists and nationalists briefly rallied to the National
Volunteers. However, the moment passed without fruition. The
National Volunteers, like other nationalist contributions to the war,
bled out over the next two years. Local Irish Party officials declined to
join the military or participate in recruiting, voluntary war work
assumed a unionist identity, and the Catholic Church remained aloof
from the entire venture. The Irish Volunteers represented small but
fierce anti-war sentiment in the city.

Public support and enlistment rates remained steady during the first year of the war, but declined in late 1915. Awakened to the fearsome toll incurred on foreign battlefields, nationalists feared the introduction of conscription to Ireland. Government legitimacy was undermined by the continued suspension of Home Rule, DORA prosecutions, and the inflammatory use of self-determination rhetoric by the British government. As war costs steadily rose in blood and treasure, the Cork public increasingly questioned its participation in the conflict. In the months prior to the Easter Rising, the Irish Party in Cork haemorrhaged members, while the Irish Volunteers slowly but steadily expanded.

The Easter rebellion provided a catalyst for anti-government sentiment in Cork. The execution of rebel leaders provoked widespread condemnation from constitutionalists, even as they were going on. Public sympathy was initially channelled into the INAVDF, which offered separatists a propaganda platform to recruit new supporters. The proposed partition of Ireland in the summer of 1916 further outraged Cork opinion. As local conditions stabilised, existing separatist organisations Sinn Féin, the Irish Volunteers and Cumann na mBan provided robust structures to accommodate new converts. Republicanism became a mass movement, as its message of self-reliance and abstention from the war resonated. Rather than defeat the new movement, state coercion only further delegitimised Dublin Castle.

Increasing anti-government sentiment manifested itself through a series of violent street clashes in the second half of 1917. Spontaneous and undirected, these riots frequently targeted symbols of the state. The clashes dissipated with the renewal of the Irish Volunteer organisation, which channelled unfocused youthful aggression into structured paramilitary activity. Years of pro-war propaganda created fertile ground for republican physical-force rhetoric. Methodically, Volunteer organisers built units in the city and county. Arms were secured and a republican prison culture established. The Cork Volunteers' most notable activity prior to the conscription crisis was a series of electrifying civil disobedience parades. By the end of 1917, police authorities recognised that they alone could no longer contain the Volunteers on city streets.

Cork's Sinn Féin organisation was re-launched at the end of 1916, despite pre-rising disputes over its commitment to republicanism. The new party pushed aside nascent challenges from the established AFIL party, positioning itself to harness growing anti-government sentiment. Sinn Féin represented a political departure in the city, led by activists with lower social status than the Irish Party elite. They faced aloofness from the Irish Volunteers, confusion over national policy, and competition from Count Plunkett's Liberty League. However, years of organising experience enabled the republican leadership to meet the challenge. Once separatists unified under Éamon de Valera, Sinn Féin blossomed in Cork. Branches rapidly grew in the latter half of 1917, and the party commanded a strong voice in the Cork Poor Law Guardians.

Cumann na mBan expanded at the same time, remaining closely associated with the Irish Volunteers. During 1917 and 1918, Cumann na mBan largely administered republican fundraising, and often defied authorities. Initially omitted from the local republican power structure, the organisation asserted itself during 1918. Cumann na mBan played a vital role in the general election mobilising women voters, Sinn Féin's key swing constituency. It remained primarily a republican rather than feminist organisation, though its members displayed a gender consciousness that followed from their politicisation.

Shortly after the Easter Rising, Cork Labour patched up its internal AFIL/UIL split, enabling the seizure of unique wartime opportunities. Employers no longer enjoyed the advantage of surplus unskilled labour. Staggering inflation motivated workers to organise across employment sectors. Binding arbitration mandated by the Munitions Act and Corn Production Act encouraged further unionisation. Industrial unrest struck the city in late 1917 and early 1918, led by the resurgent and republican-allied ITGWU. Food prices and shortages aroused anxiety among the city's working classes, which Cork labour addressed through the People's Food Committee agitation. When military conscription threatened, labour held the largest demonstration in city history and conducted a successful one-day general strike. Close relations with the independence movement were apparent with the Labour Party's decision to stand down from the 1918 general election, a move dictated by its rank and file.

The Irish Party could not keep pace with the rapidly evolving situation. Declining since 1914, the Redmondites shed support over the next three years, though their party apparatus continued to function and their activist base remained loyal. The National Volunteers disappeared in 1917, but the AOH and UIL limped along until the end of 1918. Ultimately, the Redmondites' collapse was political rather than structural. Party leaders lacked a compelling message relevant to the new environment. They raged against the delayed implementation of Home Rule, the coming partition of Ulster, continued government coercion, the stilted Irish Convention, the growing cost of the war, and the imposition of conscription on an unwilling public. Yet their protests were empty, and ultimately as ineffective as their constitutional tactics, which had lost credibility by 1918.

Evidence indicates that in 1917 many Cork residents no longer supported the war, and by 1918 a majority opposed it. Cork's two largest political parties (Sinn Féin and Labour) intended to cut off Britain from a major food source at the height of a true Imperial emergency. The conscription crisis featured widespread preparations for violent and non-violent resistance. Seldom has Southern Ireland been as unified as when it rejected the Military Service Bill. The ensuing public assembly ban incited thousands of city residents to join a civil disobedience campaign. Within months, Cork voters by a two to one margin returned Sinn Féin candidates who promised anti-government and pro-independence policies. Dáil Éireann was founded a few weeks later.

Challenged by the war, the British government helped create Ireland's revolutionary environment. It failed to resolve the Home Rule crisis, undermining the Irish Party. It refused to incorporate the National Volunteers into the British Army, dousing nationalist enthusiasm. It executed the Easter Rising leaders, arousing fierce opposition. It planned to partition the country, fuelling constitutionalist feelings of betrayal. It angered the public by cynically preaching democracy while approving DORA prosecutions, the public assembly ban, and the German Plot arrests. It raised Irish expectations by embracing Woodrow Wilson's promise of self-determination for small nations. Most importantly, it continued to fight a world war that required all its resources and attention. Ireland was left to stew in her own juices at a time of intense global destabilisation.

As the war continued year after year, the United Kingdom mobilised and then remobilised to finance, arm and feed its armies. Like unstable ingredients added to a chemistry experiment, wartime policies conceived in London often had unintended consequences in Cork. DORA was used to repress political speech, deficit spending generated mass inflation, mandatory arbitration encouraged workers to join trade unions, food rationing panicked a country scarred by the Potato Famine, venereal disease treatment schemes outraged the Catholic Church, army manpower requirements mandated conscription, which generated virtual rebellion. Ultimately the government prioritised winning the prolonged war, not placating Ireland. It is unclear if it could have done both. While Britain emerged victorious, its wartime policies irrevocably damaged its administration in Ireland.

The war ended on 11 November 1918, a date of symbolic synchronicity in the city of Cork. Just after the Armistice came into effect, armed Irish Volunteers broke into Cork gaol and rescued their colleague Denis MacNeilus. After years of painstaking preparations and false starts, Cork republicans had at last engaged the forces of the crown. When the triumphant Volunteers emerged from the prison gates, they must have heard celebratory bells ringing at nearby St Finbarr's Church of Ireland. In one part of the city of Cork, residents rejoiced at the end of the First World War. In another part, a new war had just begun. These two conflicts were intrinsically linked. Each was a separate act of the same play. In Cork city, the final curtain of that drama lowered four years later with the death of what some came to call 'the Munster Republic'.

Bibliography

Primary Manuscript Sources

Cork

CORK PUBLIC MUSEUM
Lil Conlon
Tomás MacCurtain
Terence MacSwiney

CORK CITY AND COUNTY ARCHIVES
George Berkeley
Head Constable Brown
Barry Egan
Seamus Fitzgerald
Robert Langford
Terence MacSwiney
Connie Neenan
Cork Coopers' Society
Cork District Trade Book
Cork City Club
Cork County Club
Liam de Róiste
    Papers
    Diaries
        U271A/19: 22 December 1915–25 April 1916
        (MS 31,146, NLI): 11 July 1917–30 December 1917
        U271A/20: 17 May 1918–13 July 1918
        U21A/21: 14 July 1918–24 October 1918
        U271A/22: 25 October 1918–17 November 1918
        U271A/23: 18 November 1918–22 January 1919
Ancient Order of Hibernians, Cork County
        County Board Letter Books
        County Convention Reports
        County Council Minute Book

Second Degree Minute Book
Second Degree Letter Book
126 Division Dues Book
Cork Corporation Meeting Minutes
Cork Corporation Public Health Committee Meeting Minutes
Cork Corporation Law and Finance Committee Meeting Minutes
Cork Corporation Working Class Dwellings Committee Meeting Minutes
Cork Poor Law Guardians Meeting Minutes

> BG69A/142: 8 November 1914–1 April 1915
> BG69A/143: 3 April 1915–16 September 1915
> BG69A/144: 18 September 1915–28 April 1916
> BG69A/145: 29 April 1916–19 August 1916
> BG69A/146: Missing
> BG69A/147: 17 March 1917–20 September 1917
> BG69A/148: 27 September 1917–28 March 1918
> BG69A/149: 4 April 1918–26 September 1918
> BG69A/150: 3 October 1918–3 April 1919

Cork Poor Law Guardians Clerk Letter Book
Cork Poor Law Union Indoor Relief Registers

UNIVERSITY COLLEGE CORK BOOLE LIBRARY
Andrew Bielenberg Collection
Annual Reports of the Medical Officer of Health (City of Cork)
British in Ireland Series, Microfilm

> RIC Inspector General and County Inspector Monthly Reports; Reports
> on Arms and Ammunition; Reports on Recruiting; Reports on the Sinn
> Féin Movement; Precis on Information Received by the Special Branch,
> RIC; Reports on Illegal Drillings; Reports of the Military Intelligence
> Officers in Ireland; Postal Censorship Reports.

Daniel Corkery Papers
Ireland Department of Agriculture and Technical Instruction Committee
    Annual Journals, 1911–1920
Murphy's Brewery Collection
Munster Printing Collection
William O'Brien Papers
Alfred O'Rahilly Papers
Reports of the President of University College Cork
Sinn Féin and Republican Suspects CD
University College Cork Official Gazette

PORT OF CORK AUTHORITY (CORK CUSTOMS HOUSE)
Cork Harbour Commission Meeting Minutes

> Volume 47: 1 May 1916–19 July 1916
> Volume 48: 26 July 1916–2 May 1917
> Volume 49: 16 May 1917–26 June 1918
> Volume 50: 3 July 1918–2 July 1919

Volume 51: 30 July 1919–11 August 1920
Volume 52: 19 August 1920–17 November 1920
Volume 53: 24 November 1920–6 October 1921

CORK CITY LIBRARY LOCAL STUDIES DEPARTMENT
Cork Local History Collection
Guy's Directory

Dublin

UNIVERSITY COLLEGE DUBLIN ARCHIVES
Éamon de Valera
Mary MacSwiney
Terence MacSwiney's Biographers
General Richard Mulcahy
Ernie O'Malley Notebooks

NATIONAL LIBRARY OF IRELAND
Robert Barton
Pierce Beaslaí
Ceant-O'Brennan
Thomas Foran
J.J. Horgan
Irish National Aid and Volunteers Fund Executive
Colonel Maurice Moore
Mrs William (Sophie) O'Brien
William O'Brien (TD)
J.J. O'Connell
Florence O'Donoghue
Count Plunkett
John Redmond
Hannah Sheehy Skeffington
UIL Meeting Books

NATIONAL ARCHIVES
Bureau of Military History (BMH) Witness Statements
Chief Secretary's Office Registered Papers (CSORP)
Dáil Éireann Department of Home Affairs
General Prison Board (GPB)

TRINITY COLLEGE DUBLIN ARCHIVES
Frank & Cecilia Gallagher
John Dillon
Liam de Róiste

MILITARY ARCHIVES, CATHAL BRUGHA BARRACKS
Bureau of Military History Contemporary Documents

IRISH LABOUR HISTORY MUSEUM (BEGGARS BUSH BARRACKS)
Cathal O'Shannon Papers

IRISH CAPUCHIN ORDER PROVINCIAL ARCHIVE, CHURCH STREET
The Capuchins and the Irish Revolution Collection
Unsorted Father Thomas Dowling Papers

London
HOUSE OF COMMONS ARCHIVES
Andrew Bonar Law Papers
David Lloyd George Papers

KEW NATIONAL ARCHIVES
War Office Papers
Colonial Office Papers

Washington DC

US NATIONAL ARCHIVES I, PENNSYLVANIA AVE.
Secretary of the Navy, General Correspondence, 1916–26, RG 80
Records Collection of the Office of Naval Records and Library, RG 45

US NATIONAL ARCHIVES IV, COLLEGE PARK MD
US Consular Records, Cork, Ireland, RG 84

Palo Alto, CA

HOOVER INSTITUTION ARCHIVES, STANFORD UNIVERSITY
George Barr Baker Papers
James Healy Papers
Tracy B. Kittridge Papers
American National Red Cross

Official Publications

1911 Census of Ireland
Report on Recruiting in Ireland, 1914–1916, HC XXXIX, CD 8168
Criminal and Judicial Statistics of Ireland for 1914, XXXII, CD 525
Criminal and Judicial Statistics of Ireland for 1916, HC, XXV, CD 9066
Criminal and Judicial Statistics of Ireland for 1917, HC, Lii, CD 43

Criminal and Judicial Statistics of Ireland for 1918, HC, LiiL, CD 438

General Annual Reports on the British Army (including the Territorial Force) for the Period from 1 October 1913 to 30 September 1919, HC, XX.469, CD 1193

Hansard, Historical Debates, 1803–2005

Report of the Royal Commission on the Rebellion in Ireland, CD 8279

The Royal Commission on the Rebellion in Ireland: Minutes of Evidence and Appendix of Documents, CD 8311

Report on the Administration of the National Relief Fund up to 30 September 1916, CD 8449,8621,8290

Report on Recruiting in Ireland, 1914–1916, HC XXXIX, CD 8168

Statement Giving Particulars of Men of Military Age in Ireland, 1916, HC XVII.581, CD 8390

Newspapers

Anglo-Celt
Cork Constitution
Cork Examiner
Cork Free Press
Freeman's Journal
Irish Citizen
Irish Independent
Irish Times
New York Times
Southern Star
Times of London
Voice of Labour

Theses

Gough, Michael J., 'A History of the Physical Development of Cork City', MA thesis, UCC, 1974

Hennessy, David, 'Ireland and the First World War: A Perspective', MPHIL thesis, UCC, 2004

Lahiff, Edward, 'Industry and Labour in Cork, 1890–1921', MA thesis, UCC, 1988

Linehan, Thomas A., 'The Development of Cork's Economy and Business Attitudes, 1910–1939', MA thesis, UCC, 1985

Lucey, Dermot J., 'Cork Public Opinion and the First World War', MA thesis, UCC, 1972

Martin, Micheál, 'The Formation and Evolution of the Irish Party Political System, with Particular Emphasis on the Cork City Borough Constituency, 1918–1932', MA thesis, UCC, 1988

MacSweeney, A.M., 'A Study of Poverty in Cork City', MA thesis, UCC, 1915

Reddick, Stephen McQuay, 'Political and Industrial Labour in Cork, 1899–1914', MA thesis, UCC, 1984

Staunton, Martin, 'The Royal Munster Fusiliers in the Great War', MA thesis, UCD, 1986

Private Sources

Ida Ní Shé, Cumann na mBan Collection
Rollie Green, Lieutenant Lucien Green Diary
James O'Shea, O'Shea Family History

Select Secondary Sources

Amery, L.S., *My Political Life, Volume II* (London: Hutchinson, 1953)

Augusteijn, Joost, *From Public Defiance to Guerrilla Warfare: The Experience of Ordinary Volunteers in the Irish War of Independence, 1916–1921* (Dublin: Irish Academic Press, 1996)

Bew, Paul, *Land and the National Question in Ireland* (Dublin: Gill & Macmillan, 1978)

Bew, Paul, 'Moderate Nationalism and the Irish Revolution, 1916–1923', *Historical Journal*, vol. 42, no. 3, September 1999, pp. 729–49

Bielenberg, Andrew, *Irish Flour Milling* (Dublin: The Lilliput Press, 2003)

Bielenberg, Andrew, 'Irish Distilling Industry Under the Union', in Dicks and Ó Gráda (eds), *Refiguring Ireland*, pp. 290–315

Bielenberg, Andrew, *Cork's Industrial Revolution, 1780–1880: Development or Decline?* (Cork: Cork University Press, 1991)

Bourke, Joanna, 'Effeminacy, Ethnicity and the End of Trauma: The Suffering of Shell-Shocked Men in Great Britain and Ireland, 1914–1939', *Journal of Contemporary History*, vol. 35, pp. 57–9

Bourke, Joanna, 'Irish Tommie: The Construction of a Martial Manhood', *Bullán, An Irish Studies Journal*, Winter 1997, pp. 13–30

Bowman, Timothy, *Carson's Army: The Ulster Volunteer Force, 1910–1922* (Manchester: Manchester University Press, 2007)

Bowman, Timothy, *Irish Regiments in the Great War: Discipline and Morale* (Manchester: Manchester University Press, 2003)

Boyce, D. George, 'British Opinion, Ireland and the War, 1916–1918', *Historical Journal*, no. 17 (1974), pp. 575–93

Boyce, D. George, *Ireland, 1828–1923: From Ascendancy to Democracy* (Oxford: Blackwell, 1992)

Boyce, D. George, *The Sure Confusing Drum: Ireland and the First World War* (Swansea: University College Swansea, 1993)

Boyce, D. George (ed. with Alan O'Day), *Ireland in Transition, 1867–1921* (London: Routledge, 2004)

Boyce, D. George (ed.), *The Revolution in Ireland, 1879–1923* (Dublin: Gill & Macmillan, 1998)

Bradley, Dan, *Farm Labourers: Irish Struggle, 1900–1976* (Belfast: Athol Books, 1988)

Branagan, W.J., 'Ireland and War Contracts', *Studies*, 1915, pp. 470–7

Broadberry, Stephen and Howlett, Peter, 'United Kingdom During World War One: Business as Usual?', in Stephen Broadberry and Mark Harrison (eds), *Economics of World War One* (Cambridge: Cambridge University Press, 2005), pp. 206–31

Browne, Charlie, *The Story of the 7th: A Concise History of the 7th Battalion, Cork No. 1 Brigade, Irish Republican Army from 1915 to 1921* (Cork: Schull Books, 2006)

Brundage, David, 'American Labour and the Irish Question, 1916–1923', *Saothar*, no. 24, 1999, pp. 59–65

Burns, Robin B, 'The Montreal Irish and the Great War', *CCHA Historical Studies*, no. 52, 1985, pp. 67–81

Buttimer, Cornelius and O'Flanagan, Patrick (eds), *Cork: History and Society. Interdisciplinary Essays on the History of an Irish County* (Dublin: Geography Publications, 1993)

Callanan, Frank, *T.M. Healy* (Cork: Cork University Press, 1996)

Campbell, Colm, *Emergency Law in Ireland, 1918–1925* (Oxford: Oxford University Press, 1994)

Campbell, Fergus, *Land and Revolution: Nationalists, Politics in the West of Ireland, 1891–1921* (Oxford: Oxford University Press, 2005)

Casey, Patrick J., 'Irish Casualties in the First World War', *Irish Sword*, no. 20 (Summer 1997), pp. 193–206

Chavasse, Moiron, *Terence MacSwiney* (Dublin: Clonmore & Reynolds, 1961)

Chatterton, E.K., *Danger Zone: The Story of the Queenstown Command* (London: Rich & Cowan, 1936)

Clarke, Olga Pyne, *She Came of Decent People* (London: Pelham Books, 1985)

Coates, Tim (ed.), *The World War I Collection: Gallipoli and the Early Battles, 1914–1915* (London: The Stationery Office, 2001)

Coleman, Marie, *County Longford and the Irish Revolution, 1910–1923* (Dublin: Irish Academic Press, 2003)

Conlon, Lil, *Cumann na mBan and the Women of Ireland* (Kilkenny: Kilkenny People, 1969)

Coolahan, John, 'The ASTI and the Secondary Teachers' Strike of 1920', *Saothar*, no. 10, 1984, pp. 43–59

Corkery, Daniel, 'Terence MacSwiney: Lord Mayor of Cork', *Studies*, 1920, pp. 512–20

Costello, Francis, *Enduring the Most: The Life and Death of Terence MacSwiney* (Dingle: Brandon, 1996)

Crean, Thomas Neilan, 'Labour and Politics in Kerry During the First World War', *Saothar*, no. 19, 1994, pp. 27–40

Cronin, Maura, 'Work and Workers in Cork City and County, 1800–1900', in Buttimer and O'Flanagan (eds), *Cork: History and Society*, pp. 699–720

Cronin, Maura, *Country, Class, or Craft? The Politicisation of the Skilled Artisan in Nineteenth-Century Cork* (Cork: Cork University Press, 1994)

Cronin, Mike, Murphy, William and Roose, Paul (eds), *The Gaelic Athletic Association, 1884–2009* (Dublin: Irish Academic Press, 2009)

D'Alton, Ian, 'Keeping the Faith: An Evocation of the Cork Protestant

Character, 1820–1920', in Buttimer and O'Flanagan (eds), *Cork: History and Society*, pp. 759–79

D'Alton, Ian, 'Educating for Ireland? The Urban Protestant Elite and the Early Years of Cork Grammar School, 1880–1914', *Éire-Ireland*, vol. 46, nos 3 & 4, Fall/Winter 2011, pp. 201–26

Davis, Richard, *Arthur Griffith and Non-Violent Sinn Féin* (Dublin: Anvil Books, 1974)

Day, Susanne, *The Amazing Philanthropists* (London: Sidgwick & Jackson, 1916)

Denman, Terence, '"The Red Livery of Shame": The Campaign Against Army Recruitment in Ireland, 1899–1914', *Irish Historical Studies*, vol. 29, November 1994, pp. 208–33

Denman, Terence, 'The Catholic Irish Soldier in the First World War: The Racial Environment', *Irish Historical Studies*, vol. XXVII, no. 108, November 1991, pp. 362–5

Denman, Terence, 'Sir Lawrence Parsons and the Raising of the 16th (Irish) Division, 1914–1915', *Irish Sword*, Winter 1987, pp. 90–104

Dewey, P.E., 'Military Recruiting and the British Labour Force During the First World War', *Historical Journal*, no. 27, 1984, pp. 199–223

De Wiel, Jerome Ann, *The Catholic Church and Ireland* (Dublin: Irish Academic Press, 2003)

De Wiel, Jerome Ann, 'Archbishop Walsh and Monsignor Curran's Opposition to the British War Effort in Dublin, 1914–1918', *Irish Sword*, vol. XXII, Winter 2000, pp. 193–204

Dicks, David and Ó Gráda, Cormac (eds), *Refiguring Ireland: Essays in Honour of L.M. Cullen* (Dublin: The Lilliput Press, 2003)

Doherty, Gabriel and Keogh, Dermot, *1916: The Long Revolution* (Cork: Mercier Press, 2007)

Donnelly, James, *The Land and the People of Nineteenth-Century Cork: The Rural Economy and the Land Question* (London: Routledge & Kegan Paul, 1975)

Dooley, Terence, *The Land for the People: The Land Question in Independent Ireland* (Dublin: UCD Press, 2004)

Dooley, Thomas, *Irishmen or English soldiers? The Times and World of a Southern Catholic Irish Man (1876–1916) Enlisting in the British Army During the First World War* (Manchester: Manchester University Press, 1995)

Dooley, Thomas, 'Politics, Bands and Marketing: Army Recruiting in Waterford City, 1914–1915', *Irish Sword*, no. 28, Winter 1991, pp. 206–19

Douglas, Roy, 'Voluntary Enlistment in the First World War and the Work of the Parliamentary Recruiting Committee', *Journal of Modern History*, vol. 42, December 1970, pp. 564–85

Downs, Margaret (in Fitzpatrick, 1986), 'The Civilian Voluntary Aid Effort', pp. 27–37

Farrell, Brian, *The Founding of Dáil Éireann: Parliament and Nation Building* (Dublin: Gill & Macmillan, 1971)

Fawsitt, J.L., 'New Industries for a Greater Cork', *Studies*, 1917, pp. 462–9

Ferriter, Diarmuid, *Occasions of Sin: Sex and Society in Modern Ireland* (London: Profile Books, 2007)

Finnan, Joseph, '"Let Irishmen Come Together in the Trenches": John Redmond and the Irish Party Policy in the Great War, 1914–1918', *Irish Sword*, no. 22, Winter 2000

Fischer, Joachim and Neville, Grace, *Cork Through European Eyes* (Cork: The Collins Press, 2005)

Fitzpatrick, David, 'The Logic of Collective Sacrifice: Ireland and the British Army, 1914–1918', *Historical Journal*, no. 38, December 1995, pp. 1017–30

Fitzpatrick, David, 'Militarism in Ireland', in Jefferey and Bartlett (eds), *A Military History of Ireland*, pp. 379–406

Fitzpatrick, David (ed.), *Ireland and the First World War* (Dublin: Trinity History Workshop, 1986)

Fitzpatrick, David, 'Strikes in Ireland, 1914–1921', *Saothar*, no. 6, 1980, pp. 26–39

Fitzpatrick, David, *Politics and Irish Life, 1913–1921: Provincial Experience of War and Revolution* (Dublin: Gill & Macmillan, 1977)

Fitzpatrick, David, 'The Geography of Irish Nationalism, 1910–1921', *Past and Present*, no. 78, February 1978, pp. 119–44

Fitzpatrick, David (ed.), *Revolution? Ireland, 1917–1923* (Dublin: Trinity History Workshop, 1990)

Folley, Terrence, 'A Catalan Trade Union and the Irish War of Independence, 1919–1922', *Saothar*, no. 10, 1984, pp. 60–7

Gallagher, John, 'Nationalism and the Crisis of Empire, 1919–1922', *Modern Asia Studies*, vol. 15, 1981, pp. 355–68

Galvin, Michael, *Kilmurray Volunteers, 1915–1921* (Midleton: Litho Press, 1994)

Garvin, Tom, *The Evolution of Irish Nationalist Politics* (Dublin: Gill & Macmillan, 1981)

Garvin, Tom, *Nationalist Revolutionaries in Ireland* (Oxford: Clarendon Press, 1987)

Gaughan, J. Anthony, *Alfred O'Rahilly. Vol. II: Public Figure* (Naas: Kingdom Books, 1989)

Girvin, Brian, *From Union to Union: Nationalism, Democracy and Religion in Ireland, Act of Union to European Union* (Dublin: Gill & Macmillan, 2002)

Greaves, C. Desmond, *The Irish Transport and General Workers' Union: The Formative Years* (Dublin: Gill & Macmillan, 1982)

Greenhalgh, Elizabeth, 'David Lloyd George, George Clemenceau and the 1918 Manpower Crisis', *The Historical Journal*, vol. 50, no. 2, June 2007, pp. 397–421

Gregory, Adrian and Paseta, Senia (eds), *Ireland and the Great War: A War to Unite Us All?* (Manchester: Manchester University Press, 2002)

Griffith, Kenneth and O'Grady, Timothy, *Curious Journey: An Oral History of Ireland's Unfinished Revolution* (London: Hutchinson, 1982)

Gullace, Nicoletta, 'White Feathers and Wounded Men: Female Patriotism and the Memory of the Great War', *Journal of British Studies*, vol. 36, April 1997, pp. 178–206

Gullace, Nicoletta, 'Sexual Violence and Family Honor: British Propaganda and International Law During the First World War', *American Historical Review*, June 1997, pp. 714–47

Gwynn, Denis, *The Life of John Redmond* (London: George G. Harrap & Co., 1935)

Halpern, Paul, *A Naval History of World War One* (London: University College London Press, 1994)

Hart, Peter (ed.), *British Intelligence in Ireland, 1920–1921* (Cork: Cork University Press, 2002)

Hart, Peter, *The IRA and Its Enemies: Violence and Community in Cork, 1916–1923* (Oxford: Oxford University Press, 1998)

Healy, Maurice, *The Old Munster Circuit* (London: Michael Joseph Ltd, 1939)

Healy, Tim, *Letters and Leaders of My Day, Vol. II* (London: Thornton Butterworth, 1928)

Hennessy, Thomas, *Dividing Ireland: World War One and Partition* (London: Routledge, 1998)

Henry, William, *Galway and the Great War* (Cork: Mercier Press, 2006)

Hopkinson, Michael (ed.), *The Last Days of Dublin Castle: The Diaries of Mark Sturgis* (Dublin: Irish Academic Press, 1999)

Hopkinson, Michael, *The Irish War of Independence* (Dublin: Gill & Macmillan, 2002)

Hoppen, Theodore K., 'Roads to Democracy: Electioneering and Corruption in Nineteenth-Century England and Ireland', *History, The Journal of the Historical Association*, Fall 1998, vol. 83

Horgan, J.J., 'The World Policy and President Wilson', *Studies*, vol. VII, 1918, pp. 553–63

Horgan, J.J., 'William Redmond, Some Personal Memories', *Studies*, 1917, pp. 417–23

Horgan, J.J., 'Precepts and Practice in Ireland, 1914–1919', *Studies*, 1919, pp. 210–26

Horgan, J.J., *From Parnell to Pearse: Some Recollections and Reflections* (Dublin: Browne & Nolan, 1948)

Horne, John, *Our War: Ireland and the Great War* (Dublin: Royal Irish Academy, 2008)

Horne, John (ed.), *State, Society, and Mobilisation in Europe duing the First World War* (Cambridge: Cambridge Univeristy Press, 1997)

Jefferey, Keith, *Ireland and the Great War* (Cambridge: Cambridge University Press, 2000)

Jefferey, Keith and Bartlett, Thomas (eds), *A Military History of Ireland* (Cambridge: Cambridge University Press, 1996)

Jefferey, Keith (ed.), *'An Irish Empire?' Aspects of Ireland and the British Empire* (Manchester: Manchester University Press, 1996)

Johnson, Nuala, *Ireland, the Great War and the Geography of Remembrance* (Cambridge: Cambridge University Press, 2003)

Johnstone, Thomas, *Orange, Green and Khaki: The Story of the Irish Regiments in the Great War, 1914–1918* (Dublin: Gill & Macmillan, 1992)

Karsten, Peter, 'Irish Soldiers in the British Army, 1792–1922', *Journal of Social History*, vol. 17, Autumn 1983, pp. 31–64

Kenneally, Ian, *The Paper Wall: Newspapers and Propaganda in Ireland, 1919–1921* (Cork: The Collins Press, 2008)

Keogh, Dermot, *The Vatican, the Bishops and Irish Politics, 1919–1939* (Cambridge: Cambridge University Press, 1986)

Kotsonouris, Mary, *Retreat from Revolution: The Dáil Courts, 1920–1924* (Dublin: Irish Academic Press, 1994)

Laffan, Michael, *The Resurrection of Ireland: The Sinn Féin Party, 1916–1923* (Cambridge: Cambridge University Press, 1999)

Lane, Fintan, 'Music and Violence in Working-Class Cork: The "Band Nuisance", 1879–1882', *Saothar*, vol. 24, 1999, pp. 17–31

Lankford, Siobhan, *The Hope and the Sadness: Personal Recollections of Troubled Times in Ireland* (Cork: Tower Books, 1980)

Lenisko, Lynn Speer, 'A Dubious Reputation? The Performance of the 16th (Irish) Division, 1916–20 March 1918', *Irish Sword*, no. 22, Summer 2000

Luddy, Maria, *Prostitution and Irish Society, 1800–1940* (Cambridge: Cambridge University Press, 2007)

Lyons, F.S.L., *Charles Stewart Parnell* (London: Routledge & Kegan Paul, 1977)

Macardle, Dorothy, *The Irish Republic, 1911–1925* (Dublin: Irish Press, 1951)

MacSweeney, A.M., 'A Study of Poverty in Cork City', *Studies*, vol. IV, 1915, pp. 92–104

MacSwiney, Mary, *History's Daughter: A Memoir from the Only Child of Terence MacSwiney* (Dublin: The O'Brien Press, 2005)

Martin, Micheál, *Freedom to Choose: Cork and Party Politics, 1918–1932* (Cork: The Collins Press, 2009)

Maume, Patrick, *The Long Gestation: Irish Nationalist Life, 1891–1918* (Dublin: Gill & Macmillan, 1999)

McArdle, Paula Connolly, 'The Munster Women's Franchise League, 1910–1918', in Bernadette Whelan, *Clio's Daughters: Essays on Irish Women's History, 1945–1939* (Limerick: University of Limerick Press, 1997)

McCarthy, Eoin and O'Sullivan, Gerard, 'Cork-Born Soldiers Who Died in World War One', *Journal of the Ballincollig Community School Local History Society*, vol. 7, 1990–1991, pp. 20–68

McCarthy, Justin, *The Story of an Irishman* (London: Chatto & Windus, 1904)

McDowell, R.B., *The Irish Convention, 1917–1918* (London: Routledge & Kegan Paul, 1970)

McKillen, Beth, 'Irish Feminism and Nationalist Separation, 1914–1923', *Éire-Ireland*, vol. XVII, Fall 1982, pp. 52–67

Mitchell, Arthur, *Labour in Irish Politics, 1890–1930* (Dublin: Irish Academic Press, 1974)

Moriarty, Theresa, 'Work, Warfare and Wages: Industrial Controls and Irish Trade Unionism in the First World War', in Gregory and Paseta (eds), *Ireland and the Great War*, pp. 73–93

Morison, Elting, *Admiral Sims and the Modern American Navy* (New York: Russell & Russell, 1968)

Morrissey, Thomas, *William O'Brien, 1881–1968* (Dublin: Four Courts Press, 2007)

Murphy, Maura, 'The Economic and Social Structure of Nineteenth-Century Cork', in David Harkness and Mary O'Dowd, *The Town in Ireland* (Belfast: Appletree Press, 1981), pp. 125–54

Murphy, William, 'The GAA During the Irish Revolution, 1913–1923', in Cronin, Murphy and Roose (eds), *The Gaelic Athletic Association* (Dublin: Irish Academic Press, 2009).

Novick, Ben, *Conceiving Revolution: Irish Nationalist Propaganda During the First World War* (Dublin: Four Courts Press, 2001)

O'Brien, John B., 'Population, Politics and Society in Cork, 1780–1900', in Buttimer and O'Flanagan (eds), *Cork: History and Society*, pp. 699–720

O'Brien, Joseph, *William O'Brien and the Course of Irish Politics, 1881–1918* (Berkeley: University of California Press, 1976)

O'Callaghan, Antoin, *The Lord Mayors of Cork, 1900 to 2000* (Cork: Inversnaid Publications, 2000)

O'Connor, Emmet, *Reds and the Green* (Dublin: University College Dublin Press, 2004)

O'Connor, Emmet, *A Labour History of Ireland* (Dublin: Gill & Macmillan, 1992)

O'Connor, Emmet, *Syndicalism in Ireland* (Cork: Cork University Press, 1988)

O'Connor, Emmet, 'Agrarian Unrest and the Labour Movement in County Waterford, 1917–1923', *Soathar*, no. 6, 1980, pp. 40–58

O'Connor, Frank, *An Only Child* (London: Pan Books, 1970)

O'Donoghue, Florence, *No Other Law* (Dublin: Anvil Press, 1986)

O'Donoghue, Florence (ed.), *Sworn to Be Free: The Complete Book of IRA Jailbreaks, 1918–1921* (Tralee: Anvil Press, 1971)

O'Donoghue, Florence, *Tomás MacCurtain: Soldier and Patriot* (Tralee: Anvil Press, 1971)

Ó Drisceoil, Diarmuid and Ó Drisceoil, Donal, *The History of Lady's Well Brewery* (Cork: Murphy's Brewery, 1997)

Ó Drisceoil, Diarmuid and Ó Drisceoil, Donal, *Serving the City: The Story of the English Market* (Cork: The Collins Press, 2005)

O'Faoláin, Seán, *Vive Moi! An Autobiography* (London: Sinclair-Stevenson, 1993)

Ó Gráda, Cormac, *Ireland: A New Economic History* (Oxford: Oxford University Press, 1994)

O'Hegarty, P.S., *The Victory of Sinn Féin* (Dublin: UCD Press, 1998)

O'Leary, Cornelius, *Irish Elections, 1918–1977* (Dublin: Gill & Macmillan, 1979)

O'Mahony, Colman, *The Maritime Gateway to Cork: A History of the Outports of Passage West and Monkstown, 1754–1942* (Cork: Tower Books, 1986)

O'Mahony, Colman, *Life in Cork, 1750–1930* (Cork: Tower Books, 1997)

O'Halpin, Eunan, *The Decline of the Union: British Government in Ireland, 1892–1920* (Dublin: Gill & Macmillan, 1987)

O'Rahilly, Alfred, 'The Social Problem in Cork', *Studies*, 1917, pp. 177–88

Paseta, Senia, *Before the Revolution: Nationalism, Social Change and Ireland's Catholic Elite, 1879–1922* (Cork: Cork University Press, 1999)

Purséil, Pádraig, *The GAA In Its Time* (Dublin: Ward River Press, 1984)

Regan, John, *The Irish Counter-Revolution, 1921–1936* (Dublin: Gill & Macmillan, 1999)

Reilly, Eileen, 'Women and Voluntary War Work', in Gregory and Paseta, *Ireland and the Great War*, pp. 49–72

Riordan, E.J., *Modern Irish Trade and Industry* (London: Methuen & Co., 1921)

Ruiseal, Liam, *Liam Ruiseal Remembers* (Cork: Tower Books, 1978)

Sanders, M.L., 'Wellington House and British Propaganda During the First World War, *The Historical Journal*, vol. XVIII, 1975

Sanders, M.L. and Taylor, Philip, *British Propaganda During the First World War* (London: Macmillan, 1982)

Townshend, Charles, 'The Irish Railway Strike of 1920: Industrial Action and Civil Resistance in the Struggle for Independence', *Irish Historical Studies*, vol. XXI, 1978–1979, pp. 265–82

Townshend, Charles, *The British Campaign in Ireland, 1919–1921* (Oxford: Oxford University Press, 1975)

Townshend, Charles, *Easter 1916: The Irish Rebellion* (London: Penguin, 2005)

Valiulis, Maryann G., *Portrait of a Revolutionary: General Richard Mulcahy and the Founding of the Irish Free State* (Dublin: Irish Academic Press, 1992)

Varley, Tony, 'Agrarian Crime and Social Control: Sinn Féin and the Land Question in the West of Ireland in 1920', in Mike Tomlinson, Tony Varley and Ciaran McCullough (eds), *Whose Law and Order? Aspects of Crime and Social Control in Irish Society* (Belfast: Sociological Association of Ireland, 1988), pp. 54–75

Ward, Alan J., 'Lloyd George and the 1918 Irish Conscription Crisis', *Historical Journal*, no. 17, 1974, pp. 107–29

Ward, Margaret, *Unmanageable Revolutionaries* (London: Pluto Press, 1983)

Ward, Margaret (ed.), *In Their Own Words: Women and Irish Nationalism* (Cork: Attic Press, 1995)

Warwick-Haller, Sally, *William O'Brien and the Irish Land War* (Dublin: Irish Academic Press, 1990)

Wheatley, Michael, *Nationalism and the Irish Party: Provincial Ireland, 1910–1916* (Oxford: Oxford University Press, 2005)

White, Gerry and O'Shea, Brendan, *Baptised in Blood: The Formation of the Cork Brigade of the Irish Volunteers* (Cork: Mercier Press, 2005)

White, Gerry and O'Shea, Brendan, *The Burning of Cork* (Cork: Mercier Press, 2006)

White, Gerry and O'Shea, Brendan, 'Easter 1916 in Cork: Order, Counter-Order and Disorder', in Doherty and Keogh, *1916: The Long Revolution*, pp. 169–96

Notes and References

INTRODUCTION

1 D.L. Kelleher, *Cork's Own Town* (Cork: Guy & Co. Ltd, 1920), Munster Printing Collection (MP), Boole Library, University College Cork (UCC).
2 Cork Harbour Commission Meeting Minutes, 5 September 1921, Port of Cork Archives (PCA).
3 Cork Harbour Commission Meeting Minutes, 7 September 1921.
4 David Fitzpatrick (ed.), *Ireland and the First World War* (Dublin: Trinity History Workshop, 1986).
5 Especially noteworthy are works by Keith Jeffery, Joanna Bourke, Nuala Johnson, Timothy Bowmen, Terence Denman, Adrian Gregory, Senia Paseta and Jerome aan de Wiel.
6 George Boyce, *The Revolution in Ireland* (London: Macmillan Press, 1988), p. 13.
7 Adrian Gregory and Senia Paseta (eds), *Ireland and the Great War: A War to Unite Us All?* (Manchester: Manchester University Press, 2002), p. 2.
8 Ben Novick, *Conceiving Revolution: Irish Nationalist Propaganda During the First World War* (Dublin: Four Courts Press, 2001), p. 18.
9 Charles Townshend, 'British Policy in Ireland, 1906–1921', pp. 173–92, in George Boyce (ed.), *The Revolution in Ireland, 1879–1923* (Basingstoke: Macmillan, 1988).
10 Marie Coleman, *County Longford and the Irish Revolution, 1910–1923* (Dublin: Irish Academic Press, 2003); Fergus Campbell, *Land and Revolution: Nationalist Politics in the West of Ireland, 1891–1921* (Oxford: Oxford University Press, 2005); Joost Augusteijn, *From Public Defiance to Guerrilla Warfare: The Experience of Ordinary Volunteers in the Irish War of Independence, 1916–1921* (Dublin: Irish Academic Press, 1996); Peter Hart, *The IRA and Its Enemies: Violence and Community in Cork, 1916–1923* (Oxford: Oxford University Press, 1998); John O'Callaghan, *Revolutionary Limerick: The Republican Campaign for Independence in Limerick, 1913–1921* (Dublin: Irish Academic Press, 2010).
11 Anne Dolan, *Commemorating the Irish Civil War: History and Memory, 1923–2000* (Cambridge: Cambridge University Press, 2003); Patrick Maume, *The Long Gestation: Irish Nationalist Life, 1891–1918* (Dublin: Gill & Macmillan, 1999); Michael Wheatley, *Nationalism and the Irish Party, Provincial Ireland, 1910–1916* (Oxford, Oxford University Press, 2005); Ferghal McGarry, *The Rising* (Oxford: Oxford University Press, 2010).
12 See Thomas Hennessey, *Dividing Ireland: World War One and Partition* (London: Routledge, 1998); Charles Townshend, *Easter 1916: The Irish Rebellion* (Chicago: Ivan Dee, 2006); Nuala Johnson, *Ireland, the Great War and the Geography of Remembrance* (Cambridge: Cambridge University Press, 2003); and Novick, *Conceiving Revolution*.
13 John Borgonovo (ed.), *Florence and Josephine O'Donoghue's War of Independence* (Dublin: Irish Academic Press, 2006), p. ix.
14 Townshend, 'British Policy in Ireland', p. 187.

249

15   Four of Hart's chapters exclusively deal with the Bandon Valley, while north Cork and east Cork rarely feature in the work. City events sometimes appear as evidence for broader points, but with little in-depth exploration.

16   Gerry White and Brendan O'Shea, *Baptised in Blood: The Formation of the Cork Brigade of the Irish Volunteers, 1913–1916* (Cork: Mercier Press, 2005).

17   John Horne (ed.), *State, Society and Mobilisation in Europe during the First World War* (Cambridge: Cambridge University Press, 1997, pp. 114–20, 145, 151, 155, 158–9, 168–9, 173, 182, 195–211, 228–9.

18   Ibid., p. 7.

CHAPTER I: CORK POLITICAL LIFE PRIOR TO EASTER 1916

1   Bureau of Military History (BMH) Witness Statement (WS) 869, Commandant P.J. Murphy, National Archives (NA), Dublin (hereafter WS).

2   From the 1911 Census of Ireland. The 1916 *Guy's Directory* uses the 1911 Census to quantify the Cork City Parliamentary Borough (encompassing the suburbs) at 102,274.

3   Andrew Bielenberg, *Cork's Industrial Revolution, 1780–1880: Development or Decline?* (Cork: Cork University Press, 1991); Maura Murphy, 'The Economic and Social Structure of Nineteenth Century Cork', in David Harkness and Mary O'Dowd, *The Town in Ireland* (Belfast: Appletree Press, 1981), pp. 125–54; John B. O'Brien, 'Population, Politics and Society in Cork, 1780–1900', in Cornelius Buttimer and Patrick O'Flanagan (eds), *Cork: History and Society. Interdisciplinary Essays on the History of an Irish County* (Dublin: Geography Publications, 1993), pp. 699–720.

4   Murphy, 'The Economic and Social Structure of Nineteenth-Century Cork', pp. 127, 129, 132; Maura Cronin, 'Work and Workers in Cork City and County, 1800–1900', in Buttimer and O'Flanagan, *Cork: History and Society*, pp. 699–720.

5   See Cronin, 'Work and Workers in Cork City and County'.

6   For further details see Diarmuid Ó Drisceoil and Donal Ó Drisceoil, *The History of Lady's Well Brewery* (Cork: Murphy's Brewery, 1997); and *Serving the City: The Story of the English Market* (Cork: The Collins Press, 2005). See also Stephen McQuay Reddick, 'Political and Industrial Labour in Cork, 1899–1914', MA thesis, UCC; Thomas Linehan, 'The Development of Cork's Economy and Business Attitudes, 1910–1939', MA thesis, UCC 1985; Michael Gough, 'A History of the Physical Development of Cork City', MA thesis, UCC, 1974; Edward Lahiff, 'Industry and Labour in Cork, 1890–1921', MA thesis, UCC, 1988; Myriam Nyahan, 'Henry Ford and Son Ltd: A History of the Cork Plant, 1917–1984', MA thesis, UCC, 2004.

7   *Ireland Department of Agriculture & Technical Instruction Committee Journals*, 1911 to 1915, UCC.

8   Eilis Stack, 'Victorian Cork', in Henry Alan Jefferies (ed.), *Cork Historical Perspectives* (Dublin: Four Courts Press, 2004), pp. 172–91.

9   D.J. Coakley, *Cork: Its Trade and Commerce* (Cork: Chamber of Commerce and Shipping Booklet, 1917), Cork City Library.

10   A.M. MacSweeney, 'A Study of Poverty in Cork City', MA thesis, UCC 1915. See also MacSweeney's article of the same name in *Studies*, vol. IV, 1915, pp. 92–104. Colman O'Mahony numbers the city's tenement population at 8,765 in 1913. See Colman O'Mahony, *The Maritime Gateway to Cork: A History of the Outports of Passage West and Monkstown, 1754–1942* (Cork: Tower Books, 1986), p. 316.

11   D.J. Coakley, *The General Principles of Housing and Town Planning* (Cork: Cork County Borough Technical Instruction Committee, 1918), MP, UCC. See also Alfred O'Rahilly, Alfred, 'The Social Problem in Cork', *Studies*, vol. VI, no. 22, June 1917, pp. 177–88.

12   O'Brien, 'Population, Politics and Society in Cork', p. 717.

13   J.C. Saunders, *Annual Report of the Medical Officer of Health, 1935* (Cork: Guy & Co. Ltd, 1936).

14 Peter Karsten, 'Irish Soldiers in the British Army, 1792–1922', *Journal of Social History*, vol. 17, Autumn 1983, pp. 31–64.

15 Maura Cronin, *Country, Class, or Craft? The Politicisation of the Skilled Artisan in Nineteenth-Century Cork* (Cork: Cork University Press, 1994); Gerard O'Brien, 'Rebel Cork', in Jefferies, *Cork Historical Perspectives*, pp. 192–205

16 Cronin, *Country, Class, or Craft*, pp. 106–7, 154–5, 260; O'Brien, 'Population, Politics and Society in Cork', p. 715; R.V. Comerford, *The Fenians in Context: Irish Politics and Society, 1842–1882* (Dublin: Wolfhound Press, 1998), pp. 41–2, 158–9; Walter McGrath, 'The Fenian Rising in Cork', *Irish Sword*, 1968, vol. VIII, no. 33, pp. 245–54.

17 James Donnelly, *The Land and the People of Nineteenth-Century Cork: The Rural Economy and Land Question* (London: Routledge & Kegan Paul, 1975), pp. 257, 264–5, 270, 290; Maura Cronin, 'Parnellism and Workers: The Experience of Cork and Limerick', in Donal Ó Drisceoil and Fintan Lane, *Politics and the Irish Working Class, 1830–1945* (New York: Palgrave Macmillan, 2005), pp. 140–53.

18 Ex-Fenian councillors included William Kelleher, Jeffery Herlihy, Paddy Meade and C.P. O'Sullivan.

19 RIC County Inspector's Monthly Report for Cork City and East Riding (hereafter CI Report) for November 1910, CO 904/82; CI Report for November 1911, CO 904/85, *British in Ireland* (Microfilm), UCC. CO denotes Colonial Office and is the identification classification for the *British in Ireland* microfilm series. That CO classification was replaced by PRO (Public Record Office) and can be found in the Kew National Archives in London (hereafter TNA) simply by swapping CO for PRO and retaining the rest of the reference. For example, CO 904/82 can be found in TNA as PRO 904/82.

20 For details on O'Brien and the AFIL, see Maume, *The Long Gestation*, pp. 107–10, 142–6; Joseph O'Brien, *William O'Brien and the Course of Irish Politics, 1881–1918* (Berkeley: University of California Press, 1976), pp. 144, 184, 187, 192–211; Sally Warwick-Haller, *William O'Brien and the Irish Land War* (Dublin: Irish Academic Press, 1990), pp. 260–2.

21 O'Brien, *William O'Brien and the Course of Irish Politics*, p. 196; Maume, *The Long Gestation*, pp. 108–9.

22 O'Brien, *William O'Brien and the Course of Irish Politics*, pp. 192, 198–9; William O'Brien, *The Irish Revolution and How It Came About* (London: George Allen & Unwin Ltd, 1923), pp. 66–7; Maume, *The Long Gestation*, pp. 107–9; Reddick, 'Political and Industrial Labour in Cork', pp. 93, 144, 174–81; Dan Bradley, *Farm Labourers: Irish Struggle, 1900–1976* (Belfast: Athol Books, 1988), pp. 26–31; Liam de Róiste *Evening Echo* Series, 23 October 1954, 6 November 1954.

23 The AFIL branches were George's Quay, Northeast Ward, West Ward, Centre Ward, Douglas, Blackrock, Thomas Davis, Blarney Street and the '98 Club. See the 1913 *Guy's Directory*, Cork City Library.

24 CI Report for May 1910, CI Report for October 1910, December 1910, CO 904/82; CI Report for January 1911, CO 904/83; CI Report for January 1914, CO 904/102.

25 Susanne Day, *The Amazing Philanthropists* (London: Sidgwick & Jackson, 1916), pp. 30–1.

26 Maume, *The Long Gestation*, p. 144.

27 Ibid., p. 172.

28 O'Brien, *William O'Brien and the Course of Irish Politics*, p. 203, 207, 211, 213, 216, 222; Maume, *The Long Gestation*, pp. 142–4, 172; Warwick-Haller, *William O'Brien and the Irish Land War*, pp. 260–1.

29 *Cork Constitution*, 8 June 1914 (hereafter referred to as *CC*).

30 Maume, *The Long Gestation*, p. 142.

31 UIL National Directory Minute Books, MS 708, National Library of Ireland (NLI).

32 For some examples, see County Council motions of loyalty to John Redmond and the Irish Party on 4 October 1914, 4 June 1916 and 6 August 1916, AOH Cork

County Council Meeting Minutes, U389a/26, Cork City and County Archives (CCCA).

33 AOH Cork County Annual Convention Reports, 1914–1919, U389a/25, CCCA.

34 AOH Cork County Council Meeting Minutes, 11 August 1912.

35 AOH Cork County Council Meeting Minutes, 9 August 1914, U389a/26, CCCA; and Gerry White and Brendan O'Shea, *Baptised in Blood: The Formation of the Cork Brigade of the Irish Volunteers, 1913–1916* (Cork: Mercier Press, 2005), p. 70. See also WS 47, Seán Healy and Liam O'Callaghan; and WS 869, P.J. Murphy, NA.

36 AOH Cork County Annual Convention, 11 February 1917; AOH Cork County Council Meeting Minutes, 13 August 1911, 15 June, 5 July 1914, 4 February, 3 October, 5 December 1915, 6 February 1916; Draft Letter from County Secretary to a Member of the Commercial and Professional Division, 24 March 1919, AOH County Board Letter Book, U838a/7, CCCA. The latter communiqué was addressed to an unidentified Hibernian member of the Cork Harbour Commission, facing disciplinary action for 'not voting at the meeting of the Cork Harbour Commissioners as per whip sent you'.

37 AOH County Council Meeting Minutes, 13 August 1911, 5 July 1914, 4 February, 5 June, 3 October 1915.

38 AOH Cork County Council Meeting Minutes, 5 July 1914, 3 January 1915. See also the Cork County Council Meetings of 15 June 1914, 9 August 1914 and 7 November 1915; Eugene Gayer to Colonel Moore, 18 November 1914, MS 10,547 (6/III), NLI; Gerald Moloney (Middleton) to T.J. Hannah, 7 October 1914, MS 10,544 (2), NLI.

39 The Cork City Regiment of the National Volunteers were led by Maurice Talbot-Crosbie, George Crosbie, John J. Horgan (J.J.) and Harry Donegan. For a listing of officers, see the 1915 *Guy's Directory*; and J.J. Horgan's Contemporary Documents (CD) 67, Bureau of Military History, Cathal Brugha Barracks, Dublin.

40 Colonel Maurice Moore to Henry Donegan, 30 May 1917, MS 10,547 (6/I). Moore was quoting Donegan's comment in a prior letter to him.

41 *Cork Examiner*, 5 April 1915 (hereafter *CE*).

42 RIC Return for Arms, Period Ending 28 February 1917, CO 904/29.

43 1916 *Guy's Directory*; AOH Cork County Council Meeting Minutes, 15 June 1914, U389a/26, CCCA.

44 See Michael Wheatley, *Nationalism and the Irish Party: Provincial Ireland, 1910–1916* (Oxford: Oxford University Press, 2005), p. 251.

45 The list comes from *CE*, 13 March 1917, but it is probably not comprehensive. Those named are: Coroner J. Horgan; Coroner J. McCabe; Coroner Murphy; John Roynane; John Hoare; J. Doherty; Thomas Kelleher; D. McGrath; M. Kenneally, TC; M. O'Riordan; Jeremiah McEnery; Timothy Lyons, DI; R.H. Geary; Pierce Bradley; John O'Brien; Hugh Martin; R. Stack; J. Conway; and S. Mahony, TC. Of those listed the following were also AOH officers: Coroner Horgan; Coroner Murphy; John Roynane; George Crosbie; John Hoare; Thomas Kelleher; D McGrath; Jeremiah McEnery; R.H. Geary; J. Conway; S. Mahony; Henry Donegan.

46 The County Cork AOH 'Watch Committee' placed Hibernians into available jobs. On 15 June 1915, the AOH County Council ordered all public board vacancies to be filled with candidates selected by the local AOH division. See the AOH Cork County Council Meeting Minutes, CCCA.

47 James McConnell, '"Jobbing with Tory and Liberal": Irish Nationalists and the Politics of Patronage, 1880–1914', *Past and Present*, no. 188, August 2005, pp. 105–31.

48 J.J. Horgan, *From Parnell to Pearse: Some Recollections and Reflections* (Dublin: Richview Press, 1948), pp. 121–5; de Róiste *Evening Echo* Series, 16 September and 18 September 1918; and Liam Ruiséal, *Liam Ruiséal Remembers* (Cork: Tower Books, 1978), pp. 12–13.

49 John Redmond to M.J. Horgan (J.J.'s father), 16 December 1909 and John Redmond to J.J. Horgan, 19 June 1914, MS 18,270, NLI. See also Tom Garvin's brief discussion of Horgan's prescient political theorising, in *Nationalist Revolutionaries in Ireland, 1858–1928* (Dublin: Gill & Macmillan, 1987), p. 122.

50 For examples, see the *CE*, 24 October, 14–15, 19, 25–26, 28–30 November 1910, 16, 17 January 1914. See also the CI Report for May 1910, CO 904/81; CI report for October and November 1910, CO 904/82; CI Report for January 1911, CO 904/83.

51 Lynch, David, *Radical Politics in Modern Ireland: The Irish Socialist Republican Party, 1896–1904* (Dublin: Irish Academic Press, 2005), pp. 105, 108; Lane, Fintan, *The Origins of Modern Irish Socialism, 1881–1896* (Cork: Cork University Press, 1997), p. 221.

52 Cronin, 'Work and Workers in Cork City and County', pp. 699–720.

53 Reddick, 'Political and Industrial Labour in Cork', pp. 44, 62, 67–8, 90, 93, 99, 124–51.

54 Bradley, *Farm Labourers*, pp. 26–31; Maume, *The Long Gestation*, p. 107.

55 Francis Devine, 'Larkin and the ITGWU, 1909–1912', in Donal Nevin (ed.), *James Larkin: Lion of the Fold* (Dublin: Gill & Macmillan, 1998), pp. 30–7.

56 Emmet O'Connor, *James Larkin* (Cork: Cork University Press, 2002), pp. 19, 23.

57 RIC County Inspector's Report for Cork City and East Riding for April 1909, CO 904/77.

58 RIC County Inspector's Report for Cork City and East Riding for May 1909, CO 904/78; Devine, 'Larkin and the ITGWU', p. 31.

59 For some details of the strike, see *CE*, 11, 18, 19, 21, 22, 23 and 24 June 1909.

60 RIC CI Report for June 1909, CO 904/78.

61 O'Connor, *James Larkin*, p. 27; CI Report for July 1909, CO 904/78.

62 RIC CI Report for June 1909 and July 1909, CO 904/78.

63 CI Report for July 1909, CO 904/78; CI Report for September 1909, CO 904/79.

64 Devine, 'Larkin and the ITGWU', p. 33; O'Connor, *James Larkin*, pp. 28–9. The two Cork branch officials, Sullivan and Patrick Coveney, were acquitted.

65 CI Report for August 1909.

66 C. Desmond Greaves, *The Irish Transport and General Workers' Union: The Formative Years* (Dublin: Gill & Macmillan, 1982), pp. 38–43; Reddick, 'Political and Industrial Labour in Cork', pp. 9–10, 174–81, 186, 190–3.

67 O'Connor, *James Larkin*, p. 46.

68 Greaves, *The Irish Transport and General Workers' Union*, pp. 70–2; Reddick, 'Political and Industrial Labour in Cork', pp. 10, 215, 222, 225, 227, 240. See also Lahiff, 'Industry and Labour in Cork', pp. 169–72.

69 CI Report for December 1913, CO 904/91; RIC Inspector General's Report for November 1914, CO 904/94; WS 21, Joseph O'Shea; WS 47, Seán Healy and Liam O'Callaghan; WS 869, P.J. Murphy, NA.

70 Cork District Trades Council Meeting Minutes, 31 August, 14, 28 September, 12, 26 October 1916, U216 (Box 1), CCCA.

71 Using the 1911 Census figures, the 1916 *Guy's Directory* lists the city's religious makeup as follows: Catholic, 67,816; Church of Ireland, 6,576; Presbyterian, 912; Methodist, 643; Baptist, Congregationalists, Lutherans (combined total), 150; other Protestant (Salvation Army, Brethren and others), 101; Jewish Congregation, 340.

72 See the 1915 *Guy's Directory*, which includes Lapp's Asylum for Aged Protestants; the Great Coat Hospital (an Alms House); Home for Protestant Incurables; Women's National Health Association; Cork Grammar School; Young Men's Christian Association (YMCA); Church of Ireland Young Men's Association; and the Church of Ireland Boys' Brigade.

73 J.J. Horgan to Joseph Devlin, 2 March 1911, MS 18,271, NLI. They still held office in 1916.

74 Ian D'Alton, 'Keeping the Faith: An Evocation of the Cork Protestant Character, 1820–1920', in Cornelius Buttimer and Patrick O'Flanagan (eds), *Cork: History and Society. Interdisciplinary Essays on the History of an Irish County* (Dublin: Geography Publications, 1993), pp. 759–80.

75 Dan Williams, Henry Beale and Alderman Richard Beamish (the brewer) served as corporation councillors; some other unionists prominent in civic life were Sharman Crawford (chairman, County Technical Instruction Committee), Benjamin

Haughton (Cork Harbour Commission), Sir John Harley Scott (former lord mayor, Cork Harbour Commission), Charles Furlong (Cork Harbour Commission), John Dinan (Poor Law Guardians) and Canon A.J. Nicholson (Cork Technical Education Committee).

76 *CC*, 2 August 1917.
77 O'Brien, *The Irish Revolution and How It Came About*, pp. 66–7.
78 WS 24, Cornelius Murphy, NLI.
79 Patrick Maume, *'Life That is Exile': Daniel Corkery and the Search for Irish Ireland* (Belfast: Institute of Irish Studies, 1993), pp. 19–37; Michael J. O'Neill, *Lennox Robinson* (New York: Twayne Publishers, 1964), pp. 52–3; Daniel Corkery in P.S. O'Hegarty, *A Short Memoir of Terence MacSwiney* (Dublin: Talbot Press, 1922), pp. 22–7; Ruiséal, *Liam Ruiséal Remembers* pp. 12–14; Moirin Chavasse, *Terence MacSwiney* (Dublin: Clonmore & Reynolds, 1961), pp. 28–9; de Róiste *Evening Echo* Series, 18 September 1954; 'T.C. Murray, 1873–1959', Pamphlet (Macroom: T.C. Murray Commemorative Group, 1974), UCC; 'The Last Warrior of Coole', Programme, 1955-111 (A-E), Terence MacSwiney Collection, Cork Public Museum. Mary MacSwiney played in the theatre orchestra.
80 *CC*, 18 January 1913; 1916 *Guy's Directory*; Neal Garnham, *Association Football and Society in Pre-Partition Ireland* (Belfast: Ulster Historical Foundation, 2004), p. 44. The cricket clubs were the Cork City Cricket Club, Cork Bohemians Cricket Club and Doneraile Cricket Club; and the rugby clubs were Dolphin, Constitution and Shannon, which all still exist today. Soccer was primarily a military game, with twelve of sixteen teams in the Munster Division being army or navy unit teams. Additional information courtesy of David Toms.
81 John P. Power, *A Story of Champions* (Cork: Lee Press, 1941), pp. 91–6; J.J. Walsh, *Recollections of a Rebel* (Tralee: Kerryman, 1944), pp. 16–19; Marcus de Burca, *The GAA: A History* (Dublin: Cumann Luthchleas Gael, 1980), pp. 87, 111, 123; Minute Book of the Reform Committee, Cork GAA County Board (1904), de Róiste Papers, 10539/268, Trinity College Dublin.
82 *CE*, 17 January 1914; de Róiste *Evening Echo* Series, 6 November 1954; Walsh, pp. 28–9.
83 War of Independence IRA battalion commanders Dan 'Sandow' O'Donovan, Mick Murphy and Connie Neenan were noted GAA players.
84 This echoes tensions identified in William Murphy's article, 'The GAA in the Irish Revolution, 1913–1923', in Mike Cronin, William Murphy and Paul Roose (eds), *The Gaelic Athletic Association, 1884–2004* (Dublin: Irish Academic Press, 2009), pp. 61–76.
85 De Róiste *Evening Echo* Series, 19 August 1954.
86 The teachers were Seán Conlon, Denis Breen, Dan Harrington, Daniel Corkery and Edward Sheehan (all national teachers) and later Cork Technical Education and Instruction Committee instructors Donal Óg O'Callaghan, Liam de Róiste and Terry MacSwiney.
87 Ruiséal, *Liam Ruiséal Remembers*, p. 10; WS 16, Robert Langford; WS 25, Pat Higgins; de Róiste *Evening Echo* Series, 11 September 1954, 18 September 1954, 2 October 1954, 7 October 1954, 16 October 1954; Daniel Corkery, 'Terence MacSwiney: Lord Mayor of Cork', *Studies*, vol. IX, no. 36, December 1920, pp. 512–20; Maume, *'Life That is Exile'*, p. 23. The 1913 *Guy's Directory* lists nine Gaelic League branches in Cork city.
88 A similar political controversy broke out in 1911, when Catholic clergy protested at James Connolly's lecture on socialism held at An Dún, but the priests 'were thrown out', reported Pat Higgins. 'Even the mildest Gaelic Leaguer would not have it.' See WS 25, Pat Higgins; WS 89, Micheál Ó Cuill.
89 De Róiste *Evening Echo* Series, 7 October 1954, 16 October 1954; WS 16, Robert Langford; WS 21, Joseph O'Shea; WS 25, Pat Higgins; WS 89, Micheál Ó Cuill; WS 869, P.J. Murphy; Florence O'Donoghue, *Tomás MacCurtain: Soldier and Patriot* (Tralee: Anvil Press, 1971), p. 20.

90 BMH WS 16, Riobard Langford.

91 WS 16, Robert Langford; WS 21, Joseph O'Shea; WS 89, Micheál Ó Cuill.

92 WS 21, Joseph O'Shea; WS 47, Seán Healy and Liam O'Callaghan; WS 89, Micheál Ó Cuill; WS 869, P.J. Murphy; de Róiste *Evening Echo* Series, 30 October 1954. Other IRB organisers involved were Donal Óg O'Callaghan, Seán O'Sullivan and Martin Donovan. O'Sullivan was especially prominent. Robert Langford was also active in the Fianna, prior to his joining the IRB.

93 For an excellent discussion of the movement, see Marnie Hay, 'The Foundation and Development of Na Fianna Éireann, 1909–1916', *Irish Historical Studies*, vol. XXXVI, no. 141, May 2008, pp. 53–71.

94 WS 739, Felix O'Doherty; O'Donoghue, *Tomás MacCurtain*, p. 25.

95 For details on the Irish scouting movement of this period, see Johnny Conn, 'The Dublin Battalion of the Church Lads' Brigade', pp. 70–3 and 'A Note on the History and Martial Attributes of the Boys' Brigade', pp. 66–9, *Irish Sword*, vol. XXVI, Winter 2006.

96 WS 21, Joseph O'Shea; WS 47, Seán Healy and Liam O'Callaghan; WS 739, Felix O'Doherty; O'Donoghue, *Tomás MacCurtain*, pp. 24–5.

97 For examples see Tadhg O'Sullivan, Seán Healy, Liam O'Callaghan, Dick Murphy, Jeremiah Mullane, Seamus Courtney and Walter Furlong. O'Sullivan and Mullane were both killed by police in 1921, while Courtney died of illness after a 1918 jail term. Walter Furlong became lord mayor of Cork in 1951.

98 De Róiste *Evening Echo* Series, 21 August 1954; Terence Denman, '"The Red Livery of Shame": The Campaign Against Army Recruitment in Ireland, 1899–1914', *Irish Historical Studies*, vol. 29, November 1994, pp. 208–333; *CE*, 12 November 1899. The Cork meeting was attended by Lord Mayor J.C. Flynn, MP; E. Crean, MP; five city councillors; Maude Gonne; Arthur Griffith; and six marching bands. For further discussion of the Irish Transvaal Committee, see Keith Jeffery, 'The Irish Military Tradition in the British Empire', in Keith Jeffery (ed.), *An Irish Empire? Aspects of Ireland and the British Empire* (Manchester: Manchester University Press, 1996), pp. 95–7.

99 WS 1, Tom Barry; de Róiste *Evening Echo* Series, 19 August 1914, 14 October 1954; P.S. O'Hegarty, *A Short Memoir of Terence MacSwiney* (Dublin: Talbot Press, 1922), pp. 14–15; Maume, *'Life That is Exile'*, p. 24.

100 Orlaith Mannion, '"Silent but Eloquent Reminders": The Nationalist Monuments in Cork and Skibbereen', in Laurence Geary, *Rebellion and Remembrance in Modern Ireland* (Dublin: Four Courts Press, 2001), pp. 185–95.

101 Horgan, *From Parnell to Pearse*, p. 121.

102 De Róiste *Evening Echo* Series, 26 August 1954, 28 August 1954; O'Donoghue, *Tomás MacCurtain*, p. 18; P.S. O'Hegarty, *A Short Memoir of Terence MacSwiney*, pp. 16–17; Chavasse, *Terence MacSwiney*, pp. 22–7.

103 WS 869, P.J. Murphy, NLI; Pauline Healy to Etienette Beauque, 21 January 1928, Papers of Terence MacSwiney's Biographers, P48c/60, University College Dublin (UCD) Archives; Antoin O'Callaghan, *Of Timber, Iron and Stone: A Journey Through Time on the Bridges of Cork* (Ballinhassig: Inversnaid Publications, 1991), pp. 39–41; Chavasse, *Terence MacSwiney*, p. 24. The society mainly persuaded the corporation to post Irish translations of Cork streets and rename Wellington and George IV bridges after Thomas Davis and Peter O'Neill Crowley (a local Fenian hero).

104 De Róiste *Evening Echo* Series, 25 November 1954; O'Donoghue, *Tomás MacCurtain*, p. 18.

105 *Report of the Royal Commission on the Rebellion in Ireland*, p. 111.

106 De Róiste *Evening Echo* Series, 16 September 1954; Horgan, *From Parnell to Pearse*, pp. 121–4; Seán Ó Cuiv to Etienette Beauque, 24 August 1928, P48c/106/54, UCD Archives; E.J. Riordan, *Modern Irish Trade and Industry* (London: Methuen & Co., 1921), pp. 265–7; Maume, *The Long Gestation*, pp. 58–9; Cork Industrial Development Association (IDA), 1913 Annual Meeting, MP 582, UCC; Cork IDA

1914 Annual Meeting, MP 578; Cork IDA 1915 Annual Meeting, MP 581; Cork IDA 1916 Annual Meeting, MP 352; Cork IDA 1917 Annual Meeting, MP 353A; 1905 Cork Industrial Exhibit Programme, MP 717; 1910 All Ireland Industrial Conference, MP 417; 1905 All Ireland Industrial Conference, MP 732; 1908 Directory of Irish Manufacturers (Published by Cork IDA), MP 105.

107   De Róiste *Evening Echo* Series, 16 September 1954; 1905 Cork Industrial Exhibit Programme, MP 717, UCC.

108   Horgan, *From Parnell to Pearse*, p. 122. See also the de Róiste *Evening Echo* Series, 16 September 1954.

109   1910 All Ireland Industrial Conference Proceedings, MP 417, UCC.

110   Riordan, *Modern Irish Trade and Industry*, pp. 275–279; Horgan, *From Parnell to Pearse*, p. 123; de Róiste *Evening Echo* Series, 16 September 1954.

111   1905 Cork Industrial Exhibition Programme, MP 717, UCC; CI Report for November 1912, CO 904/88.

112   1905 Cork Industrial Exhibit Programme, MP 717; Cork IDA 1917 Annual Meeting, MP 353A.

113   Cork IDA 1913 Annual Meeting, MP 582; Cork IDA 1917 Annual Meeting, MP 353A.

114   Cork IDA 1916 Annual Meeting, MP 352; Cork IDA 1917 Annual Meeting. The latter report lists queries from Great Britain, Scandinavia, France, Spain, Italy, Switzerland, Egypt, India, New Zealand, Australia, South Africa, Japan and North and South America.

115   J.L. Fawsitt, 'New Industries for a Greater Cork', *Studies*, vol. VI, no. 23, September 1917, pp. 462–9; RIC Inspector General's Report for January 1917, CO 904/102; Cork IDA 1916 Annual Meeting.

116   RIC Inspector General's Report for January 1917, CO 904/102; de Róiste Diary, 19 September 1919, 8 November 1919, 2 December 1919. For details of the negotiations see the Cork Harbour Commission Meeting Minutes, 20 November 1916, PCA (hereafter referred to as CHCMM).

117   CHCMM 8, 15 January 1919, 5 January 1920; *CE*, 16, 17 October 1919; de Róiste Diary, 29 November 1919, 3 January 1920.

118   Garvin, *Nationalist Revolutionaries in Ireland*, pp. 123–7, 133–8. Garvin's analysis on pre-Revolutionary Sinn Féin's economic outlook largely neglects the industrial revival movement.

119   See Mary E. Daly, *Industrial Development and the Irish National Identity, 1922–1939* (Syracuse: Syracuse University Press, 1992), p. 6.

120   WS 26, P.S. O'Hegarty. The old-time Fenian and GAA leader P.N. Fitzgerald headed the Cork city circle.

121   WS 26, P.S. O'Hegarty; WS 89, Micheál Ó Cuill; WS 16, Robert Langford; WS 1, Tom Barry [Tom Barry, Cork city, rather than the west Cork flying column commander].

122   WS 26, P.S. O'Hegarty; and WS 4, Diarmuid Lynch. Early IRB members included Sinn Féin and GAA leader Tadhg Barry; IDA secretary and AOH American Alliance member Diarmuid (J.L.) Fawsitt; and Gaelic League teacher and branch president Donal Óg O'Callaghan. According to Pat Higgins, 'A small number of people were responsible for the separatist activities, including the Gaelic League, AOH American, IDA, Fianna, Inghinidhe na hÉireann. The main movers were Martin Donovan, Tomás MacCurtain, Seán O'Hegarty, Micheál Ó Cuill. They were all in the O'Growney Branch.' They were also all in the IRB. See WS 25, Pat Higgins.

123   Referencing his 1947 interview with John Good mentioned below, Florrie O'Donoghue wrote, 'This bears out Seán and P.S. O'Hegarty in their statements that this group was allowed to carry on at the same time that new circles of younger men were being organised without their knowledge.' See O'Donoghue's BMH Diary, 1947–8, 15 December 1947 Entry, MS 31,555 (2), NLI.

124   Ibid. The IRB veteran was republican labour leader John Good. City Alderman Paddy Meade seems to have been another member of the Old IRB and was likewise

unaware of the younger members of the Brotherhood. See the Liam de Róiste Diary, 2 December 1918.

125 WS 89, Micheál Ó Cuill; WS 16, Robert Langford; WS 24, Cornelius Murphy; WS 25, Pat Higgins.

126 WS 89, Micheál Ó Cuill.

127 Florence O'Donoghue, Notes on a Manuscript Draft of Moiron Chavasse's *Terence MacSwiney*, circa 1954, p. 4, MS 31,282 (2), NLI.

128 WS 16, Robert Langford; WS 24, Cornelius Murphy; WS 25, Pat Higgins; WS 77, Harry Lorton; WS 89, Micheál Ó Cuill; RIC CI Report for July 1911, CO 904/84; CI Report for January 1916, CO 904/100; Precis of Information, April 1915, RIC Crime Special Branch, CO 904/120.

129 WS 16, Robert Langford; Terence Denman, '"The Red Livery of Shame"'.

130 *CE*, 8–10 June 1911; WS 79, Diarmuid Ó Donneabhain; CI Report for April 1911, CO 904/83; CI Reports for May and June 1911; CI Report for July 1911, CO 904/84.

131 *CE*, 9, 10 June 1911; WS 79, Diarmuid Ó Donneabhain; WS 89, Micheál Ó Cuill; O'Donoghue, *Tomás MacCurtain*, p. 24.

132 Statement of Captain [Thomas] O'Donovan, MS 31,369, NLI; *Southern Star*, 21 August 1909; *Irish Independent* (hereafter *II*) 19, 21 August 1909; RIC Inspector General's Report for August 1909, CO 904/98; Hansard, HC Debates, 31 August 1909, vol. 10, c. 182.

133 Richard Davis, *Arthur Griffith and Non-Violent Sinn Féin* (Dublin: Anvil Books, 1974), pp. 17–18, 82–3. Three of the six county branches were in good standing and membership totalled thirty-nine members.

134 Liam de Róiste *Evening Echo* Series, 23 October 1954; O'Donoghue, *Tomás MacCurtain*, p. 21; Davis, *Arthur Griffith and Non-Violent Sinn Féin*, pp. 61–2; Report of Sergeant A. Young, 4 April 1910; Memorandum on Information Provided to the Secretary, General Post Office, 25 August 1914, CO 904/212/351, Colonial Office Records Series, Volume I; 'Sinn Féin and Republican Suspects', Dublin Castle Special Branch Files, Eneclann Ltd., Dublin, 2006 (hereafter 'Sinn Féin and Republican Suspects').

135 De Róiste *Evening Echo* Series, 21 October 1954.

136 Frank Callanan, *T.M. Healy* (Cork: Cork University Press, 1996), p. 465; Richard Davis, *Arthur Griffith* (Dundalk: Dublin Historical Association, 1976), p. 15.

137 O'Donoghue, *Tomás MacCurtain*, pp. 21–2.

138 Ibid., p. 22; Michael Laffan, *The Resurrection of Ireland: The Sinn Féin Party, 1916–1923* (Cambridge: Cambridge University Press, 1999), pp. 31–2; de Róiste *Evening Echo* Series, 6 November 1954; CI Report for August 1913, CO 904/90; CI Report for September 1914; CI Report for November 1914, CO 904/94; CI Report for November 1915, CO 904/98.

139 For an insightful discussion of the Belfast separatist community, see Marnie Hay, *Bulmer Hobson and the Nationalist Movement in Twentieth-Century Ireland* (Manchester: Manchester University Press, 2009), pp. 23–45.

140 The North Mon alumni included MacCurtain, Terence and Seán MacSwiney, Seán and P.H. O'Hegarty, Tadhg Barry and Donal Óg O'Callaghan.

141 Only two members of faculty joined the separatist community before 1916: Alfred O'Rahilly and literature lecturer W.F. Stockley. Both were late arrivals to the Cork group.

142 Ruiséal, *Liam Ruiséal Remembers*, p. 14.

143 David Fitzpatrick, *Harry Boland's Irish Revolution* (Cork: Cork University Press, 2003), pp. 128, 206.

144 Borgonovo, *Florence and Josephine O'Donoghue's War of Independence*, p. 64.

145 Among other possibilities were Donal Óg O'Callaghan and Tadhg Barry. Donal Óg was quarrelsome, indiscreet and performed poorly in the 1920–1 period. Tadhg Barry was a socialist whose revolutionary career was dogged by sheer bad luck.

146 Thomas O'Donovan to Florrie O'Donoghue, Undated Statement, MS 31,369, NLI.

147 White and O'Shea, *Baptised in Blood*, pp. 16–26; O'Donoghue, *Tomás MacCurtain*, pp. 26–8; WS 15, Fred Murray; WS 16, Robert Langford; WS 19, Liam Murphy; WS 24, Cornelius Murphy; WS 25, Pat Higgins; WS 77, Harry Lorton; WS 89, Micheál Ó Cuill; WS 91, J.J. Walsh; de Róiste *Evening Echo* Series, 4 November 1954.

148 O'Donoghue, *Tomás MacCurtain*, pp. 26–8; Walsh, *Recollections of a Rebel*, pp. 22–4; O'Hegarty, *A Short Memoir of Terence MacSwiney*, pp. 44–6; de Róiste *Evening Echo* Series, 4 November 1954; Robert Langford Statement, U156/2, CCCA; Ruiséal, *Liam Ruiséal Remembers*, p. 16; Frank Gallagher, *Four Glorious Years* (Dublin: Blackwater Press, 2005), pp. 219–22.

149 Walsh, *Recollections of a Rebel*, p. 24

150 This membership list contains occupations for only about 200 of the 1,400 listed members, with city officers only recording that information after June 1914.

151 AOH Cork County Council Meeting Minutes, 15 June 1914, 5 July 1914, U389a/26, CCCA.

152 AOH Cork County Council Meeting Minutes, 5 July 1914.

153 WS 25, Pat Higgins; de Róiste *Evening Echo* Series, 13 November 1954; Cork City Regiment Irish Volunteers Roster, U/271A, CCCA. Florrie O'Donoghue numbered the county Volunteers at 6,000 in *Tomás MacCurtain*, p. 34.

154 White and O'Shea, *Baptised in Blood*, pp. 36–40; O'Donoghue, *Tomás MacCurtain*, pp. 33–7.

Chapter II: Cork and the First World War, 1914 to Easter 1916

1 *Fianna Fáil*, 19 September 1914.

2 *CE*, 5, 6 August 1914. Stone-throwing erupted after police made bayonet and baton charges to keep back the throng.

3 *CE*, 3 September 1914. O'Brien later claimed over 500 city men enlisted in the British Army in the two weeks following the meeting. See the *Cork Free Press*, 6 January 1915. Despite the extraordinary events, the Irish Party refused to share the recruiting platform with their AFIL enemies. See Report for September 1914, CO 904/94; *CC*, 3 September 1914.

4 Hansard, HC Debates, 03 August 1914, vol. 65, cc 1829.

5 Hansard, HC Debates, 10 August 1914, vol. 65, cc 2264–5; *The The Irish Times*, 22 August 1914.

6 Dated 17 August 1914, Liam de Róiste Papers, 10539/524, Trinity College Dublin; *The Irish Times*, 29 July 1914.

7 CI Report for Cork City and East Riding, August 1914, CO 904/94.

8 Gerry White and Brendan O'Shea, *Baptised in Blood: The Formation of the Cork Brigade of the Irish Volunteers, 1913–1916* (Cork: Mercier Press, 2005), pp. 45–53.

9 Ibid., pp. 50–5.

10 Cork City Regiment, Irish National Volunteers Fundraising Circular, 30 November 1914, Contemporary Documents (CD) 67, John J. Horgan, Bureau of Military History, Cathal Brugha Barracks.

11 *CE*, 6 August 1914.

12 Ibid., 1 September 1914.

13 Ibid., 2 September 1914.

14 Ibid., 19 October 1914.

15 AOH Cork County Council Meeting Minutes, 4 October 1914.

16 *Cork Free Press*, 13 January 1915.

17 Ibid., 3 March 1915.

18 John Horne (ed.), *State, Society and Mobilisation in Europe during the First World War* (Cambridge: Cambridge University Press, 1997, p. 7.

19 RIC 1915 Intelligence Notes, PRO 903/19/1, TNA, London; CI Report for June 1915, CO 904/96.

20 *CE*, 21 October 1914, 26 May, 1 June 1915.

21   CI Report for November 1914, CO 904/95; CI Report for November 1915; RIC Crime Special Branch Report for March 1915 and July 1915.
22   CI Report for September 1914, CO 904/94.
23   Report of Constable Michael P. O'Sullivan, 22 October 1914, CO 904/206/233B, Jim Larkin, *Sinn Féin and Republican Suspects*.
24   WS 21, Joseph O'Shea; Robert Langford's Draft BMH Statement, U156/3, CCCA.
25   WS 24, Cornelius Murphy.
26   'History of the Irish Volunteers in County Cork to 1916', by Florence O'Donoghue, MS 31,437, NLI.
27   General Post Office Director Arthur Norway to Undersecretary Nathan, 12 November 1914, CO 904/212/351, T. O'Neill, *Sinn Féin and Republican Suspects*.
28   *CE*, 31 October 1914.
29   *II*, 26 December 1914; *Freeman's Journal*, 4 January 1915.
30   *Freeman's Journal*, 9 January 1915; *II*, 9 January 1915. Five councillors opposed to the motion discreetly exited the chambers to avoid recording their vote. Four of the five were AFIL councillors. See also Daniel Corkery, 'Professor W.F.P. Stockley, 1859–1943', *Capuchin Annual*, 1948.
31   Captain R.E. Roberts to Colonel Moore, 5 February 1915, MS 10,547 (6/I), NLI; *CC*, 23 January 1915, 3 February 1915; *Cork Free Press*, 6, 7 January 1915. Only sixteen of the fifty-six councillors attended the freedom of the city vote, with the majority remaining outside the chamber to avoid stating their preference one way or another.
32   *Cork Free Press*, 5 March 1915.
33   *CE*, 18 March 1915; *Cork Free Press*, 18 March 1915.
34   Martin Staunton, 'The Royal Munster Fusiliers in the Great War', MA thesis, UCD, 1986, Appendix III.
35   Statement Giving Particulars of Men of Military Age in Ireland, 1916, HC XVII.581, CD 8390.
36   Keith Jeffery, *Ireland and the First World War* (Cambridge: Cambridge University Press, 2000), pp. 18–19; P.E. Dewey, 'Military Recruiting and the British Labour Force During the First World War', *Historical Journal*, no. 27 (1984), pp. 199–223; Staunton, 'The Royal Munster Fusiliers'; Thomas Hennessey, *Dividing Ireland: World War One and Partition* (London: Routledge, 1998), pp. 97–103; Patrick J. Casey, 'Irish Casualties in the First World War', *Irish Sword*, no. 20 (Summer 1997), pp. 193–206; Terence Denman, '"The Red Livery of Shame": The Campaign Against Army Recruitment in Ireland, 1899–1914', *Irish Historical Studies*, vol. 29, November 1994, pp. 208–33; Terence Denman, 'Sir Lawrence Parsons and the Raising of the 16th (Irish) Division, 1914–1915, *Irish Sword*, Winter 1987, vol. XVII, pp. 90–104; Fitzpatrick, David, 'The Logic of Collective Sacrifice: Ireland and the British Army, 1914–1918', *Historical Journal*, no. 38, December 1995, pp. 1017–30; Peter Murray, 'The First World War and a Dublin Distillery Workforce: Recruiting and Redundancy at John Power and Son, 1915–1917', *Saothar*, no. 15 (1990), pp. 128–37.
37   *Cork Free Press*, 17 March 1915.
38   *CE*, 28 October 1915.
39   'Report on the Administration of the National Relief Fund up to 30 September 1916', Command Papers, Reports of Commissioners, CD 8449, 8621, 8290, vol. XVII, 753, 793, 802, 20th Century House Sessional Papers. The breakdown was 541 wives, 1,441 children and 1,152 widows' dependents (dependents of killed servicemen).
40   See Table 2.4.
41   For examples, see the *CE*, 11–17 May 1915.
42   Ibid., 11, 13–15 May 1915.
43   Ibid., 11 May 1915.
44   Francis Costello, *Enduring the Most: The Life and Death of Terence MacSwiney* (Dingle: Brandon Books, 1995), pp. 51–4.
45   White and O'Shea, *Baptised in Blood*, pp. 56, 66.

46   John Borgonovo (ed.), *Florence and Josephine O'Donoghue's War of Independence* (Dublin: Irish Academic Press, 2006), p. 16.

47   Terence Dooley attributes the surges in nationalist enlistments during 1915 to these campaigns. See Dooley, 'Politics, Bands, and Marketing: Army Recruiting in Waterford City, 1914–1915', *Irish Sword*, no. 28, Winter 1991, pp. 206–19.

48   Borgonovo, *Florence and Josephine O'Donoghue's War of Independence*, p. 16.

49   *CC*, 15 March 1915.

50   *CE*, 13 May 1915.

51   *Cork Free Press*, 22 March 1915. Moore was Professor of Pathology at UCC from 1909 to 1940.

52   See James McConnell, 'Recruiting Sergeants for John Bull? Irish Nationalist MPs and Enlistment during the Early Months of the Great War', *War in History*, no. 14, 2007, pp. 408–29. For a discussion of British First World War propaganda's emphasis on German sexual violence, see Nuala Johnson, *Ireland, the Great War and the Geography of Remembrance* (Cambridge: Cambridge University Press, 2003), pp. 28–31; Nicolletta Gullace, 'Sexual Violence and Family Honor: British Propaganda and International Law During the First World War', *American Historical Review*, June 1997, pp. 714–47; Edward Demm, 'Propaganda and Caricature in the First World War', *Journal of Contemporary History*, vol. 28, no. 2, 1993, pp. 163–92; Lucy Noakes, 'Gender, War and Memory: Discourse and Experience in History', *Journal of Contemporary History*, vol. 36, no. 4, 2001, pp. 663–72; Ruth Harris, '"The Child of the Barbarian": Rape, Race and Nationalism in France During the First World War', *Past and Present*, no. 141, November 1993, pp. 170–206; M.L. Sanders and Philip Taylor, *British Propaganda During the First World War* (London: Macmillan, 1982), pp. 142–4. See also John Horne and Alan Kramer, 'German "Atrocities" and Franco-German Opinion, 1914: The Evidence of German Soldiers' Diaries', *Journal of Modern History*, no. 66, 1994, pp. 1–33; and *German Atrocities 1914: A History of Denial* (New Haven and London: Yale University Press, 2001).

53   *CC*, 19 August 1915. Giusani was killed in combat the following year. See the *CE*, 23 November 1916.

54   *CC*, 19 August 1915.

55   *Cork Free Press*, 18 February 1915. See also Johnson, *Ireland, the Great War and the Geography of Remembrance*, pp. 51–2.

56   *CE*, 27 October 1915.

57   *CC*, 6 March 1916.

58   *The Irish Times*, 6 December 1915.

59   Ibid., 15 March 1915.

60   *Cork Free Press*, 15 March 1915.

61   *CC*, 19 August 1915.

62   *The Irish Times*, 7 December 1915; *CC*, 7 December 1915. If belligerence is an indicator, Kettle may have been drunk. For further details about this period of Kettle's career, see Senia Paseta's *Thomas Kettle* (Dublin: UCD Press, 2008), pp. 81–7.

63   See RIC CI Reports for August 1914 to December 1915, CO 904/94–8; and Precis of RIC Crime Special Branch Reports, August 1914 to December 1915, CO 904/120.

64   McConnell, 'Recruiting Sergeants for John Bull'. See also Michael Wheatley, *Nationalism and the Irish Party: Provincial Ireland, 1910–1916* (Oxford: Oxford University Press, 2005), p. 215; and Hennessey, *Dividing Ireland*, pp. 99–103. For a contrary view of the Irish Party, see John Ellis, 'The Degenerate and the Martyr: Nationalist Propaganda and the Contestation of Irishness, 1914–1918', *Éire-Ireland*, vol. XXXV, 2000–2001, pp. 7–33.

65   *CC*, 3 September 1914, 15, 22, 25 March, 10 April, 13 May, 19 August, 6, 7 December 1915, 3 January, 6 March 1916; *CE*, 12 April, 31 May 1915.

66   Henry Donegan to Moore, 25 February 1915, MS 10,547 (6/I). For a committee list, see the *Cork Free Press*, 17 March 1915; *CC*, 5 March, 1, 8 April, 13 May 1915; and *CE*, 5 March 1915. Lord Mayor Sir Henry O'Shea only attended the first meeting.

67   J.J. Horgan to John Dillon, 30 March 1915, John Dillon Papers, 6772/269, Trinity College Dublin (TCD) Archives. Horgan wrote, 'I told the rather stupid English recruiting officer here that O'Leary might be worth 200 recruiting sergeants if they brought him home.'

68   *CC*, 13 April 1915. This quotation differs from Frank Gallagher's in *The Four Glorious Years* (Dublin: Blackwater Press, 2005), p. 43.

69   Henry Donegan to Moore, 25 February 1915, MS 10,547 (6/I), NLI.

70   The officers who served in the British Army were: Maurice Talbot-Crosbie, John O'Brien, Michael O'Callaghan, W. Perry and R.E. Roberts. Roberts was a reservist recalled to service. The listed NV officers are: J. Smith-Sheehan; Henry Donegan; C.J. Flynn; George Devlin; J.J. Horgan; M. O'Callaghan; T. McGrath; T. Hogan; W. Perry; J. Keating; T. Byrne; M. Hill; George Hutchinson; P.J. Egan; Barry Egan; J.W. Skuce; W.T. Daunt; George Murphy; J. O'Connell; M. Bulmer; F.J. O'Riordan; C.P. Murphy; F. Cotter; Jeremiah Riordan; Maurice Talbot-Crosbie; R.E. Roberts; John O'Brien. There were also numerous other Redmondites serving in administrative functions for the NV (branch treasurers and secretaries) who likewise did not enlist. See the 1915 and 1916 *Guy's Directory*.

71   Tadhg Barry to Liam de Róiste, 24 November 1918, U271/C/15, CCCA.

72   *CC*, 19 August 1915.

73   *Dictionary of Irish Biography, vol. VIII* (Cambridge: Cambridge University Press, 2009). The third son became a general in the British Army.

74   *Southern Star*, 20 February 1915.

75   *CE*, 14 August 1914.

76   *Cork Free Press*, 3 September 1914; *CE*, 19 August 1915. At the City Hall recruiting meeting of 1 September 1914, Dowse attended, along with Rev. A.E. French (CI Rector, Passage West) and Rev. R.H. Broughman (CI Minister, Ross Cathedral).

77   *CC*, 11 August 1914.

78   For examples, see *CC*, 11 August 1914, 5 August 1916, 7 January 1918.

79   For a discussion of voluntary war work see Margaret Downs, 'The Civilian Aid Effort', in David Fitzpatrick, (ed.), *Ireland and the First World War* (Dublin: Trinity History Workshop, 1986), pp. 37–47; and Eileen Reilly, 'Women and Voluntary War Work', in Adrian Gregory and Senia Paseta (eds), *Ireland and the Great War: A War to Unite Us All?* (Manchester: Manchester University Press, 2002), pp. 49–72.

80   *CE*, 12, 21, 25 August 1914.

81   *CC*, 29 March, 9 April 1915, 23 October, 7 December 1916, 12 April 1917, 10 May 1919; *CE*, 30 October 1914; *Cork Free Press*, 15 January 1915.

82   *CC*, 14 November 1916, 21 February, 14 April 1917, 2, 18 January 1918; *CE*, 4 December 1915.

83   *CE*, 26 October 1914; RIC Crime Special Branch Report, June 1915, CO 904/97.

84   *CE*, 31 October 1914.

85   For additional information, see Maume, *The Long Gestation*, pp. 73–9, 147–9; Joseph Finman, '"Let Irishmen Come Together in the Trenches": John Redmond and the Irish Party Policy in the Great War, 1914–1918', *Irish Sword*, no. 22, Winter 2000; Hennessey, *Dividing Ireland*, pp. 73–80; J.J. Lee, *Ireland 1912–1985: Politics and Society* (Cambridge: Cambridge University Press, 1989), pp. 21–2; David Fitzpatrick, *The Two Irelands* (Oxford: Oxford University Press, 1998), pp. 51–4.

86   Boyce, in Paseta and Gregory, *Ireland and the Great War*, p. 191.

87   The Irish Volunteers split at the end of August, but the National Volunteers did not form until a few weeks later.

88   *CE*, 11, 14, 15 August 1914. David Fitzpatrick reports similar unionist support of the National Volunteers in Clare during the war's first weeks. See *Politics and Irish Life* (Dublin: Gill & Macmillan, 1977), pp. 53–4.

89   Philip Harold Barry to Colonel Moore, 15 May 1915; Colonel James Grove-White to Colonel Moore, 15 August 1914; Talbot-Crosbie to Moore, 13 August 1914, 20 August 1914, MS 10,547 (6/II), NLI.

90   Maurice Talbot-Crosbie to Colonel Moore, 7 September 1914, MS 10,550; Henry Donegan to Fitzroy-Hemphill, 26 October 1914, MS 10,547 (6/I).

91   R.E. Roberts to Colonel Moore, 10 October 1914, MS 10,547 (6/III).

92   Timothy Bowman, *Carson's Army: The Ulster Volunteer Force, 1910–1922* (Manchester: Manchester University Press, 2007), pp. 47–8, 51. Bowman shows more egalitarian leadership in urban UVF units.

93   *CE*, 13 October 1914.

94   *II*, 14 September 1914.

95   White and O'Shea, *Baptised in Blood*, p. 70; CI Report for November 1914, CO 904/95.

96   RIC 1915 Intelligence Notes, PRO 903/19/1, TNA. The total was 2,256. David Fitzpatrick gives the ratio of Irish Catholic recruits with prior Volunteer service at 1:3. See Fitzpatrick, 'The Logic of Collective Sacrifice', pp. 1027–9.

97   CI Report for November 1914, 904/5; Fitzpatrick, 'The Logic of Collective Sacrifice', pp. 1028–9. Fitzpatrick puts the national enlistment percentage for the National Volunteers at 17 per cent and the Munster percentage as 13.6 per cent.

98   In a 1914 fundraising circular the Cork City Regiment, NV claimed 200 members enlisted, but that number seems seriously inflated and probably accounted for called-up reservists. As Daunt mentioned in his second letter to the editor (*CC*, 30 March 1915), reservists should not be included in the enlistment total since they left Cork prior to the establishment of the NV. See the Cork City Regiment, Irish National Volunteers Fundraising Circular, 30 November 1914, BMH CD 67, J.J. Horgan, Cathal Brugha Barracks, Dublin.

99   *CE*, 27 March 1915; *CC*, 30 March 1915. Daunt claimed they had 300 reliable members.

100 See *CC*, 29, 30 March 1915.

101 *CC*, 30 March 1915.

102 *CE*, 23 October 1914.

103 White and O'Shea, *Baptised in Blood*, pp. 77–9; *Cork Free Press*, 13, 16 January 1915.

104 J.J. Horgan and Eugene Gayer to T.A. Howe, RIC County Inspector, 12 December 1914; Henry Donegan to Colonel Moore, 31 December 1914; MS 10,547 (6/III), NLI.

105 For an exchange of letters between the military and NV, see the *Southern Star*, 13 February 1915.

106 Horgan, *From Parnell to Pearse*, p. 268–9, cited in White and O'Shea, *Baptised in Blood*, p. 78.

107 Henry Donegan to Moore, 25 February 1915, MS 10,547 (6/II).

108 Henry Donegan to Moore, 2 March 1915, MS 10,547 (6/II).

109 *Cork Free Press*, 17 March 1915.

110 Fitzpatrick, *Politics and Irish Life*, p. 54; Wheatley, *Nationalism and the Irish Party*, pp. 213–15.

111 *The Irish Times*, 6, 7 December 1915; *CC*, 7 December 1915.

112 John Redmond to J.J. Horgan, 4 December 1915, MS 18,270, NLI. The lord lieutenant appeared at a recruiting rally in Waterford the same week.

113 J.J. Horgan, draft reply to John Redmond, circa 4 December 1915, MS 18, 270, NLI.

114 Ibid.

115 See Patrick Casey, 'Irish Casualties in the First World War', in Tim Coates (ed.), *The World War I Collection: Gallipoli and the Early Battles, 1914–1915* (London: The Stationery Office, 2001); Bryan Cooper, *The Tenth (Irish) Division in Gallipoli* (Dublin: Irish Academic Press, 1993); Myles Dungan, *Irish Soldiers and the Great War* (Dublin: Four Courts Press, 1997); Henry Harris, *The Irish Regiments in the First World War* (Cork: Mercier Press, 1968); John Horne (ed.), *Our War: Ireland and the Great War* (Dublin: Royal Irish Academy, 2008); Keith Jeffery, *Ireland and the Great War* (Cambridge: Cambridge University Press, 1999); Thomas Johnstone, *Orange, Green, and Khaki: The Story of the Irish Regiments in the Great War, 1914–1918* (Dublin: Gill & Macmillan, 1992).

116 See Gerry White and Brendan O'Shea, *A Great Sacrifice: Cork Servicemen Who Died in the Great War* (Cork: Echo Publications, 2010). See also Eoin McCarthy and Gerard O'Sullivan, 'Cork-Born Soldiers Who Died in World War One', *Journal of the Ballincollig Community School Local History Society*, vol. 7, 1990–1991, pp. 20–68.

117 RIC Inspector General's Report for May 1915, CO 904/97; RIC Inspector General's Report for September 1915, CO 904/98.

118 *CC*, 13 January 1916; Reports of Sergeant Young, 13 and 17 January 1916, CO 904/211/334, Fr Michael O'Flanagan, *Sinn Féin and Republican Suspects*.

119 Charles Townshend, *Easter 1916: The Irish Rebellion* (Chicago: Ivan Dee, 2006), p. 60.

120 'General Annual Reports on the British Army (Including the Territorial Force) for the Period from 1 October 1913 to 30 September 1919', Parliamentary Papers, XX.469, Cmd. 1193.

121 Keith Jeffery, 'The Irish Military Tradition in the British Empire', in Keith Jeffery (ed.), *An Irish Empire? Aspects of Ireland and the British Empire* (Manchester: Manchester University Press, 1996), pp. 99.

122 Fitzpatrick, 'The Logic of Collective Sacrifice', p. 1030. Fitzpatrick's enlistment data excludes agriculture workers, who comprised over half the Irish workforce. For this reason, historian Peter Dewey omitted Ireland from his study of the same data set, 'Military Recruiting and the British Labour Force During the First World War'. In addition, Fitzpatrick depends on the Z8 employer surveys, from businesses employing 100 staff or more. This skews results towards urban centres, especially Belfast.

123 Jeffery, 'The Irish Military Tradition in the British Empire', pp. 97–9.

124 Jeffery, 'The Irish Military Tradition in the British Empire', p. 100.

125 CI Report for February 1916, CO 904/100; Royal Commission on the Rebellion in Ireland Report, p. 111. Kent was acquitted and MacSwiney convicted but handed a nominal one-shilling fine.

126 CI Reports for May, August, September and December 1915.

127 WS 1, Tom Barry; WS 15, Fred Murray; WS 16, Robert Langford; WS 19, Liam Murphy; WS 24, Cornelius Murphy; Company list of pre-Rising Volunteers, MacSwiney Collection, 1955-208-11, Cork Public Museum.

128 This seemed in contrast with the Dublin Volunteers. For examples of Cork clerks see: Seán Murphy, Tomás MacCurtain, Pat Higgins, Seán O'Sullivan; shop assistants: Tadhg O'Sullivan, Seán Lucey, Seán Culhane; artisans: Robert Langford, Fred Murray, Mark Wickham, Harry Lorton; teachers: Liam de Róiste, Terry MacSwiney, Donal Óg O'Callaghan, Edward Sheehan; small shop owners: Seán O'Cuill, Edward Coughlan, Liam Ruiséal. Maurice O'Connor, Edward Sheehan and Terence MacSwiney graduated from UCC, though MacSwiney did so as a mature student. Mathematics Professor Alfred O'Rahilly and Literature Professor W.F.P. Stockley joined the movement after the Easter Rising. See Corkery, 'Professor W.F.P. Stockley', pp. 257–67; J. Anthony Gaughan, *Alfred O'Rahilly. Vol. II: Public Figure* (Naas: Kingdom Books, 1989), p. 16. For details of University College Dublin staff and alumni involvement in the Easter Rising see F.X. Martin (ed.), *The Easter Rising 1916 and University College Dublin* (Dublin: Browne & Nolan, 1966).

129 Report of T.A. Howe, Chief Inspector, Cork RIC, June 1916, in the *Report of the Royal Commission on the Rebellion in Ireland*, pp. 111–12.

130 Peter Hart's survey of IRA leadership and levels of violence offers few unequivocal conclusions, except that a strong Gaelic League presence was the indicator of high levels of violence during 1919–23. See Peter Hart, 'The Geography of Revolution in Ireland, 1917–1923', *Past and Present*, vol. 155, no. 1, 1997, pp. 163–73.

131 *The Irish Times*, 15 March 1915.

132 *CC*, 10 March 1916.

133 Ibid., 11 March 1916.

134 Ibid., 13–15 March 1916.

135   CI Report for March 1916, CO 904/100.

CHAPTER III: THE RISING AND AFTER

1   Liam de Róiste Bureau of Military History Draft Statement, U271/L4, CCCA.
2   John Borgonovo (ed.), *Florence and Josephine O'Donoghue's War of Independence* (Dublin: Irish Academic Press, 2006), p. 25.
3   See also Florence O'Donoghue, *Tomás MacCurtain: Soldier and Patriot* (Tralee: Anvil Press, 1971), pp. 67–102.
4   BMH WS 89, Micheál Ó Cuill. The officer was Seán O'Sullivan.
5   Lewis Bayly, *Pull Together! The Memoirs of Admiral Sir Lewis Bayly* (London: George G. Harrap, 1939), pp. 201–3; undated statement of Harbour Pilot Michael Walsh, Cobh, PR6-49-1, Seamus Fitzgerald Papers, CCCA.
6   O'Donoghue, *Tomás MacCurtain*, p. 94–5; Gerry White and Brendan O'Shea, *Baptised in Blood: The Formation of the Cork Brigade of the Irish Volunteers, 1913–1916* (Cork: Mercier Press, 2005), p. 102. In his excellent *The Rising* (p. 214), Ferghal McGarry puts the Cork mobilisation at 60 per cent. However, precise Cork company mobilisation returns gathered by Florrie O'Donoghue for his Tomás MacCurtain biography report a turnout of 70 per cent (See MS 31,439, NLI). For a list of pre-Rising Cork Volunteers and officers, see the MacSwiney Papers, 1955-208-11, Cork Public Museum. According to O'Donoghue's and the Cork Public Museum lists, the four Cork city companies numbered 180 men, which would mean 89 per cent turned out for the Easter mobilisation. However, these seem to provide only 'reliable' Volunteers. Company mobilisation returns count 300 men in the Cork city companies.
7   The County Cork armaments totalled 201 rifles, including 100 single-shot Martinis and 50 single-shot 'Howth rifles'. The latter (black-powder Mausers) had only twenty rounds of ammunition per rifle. The Volunteers also held 518 shotguns and 768 pistols. See total returns, MS 31,439.
8   Ferghal McGarry, *The Rising* (Oxford: Oxford University Press, 2010), pp. 212–15.
9   MS 31,439.
10   The figures are even more striking when examining each city company individually. A Company held thirty rifles and mobilised thirty-one men; B Company, thirty-two rifles and thirty-five men; C Company, thirty-two rifles and thirty-seven men; D Company, forty rifles and forty men. A few city Volunteers were used as cyclists and dispatch riders, which might account for the disparity. See MS 31,439 and MS 31,437.
11   BMH WS 19, Liam Murphy.
12   For some additional details see: WS 78, John Manning; WS 103, Statement of Seán O'Hegarty, Seán Lynch, Tadhg Twomey and Jeremiah O'Shea; WS 89, Micheál Ó Cuill; WS 637, Muriel MacSwiney; WS 47, Seán Healy and Liam O'Callaghan; WS 1737, Seamus Fitzgerald; WS 19, Liam Murphy; WS 1561 Margaret Lucy; WS 90, Con Collins; WS 869, Commandant P.J. Murphy; WS 15, Fred Murray; WS 16, Riobárd Langford; WS 33, Daniel Hegarty, WS 46, Patrick Twomey; WS 54, Seán O'Hegarty; WS 119, Eitne MacSwiney, WS 1224, Thomas Delarue; WS 1521, Michael Walsh.
13   WS 25, Pat Higgins.
14   WS 24, Cornelius Murphy.
15   WS 1737, Seamus Fitzgerald.
16   De Róiste BMH Draft Statement.
17   John F. Boyce, *The Irish Rebellion of 1916* (London: Constable & Company Ltd., 1916), p. 146.
18   WS 19, Liam Murphy.
19   Undated Statement of Tom O'Donovan to Florrie O'Donoghue, MS 31,369, NLI.
20   WS 16, Robert Langford; 'Comments on Florence O'Donoghue's Life of Tomás MacCurtain', pamphlet issued by the Cork 1916 Men's Association, with handwritten

notes by Robert Langford, MS 31,434, NLI; Liam de Róiste's wife Nora quoted MacSwiney as saying, 'It was only the scum of Dublin, Larkin's crowd, who were fighting.' See the de Róiste BMH Draft Statement, U271/L4. Florrie O'Donoghue believed Robert Langford 'may be a bit prejudiced against the MacSwiney women folk', but was ultimately honest, adding, 'what he has said is what many people know in a vague way but avoid saying.' See his 'Notes on Witnesses, Private', Bureau of Military History notebook, circa 1948, MS 31,368, NLI; and letter from 'A Cork Nationalist', *Cork Free Press*, 9 December 1916.

21 WS 637, Muriel MacSwiney; WS 1598, Seán Murphy, Thomas Barry, Patrick Canton, James Wickham; Liam de Róiste Diary, 13 August 1916.

22 WS 89, Micheál Ó Cuill.

23 'Comments on Florence O'Donoghue's Life of Tomás MacCurtain', p. 14; Micheál Ó Cuill to Moirin Chavasse, 12 June 1952, Papers of Terence MacSwiney's Biographers, 48c/218, UCD Archives; WS 24, Cornelius Murphy; WS 1561, Margaret Lucy; WS 1547, Mick Murphy; WS 1656, Daniel Healy; WS 1584, Patrick Murray; WS 637, Muriel MacSwiney. The RIC reported that the Volunteers surrendered 76 rifles and shotguns from their known arsenal of 126 firearms, but failed to turn in ammunition or revolvers. See *Report of the Royal Commission on the Rebellion in Ireland*, p. 112.

24 WS 24, Cornelius Murphy.

25 *Report of the Royal Commission on the Rebellion in Ireland*, p. 112; J.J. Horgan to Maurice Moore, 31 May 1916, MS 10,561, NLI.

26 J.J. Horgan to Maurice Moore, 31 May 1916, MS 10,561.

27 *Cork Free Press*, 23 September 1916.

28 Meeting of 4 May 1916, reported in *CC*, 8 May 1916.

29 William O'Brien to Frank Gallagher, 26 April 1916, UC/UOB/PP/AS/87, William O'Brien Papers, UCC.

30 *CE* editorial, 29 April 1916.

31 CHCMM, 1 May 1917.

32 This untabled amendment was proposed by William Dennehy and supported by Captain Collins and Jeremiah O'Sullivan.

33 *Cork Free Press*, 13 May 1916.

34 *CE*, 28–9 April, 1, 4, 6 May 1916.

35 Ibid., 29 April 1916.

36 J.J. Horgan to Maurice Moore, 31 May 1916, MS 10,561, NLI.

37 Ibid. Other councillors echoed O'Gorman.

38 *CE*, 29 April 1916.

39 *CC*, 15 May 1916; *CE*, 15 May 1916.

40 1916 RIC Intelligence Notes, County Cork E.R. [East Riding] and Cork City, PRO 904/19 Part 2, TNA (hereafter 1916 RIC Intelligence Notes).

41 *CE*, 1 May 1916.

42 Ibid., 4 May 1916.

43 Ibid., 6 May 1916.

44 Cork Poor Law Guardian (PLG) Meeting Minutes, 6 May 1916, CCCA.

45 *CE*, 10 May 1916.

46 *Cork Free Press*, 13 May 1916.

47 *CE*, 11 May 1916. The letter was signed by Assistant Bishop Cohalan, Lord Mayor Butterfield, High Sheriff Hart and officers of the UIL City Executive: George Crosbie, Coroner William Murphy, Coroner John J. Horgan and Coroner James J. McCabe.

48 CHCMM, 10 May 1916, CP/C/A/12, CCCA.

49 *CE*, 12 May 1916.

50 Cork Corporation Meeting Minutes, 11 May 1916 (hereafter, CCMM).

51 *CE*, 11 May 1916.

52 Report of the US Consul, Queenstown, Charles Hathaway, 'The Irish Question at

the Beginning of 1917', 23 February 1917, US Consular Records, Cork, Ireland, vol. 112, RG 84, US National Archives IV.

53   *CE*, 12, 17 May 1916; AOH Cork Council Minute Book, 4 June 1916, U389a/26, CCCA.

54   *CC*, 25 May 1916. For details on the imperialist holiday, see David Hume, 'Empire Day in Ireland, 1896–1962', in Keith Jeffery (ed.), *An Irish Empire? Aspects of Ireland and the British Empire* (Manchester: Manchester University Press, 1996), pp. 149–68.

55   CI Report for May 1916, CO 904/100.

56   *CE*, 1 July 1916.

57   Ibid., 27 July 1916.

58   Cork PLG Meeting Minutes, 29 July 1916 (hereafter CPLGMM).

59   *CC*, 4 August 1916; CO 904/195, Roger Casement File, *Sinn Féin and Republican Suspects*.

60   *Cork Free Press*, 12 August 1916.

61   Defence of the Realm Act Search Warrant, To Cork County Inspector Thomas Howe, From Sir John Maxwell, 22 September 1916; Major General J. Doran (Commander, Southern District) to Headquarters Irish Command, 28 September 1916; Lieutenant General G.J. Maxwell to Chief Secretary, 29 September 1916, War Office (WO) 35/69, TNA; Southern District Military Intelligence Monthly Reports, September 1916, November 1916, CO 904/157, *British in Ireland Series* (hereafter Southern District Military Intelligence Report).

62   *CC*, 10 June 1916.

63   *CE*, 2, 24, 26 June 1916; *CC*, 26 June 1916.

64   *CC*, 26 June 1916.

65   *CE*, 30 June 1916. No Mansion House Fund branch appeared in Cork, while the Irish National Aid established a provisional branch prior to the Mansion House Flag Day. See the *Cork Free Press*, 24 June 1916.

66   *Cork Free Press*, 24 June 1916.

67   *CE*, 30 June 1916.

68   For examples of attendees, see the *CE*, 1, 14 July, 17 August, 2 November 1916, 5 January, 18 April, 6 July 1917; *Cork Free Press*, 26 August, 9, 23 September, 14 October 1916.

69   *CE*, 1, 8, 14 July, 4 August 1916.

70   *CE*, 17 August 1916.

71   This occurred on 11 August 1916. See the Irish National Aid and Volunteers Fund (INAVF) Executive Minute Book, MS 24,469, NLI; *CE*, 19 August 1916; Liam de Róiste Diary, 11 August 1916, U271A/18; WS 687, Monsignor M. Curran.

72   F.S.L. Lyons, 'Dillon, Redmond and the Irish Home Rulers', in F.X. Martin (ed.), *Leaders and Men of the Easter Rising: Dublin 1916* (London: Methuen & Co., 1967), pp. 29–41; David Lloyd George, *The War Memoirs of David Lloyd George* (London: Oldhams Press, 1938), pp. 421–3; For the specific Lloyd George proposals presented to the Irish Party Executive, see Joseph Devlin to J.J. Horgan, 30 June 1916, MS 18,271, NLI.

73   *CC*, 19 June 1916.

74   Ibid., 19, 21 June 1916.

75   Meeting of 4 June 1916, AOH Cork County Council Minute Book, U389a/26.

76   *CE*, 19, 24 June 1916.

77   Ibid., 22 June 1916.

78   Cork Corporation Meeting Minutes, 21 July 1916.

79   Meeting of 2 July 1916, AOH Cork County Council Minute Book, U389a/26.

80   J.J. Horgan to Joe Devlin, 1 July 1916, MS 18,271, NLI.

81   John Dillon to J.J. Horgan, 25 June 1916, MS 18,271, NLI.

82   CI Report for June 1916, CO 904/100.

83   CI Report for July 1916, CO 904/100.

84 *CC*, 21 June 1916.
85 *CE*, 19 June 1916.
86 *CC*, 19 June 1916.
87 William O'Brien to Fr Madden, 10 June 1916, UC/UOB/PP/AS/100, William O'Brien Papers, UCC.
88 *CC*, 20 June 1916.
89 Mrs William O'Brien Draft Memoir, MS 8507 (7), NLI.
90 *CE*, 24 June 1916.
91 *CC*, 24 June 1916.
92 *CE*, 24 June 1916.
93 *CC*, 24 June 1916.
94 *Cork Free Press*, 1 July 1916.
95 Muriel Murphy to Tomás MacCurtain, 27 June 1916, MacCurtain Collection, L1966-168, Cork Public Museum.
96 William O'Brien, *The Irish Revolution and How It Came About* (London: George Allen & Unwin Ltd, 1923), p. 45. O'Brien's wife Sophie echoed this version in her unpublished memoir. See the Mrs William O'Brien Papers, MS 8507 (7), NLI.
97 RIC Inspector General's Report, June 1916, CO 904/100.
98 Comments submitted to American Consul Wesley Frost's report on conditions in Ireland, December 1916, U271/F8, CCCA.
99 Report of County Inspector Walsh, 20 July 1916, Chief Secretary's Office Registered Papers (CSORP) 1916/12,669, NA.
100 *CC*, 22 July 1916.
101 CI Report for July 1916, CO 904/100; *CC*, 22 July 1916.
102 *Southern Star*, 5 August 1916.
103 *CE*, 9 August 1916.
104 J.J. Lee, *Ireland 1912–1985: Politics and Society* (Cambridge: Cambridge University Press, 1989), p. 37. See also Thomas Hennessey, *Dividing Ireland: World War One and Partition* (London: Routledge, 1998), pp. 144–52.
105 RIC Cork County Inspector to Chief Secretary's Office, 18 July 1916, CSORP 1916/14,512, NA.
106 *Cork Free Press*, 15 July 1916.
107 Undersecretary's Telegram, 20 July 1916, CSORP 1916/25,309, NA.
108 CI Report for July 1919, CO 904/100.
109 *CC*, 30 September 1916.
110 North Cork City District Inspector to Under Secretary, 24 July 1916, CSORP, 1916/25,969, NA.
111 Resident Magistrate's Report, 23 July 1916, CSORP, 1916/25,969.
112 *CC*, 30 September 1916.
113 Notice of Question in Parliament, 25 July 1916, CSORP, 1916/25,969.
114 North Cork City District Inspector to Under Secretary, 24 July 1916, CSORP, 1916/25,969.
115 *CC*, 26 August 1916.
116 Ibid., 2 September 1916.
117 Ibid., 14 August 1916.
118 Ibid., 11, 29 August 1916.
119 *Cork Free Press*, 11 November 1916; RIC Inspector General's Report for September 1916, CO 904/101.
120 *CE*, 11 December 1916.
121 Southern District Military Intelligence Report for October 1916, CO 904/157.
122 Southern District Military Intelligence Report for October 1917.
123 Southern District Military Intelligence Report for July 1917. See also the Southern District Reports for August 1917 and October 1917.
124 CI Report for November 1910, CO 904/82; CI Report for November 1914, CO

904/95; CI Report for November 1915, CO 904/98. In the pre-war years, the corporation typically attended.

125   CI Report for November 1916, CO 904/101. See also the *CC*, 27 November 1916.

126   *CC*, 27 November 1916; Seán Ó Muirthile Memoir, Richard Mulcahy Papers, P7a/201, UCD Archives.

127   *CC*, 10 January 1917.

128   *CE*, 13 December 1916, 17 January 1917; *CC*, 10 January, 9 March 1917.

129   *CE*, 27 November 1916.

130   CI Report for November 1916.

131   *CE*, 27 November 1916, 7 March 1936 ('An appreciation of Birdie Conway', by Lil Conlon); *CC*, 27 December 1916; WS 47, Seán Healy and Liam O'Callaghan; CI Report for November 1916; CI Report for December 1916, CO 904/101.

132   WS 47, Seán Healy and Liam O'Callaghan.

133   *CC*, 27 November 1916.

134   CI Report for December 1916, CO 904/101; RIC Inspector General's Report for December 1916, CO 904/101.

135   Letter from Major General Beauchamp John Colcough Doran, Headquarters Southern Command, to Liam de Róiste, 23 December 1916, de Róiste Papers, U27/F9, CCCA.

136   *CE*, 2 January 1917; CCMM, 12 January 1917.

137   CO 904/197/97, Patrick Corcoran, *Sinn Féin and Republican Suspects*.

138   *CC*, 3 January 1917; *CE*, 3 January 1917; Liam de Róiste Diary, 20 December 1916; Sinn Féin pamphlets, F1, U271A, CCCA.

139   *CE*, 24 January 1917; *CE*, 20 March 1920; RIC Inspector General's Report for September 1914, CO 904/94; Inspector General's Report for January 1917, CO 904/102; CO 904/197/97, Patrick Corcoran, *Sinn Féin and Republican Suspects*.

140   For some examples, see the *CE*, 21 May 1915, 3 April 1916, 14 December 1917, 15 November 1918, 16 May 1919; CHCMM, 28 November 1917.

141   *CC*, 23 February 1917; *CE*, 23 February 1917.

142   *CE*, 5 March 1917.

143   *CC*, 23 February 1917.

144   *CC*, 23 February 1917; *CE*, 23 February 1917.

145   *CC*, 23 February 1917.

146   Ibid., 8, 14 February 1917.

147   Ibid., 23 February 1917.

148   *CE*, 23 February 1917.

149   *CC*, 5 March 1917.

150   *CE*, 19, 21 March 1917.

151   *CC*, 24 April 1917.

152   Ibid., 13 July 1917.

153   John Horne, *State, Society and Mobilisation in Europe during the First World War* (Cambridge: Cambridge University Press, 1997), p. 7.

154   CPLGMM, 1 November 1917.

155   RIC 1916 Intelligence Notes, PRO 903/19/2, TNA; CI Reports for July and August 1916, CO 904/100, September, November, December 1916, CO 904/101.

156   Southern District Military Intelligence Reports for September 1916, October 1916 and December 1916, CO 904/156.

157   De Róiste Diary, 24 September 1916; Barry to Tomás MacCurtain, 28 September 1916, courtesy Donal Ó Drisceoil.

158   CCMM, 27 October 1916; *CE*, 17 October 1916.

159   Southern District Military Intelligence Monthly Report for September 1916. See also the Southern District Intelligence Report for October 1916.

160   Southern District Military Intelligence Report for December 1916.

161   CI Report for November 1916, CO 904/101.

162   *CC*, 28 December 1916; Major General B. Doran, Southern Command, to Headquarters, Irish Command, 10 January 1917, WO 35/69, TNA.

163 RIC 1916 Intelligence Notes, PRO 903/19/2; *CC*, 30 December 1916.
164 CI Report for December 1916.

CHAPTER IV: 'THOUGHTLESS YOUNG PEOPLE' AND THE CORK CITY RIOTS OF 1917

1 De Róiste Diary, 14 July 1917.
2 For examples, see the *CE*, 24, 30 June 1916, 17, 19 August 1916 and 2 November 1916.
3 John B. O'Brien, 'Population, Politics, and Society in Cork, 1780–1900', in Cornelius Buttimer and Patrick O'Flanagan (eds), *Cork: History and Society. Interdisciplinary Essays on the History of an Irish County* (Dublin: Geography Publications, 1993) p. 715.
4 Seán Daly, *A City in Crisis: A History of Labour Conflict and Social Misery, 1870–1872* (Cork: Tower Books, 1978), pp. 39–78.
5 O'Brien, 'Population, Politics, and Society in Cork', pp. 699–720.
6 Fintan Lane, 'Music and Violence in Working-Class Cork: The "Band Nuisance", 1879–1882', *Saothar*, vol. 24, 1999, pp. 59–65.
7 Justin McCarthy, *The Story of an Irishman* (London: Chatto & Windus, 1904), pp. 348–54.
8 For examples, see the *CE*, 24 October 1910, 14, 15, 19, 25, 26, 28, 30 November 1910, 1, 3, 5 December 1910.
9 *CE*, 16–17 January 1914. The offending marching bands were the Parnell Fife Band, the Workingman's Drum and Fife Band, the Roche's Guard Band and the Barrack Street Band.
10 Emmet O'Connor, *James Larkin* (Cork: Cork University Press, 2003), p. 46.
11 John O'Callaghan, '"A Centre of Turbulence and Rioting": The Republican Movement in Limerick, 1917–1918', in William Sheehan and Maura Cronin, *Riotous Assemblies: Rebels, Riots and Revolts in Ireland* (Cork: Mercier Press, 2011), pp. 179–86; Peter Hart, *The IRA and Its Enemies: Violence and Community in Cork, 1916–1923* (Oxford: Oxford University Press, 1998), p. 54.
12 *CE*, 9 April 1917.
13 See the *CE*, 3, 24 January 1917; RIC Inspector General's Report for January 1917; de Róiste Diary, 3 January 1917.
14 *CC*, 16 April 1917.
15 Ibid., 20 April 1917.
16 Ibid., 16 April 1917.
17 *CE*, 16 April 1917.
18 CI Report for April 1917, CO 904/102.
19 *CC*, 20 April 1917.
20 Lil Conlon, *Cumann na mBan and the Women of Ireland* (Kilkenny: Kilkenny Press, 1969), p. 45.
21 Report of DI Walsh to RIC Special Branch, 25 April 1917, CO 904/214/401, Peter Sheehan, *Sinn Féin and Republican Suspects*.
22 Attorney General to Chief Secretary, 3 May 1917, CO 214/401. See the entire file for various comments from Dublin Castle officials.
23 Report of Constable James Downey, 24 April 1917, CO 904/214/401, *Sinn Féin and Republican Suspects*.
24 *CC*, 23 April 1917.
25 RIC Inspector General's Report for April 1917, CO 904/102.
26 CI Report for May 1917, CO 904/103.
27 *CC*, 4 May 1917.
28 Seán Healy to Florrie O'Donoghue, 21 July 1965, MS 31,324, NLI.
29 CI Report for May 1917.
30 *CC*, 11 May 1917.
31 Ibid., 23 June 1917.

32 CCMM, 22 June 1917, CCCA; *CC*, 23 June 1917.

33 RIC Report of 'Demonstrations of Sinn Féin and Deportees in June 1917', CO 904/23, *British in Ireland Series*.

34 The eight prisoners were: Diarmuid Lynch, David Kent, J.J. Walsh, Maurice Brennan, Fergus O'Connor, William Tobin, Con Donovan and Thomas Hunter. See the *CE*, 25 June 1917.

35 CI Report for June 1917, CO 904/103; *CC*, 25 June 1917.

36 *CE*, 25 June 1917.

37 *CC*, 25 June 1917.

38 *CE*, 25 June 1917.

39 *CC*, 25 June 1917.

40 *CE*, 25 June 1917.

41 Information about the civic fire escapes comes courtesy of Cork Fire Brigade historian Pat Poland.

42 *CC*, 25 June 1917.

43 The scales were subsequently replaced and can be seen today on the front (Washington Street) of the Courthouse. During a 2009 lecture by the author in Clonakilty, County Cork, Sinead Cripps relayed her family's oral tradition that attributed her grandfather with scaling the building. She reported her grandfather claimed he was the only man in Cork not to get a piece of the scales of justice.

44 *CE*, 25 June 1917.

45 *CC*, 25 June 1917.

46 Ibid., 14 May 1917, 11 June 1917.

47 *CC*, 25 June 1917. The purpose of the meeting was 'To voice the opinion of Cork City and County regarding the proposed Government Convention'. See the Liam de Róiste Papers, F3, CCCA.

48 WS 446, Frank Haynes.

49 *CE*, 25 June 1917.

50 *CC*, 26 June 1917.

51 Ibid., 25 June 1917.

52 WS 446, Frank Haynes; *CC*, 25 June 1917; *CE*, 25 June 1917.

53 CSORP 1917/24,223, NA; *CC*, 26 June 1917.

54 Statement of 3 July 1917, Papers of RIC Head Constable Brown, U97, CCCA. Brown's statement includes post-edit insertions in different handwriting, mentioning that his party came under revolver fire as it reached the recruiting office. I removed one such edit from the above quote, as the handwriting authorship is unclear. Brown wrote this statement for a malicious injury application and I suspect it was edited with this in mind. Various newspaper accounts claim shots began later in the evening, after bayonet charges began. (See the *CC*, 27 June 1917).

55 WS 446, Frank Haynes.

56 Statement of 3 July 1917, Papers of Head Constable Brown.

57 This was most likely unauthorised fire from individual Irish Volunteers, though IRA records fail to mention the incident.

58 Report of the Coroner's Inquest, *CC*, 27 June 1917.

59 *CE*, 25 June 1917.

60 Ibid., 25 June 1917.

61 Statement of 3 July 1917, Papers of Head Constable Brown.

62 *CC*, 27 June 1917.

63 Ibid., 25 June 1917.

64 The Cork INAVDF attempted to pay the young man £7, along with the family of Abraham Allen who was bayoneted by the police. See the meeting of 17 July 1917, INAVDF Executive Minutes, MS 23,469, NLI.

65 *CE*, 25 June 1917.

66 Ibid., 26 June 1917.

67 CI Report for June 1917.

68 *CC*, 19 September 1917.
69 Ibid., 26 June 1917. MacCurtain, MacSwiney and Murphy commanded the city Volunteers, while Walsh and Lynch were both veterans of the rising fighting.
70 *CC*, 26 June 1917; *CE*, 26 June 1917; Cork County Inspector to Undersecretary, 6 September 1917, CSORP 1917/23,333, NA.
71 *CC*, 26 June 1917
72 *CE*, 26 June 1917.
73 County Inspector to Undersecretary, 27 June 1917, CSORP 1917/24,213.
74 County Inspector Telegram to Undersecretary, 28 June 1917, CSORP 1917/24,213; Hansard, HC Debates, 28 June 1917, vol. 95, cc 506–7.
75 *CC*, 25–26 June 1917.
76 *CE*, 26 June 1917.
77 *CE*, 27 June 1917, 2, 26 July 1917; Michael Collins to Cork Secretary Tadhg O'Shea, 18 July 1917, INAVDF Letter Books, MS 23,465, NLI.
78 *CC*, 27 June 1917; CPLGMM, 28 June 1917, BG 69A/147, CCCA.
79 CI Cork to Undersecretary, 6 September 1917, CSORP 1917/23,333, NA.
80 WS 869, P.J. Murphy.
81 Liam de Róiste Diary, 29 September 1917, MS 31,146, NLI.
82 Letter from 'An Irish Cockney', *CC*, 26 June 1917.
83 *CC*, 27 June 1917; WS 446, Frank Haynes.
84 *CE*, 26 June 1917.
85 *CC*, 15 May, 22 September 1917, 31 May, 3 June, 19 July 1918; de Róiste Diary, 29 September and 3 October 1917, MS 31,1446I.
86 'Found on Jerh Mullane on 21st July 1917', Papers of Head Constable Brown.
87 See the *CC*, 16 April (concerning incidents on 14–15 April), 24–25 June, 4, 24, 28 September, 12, 23 November 1917.
88 There were no reports of looting or vandalism.
89 See the *CC*, 25, 26 June 1917, 4, 24, 28 September 1917, 12, 21 November 1917, 16 April 1918.
90 *CC*, 10, 27–28 July 1917, 28 September 1917; *CE*, 27–28 July 1917, 28 September 1917; CI Report for July 1917, CO 904/103.
91 Chief Secretary to Undersecretary, 18 July 1917, CSORP 1917/23,725, NA. See also Judgement of Royal Magistrate Starkie, 29 September 1917, CSORP 1917/25,209, NA.
92 *CE*, 27 July 1917.
93 Ibid., 28 July 1917.
94 *CC*, 27 July 1917.
95 Ibid., 27 September 1917; *CE*, 27 September 1917.
96 *CC*, 28 September 1917. Liam de Róiste heard another colourful version of the speech. See his diary, 3 October 1917.
97 *CE*, 28 September 1917. See also the CI Report for September 1917, CO 904/104.
98 *CC*, 28 September 1917.
99 'Application of Head Constable John Brown for Sustaining Malicious Injury on 27 September 1917' under the Criminal Injuries Act, 1919, Papers of Head Constable John Brown.
100 WS 869, P.J. Murphy.
101 *CC*, 1 October 1917; *CE*, 28 September 1917.
102 *CE*, 29 September 1917.
103 Ibid; *CC*, 29 September 1917.
104 *CC*, 1 October 1917.
105 Ibid., 12 July 1917; *CE*, 2 October 1917.
106 *CE*, 23 November 1917.
107 *CC*, 23 November 1917.
108 Brief for Counsel, 14 November 1918, Cork Summer Assizes Appeal No. 24, Thomas Dinan vs. Daniel Harrington, CSORP 1918/30,770, NA; *CE*, 23 November 1917.

109   *CC*, 19, 26 November 1917; *CE*, 22 November 1916, 25 June 1917; CI Report for November 1917, CO 904/104; *CC*, 19 November 1917; Hansard, HC Debates, 22 November 1917, vol. 99, c. 1337.

110   For details see Dinan vs Harrington, CSORP 1918/30,770; The victims' joint statement, 28 November 1917, MS 31,148, NLI; de Róiste diary, 23 and 25 November 1917; *CC*, 23 November 1917, 10–11 April 1918; *CE*, 23 November 1917, 10–11 April 1918.

111   Victims' joint statement.

112   *CC*, 10 April 1918; *CE*, 10 April 1918.

113   *CC*, 10 April 1918.

114   De Róiste took the statements. See the de Róiste Diary, 25 November 1917; and the CCMM, 14 December 1917 and 11 January 1918, CCCA.

115   Assistant Undersecretary to Crown Solicitor Jasper Wolfe, 20 August 1918; Dinan vs Harrington; Patrick Brady to David Lloyd George, 21 January 1918, CSORP 1918/4380, NA; Press Censor to All Newspapers in Ireland, 5 December 1917, Terence MacSwiney Papers, 1945-369, Cork Public Museum. See also the *CC*, 23 November 1917, which reported Patrick Brady being 'treated for two ____ wounds in the leg'.

116   Undersecretary to Crown Solicitor Wolfe, 20 August 1918; Crown Solicitor Wolfe to Undersecretary, 25 November 1918, Dinan vs Harrington; *CC*, 23 July 1918; *CE*, 11 April 1918, 21 October 1918.

117   Wolfe to Undersecretary, 25 July 1918, Dinan vs Harrington.

118   Denis Garvey and Daniel Harrington were shot together on a streetcar in Cork city in May 1920. See John Borgonovo, *Spies, Informers and the Anti-Sinn Féin Society: The Intelligence War in Cork City 1920-1921* (Dublin: Irish Academic Press, 2007), pp. 86, 118–19, 138. Constable Joseph Murtagh, whose 1920 assassination seemingly sparked the MacCurtain killing, was also present.

119   De Róiste Diary, 3 October 1917.

120   *CC*, 5 October 1917. The cost of police drafts were charged to local ratepayers.

121   *CC*, 5 October 1917.

122   WS 869, P.J. Murphy.

123   See the *CE*, 22 October 1917, 5, 19 November 1917.

124   Bishop Cohalan to Liam de Róiste, 7 December 1917, C48, de Róiste Papers, CCCA.

125   *CC*, 14 February 1918; *CE*, 14 February 1914; CI Report for February 1918, CO 904/105.

126   Two soldiers rescued from military police, *CC*, 11 February 1918; a mob strikes two police trying to arrest a man during the *Evening Echo* newsboy strike, *CC*, 30 May 1918; Blackpool residents assault police arresting an army deserter, *CC*, 26–27 August 1918; Police stoned while trying to arrest a shoplifter on Washington Street, *CE*, 22 October 1918.

127   Peter Hart makes a similar observation in *The IRA and Its Enemies*, p. 54.

CHAPTER V: THE REPUBLICAN FRONT: SINN FÉIN, THE IRB, AND THE IRISH VOLUNTEERS IN 1917

1   John Borgonovo (ed.), *Florence and Josephine O'Donoghue's War of Independence* (Dublin: Irish Academic Press, 2006), p. 41.

2   *CE*, 6 July 1917. The county contributed £3,466 to the Red Cross in 1917 and £2,563 in 1918. For details, see Margaret Downs, 'The Civilian Aid Effort', in David Fitzpatrick, (ed.), *Ireland and the First World War* (Dublin: Trinity History Workshop, 1986), pp. 27–37.

3   *CC*, 10, 24 September 1917; *CE*, 23 August 1916, 18 April, 29 May, 2 June, 24 September 1917; *Cork Free Press*, 11 November 1916; *Southern Star*, 26 January 1918; Irish National Aid and Volunteers Dependents' Fund Executive Minute Book, 16 January 1917; CI Reports for November, December 1916; Southern District Military Intelligence Report for December 1916, CO 904/157; WS 1561, Margaret Lucy; Connie Neenan Memoir, CCCA.

4   BMH, Contemporary Documents (CD) 250-3-1, Military Archives, Cathal Brugha
    Barracks.
5   CPLGMM, 30 August 1917.
6   CCMM, 12 October 1917.
7   *CE*, 23 February 1917; *CC*, 25 June 1917; Southern District Military Intelligence
    Report for February 1917; CI Report for February 1917, CO 904/102; Florence
    O'Donoghue, *Tomás MacCurtain: Soldier and Patriot* (Tralee: Anvil Press, 1971), pp.
    125–7.
8   *CE*, 31 May 1917.
9   *CE*, 6 July 1917. Coroner Murphy was the most prominent dropout.
10 Meeting of 17 July 1917, INAVDF Executive Minutes.
10 Collins to Tim O'Shea, 18 July 1917, INAVDF Letter Books.
12 Meeting of 4 September 1917, INAVDF Executive Minutes.
13 Collins to O'Shea, 5 September 1917, INAVDF Letter Books; Collins to O'Shea, 31
    October 1917, INAVDF Letter Books. Collins informed O'Shea on 7 November that
    during his next visit to Cork he would reconsider the £10 grant to Corcoran.
14 Collins to Tadhg Barry, 27 March 1918, INAVDF Letter Books.
15 Michael Laffan, *The Resurrection of Ireland: The Sinn Féin Party, 1916–1923*
    (Cambridge: Cambridge University Press, 1999), pp. 70–93.
16 Patrick Maume, *The Long Gestation: Irish Nationalist Life, 1891–1918*, (Dublin: Gill &
    Macmillan, 1999), p. 189; WS 16, Robert Langford; CI Report for November 1910.
    Healy was a former president of the Cork AOH American Alliance. See the *Southern
    Star*, 4 November 1916.
17 *Cork Free Press*, 28 October 1916, 4, 11 November 1916.
18 *CE*, 11 November 1916; *II*, 11, 13 November 1916; *Southern Star*, 28 October 1916;
    Tadhg Barry to Tomás MacCurtain, 26 October 1916; MacCurtain to Barry, 1
    November 1916, MacCurtain Collection, L1966-158-2, Cork Public Museum. Fellow
    Reading prisoner Arthur Griffith complained to William O'Brien that MacCurtain
    had 'hideously mismanaged' the episode. Letter from 'A Cork Nationalist', *Cork
    Free Press*, 9 December 1916; William O'Brien, *The Irish Revolution and How It Came
    About* (London: George Allen & Unwin Ltd, 1923), p. 383.
19 *Cork Free Press*, 9, 25 November 1916. See also Laffan, *The Resurrection of Ireland*, pp.
    72–5; Maume, *The Long Gestation*, pp. 189–90; Arthur Griffith, Tomás MacCurtain,
    Seán Milroy to Unknown, 24 November 1916, 1945-214, Cork Public Museum; *II*, 6,
    8, 27 November 1916.
20 Sophie O'Brien's Manuscript, MS 8507 (7); Frank Gallagher to Celia Saunders, 13
    December 1916, Frank Gallagher Papers, 10050/17, TCD Archives.
21 Seán Nolan to Herbert Pim, 18 December 1916, RIC Crimes Special Branch Report
    to the Undersecretary, Notes of Papers Found in the Possession of John Nolan,
    Cork, Arrested 2 February 1917, CO 904/29, *British in Ireland Series*. See also Nolan's
    comments at the Manchester Martyr Commemoration, *CE*, 27 November 1916.
22 De Róiste Diary, 16 December 1916. The provisional committee was Chairman Seán
    Nolan; treasurer Liam de Róiste; secretaries Seán Conlon and Pat Barrett; and exec-
    utive members Seán Jennings, Maurice Conway, Liam Murphy and Denis O'Neill.
23 Ibid.
24 De Róiste Diary, 20 December 1916; CI Reports for January, February, April and
    May 1917.
25 'The Irish Question at the Beginning of 1917', RG 84.
26 De Róiste Papers, U271/F1, CCCA.
27 De Róiste Diary, 20 January 1917; Corporation Meeting Minutes, 12 January 1917.
28 CI Reports for January, February, April and May 1917; Laffan, *The Resurrection of
    Ireland*, p. 94.
29 Laffan, *The Resurrection of Ireland*, pp. 85–93.
30 *CC*, 24, 30 March, 13 April 1917.
31 See the Liberty League invitation and ticket lists, MS 11,383 (1), NLI.

32 Cork City Sinn Féin Executive Resolution, 22 April 1917; and Cork City Sinn Féin Executive Circular to Mansion House Committee, 2 June 1917, MS 11,383 (6), NLI.

33 Laffan, *The Resurrection of Ireland*, pp. 90–3.

34 *CE*, 31 October 1914. See also Stephen McQuay Reddick, 'Political and Industrial Labour in Cork, 1899–1914', MA thesis, UCC, pp. 65, 88. Lane was driven from Sinn Féin in 1919 for complicity in corruption at the Cork Workhouse. See *CC*, 19 December 1919, 12 January 1920; *CE*, 28 November 1919, 23 February 1920.

35 De Róiste *Evening Echo* Series, 7 October 1954; O'Donoghue, *Tomás MacCurtain*, pp. 36, 48; *CC*, 26 February, 18 March 1916; CSORP 1916/12,669, NA. After making that remark at the Cork Corporation, another councillor warned, 'You'll lose your JP-ship for that.' See *CC*, 26 February 1916.

36 RIC Inspector General's Report for August 1916; CPLGMM, 17 June 1916, 28 April 1917; *CC*, 2, 21 June, 22 July, 28 October, 11 November 1916.

37 Lane to Plunkett, 14 May 1917, MS 11,383.

38 See Patrick Casey to Count Plunkett, 22 May 1917; William Shorten to Count Plunkett, 31 May 1917, MS 11,383.

39 Cork City Sinn Féin Executive to Mansion House Committee, 2 June 1917, MS 11,383. See also the Cork City Sinn Féin Executive to Count Plunkett, 22 May 1917; Mary MacSwiney to Count Plunkett, 30 May 1917; William Shorten to Count Plunkett, 31 May 1917, MS 11,383.

40 Lane to Plunkett, 30 May 1917, MS 11,383.

41 *CC*, 6 June 1917.

42 Statement of Professor Thomas Dillon, 24 September 1953, de Valera Papers, P150/575, UCD Archives. See also William O'Brien's (labour leader) memoir, *Forth the Banners Go* (Dublin: Three Candles Ltd, 1969), pp. 148–52.

43 J.J. Horgan to John Dillon, 19 June 1918, 6775/87/270, TCD Archives; Thomas Hallinan to J.D. Nugent, 1 November 1919, AOH County Board Letter Book, U839a/9, CCCA.

43 Sinn Féin Director of Organisation Report, 19 December 1917, MS 11,405, NLI. By December 1917, there were Sinn Féin clubs listed in the following wards: East, Northeast, North, West, South, Southeast, Middle, Centre; and in the suburbs of Blackrock, Douglas, Clogheen and Bishopstown. See L1966-141, Cork Public Museum.

45 Thomas O'Donovan to Tomás MacCurtain, 9 June 1917, L1966-160, Cork Public Museum.

46 J.J. Horgan to John Dillon, 19 June 1918, 6772/269, TCD Archives.

47 Robert Monteith, *Casement's Last Adventure* (Dublin: Michael Moynihan, 1953), p. 202.

48 The list is: Alfred O'Rahilly, Barry Egan, Donal Óg O'Callaghan, Bart Quinlan, Cathal O'Shannon, Charles Coughlan, Éamon Coughlan, Cors O'Donovan, D. Saunders, Dan Barry, Denis Lucey, Denis O'Neill, Denis Tobin, Ed Gorgan, Francis Keogh, Frank O'Neill, Fred Murray, Harry Lorton, James Allen, James Purcell, James Walsh, James Fitzpatrick, Jeremiah Kelleher, J.J. Walsh, Seán Jennings, Seán French, Seán Good, John O'Keefe, John O'Leary, John Sheehan, Liam de Róiste, Maurice Walsh, Michael Mehigan, Micheál Ó Cuill, Michael Murphy, P.A. O'Riordan, PA Barrett, Pat Higgins, Patrick O'Sullivan, Paul O'Flynn, W.P. Stockley, Richard Hawkins, Bob Daly, Seán Conlon, Seán MacCurtain, Tomás MacCurtain, Seán O'Sullivan, Simon Daly, Stephen Harrington, Stephen Heffernan, Stephen O'Riordan, Tom Donovan, Tadhg Barry, Terence MacSwiney, Thomas Daly, Thomas Forde, Timothy Geary, William Kenneally, Liam Ruiséal.

49 J.J. Walsh was a town councillor, as were Jeremiah Kelleher and Denis O'Neill, while John Good was a Poor Law Guardian.

50 Fergus Campbell, *Land and Revolution: Nationalist Politics in the West of Ireland, 1891–1921* (Oxford: Oxford University Press, 2005), pp. 296–9; Fitzpatrick, *Politics and Irish Life* (Dublin: Gill & Macmillan, 1977), pp. 107–22.

51 The list was compiled from AOH records, the 1916 UIL Executive, Cork newspapers and the 1915 and 1916 *Guy's Directory*, cross-referenced with the 1911 Census.

52 *CE*, 14, 25 June, 13–14, 27 August, 24 September 1917.

53 *CC*, 25 June 1917; *CE*, 24 September 1917.

54 *CE*, 13 August, 24 September, 8 October, 15 November, 10 December 1917; Southern District Military Intelligence Reports for August and September 1917.

55 *CC*, 25 June, 12 July, 13 August, 2 October 1917; *CE*, 27, 31 August, 24 September, 8 October 1917.

56 Tomás MacCurtain to Tadhg Barry, 24 August 1917, BMH CD 69/4/C (Michael Galvin), MA.

57 WS 4, Diarmuid Lynch; 1916 Men's Association Pamphlet; de Róiste Diary, 18, 20, 27–28 October 1917; Connie Neenan Memoir, CCCA.

58 Borgonovo, *Florence and Josephine O'Donoghue's War of Independence*, p. 41.

59 Ibid.

60 De Róiste Diary, 2 December 1917; Florrie O'Donoghue Cork City Chronology, MS 31,398 (1), NLI.

61 De Róiste Diary, 1 January 1918; Sinn Féin City Executive Department list, circa December 1917, MacCurtain Collection, L1966-141, Cork Public Museum.

62 *CE*, 19 January 1918; *Southern Star*, 26 January 1918; Cork Summer Assizes Appeal No. 24, Dinan vs Harrington; Eveline Murphy to Prime Minister Lloyd George, 23 January 1918, CSORP 1918/2473, NA.

63 De Róiste Diary, 18 November 1917.

64 Gerry White and Brendan O'Shea, *Baptised in Blood: The Formation of the Cork Brigade of the Irish Volunteers, 1913–1916* (Cork: Mercier Press, 2005), Appendix B, pp. 115–16.

65 Translated Text of Tomás MacCurtain Diary, 19 June 1916, L1966-145-2, MacCurtain Collection, Cork Public Museum.

66 WS 719, E Company (Blackpool), 1st Battalion, Cork No. 1 Brigade Joint Statement, Maurice Forde, Peadar McCann, Thomas Daly, Seán Kenny, Michael Keogh, Joseph O'Shea and Tim O'Sullivan; WS 1598, Seán Murphy, Thomas Barry, Patrick Canton and James Wickham; Monteith, *Casement's Last Adventure*, p. 202; T. Ryle Dwyer, *Tans, Terror and Troubles: Kerry's Real Fighting Story, 1913–1923* (Cork: Mercier Press, 2003), p. 98; *CE*, 1 May 1916.

67 WS 187, Annie Fanning; WS 1207, Alfred White; WS 1598, Seán Murphy, Thomas Barry, Patrick Canton and James Wickham; Desmond Greaves, *Liam Mellowes and the Irish Revolution* (London: Lawrence & Wishart, 1971), p. 97.

68 Pat Higgins to Florrie O'Donoghue, 17 September 1936, MS 31,340 (7), NLI; WS 1521, Michael Walsh.

69 13 August 1916, de Róiste Diary 1916; WS 150, Gregory Murphy; WS 1521, Michael Walsh; WS 1200, Cornelius O'Regan; WS 668, Garry Byrne; WS 1584, Patrick Murray; WS 116, Dan Dennehy; Richard Mulcahy, 'The Irish Volunteer Convention, 27 October 1917', *Capuchin Annual*, 1967, pp. 400–10.

70 Barry to MacCurtain, 28 September 1916, original courtesy Donal Ó Drisceoil.

71 *CC*, 6 October 1916; *CE*, 27 November 1916.

72 Borgonovo, *Florence and Josephine O'Donoghue's War of Independence*, pp. 29–30; Seán Healy to Florrie O'Donoghue, 17 September 1965, MS 31,342 (2); WS 1584, Pa Murray; WS 1737, Seamus Fitzgerald; Translated Tomás MacCurtain Diary.

73 O'Hegarty had been ordered out of the city by the military authorities prior to the rising and thus lost his Volunteer rank.

74 WS 25, Pat Higgins; WS 79, Diarmuid Ó Donneabhain; de Róiste Diary, 20 January 1917.

75 De Róiste Diary, 20 January 1917; RIC Inspector General's Report, February 1917, CO 904/102.

76 Statement of Cathal Brugha, 8 April 1922, Papers of Terence MacSwiney's Biographers, 48C/361/97, UCD Archives; WS 1598, Seán Murphy, Thomas Barry,

Patrick Canton, James Wickham; WS 136, Pat Crowley; WS 79, Diarmuid Ó Donneabhain; WS 63, Michael O'Sullivan, Seán Butler, David O'Callaghan; WS 46, Patrick Twomey; WS 20, Tom Hales; WS 25, Pat Higgins; WS 16, Robert Langford; Diarmuid Lynch to Florrie O'Donoghue, 27 November 1944, Folder One; Michael Lynch Questionnaire, circa June 1947, Folder Three; Florrie O'Donoghue to Diarmuid Lynch, 3 January 1944, Michael Lynch to Diarmuid Lynch, 2 December 1944, Folder Six, U179, CCCA.

77   WS 46 Patrick Twomey. Twomey says the charge was against 'the Brigade officers'.
78   WS 20, Tom Hales; WS 25, Pat Higgins.
79   WS 16, Robert Langford; WS 25, Pat Higgins; WS 46, Patrick Twomey; WS 136, Pat Crowley.
80   WS 16, Robert Langford.
81   WS 20, Tom Hales. For additional correspondence relating to the inquiry, see Diarmuid Lynch to Florrie O'Donoghue, 27 November 1944, Folder One; Michael Lynch Questionnaire circa June 1947, Folder Three; Diarmuid Lynch to Florrie O'Donoghue, 5 September 1950; F. O'Donoghue to D. Lynch, 2 July 1950, Folder Four; F. O'Donoghue to D. Lynch, 3 January 1944; Michael Lynch to D. Lynch, 2 December 1954, Folder Six, U179, CCCA.
82   WS 63, Michael O'Sullivan, Seán Butler, David O'Callaghan.
83   Pauline Healy to Etienette Beauque, 21 January 1928, P48c/60, Papers of Terence MacSwiney's Biographers, UCD.
84   WS 1351, Humphrey O'Donoghue; WS 1063, Jerome Buckley; WS 1200, Cornelius O'Regan; WS 1418, Michael Kearney; WS 1456, John Kelleher; WS 1063, Jerome Buckley; WS 621, Samuel Kingston; Robert Langford Papers, U156/3, CCCA; WS 810, 3rd Battalion Joint Statement; WS 965, Tadhg MacCarthy; WS 759, John Jones; WS 1270, Joseph Cashman.
85   For one example, see Borgonovo, *Florence and Josephine O'Donoghue's War of Independence*, p. 155.
86   'Notes of Papers Found in Possession of John Nolan of Cork', Arrested 22 February 1917, Crime Special Branch Reports, CO 904/29.
87   WS 1584, Pa Murray.
88   Borgonovo, *Florence and Josephine O'Donoghue's War of Independence*, p. 25.
89   CI Report for February 1917, March 1917, April 1917, CO 904/102; Southern District Report for March 1917, CO 904/157; Connie Neenan Memoir, CCCA.
90   White and O'Shea, *Baptised in Blood*, p. 102; Undated Notes, 1955-208-11, Terence MacSwiney Collection, Cork Public Museum; O'Donoghue, *Tomás MacCurtain*, p. 94.
91   Frank Gallagher to William O'Brien, 31 December 1917, AS/157, William O'Brien Papers, UCC; WS 1707, Patrick Collins; WS 1521, Michael Walsh; WS 1579, Seán Lucey; WS 558, B Company, 2nd Battalion Joint Statement (Mark Wickham, John J. Lucey, Patrick Deasy and Maurice Fitzgerald); WS 1708, William Barry; WS 719, E Company, 1st Battalion Join Statement; O'Donoghue, *Tomás MacCurtain*, p. 131. The city briefly boasted a third battalion in the south city suburbs, but it was disbanded owing to unauthorised seizures and perhaps robberies committed by its commanders.
92   See 1950 correspondence between Diarmuid Lynch and Florrie O'Donoghue, Folder 4, U179, CCCA. MacSwiney may have been influenced by the church's opposition to secret societies. See 'Rossa's Recollections', undated notes, 1955-252, Terence MacSwiney Collection, Cork Public Museum. Diarmuid Lynch reported that in 1912 he had been advised against recruiting MacSwiney for the IRB membership and thought, 'The religious ban may have been the obstacle.' See WS 4, Diarmuid Lynch.
93   WS 4, Diarmuid Lynch; WS 104, George Lyons; WS 279, Seamus Dobbin; WS 339, Patrick McCormack.
94   See WS 1521, Michael Walsh; WS 1584, Patrick 'Pa' Murray; WS 1656, Daniel Healy; Ray Kennedy, P17b/111, Ernie O'Malley Notebooks, UCD Archives; Seán Breen,

O'Malley Notebooks, P17b/124; Borgonovo, *Florence and Josephine O'Donoghue's War of Independence*, p. 31; Robert Langford Draft IRA Pension Application, circa 1937, Langford Papers, U156/3(iii), CCCA; and Seán Healy to Florence O'Donoghue, 10 July 1965, MS 31,342 (2), NLI.

95   Borgonovo, *Florence and Josephine O'Donoghue's War of Independence*, pp. 31–2.

96   Ibid., p. 32.

97   For conflicting interpretations about whether this occurred in the pre-rising Volunteers, see WS 15, Fred Murray and WS 19, Liam Murphy.

98   WS 25, Pat Higgins.

99   Robert Langford response to 'Comments on Florence O'Donoghue's Life of Tomás MacCurtain', p. 9; WS 561, Matt O'Callaghan; WS 558, B Company, 1st Battalion, Joint Statement; WS 719, E Company, 1st Battalion, Joint Statement; WS 1561, Michael Walsh.

100   For details, see my paper '"The Lid Came Off": The IRB, The IRA and Dual Control in Cork City, 1917–1921', delivered to the 2008 conference, 'The Black Hand of Republicanism, The Fenians and History', Queen's University Belfast.

101   Borgonovo, *Florence and Josephine O'Donoghue's War of Independence*, pp. 26–7.

102   Barry Coldrey, *Faith and Fatherland: The Christian Brothers and the Development of Irish Nationalism, 1838–1921* (Dublin: Gill & Macmillan, 1988).

103   Peter Hart, 'The Geography of Revolution in Ireland, 1917–1923', *Past and Present*, vol. 155, no. 1, 1997, p. 171.

104   Past pupils of the 'South Mon' included Tomás MacCurtain, Tadhg Barry, Donal 'Óg' O'Callaghan, Terence MacSwiney, Tom Crofts, Seán O'Hegarty and P.S. O'Hegarty.

105   John O'Callaghan, *Revolutionary Limerick: The Republican Campaign for Independence in Limerick, 1913–1921* (Dublin: Irish Academic Press, 2010), pp. 152–5; Report of RIC District Inspector Cork North, 15 January 1919, CO 904/204/214 (J.J. Keane), Sinn Féin and Republican Suspects; *II*, 30 August 1915; *Southern Star*, 4 September 1915; *The Irish Times*, 15 March 1942; *Irish Press*, 16 March 1942; Coldrey, *Faith and Fatherland*, pp. 193–4.

106   Barry Coldrey, 'The Social Classes Attending Christian Brothers Schools in the Nineteenth Century', *British Journal of Educational Studies*, vol. 38, no. 1 (Feb. 1990), pp. 67–71.

107   O'Callaghan, *Revolutionary Limerick*, p. 48. See also Ian d'Alton, 'Educating for Ireland? The Urban Protestant Elite and the Early Years of Cork Grammar School, 1880–1914', *Éire-Ireland*, vol. 46, nos 3 & 4, Fall/Winter 2011, pp. 201–26.

108   Peter Hart, *The IRA and Its Enemies: Violence and Community in Cork, 1916–1923* (Oxford: Oxford University Press, 1998), pp. 202–25; Fitzpatrick, David, 'The Geography of Irish Nationalism, 1910–1921', *Past and Present*, no. 78, February 1978, pp. 119–44.

109   See P.E. Dewey, 'Military Recruiting and the British Labour Force During the First World War', *Historical Journal*, no. 27 (1984); Roy Douglas, 'Voluntary Enlistment in the First World War and the Work of the Parliamentary Recruiting Committee', *Journal of Modern History*, vol. 42, December 1970, pp. 564–85; Fitzpatrick, David, 'The Logic of Collective Sacrifice: Ireland and the British Army, 1914–1918', *Historical Journal*, no. 38, December 1995, pp. 1017–30; Keith Jeffery, *Ireland and the Great War* (Cambridge: Cambridge University Press, 1999); Peter Karsten, 'Irish Soldiers in the British Army, 1792–1922', *Journal of Social History*, vol. 17, Autumn 1983.

110   David Fitzpatrick, 'Militarism in Ireland, 1900–1922', in Thomas Bartlett and Keith Jeffery (eds), *A Military History of Ireland* (Cambridge: Cambridge University Press, 1996), p. 389.

111   See Hart, 'The Geography of Revolution in Ireland', p. 161. For one recruit's perception of threat to his economic future, see Borgonovo, *Florence and Josephine O'Donoghue's War of Independence*, p. 29.

112   Marie Coleman, *County Longford and the Irish Revolution, 1910–1923* (Dublin: Irish

Academic Press, 2003), pp. 162, 177–8. For British praise of the Cork Volunteer leadership, see Peter Hart (ed.), *British Intelligence in Ireland, 1920–1921: The Final Reports* (Cork: Cork University Press, 2002), p. 39.

113 Fitzpatrick, 'Militarism in Ireland', pp. 382–5.

114 Michael Sanders and Philip Taylor, *British Propaganda During the First World War* (London: Macmillan, 1982), pp. 137–40.

115 Nuala Johnson, *Ireland, the Great War and Geography of Remembrance* (Cambridge: Cambridge University Press, 2003), p. 31.

116 Hopkin, 'Domestic Censorship in the First World War', *Journal of Contemporary History*, vol. 5, no. 4 (1970), pp. 151–69; Nicolletta Gullace, 'White Feathers and Wounded Men: Female Patriotism and the Memory of the Great War', *Journal of British Studies*, vol. 36, April 1997, pp. 178–206.

117 See, '"Irish Tommie": The Construction of a Martial Manhood', *Bullán, An Irish Studies Journal*, Winter 1997, pp. 13–30.

118 For many examples, see the 'Code words and Nicknames Used in the Correspondence of the Irish Internees' in the Directory of Military Intelligence Postal Censorship Third and Fourth Report, 16 November 1918–15 December 1918, Directorate of Military Intelligence, CO 904/164, *British in Ireland Series*. Note also Florrie O'Donoghue's casual employment of British military terms in Borgonovo, *Florence and Josephine O'Donoghue's War of Independence*, Chapter 9.

119 CI Report for February 1917; O'Donoghue, *Tomás MacCurtain*, pp. 123–5; Seán Ó Cuiv to Etienette Beuque, 24 August, 1929, P48c/106/54; Translated MacCurtain Diary. See also Billy Mullins, *Memoir of Billy Mullins* (Tralee: Kenno Ltd, 1983), pp. 76–98.

120 CI Report for March 1917, CO 904/102; Southern District Intelligence Report for March 1917; *CC*, 8, 26 March, 17 April 1917.

121 *CC*, 26 March, 17, 26 April 1917; CI Report for April 1917.

122 Copy of the Order Issued 11 May 1917, 1955-208-11, Terence MacSwiney Collection, Cork Public Museum.

123 Borgonovo, *Florence and Josephine O'Donoghue's War of Independence*, p. 33.

124 *CC*, 14, 17 May, 4, 11 June 1917; *CE*, 4 June 1917.

125 WS 719, E Company, 1st Battalion, Joint Statement. See also WS 775, Patrick Crowe; WS 1675, Joe O'Shea; WS 1579, Seán Lucey.

126 Borgonovo, *Florence and Josephine O'Donoghue's War of Independence*, p. 80.

127 De Róiste Diary, 20 December 1916; de Róiste BMH Statement; WS 1707, Patrick Collins.

128 *CC*, 26–27 January, 10 February 1917; RIC Inspector General's Report for January 1917.

129 Ibid.

130 WS 869, P.J. Murphy.

131 WS 1584, Pa Murray.

132 RIC Inspector General's Report for January 1918, CO 904/105.

133 Southern District Intelligence Report for September 1917; CI Report for September 1917; *CC*, 4, 6 September 1917; Robert Langford Statement; WS 869, P.J. Murphy; WS 1547, Mick Murphy; WS 1656, Dan Healy; Florence O'Donoghue, *Tomás MacCurtain*, p. 133.

134 There were multiple reports of size of the seizure. The *Constitution* reported that twenty-five Lee Enfields and twenty-six Martini Henry carbines were taken (a total of fifty-one rifles), but the Cork Grammar School itself recorded a loss of fifty-five rifles (see *CC*, 4 September 1917 and the Cork Grammar School Annual Report in the *CC*, 20 December 1917). Volunteer Mick Murphy recalled forty-seven rifles taken (WS 1547), as did Robert Langford. Florrie O'Donoghue used that number in *Tomás MacCurtain* (p. 133). The Southern Command intelligence officer reported fifty-seven rifles taken (Southern District Intelligence Report for September 1917) and the RIC claimed fifty-six were lost (CI Report for September 1917). The RIC stated that 'Nearly all the rifles were useless', but raid leader Robert Langford

called them 'serviceable'. I would suggest many of the rifles were in poor shape, but others were functioning or repairable.

135 Robert Langford to Florrie O'Donoghue, 11 January 1953, MS 31,423 (9).

136 *CC*, 11 May, 12 July 1917; *CE*, 11 May, 12 July 1917.

137 Seán Healy to Florrie O'Donoghue, 17 September 1965, MS 31,342 (2), NLI.

138 *CE*, 18 May 1917; CI Report for May 1917.

139 See his excellent *From Public Defiance to Guerrilla Warfare: The Experience of Ordinary Volunteers in the Irish War of Independence, 1916–1921* (Dublin: Irish Academic Press, 1996), pp. 65–72.

140 *CC*, 28–29 September 1917; *CE*, 28–29 September 1917; CI Report for September 1917; Criminal Injuries Act of 1919 Statements, Papers of Head Constable John Brown.

141 *CE*, 2 October 1917.

142 Pat Higgins to Florrie O'Donoghue, 17 September 1936, MS 31,340 (7), NLI.

143 RIC Inspector General's Report for October 1917, CO 904/104.

144 Translated Tomás MacCurtain Diary; *CC*, 17 November 1917. Murray was quoted in the *Constitution* by one of his police escorts.

145 RIC Inspector General's Report for October 1917; Southern District Intelligence Report for October 1917; GHQ Ireland to Undersecretary, 12 August 1919, Special Branch Files, Edward Lynch, CO 904/207/252, Sinn Féin and Republican Suspects; *CC*, 22 October 1917; *CE*, 22 October 1917.

146 *CC*, 22 October 1917.

147 Borgonovo, *Florence and Josephine O'Donoghue's War of Independence*, p. 34.

148 *CC*, 22 October 1917; *CE*, 22 October 1917.

149 *CE*, 1 November 1917; *CC*, 1 November 1917. The arrested were: Tomás MacCurtain, Terence MacSwiney, Ned Lynch, Tim O'Sullivan, Seán O'Sullivan, Patrick Corkery, Fred Murray, Seán Healy, Seamus Courtney and Pat Higgins.

150 *CC*, 5 November 1917; *CE*, 5 November 1917.

151 *CC*, 5 November 1917.

152 Ibid., 20 November 1917.

153 Ibid.

154 See assorted RIC reports on drilling, Southern District, 19 November, 13, 18, 21, 24, 29 December 1917, CO 904/122, *British in Ireland Series*.

155 'IRA Prisoners of War, Cork Male Prison, 2 November 1917, Duties of Orderlies'; 'General Rules to be Observed by Prisoners, 2 November 1917'; MacCurtain Collection, L1945-233; Undated letter from Tommy O'Grady, D9-8, Cork Public Museum.

156 Clare's Brennan brothers were the first recorded prisoners to refuse to recognise the court in Cork. Their example was promptly followed by two batches of prisoners from Clare and Kerry. See *CE*, 11, 30–31 August 1917.

157 O'Donoghue, *Tomás MacCurtain*, p. 134; Seán Healy Draft Article, circa 1959, MS 31,324, NLI; Translated MacCurtain Diaries, MS 31,140.

158 *CC*, 17 November 1917; de Róiste Diary, 18 November 1917; Seán Healy Draft Article.

159 O'Donoghue, *Tomás MacCurtain*, pp. 134–5; Healy Draft Article, MS 31,140, NLI; de Róiste Diary, 18 November 1917; *CC*, 19 November 1917.

160 CCMM, 23 November 1917; CPLGMM, 22 November 1917; CI Report for November 1917; Hansard, HC Debates, 28 November 1917, vol. 99, cc 1992–3.

161 Supplement to Report Number Four on the Correspondence of Irish Internees, Code Words and Nicknames, 24 January 1919, Postal Censorship First and Second Report, CO 904/164, *British in Ireland Series*; *CE*, 24 November 1917; Seán Healy Draft Article.

162 Tomás MacCurtain to Cork Men's Prison Medical Officer, 1 November 1917, General Prison Board (GPB) 1917/4996, NA; *CC*, 19 November 1917; *CE*, 19 November 1917.

163 *CC*, 20 November 1917; *CE*, 20 November 1917.

164   *CC*, 20–21 November 1917; *CE*, 20 November 1917.
165   *CC*, 21–22 November 1917; *CE*, 22 November 1917; General Prison Board to Undersecretary, 23 November 1917, GPB 1917/4996.
166   Acting Governor L.J. Blake to GPB, 5 December 1917, GPB 1918/9.
167   See the General Prison Board letter books for 1917, 1918, 1919 and 1920, NA.
168   *CE*, 26 November 1917; *CC*, 26 November 1917.
169   *CC*, 26 November 1917.
170   CI Clayton to RIC Special Branch, 5 December 1917, CO 904/199, Éamon de Valera, Sinn Féin and Republican Suspects. See also RIC Inspector General to CI Clayton, 8 December 1917; CI Clayton to RIC Inspector General, 9 December 1917; Sgt Young Reports to Special Branch Headquarters, 2 December 1917, 11 December 1917, CO 904/199.
171   RIC Inspector General to CI Cork, 8 December 1917, CO 904/199, Sinn Féin and Republican Suspects.
172   *CE*, 10 December 1917; *CC*, 10 December 1917; CI Report for December 1917, CO 904/104; Southern District Intelligence Report for December 1917.
173   *CE*, 10 December 1917.

CHAPTER VI: TWILIGHT OF THE MOLLIES: THE DECLINE OF THE IRISH PARTY IN 1917

1   Colonel Maurice Moore to Henry Donegan, 30 May 1917, MS 10,547 (6/ii), NLI.
2   Frequent attendees included advanced nationalists Fred Cronin, Peter Casey, C.P. O'Sullivan and Paddy Meade; social activists Marie Lynch, Susanne Day, John Dorgan and J.J. Goggin; and trade unionists Alderman Kelleher, Denis Delea, John Callanan and Jerry Lane.
3   For a party breakdown of elected Guardians, see *CC*, 6 June 1914.
4   CPLGMM, 25 May 1916.
5   Ibid., 17 June 1916.
6   Ibid., 29 June 1916.
7   Ibid., 28 June, 9 August, 29 October 1917.
8   Ibid., 28 April, 7 July 1917; *CC*, 14 April 1917. They also empowered PLG members to act as delegates to Count Plunkett's Liberty Club meeting in Cork. See the CPLGMM, 7 April, 26 May 1917.
9   CPLGMM, 28 April, 9, 16 June, 30 August, 27 September, 11 October, 1 November 1917.
10   Ibid., 22 November 1917.
11   Ibid., 27 September 1917.
12   Storekeeper Patrick Sullivan resigned after the LGB called for his dismissal owing to irregularities with the workhouse accounts. See the CPLGMM, 2 August 1917. For an account of corruption among the Poor Law Guardians, see Susanne Day's often hilarious *The Amazing Philanthropists*.
13   CPLGMM, 30 August, 6 September, 25 October 1917; *CC*, 12–13 September 1917.
14   *CC*, 13 September 1917. In *The IRA and Its Enemies* (p. 206, footnote 106), Peter Hart suggested O'Hegarty secured the storekeeper position through his 'ability at intrigue', using the 'IRB to outmanoeuvre the Ancient Order of Hibernians'. That interpretation is not borne out by the LGB inquiry. O'Hegarty was uninvolved with the canvassing, though Tadhg Barry and Fred Cronin lobbied individual Guardians on O'Hegarty's behalf. C.P. O'Sullivan threatened to reveal the Hibernian candidate's collusion in the endemic corruption inside the workhouse, if he did not step aside.
15   *CC*, 3 April 1920. For O'Hegarty's public denunciation of corrupt practices in the workhouse, see *CE*, 8 October 1918, 31 January, 9 May, 28 November 1919; *CC*, 15 November 1918, 18 July, 13 August, 12 September, 19–20 December 1919. For coverage of the LGB inquiries see *CC*, 19 December 1919, 3, 10, 12–13 January 1920.
16   *CE*, 23 November 1917; CPLGMM, 22 November 1917.

17 These were Alderman Forde, Alderman John Cronin, Denis Delea, John Callanan, T.S. Doody, Michael Egan. The sympathetic labour-affiliated councillors were Delea, Callanan and Cronin.

18 Report of the US Consul at Queenstown, *The Irish Question at the Beginning of 1917*.

19 CCMM, 22 June, 21 July, 27 October 1916.

20 *CC*, 11 September 1916.

21 CCMM, 25 August 1916.

22 *Cork Free Press*, 16 September 1916.

23 *CC*, 11 September 1916.

24 *Cork Free Press*, 16 September 1916. The *Constitution* quoted O'Riordan's response as, 'you are descended from the planters and squatters.'

25 *Cork Free Press*, 16 September 1916.

26 CCMM, 21 July 1916.

27 Courtesy of Donal Ó Drisceoil.

28 *Southern Star*, 5 August 1916.

29 CCMM, 28 September, 9 November 1917.

30 CCMM, 10 November 1916, 12 January, 28 September 1917, 12 July, 23 August and 27 September 1918.

31 CCMM, 26 January, 27 April, 25 May, 8 June, 21, 28 September, 12 October, 23 November 1917.

32 'Civilian', *The Irish Canadian Rangers* (Montreal: Gazette Printing, 1916).

33 Robin B. Burns, 'The Montreal Irish and the Great War', *CCHA Historical Studies*, no. 52 (1985), pp. 67–81; Jerome aan de Wiel, *The Catholic Church and Ireland* (Dublin: Irish Academic Press, 2003), pp. 166–7; *CE*, 7 August 1917.

34 Burns, 'The Montreal Irish and the Great War', pp. 68–9, 72; 'Civilian', *The Irish Canadian Rangers*, pp. 48–57.

35 Burns, 'The Montreal Irish and the Great War', p. 75.

36 Michael Sanders and Philip Taylor, *British Propaganda During the First World War* (London: MacMillan, 1982), p. 154. See also the National Film Board of Canada website, http://onf-nfb.gc.ca/eng/collection/film/?id=54462 and the *Ottawa Citizen*, 12 April 1917.

37 John Redmond to J.J. Horgan, 16 December 1916, MS 18,270, NLI.

38 Joseph Devlin to J.J. Horgan, 2, 6, 8 January 1917, MS 18,271, NLI.

39 *CC*, 12–13, 30 January 1917; *CE*, 12, 30 January 1917.

40 *CC*, 1 February 1917.

41 *CE*, 24 May 1918. See O'Donahoe's entries in the Commonwealth War Graves Commission website, www.cwgc.org; and 'Attestation Papers', Canadian Expeditionary Force, Database for the First World War, Archivia Net, Library Archives of Canada (www.collections.canada.com). Cork newspapers also spelled his name as O'Donoghue.

42 *CC*, 31 January 1917; *CE*, 31 January 1917.

43 *CE*, 1, 26 February 1917. See Harbour Commission Secretary Sir James Long's similar sentiments, *CC*, 6 March 1917.

44 RIC Inspector General's Report for January 1917.

45 Hansard, *HC Debates, 15 February 1917, vol. 90, c. 789*; *CC*, 16 February 1917. Police reported similar notices on homes that flew the Union Jack during the Rangers' visit. See the CI Report for February 1917.

46 Reprinted in the *CC*, 27 February 1917.

47 *CC*, 27 February, 1 March 1917.

48 Ibid., 1 March 1917.

49 Ibid., 2 March 1917; Hansard, *HC Debates, 08 March 1917, vol. 91, cc 575-6W*.

50 *CC.*, 2 March 1917.

51 Ibid., 1 March 1917.

52 Ibid., 6 March 1917; *CE*, 6 March 1917; Cork Corporation Law and Finance Committee Meeting Minutes, 28 February 1917, CP/C/CM/LF/A14, CCCA.

53   *CE*, 26 February, 2, 6 March 1917; CCMM, 9 March 1917.

54   *CE*, 8 March 1917.

55   Ibid., 8–14 March 1917.

56   Ibid., 13 March 1917; *Southern Star*, 17 March 1917; CI Report for March 1917.

57   *CE*, 13 March 1917.

58   Southern District Military Intelligence Report for March 1917.

59   *CC*, 9 March 1917.

60   CI Report for March 1917.

61   For details on the Irish Convention, see R.B. McDowell, *The Irish Convention, 1917–1918* (London: Routledge & Kegan Paul, 1970); David G. Boyce, 'British Opinion, Ireland and the War, 1916–1918', *Historical Journal*, no. 17 (1974), pp. 575–93.

62   William O'Brien to David Lloyd George, 18 June 1917, F/41/9/2, Lloyd George Papers, House of Commons Archives [HCA] London.

63   J.J. Horgan, 'Precepts and Practice in Ireland, 1914–1919', *Studies*, 1919, pp. 210–26; J.J. Horgan, *From Parnell to Pearse: Some Recollections and Reflections* (Dublin: Richview Press, 1948), p. 302.

64   Tomás MacCurtain to Eilis MacCurtain, 24 May 1917, MacCurtain Collection, 1945-215, Cork Public Museum.

65   O'Brien to Lloyd George, 17 May and 18 June 1917, F/41/9/2; Lloyd George to O'Brien, 20 July 1917, F/41/9/4; O'Brien to Lloyd George, 21 July 1917, F/41/9/5, all found in the David Lloyd George Papers, HCA. See also David Lloyd George to William O'Brien, 20 July 1917, AS/154 and the AFIL pamphlet 'Correspondence with the Prime Minister', William O'Brien Papers, UCC.

66   Arthur Mitchell, *Labour in Irish Politics, 1890–1930* (Dublin: Irish Academic Press, 1974), p. 86.

67   CCMM, 25 May 1917.

68   *II*, 2 July 1917.

69   See advertisements in *CC* and *CE*, 14 June 1917.

70   *CE*, 14 June 1917.

71   Ibid., 25 June 1917.

72   Ibid., 14 June 1917.

73   *CC*, 15 June 1917; *CE*, 15 June 1917; CI Report for June 1917.

74   *CE*, 15 June 1917. The attending councillors were Lord Mayor Butterfield, Alderman Henry Dale, M. Kenneally, John Horgan, Peter Stack and Henry Beale.

75   *CC*, 15 June 1917.

76   *CE*, 15 June 1917.

77   *CC*, 15, 19 June 1917. Writing to the *Constitution*, Sinn Féin leader Tadhg O'Shea corrected its report that the hecklers shouted 'Down with Catholicity'. 'The expression used was, "Down with Capitalism".'

78   'Cork Past and Present: Handbook for the Irish Convention', MP 855, UCC; *CC*, 25–26 September 1918.

79   CHCMM, 5 September 1917; *CE*, 25 September 1917.

80   *CE*, 26 September 1918. Unionists included Sir Alfred Dobbin, Sir Stanley Harrington, Alderman Richard Beamish, James Murphy, Joseph Pike, Sir E.W.W. Becher, Sharman Crawford, A.R. MacMullen, Sir William Newsom. Representing the Irish Party were Willie O'Connor, Sir B.C. Windle, George Crosbie, James Crosbie, Coroner William Murphy, Coroner J.J. Horgan, D. Gamble, William Hart, Daniel Horgan.

81   *CE*, 24 September 1917.

82   *CC*, 24 September 1917.

83   *CE*, 24 September 1917.

84   CCMM, 25 November 1917.

85   *CC*, 25 September 1917; *CE*, 25 September 1917.

86   *CC*, 26 September 1917.

87   See the Convention Schedule, *CE*, 25 September 1917.

88   *CE*, 26 September 1917.
89   Chairman's Report on the Luncheon, CHCMM, 12 September 1917.
90   *CC*, 27 September 1917.
91   *CC*, 8 June 1918; *CE*, 12 June 1918.
92   *CC*, 27 September 1917; *CE*, 27 September 1917.
93   *CC*, 27 September 1917; *II*, 27 September 1917; WS 719, Company E (Blackpool) Joint Statement.
94   *CC*, 27 September 1917; *II*, 27 September 1917; Southern District Military Intelligence Report for September 1917; CI Report for September 1917. Liam de Róiste reported the crowd included non-republicans. See the de Róiste Diary, 27 September 1917.
95   *II*, 27 September 1917.
96   *CC*, 27 September 1917.
97   *II*, 27 September 1917.
98   *CC*, 27 September 1917.
98   *CC*, 28 September 1917; *The Irish Times*, 28 September 1917.
100 Horgan, *From Parnell to Pearse*, p. 315. See also Lyon's RIC Crime Special Branch File, CO 904/207/257, Malcolm Lyon, *Sinn Féin and Republican Suspects*.
101 Report of Dublin Metropolitan Police Detective Sergeant S. Fagan, 8 September 1917 and Lieutenant General Shaw to Chief Secretary, 30 May 1918, CO 904/207/257.
102 Report of Detective Inspector W. O'Donnell, New Scotland Yard, 27 June 1918, CO 904/207/257; Malcolm Lyon telegram to Fr Thomas Dowling, 27 September 1918, Unsorted Fr Thomas Papers, Capuchin Archives, Dublin.
103 *CE*, 6 September 1917. See also a copy of Lyon's petition to solve the conscription crisis through the 'International Magna Carta', circulated in Dublin in May 1918, US Consul, Cork, to US Ambassador Walter Hines Page, 17 May 1918, US Consul Records, Cork, Ireland, RG 84, vol. 118.
104 Report of Detective Inspector W. O'Donnell, 27 June 1918.
105 Lieutenant General Shaw to Chief Secretary, 30 May 1918; Frank Gallagher to Celia Saunders, 1 December 1917, 10055/34; Gallagher to Saunders, 12 December 1917, 10055/35.
106 *CE*, 6 September 1917; *Southern Star*, 15 September 1917; de Róiste Diary, 3 October 1917, 19 May 1918; Horgan, *From Parnell to Pearse*, p. 315; Report of Detective Sergeant S. Fagan, 8 September 1917.
107 Lyon to Fr Thomas, 25 August, 29 September 1917, Unsorted Fr Thomas Papers. Fr Thomas recalled that 'for almost 12 months I was fairly well prosecuted by his attentions'. For examples, see Lyon's telegrams to Fr Thomas 11, 22, 25, 30 August 1917, 6, 8, 13, 17, 27 and 29 September 1917, Unsorted Fr Thomas Papers.
108 Gallagher to Saunders, 1 December 1917; de Róiste Diary, 3 October 1917.
109 Lieutenant General Shaw to Chief Secretary, 30 May 1918.
110 De Róiste Diary, 19 May 1918; Report of Detective Sergeant S. Fagan, 8 September 1917.
111 Report of Detective Sergeant S. Fagan, 8 September 1917.
112 CCMM, 12 October 1917.
113 *CC*, 25 October 1917.
114 Ibid., 26, 30–31 October, 6 November 1917.
115 Ibid., 31 October, 6 November 1917.
116 Ibid., 28 October 1917.
117 CCMM, 9 November 1917.
118 *CE*, 10 November 1917.
119 *CC*, 10 November 1917.
120 *CE*, 10 November 1917.
121 CCMM, 9 November 1917.
122 *CE*, 10 November 1917.

123   *CC*, 12 November 1917.
124   De Róiste Diary, 27 November 1917; *CC*, 23 November 1917.
125   *CE*, 24 November 1917.
126   CCMM, 23 November 1917.
127   *CC*, 24 November 1917.
128   Southern District Military Intelligence Report for November 1917.
129   *CC*, 24 November 1917.
130   Ibid., 28 November 1917.
131   Corporation Law and Finance Committee Meeting Minutes, 28 November 1917; *CE*, 29 November 1917.
132   *CC*, 27 November 1917.
133   Ibid., 28 November 1917.
134   De Róiste Diary, 27 November 1917, MS 31,146, NLI.
135   *CE*, 29 November 1917.
136   Corporation Law and Finance Committee Meeting Minutes, 28 November 1917.
137   *CC*, 20 December 1917; *CE*, 21 December 1917; Corporation Law and Finance Committee Meeting Minutes, 19 December 1917.
138   *CC*, 20 December 1917.
139   CHCMM, 5 December 1917.
140   *CC*, 14, 16 January 1919; *CE*, 15–17 January 1919.
141   *CC*, 23 January 1919; *CE*, 23 January 1919.
142   *CC*, 30 January 1919; *CE*, 31 January 1919.
143   1915 RIC Intelligence Notes, PRO 903/19, TNA.
144   Philip Harold Barry to Colonel Moore, 15 May 1915; Diarmuid Coffey to Henry Donegan, 27 May 1915; Gerald Moroney to Colonel Moore, 14 August 1915, all found MS 10,547 (6II), NLI.
145   *CE*, 5 April 1915; CI Monthly Report for April 1915, CO 904/96; CI Monthly Report for August and September 1915, CO 904/97; CI Report for December 1915, CO 904/98; Draft Reply, J.J. Horgan to John Redmond, Circa 4 December 1915, MS 18,270, NLI.
146   Redmond to Moore, 11 December 1916, MS 16,262 (5), NLI.
147   Southern District Military Intelligence Reports for October and November 1916.
148   Patrick Rooney to John Redmond, 8 December 1916, MS 16,262 (5).
149   J.J. Horgan to Colonel Moore, 3 October 1916, MS 10,550, NLI.
150   Southern District Military Intelligence Report for January 1917.
151   Henry Donegan to Colonel Moore, 16 May 1917; Moore to Donegan, 30 May 1917, MS 10,547 (6/I).
152   Moore to Donegan, 30 May 1917.
153   Report to the Chief Secretary, 7 August 1917, Crime Special Branch Reports on Arms, CO 904/29, *British in Ireland Series*; *CC*, 23 July 1917; Laurence, Kettle to Moore, 19 July 1917, MS 10,544 (2), NLI.
154   *CC*, 19 July, 6–7 August 1917; *CE*, 6 August 1917.
155   Special Crime Branch Report to Undersecretary, 12 March 1917, CO 904/29.
156   Report to the Chief Secretary, 7 August 1917, CO 904/29.
157   *CE*, 16 August 1917; de Róiste Diary, 16 August 1917.
158   *CE*, 29 August 1917. The county council did denounce the seizure.
159   Special Branch Report from Cork, 29 August 1917, RIC Reports on Recruiting, CO 904/123, *British in Ireland Series*.
160   *CE*, 1 September 1917.
161   *II*, 29 September 1917.
162   Special Branch Report from Cork, 29 August 1917, RIC Reports on Recruiting.
163   *CE*, 9 December 1918.
164   UIL National Directory Minute Books, MS 708, NLI.
165   For examples, see City Executive meetings, *CE*, 13 March, 12 May, 15 October 1917; West Ward Branch, *CE*, 17 January 1917; Northwest Ward Branch, *CE*, 5 February, 17

October 1917; Central Branch, *CE*, 23 November 1917. The *II* reported UIL Cork City Executive meetings on 13 April, 12 June, 13 August and 22 September 1917.

166 *II*, 9 November 1917.

167 *CE*, 23 November 1917.

168 For examples see the CPLGMM, 1, 22 November 1917; CCMM, 27 September, 25 November 1918; CHCMM, 17 April 1918; *CE*, 17 April 1918.

169 For examples, see the *CE*, 26 January, 9 March, 27 June, 3 September, 5 November 1917.

170 *CE*, 26 June 1917.

171 *CC*, 11 May, 12 July 1917.

172 *CC*, 12 July 1917.

173 For examples, see the *CE*, 5 February, 17 October and 23 November 1917.

174 *CE*, 12 May, 15 October 1917.

175 1918 RIC Intelligence Notes, PRO 903/19/4, TNA.

176 *CC*, 19 January 1920.

177 AOH Cork County Annual Convention Report, 26 March 1916, CCCA.

178 AOH Cork County Annual Convention Report, 11 February 1917.

179 AOH CCCMM, 3 September 1916, CCCA.

180 AOH Cork County Annual Convention Report, 11 February 1917.

181 AOH Cork County Annual Convention Reports, 10 February 1918, 9 February 1919. The number of members dropped in 1917 from 3,117 to 2,454, while Board revenue declined from £50.00.06 to £34.7.2

182 AOH Cork County Annual Convention Report, 10 February 1918.

183 County Secretary Thomas Hallinan to National Secretary J.D. Nugent, 18 October 1919, AOH Cork County Letter Book, U839a/7, CCCA.

184 AOH Cork County Annual Convention Reports, 10 February 1918, 9 February 1919; Hallinan to J.D. Nugent, 24 February 1919, AOH County Board Letter Book.

185 AOH Cork County Annual Convention Report, 9 February; John Foley to J.D. Nugent, 30 January; Hallinan to Nugent, 9 August; Hallinan to Nugent, 2 October; Hallinan to J. Donovan, 7 October; Hallinan to Nugent, 9 December; Hallinan to Nugent, 9 December, all dated 1919 and found in the AOH County Board Letter Book.

186 Hallinan to Nugent, 1 November 1919, AOH County Board Letter Book.

187 AOH Cork County Annual Convention Report, 11 February 1917.

188 AOH CCCMM 15 May 1918, AOH Second Degree Meeting Book, U389a/6.

189 Council meetings of 21 March, 15 May 1918, 26 June, 22 July 1919; General Membership meetings of 26 June, 18 September 1918, 25 March, 5 November 1919, AOH Second Degree Meeting Book.

190 AOH Cork County Annual Convention Report, 10 February 1918; Thomas Byrne to J.D. Nugent, 11 December 1918, AOH Second Degree Letter Book; Second Degree General Membership Meeting, 11 March 1919, AOH Second Degree Meeting Book.

191 Second Degree Council meetings of 21 August, 8 October 1918; Second Degree General Membership Meeting of 18 September 1918; Second Degree Special Membership Meeting of 21 October 1918; Provisional Council Meeting of 13 March 1919, all found AOH Second Degree Meeting Book; 2nd Division Secretary Joseph Bransfield to J.D. Nugent, 29 October 1921, AOH Second Degree Letter Book.

192 AOH Cork County Annual Convention Reports, 10 February 1918, 9 February 1919.

193 For examples, see Hallinan to Nugent, 2 May, 29 September, 6, 18 October 1919.

194 AOH Division 226, Book of Attendance, Secretary John Ronayne, U389a/4, CCCA.

195 AOH Cork County Annual Convention Report, 10 February 1918; Hallinan to Nugent, 3, 15 March 1919, AOH County Board Letter Book.

196 Second Degree General Membership Meeting, 11 March 1919; Hallinan to Nugent, 24 February 1919.

197 AOH Cork County Annual Convention Report, 18 January 1920; Hallinan to Nugent, 18 October 1919.

198 Report of the Biennial National Convention, 19–20 August 1919, Submitted by Cork

Delegates Thomas Hallinan and Michael Lynch, U389a/22; Hallinan to Nugent, 8 April 1919, AOH County Board Letter Book.
199   Hallinan to Nugent, 9 August 1919, AOH Cork County Board Letter Book.
200   Hallinan to Nugent, 17 November 1919, AOH Cork County Board Letter Book.
201   AOH Cork County Annual Convention Report, 19 February 1921.
202   Ibid., 15 January 1922.
203   Ibid., 14 February 1926.

CHAPTER VII: CORK WOMEN, AMERICAN SAILORS AND CATHOLIC VIGILANTES, 1917–18

1   *New York Times*, 3 November 1919.
2   See *CC*, 11, 12, 14, 16, 20 December 1916; and *CE*, 11, 13,18 December 1916.
3   *CE*, 13 December 1916.
4   Ibid., 11 December 1916. The 'Up the Mollies' cheer indicates the presence of AOH members.
5   *CC*, 11 December 1916.
6   *CE*, 11 December 1916.
7   5 December 1915, AOH Cork County Council Minute Book; Fr Russell's Letter to the Editor, *CE*, 13 December 1916. Irish Party MP John O'Connor likewise denied Sinn Féin sentiments were voiced during the protest. See Hansard, HC Debates, 31 December 1916, vol. 88, cc 1638–9.
8   See letter of 'A City Priest', *CE*, 13 December 1916.
9   Statement of Henry Standish Barry to the Irish Grants Committee, 21 January 1926, PRO 762/70/11, TNA.
10   *CC*, 16 December 1916; *CE*, 18 December 1916.
11   Cork County Inspector to Chief Secretary's Office, undated, CSORP 1916/26,190, NA.
12   *CC*, 20 December 1916.
13   Paul Halpern, *A Naval History of World War One* (London: University College London Press, 1994), p. 359; Cork Harbour Commission Meeting Minutes, 6 June 1917, PCA.
14   Halpern, *A Naval History of World War One*, p. 359; E.K. Chatterton, *Danger Zone: The Story of the Queenstown Command* (London: Rich & Cowan, 1936), p. 329; *CC*, 8 January 1919; Elting Elmore Morison, *Admiral Sims and the Modern American Navy* (New York: Russell & Russell, 1968), p. 382.
15   Lewis Bayly, *Pull Together! The Memoirs of Admiral Sir Lewis Bayly* (London: George G. Harrap, 1939), p. 233; Chief Secretary for Ireland Memorandum to War Cabinet, 'Attitude of Civil Population Towards Men of United States Naval Forces at Cork and Queenstown', 23 September 1917, Cabinet Papers (henceforth cited as CAB) 24/27, TNA.
16   Chatterton, *Danger Zone*, p. 255–6.
17   WS 1741, Michael O'Donoghue. See also WS 1737, Seamus Fitzgerald.
18   *New York Times*, 3 November 1919.
19   For an example, see *CE*, 30 November 1918.
20   *CC*, 11 March 1916.
21   Maria Luddy, *Prostitution and Irish Society, 1800–1940* (Cambridge: Cambridge University Press, 2007), pp. 25–6, 138–40, 156–62, 209; Diarmaid Ferriter, *Occasions of Sin: Sex & Society in Modern Ireland* (Dublin: Royal Irish Academy, 2007), pp. 27–9, 59–60.
22   Luddy, *Prostitution and Irish Society*, pp. 22, 24, 32, 37, 51, 57, 112–13. See also Colman O'Mahony, *In the Shadows: Life in Cork 1750–1930* (Cork: Tower Books, 1997), pp. 245–54. The military bases were Victoria Barracks, Ballincollig Barracks and Queenstown Naval Station.
23   Maria Luddy, 'Women and the Contagious Diseases Acts 1864–1886', *History Ireland*, vol. 1, no. 1, Spring 1993, pp. 32–4; Ferriter, *Occasions of Sin*, pp. 27–9.
24   Luddy, *Prostitution and Irish Society*, pp. 112–13, 145; Frances Finnegan, *Do Penance or*

Perish: A Study of Magdalen Asylums in Ireland (Co. Kilkenny: Congrave Press, 2001), pp. 159–65, 168, 202.

25   Luddy, *Prostitution and Irish Society*, p. 180. See also *The Irish Citizen*, 15 May 1915 (reference courtesy of Sarah-Anne Buckley); *CE*, 21 May 1915; *CC*, 21 May 1915.

26   *CC*, 21 May 1915.

27   Ibid., 11 March 1916.

28   *CE*, 21 August 1916.

29   *CC*, 9 June 1917.

30   CCMM, 8 June 1917.

31   *CC*, 14 June 1917.

32   Letter from 'Corkonian', *Irish Independent*, 15 September 1917.

33   *CC*, 10 June 1917.

34   See CHCMM, 30 May 1917, 4 July 1917 and 17 July 1917.

35   Arthur Julian to Cork Harbour Commission, CHCMM, 25 July 1917.

36   *CC*, 26 July 1917.

37   RIC 1917 Intelligence Notes, PRO 903/19, TNA.

38   Luddy, *Prostitution and Irish Society*, pp. 162–3, 165, 172–6, 179; *II*, 2 July 1912, 14 December 1914, 5 April 1919; *Anglo-Celt*, 18 October 1919.

39   *Southern Star*, 16 November 1911, 6 January 1912; *II*, 5–6 December 1911, 1 January, 2 July 1912; *Sunday Independent*, 7 July 1912.

40   Cork Corporation Law and Finance Committee Meeting Minutes, 20 December 1916, 17 April, 9 May, 13 June 1917, CP/C/CM/F/A14, CCCA.

41   Lucy Bland, 'In the Name of Protection: The Policing of Women in the First World War', in Julia Brophy and Carol Smart (eds), *Women in Law: Explorations in Law, Family and Sexuality* (London: Routledge & Kegan Paul, 1985), pp. 23–49; Philippa Levine, '"Walking the Streets in a Way No Decent Woman Should": Women Police in World War One', *Journal of Modern History*, March 1994, pp. 34–78. For further discussions of British 'moral panic', see Susan Pederson, 'Gender, Welfare and Citizenship in Britain During the Great War', *American Historical Review*, vol. 95, no. 4, October 1990, pp. 983–1,006; Janis Lomas, '"Delicate Duties": Issues of Class and Respectability in Government Policy Towards the Wives and Widows of British Soldiers in the Great War', *Women's History Review*, no. 9, March 2000, pp. 123–47; and Angela Wollacott, '"Khaki Fever" and its Control: Gender, Class, Age and Sexual Morality on the British Homefronts in the First World War', *Journal of Contemporary History*, vol. 29, no. 2, April 1994, pp. 325–47.

42   Luddy, *Prostitution and Irish Society*, pp. 39–40, 153–4, 174–7; *Irish Citizen*, 23 October 1915, January 1917; *The Irish Times*, 2, 14 January, 15 April 1915, 18, 26 January 1916, 19 January 1918.

43   'Attitudes of Civil Population', CAB 24/26.

44   Southern District Military Intelligence Report, September 1917; CI Report for September 1917, CO 904/104.

45   CI Report for September 1917; Southern District Military Intelligence Report for September 1917.

46   *CC*, 3 September 1917.

47   Ibid., 3 September 1917

48   Ibid., 4, 22 September 1917.

49   Ibid., 4 September 1917.

50   Ibid., 25 June, 4, 28 September 1917.

51   *CE*, 4 September 1917.

52   *New York Times*, 23 June 1921.

53   William N. Still (ed.), *The Queenstown Patrol, 1917: The Diary of Commander Joseph Knefler Taussig, U.S. Navy* (Newport: Naval War College Press, 1996), p. 113.

54   Diary of Lieutenant Lucien Byron Green, US Navy, Volume II, 4, 26 September, and 27 October 1917. Courtesy Rollie Green, Carrigaline, Co. Cork.

55   *CC*, 5 September 1917, 6 October 1917; Southern District Military Intelligence

Report for September 1917; Vice-Admiral Lewis Bayly to Vice-Admiral William Sims, 23 October 1917, CAB 24/30, TNA; Green Diary, 4, 26 September, 27 October, 1917.

56   Sims, Rear-Admiral William Sowden, *The Victory at Sea* (London: John Murray, 1920), p. 72; Bayly, *Pull Together!*, p. 233; Chatterton, *Danger Zone*, pp. 255–6.

57   Green Diary, 26 September 1917.

58   *CC*, 6 October 1917.

59   Letter from 'Uncle Bob', *CE*, 25 September 1917.

60   Letter from M.J. Crimmins, *CE*, 28 November 1917.

61   *CE*, 24 June, 1, 11 July 1918.

62   *CC*, 22 September 1917.

63   CI Report for September 1917; *CC*, 6 October 1917.

64   Cork delegates 'appointed at an influential meeting of citizens' to Vice-Admiral Sir L. Bayly, 22 October 1917, CAB 24/30.

65   Bayly to Sims, 23 October 1917, CAB 24/30.

66   Admiral Bayly to Admiral Sims, 'Questions Asked by the Lord Mayor of Cork in the Presence of Captain Pringle, USA and the Deputation', 23 October 1917, CAB 24/30.

67   Bayly to Sims, 23 October 1917.

68   Chatterton, *Danger Zone*, p. 257; Dr J.M. Barry, *Old Glory at Queenstown: The US Maritime Presence at Queenstown, 1840–1920* (Cork: Sidney Publishing, 1999); Sims, *The Victory at Sea*, pp. 71–2.

69   Admiralty Memorandum for the War Cabinet, 19 September 1917, CAB 24/26.

70   CI Report for December 1917, CO 904/104; RIC Inspector General's Report for January 1918, CO 904/105, *British in Ireland Series*; Bishop Cohalan to Liam de Róiste, 7 December 1917, C48, de Róiste Papers, CCCA.

71   Sims, *The Victory at Sea*, pp. 71–2.

72   *CC*, 21 March 1918.

73   CHCMM, 10 July 1918.

74   *II*, 6 October 1917.

75   Luddy, *Prostitution and Irish Society*, pp. 190–91; Ben Novick, *Conceiving Revolution: Nationalist Propaganda during the First World War* (Dublin: Four Courts Press, 2001), pp. 154–7.

76   Lucy Bland, '"Purifying the Public World": Feminist Vigilantes in Late Victorian England', *Women's History Review*, vol. 1, no. 3, 1992, pp. 397–412.

77   *CE*, 8 September 1917; *II*, 12 September 1917; *Anglo-Celt*, 15 September 1917.

78   *CE*, 8 September 1917.

79   *CC*, 12 September 1917, 6 October 1917; *II*, 12 September 1917; Case notes, Parente vs. the Crown, 28,979-100-9, Box 2492, Secretary of the Navy General Correspondence, 1916-1926, RG 80, National Archives I, Washington DC.

80   Case notes, Parente vs. the Crown.

81   Southern District Military Intelligence Report for October 1917.

82   Ensign Dennis Ryan, USS *Conyngham*, to Senior Officer Present, 9 September 1917, P Bases – Queenstown, General Correspondence, Folder 1, Box 452, RG 45, Records Collection of the Office of Naval Records and Library, National Archives I; Admiralty Memorandum for the War Cabinet, 19 September 1917, CAB 24/26; Sims, *The Victory at Sea*, p. 71.

83   *II*, 12 September 1917.

84   Memorandum of Associated Press of America Correspondent to US Consulate, Cork, 14 September 1914, vol. 113, US Consular Records, Cork, Ireland, RG 84.

85   Copy of Notes in the Case of Parente vs. the Crown, 28,979-100-9, Box 2492.

86   Captain J.R.P. Pringle, Senior Officer Present, US Naval Forces Europe, to US Consul, Queenstown, 4 October 1917, vol. 113, RG 84. See also same file, Captain J.R.P. Pringle to RIC District Inspector, Queenstown, 27 September 1917.

87   Attorney General to RIC Cork County Inspector, 20 September 1917, CSORP 1917/23,039, NA.

88 Assistant Secretary of the US Navy Gordon Woodbury to Francis Healy, Queenstown, 3 March 1921, 26,524-451, Box 1941, RG 80.

89 Letter and attachments of Acting Secretary of the Navy to Chief of Bureau of Navigation, 8 June 1920, 28478-100-9, Box 2492, RG 80. See also US Consul's Charles Hathaway's undated notes, RG 84, vol. 113.

90 *CE*, 29 September 1917; *The Irish Times*, 13 October 1917; *II*, 15 December 1917.

91 Cobh Urban District Council to Secretary of the Navy Josephus Daniels, 20 February 1920, 28478-100-9; Sims, *The Victory at Sea*, p. 71.

92 For examples, see the *CC*, 9, 21 July 1920.

93 *CC*, 17, 26 July 1917.

94 Luddy, *Prostitution and Irish Society*, pp. 36–7.

95 Southern District Military Intelligence Report for October 1917.

96 *NYT*, 3 November 1919.

97 Irish Chief Secretary to War Cabinet, 23 September 1916, CAB 24/27.

98 J.L. Fawsitt to Liam de Róiste, 12 February 1919, MS 10539/449, Trinity College Dublin Archives; Senator James Phelan to Charles Hathaway, US Consul, Queenstown, 20 January 1919, and Charles Hathaway to Senator James Phelan, 11 July 1919, vol. 128, US Consular Records, Cork, Ireland, RG 84; Liam de Róiste Diary entry, 14 July 1919, U271A/27, CCCA. Phelan's letter refers to a 'marine' rather than a 'naval rating'.

99 Letter from J.P. O'B', *CC*, 9 December 1918; Letter from 'Doughboy', *CC*, 24 December 1918; letters from 'A Sailor Who Has Been There' and 'Common Sense', *NYT*, 6 July 1919; letter from Wallace Irwin, George Barr McCutcheon and Julian Street, *NYT*, 14 June 1921; letters from 'An Ex-Serviceman' and Frank M. Taylor, *New York Tribune*, 1 December 1920.

100 Memorandum of Associated Press of America Correspondent, 14 September 1917; Admiral Bayly to Admiral Sims, 'Questions Asked by the Lord Mayor of Cork in the Presence of Captain Pringle, USA and the Deputation', 23 October 1917, CAB 24/30.

101 *CC*, 21 June 1917.

102 Taussig, *The Queenstown Patrol*, p. 21.

103 Sims, *The Victory at Sea*, p. 69.

104 Letter from Lieutenant (JG) Kenneth B. Keyes and Lieutenant (JG) King Whitney, *NYT*, 8 November 1919. See also letters from Henry Beston Sheahan and J.T. Rowland, *NYT*, 5 November 1919; letter from J.P. O'B, *CC*, 9 December 1918; letter from 'Doughboy', *CC*, 24 December 1918.

105 Paul McMahon, *British Spies and Irish Rebels: British Intelligence and Ireland, 1916–1945* (Woodbridge: Boydell Press, 2008), pp. 23–5; Bayly, *Pull Together!*, p. 195; Sims, *The Victory at Sea*, p. 72.

106 Bayly, *Pull Together!*, p. 195.

107 RIC Cork County Inspector to District Inspector, Queenstown, 3 March 1920; Commander in Chief Coast of Ireland Admiral Lewis Bayly to Secretary of the Admiralty, 29 June 1918; W.F. Nicholson, Secretary of the Admiralty, to Undersecretary, Dublin Castle, 6 August 1918, CO 904/123, *British in Ireland Series*.

108 Captain R.C. Russell, American Red Cross, Queenstown, to American Red Cross Committee, London, 5 August 1918, Queenstown Office, Ireland, 1919, American National Red Cross Papers, Box 55, Hoover Institute Library.

109 Luddy, *Prostitution and Irish Society*, pp. 172–8; Novick, *Conceiving Revolution*, pp. 150–7.

110 Luddy, *Prostitution and Irish Society*, pp. 170–2.

111 Margaret Ó hÓgartaigh, *Kathleen Lynn: Irishwoman, Patriot, Doctor* (Dublin: Irish Academic Press, 2006), pp. 38–9.

112 *CE*, 19 September 1917.

113 Ferriter, *Occasions of Sin*, pp. 59–60.

114 Cork Corporation Public Health Committee Meeting Minutes, 13 November 1917,

27 November 1917, 8 January 1918, CP/C/CM/PH/A27, CCCA; CPLGMM, 17 January 1918, CCCA.

115 Cork Corporation Public Health Committee Meeting Minutes, 15 February 1918; CPLGMM, 21 February 1918.

116 Cork Corporation Public Health Committee Meeting Minutes, 12 March 1918; CPLGMM, 6 December 1917, 17 January 1918, 18 July 1918. See also Luddy, *Prostitution and Irish Society*, pp. 187–91.

117 Ó hÓgartaigh, *Kathleen Lynn*, p. 39.

118 Levine, '"Walking the Streets in a Way No Decent Woman Should"', pp. 52–7; Luddy, *Prostitution and Irish Society*, pp. 192–3; Ferriter, *Occasions of Sin*, pp. 59–60.

119 Hansard 5, vol. 103, cc 1096–7 (25 February 1918); vol. 104, c. 783 (19 March 1918).

120 *CE*, 15 March 1918.

121 *CC*, 21 March 1918.

122 Ibid., 19 April 1918.

123 CPLGMM, 21 March 1918.

124 CI Report for March 1918, CO 904/105

125 Sims, *The Victory at Sea*, p. 72.

126 *CE*, 19 March 1918.

127 *CC*, 19 March 1918.

128 CI Report for March 1918.

129 *CC*, 19 March 1918.

130 Ibid., 20 March 1918.

131 *CE*, 26 March 1918.

132 John O'Callaghan, *Revolutionary Limerick: The Republican Campaign for Independence in Limerick, 1913–1921* (Dublin: Irish Academic Press, 2010), pp. 73–4.

133 See the Secretary's and Caretaker's Reports, CHCMM, 10 July 1918. 'Revolting acts' comes from the 17 July 1918 meeting.

134 CHCMM, 17 July 1918.

135 *CE*, 5 July 1918.

136 CCMM, 27 September 1918.

137 Ibid., 20 December 1918, 10 January 1919.

138 Letters from 'Doughboy' and 'Curious', *CC*, 24 December 1918.

139 *CC*, 7 November 1918.

140 Morison, *Admiral Sims*, pp. 276–84.

141 Sims, *The Victory at Sea*, pp. 69–72.

142 *New York Times*, 3, 17 November 1919.

143 'Sims-Daniels Controversy', newspaper clipping collection, Box 13, George Barr Baker Papers, Hoover Institute; and Sims draft statements and assorted preparation material, circa 1919–20, in connection with his testimony to the US Senate Committee of Investigation into the Naval Conduct of the War, circa 1919–20, Box 11, Tracy B. Kittridge Papers, Hoover Institute.

144 *New York Times*, 16, 26 January 1921. See also Alan Ward, *Ireland and Anglo-American Relations, 1899–1921* (London: Weidenfeld & Nicolson, 1969), pp. 246–7.

145 Morison, *Admiral Sims*, p. 482; *NYT*, 23 June 1921; and the US Navy File on the episode, 28,478-210, Box 2493, RG 80.

146 Morison, *Admiral Sims*, pp. 482–6; *NYT*, 11, 22, 23 June 1921.

147 For a Second World War comparison, see Leane McCormick, '"One Yank and They're Off": Interactions between US Troops and Northern Irish Women, 1942–1945', *Journal of the History of Sexuality*, vol. 15, no. 2 (May 2006), pp. 228–57.

148 M. O'Leary to Con O'Donovan, 8 January 1919, p. 1088, Postal Censorship First and Second Report, CO 904/164, *British In Ireland Series*. See also *CC*, 23 November 1918; and 1918 Navy Thanksgiving Concert Programme, Palace Theatre, Cork, courtesy Michael Lenihan, Cork.

149 *CE*, 1, 3 April 1919.

150 Ibid., 3 April 1919.

CHAPTER VIII: GENDER, NATIONALISM AND CORK CUMANN NA MBAN, 1916–18

1   Cumann na mBan, Poblachta na hÉireann Branch Concert Programme, circa January 1919, 2007-38-16, Lil Conlon Collection, Cork Public Museum.
2   *CE*, 11 August 1914; *Irish Citizen*, 26 September, 12 December 1914.
3   *Irish Citizen*, 22 May 1915.
4   Ibid., September 1917.
5   Rosemary Cullen Owens, *Louise Bennett* (Cork: Cork University Press, 2001), p. 31; Margaret Ward, '"Suffrage First, Above All Else": An Account of the Irish Suffrage Movement', *Feminist Review*, no. 10 (Spring 1982), p. 33; Susanne Day, *Round About Bar-Le-Duc* (London: Skeffington & Son, 1918); *Irish Citizen*, 5 June 1915.
6   *Irish Citizen*, 17 October, 21 November 1914, 23, 30 January 1915.
7   Ibid., September, October 1917. For criticism of Susanne Day's departure, see *Irish Citizen*, 5 June 1915.
8   Ibid., 21, 28 November 1914, September 1917. MWFL submissions to the *Irish Citizen* disappeared (with one exception) after January 1915.
9   *Irish Citizen*, September and October 1917.
10 Timothy Bowman, *Carson's Army: the Ulster Volunteer Force, 1910–1922* (Manchester: Manchester University Press, 2007), pp. 60–1, 84.
11 Paula Connolly McArdle, 'The Munster Women's Franchise League, 1910–1918', in Bernadette Whelan (ed.), *Clio's Daughters: Essays on the Irish Women's History, 1845–1939* (Limerick: Limerick University Press, 1997), pp. 32–51.
12 *CE*, 9 November 1910.
13 De Róiste *Evening Echo* Series, 25 November 1954. For details of Inghinidhe na hÉireann, see Sinead McCoole, *No Ordinary Women: Irish Female Activists in the Revolutionary Years, 1900–1923* (Madison, WI: University of Wisconsin Press, 2006), pp. 20–5.
14 Florence O'Donoghue, *Tomás MacCurtain: Soldier and Patriot* (Tralee: Anvil Press, 1971), p. 18.
15 Robert Langford Draft BMH Statement.
16 Of seventy-three profiles, I count: fifty-eight Dubliners, fifty-seven women from middle or upper-class backgrounds and just sixteen from the working or lower-middle classes.
17 *CC*, 5 March 1918.
18 See the Cumann na mBan Cork District Council (CDC) Meeting Minutes 1918–20, 2007-38-21 and 1920–1, 2007-38-23, Cork Public Museum. For the inactive UCC branch, see the meetings of 2 December 1920 and 28 August 1921.
19 Undersecretary Passports, Dublin Castle to Officer in Charge, Passport Office, Liverpool, 3 December 1920, PRO 904/170 (4), TNA.
20 WS 446, Frank Haynes; WS 637, Muriel MacSwiney.
21 WS 1561, Margaret Lucy.
22 WS 1576, Peg Duggan; Interview with Ida Ní Shé, 14 March 2009; 25 January 1920, Fourth Annual General Meeting, CDC Meeting Minutes.
23 Margaret Ward (ed.), *In Their Own Voice: Women and Irish Nationalism* (Cork: Attic Press, 1995), pp. 42–6; Rosemary Cullen Owens, 'Constance Markievicz's "Three Great Movements" and the 1916 Rising', in Gabriel Doherty and Dermot Keogh, *1916: The Long Revolution* (Cork: Mercier Press, 2007), pp. 197–224.
24 WS 1561, Margaret Lucy; *CC*, 9 June 1914; *CE*, 9 June 1914. The Limerick Cumann na mBan started the same month. See Deirdre McCarthy, 'Cumann na mBan: The Limerick Link, 1914–1921', in Paula C. McArdle (ed.), *Daughters of Erin* (Limerick: University of Limerick, 1997), pp. 52–73.
25 Miss A. O'Leary (AFIL Ladies Club) to Mary MacSwiney, 19 May 1914, P48a/8/3; Maurice Talbot-Crosbie to Mary MacSwiney, 24 May 1914, P48a/8/4; Coroner J.J. Horgan to Mary MacSwiney, 25 May 1914, P48a/8/8; 6 June 1914, John Hoare to Mary MacSwiney, P48a/8/22, all found in the Mary MacSwiney Papers, UCD Archives.

26   *CC*, 9 June 1914.
27   WS 1561, Margaret Lucy; de Róiste *Evening Echo* Series, 25 November 1914; Gerry White and Brendan O'Shea, *Baptised in Blood: The Formation of the Cork Brigade of the Irish Volunteers, 1913–1916* (Cork: Mercier Press, 2005), p. 36.
28   WS 1576, Peg Duggan; Cumann na mBan Provisional Committee Memo, Circa 1914, P48a/8/26, Mary MacSwiney Papers.
29   WS 1561, Margaret Lucy; WS 1576, Peg Duggan. At the outbreak of the war, MacSwiney and Madelaine O'Hegarty reiterated the organisation as 'solely national' and committed to supporting the Irish Volunteers and retaining local food supplies. See *CE*, 26 August 1914.
30   WS 1576, Peg Duggan; Cumann na mBan Provisional Committee Memo, Circa 1914.
31   WS 1561, Margaret Lucy; Department of Agriculture and Technical Instruction for Ireland (DATII) to Mary MacSwiney, 22 March 1915, P48a/8/24; 7 July 1915, DATII to Mary MacSwiney, P48a/8/28; DATII to Mary MacSwiney, 24 July 1915, P48a/8/30, all found in the Mary MacSwiney Papers.
32   Lil Conlon, *Cumann na mBan and the Women of Ireland* (Kilkenny: Kilkenny People, 1969), pp. 13–14, 17, 18, 20; *CC*, 18 March 1916.
33   WS 1561, Margaret Lucy.
34   O'Donoghue, *Tomás MacCurtain*, p. 80. See also Cork Cumann na mBan to Mary MacSwiney, 24 February 1916, P48a/8/37.
35   Gerry White and Brendan O'Shea, 'Easter 1916 in Cork: Order, Counter-Order and Disorder', in Doherty and Keogh, *1916: The Long Revolution*, pp. 169–96; WS 119, Eitne MacSwiney; Eithne Nic Shuibhne (Annie MacSwiney), 'The 1916 in the South: A Refutation of P.S. O'Hegarty's Version', *The United Irishman*, December 1949 (Courtesy Ide Ní Shé); WS 119, Eitne MacSwiney; de Róiste Draft BMH Statement, p. 438.
36   WS 1561, Margaret Lucy; Translated Tomás MacCurtain Diary, 1 May 1916; White and O'Shea, *Baptised in Blood*, p. 112.
37   Charlotte Fallon, *Soul on Fire: A Biography of Mary MacSwiney* (Cork: Mercier Press, 1986), pp. 32–4; de Róiste Draft BMH Statement, p. 449.
38   Home Office Report, 9 July 1916; Mary MacSwiney to Home Secretary Herbert Samuel, 19 July 1916; Governor His Majesty's Prison, Reading to Undersecretary of State, Home Office, 14 July 1916, all found in the Terence MacSwiney Home Office File, HO 144/10308, hard copy, Cork Public Museum.
39   Governor His Majesty's Prison, Reading to Undersecretary of State, Home Office, 14 July 1916.
40   *CE*, 16 April 1917; *CC*, 16, 20 April 1917; Conlon, *Cumann na mBan and the Women of Ireland*, p. 45.
41   *CC*, 25–26 June, 5, 23 November 1917; *CE*, 25 June 1917, 10 April 1918. See also Town Councillor J.J. Goggin's letter to the *II*, 24 September 1917.
42   WS 446, Frank Haynes.
43   CI Report for June 1917; CI Report for July 1918, CO 904/106; *CE*, 5 November 1917, 6 March, 24 July 1918; de Róiste Diary, 23 October 1917; WS 446, Frank Haynes.
44   *CE*, 16 April, 14 August 1917; *CC*, 11 May, 25 June, 4 September 1917.
45   Susan Pederson, 'Gender, Welfare and Citizenship in Britain During the Great War,' *American Historical Review*, October 1990, pp. 983–1,006.
46   *CC*, 11 May 1917.
47   Ibid., 25–26 June 1917; WS 446, Frank Haynes.
48   *CC*, 12 November, 16 December 1918; de Róiste Diary, 11–12 November 1918.
49   For Offaly, see Marnie Hay, *Bulmer Hobson and the nationalist movement in twentieth-century Ireland* (Manchester: Manchester University Press, 2009), p. 185. For Limerick, John O'Callaghan, *Revolutionary Limerick: The Republican Campaign for Independence in Limerick, 1913–1921* (Dublin: Irish Academic Press, 2010), p. 37 and White and O'Shea, *Baptised in Blood*, p. 84. For Waterford see *II*, 15, 21 and 23 March 1918; BMH WS 990, John Fanning; WS 1224, Thomas Delarue; WS 832,

William Desmond, WS 1006, Martin Kealy; WS 1269, John Ronayne; WS 1638, Mick Riordan. For Dublin, see Ferghal McGarry, *The Rising* (Oxford: Oxford University Press, 2010), p. 91, 132, 142–4, 164, 253. Separation women seem to have been responsible for much of the civilian hostility directed towards the Easter Rising rebels in Dublin after their surrender.

50 Ben Novick, *Conceiving Revolution: Irish Nationalist Propaganda During the First World War* (Dublin: Four Courts Press, 2001), pp. 158–60; Maria Luddy, *Prostitution and Irish Society, 1800–1940* (Cambridge: Cambridge University Press, 2007), pp. 178–81.

51 *CE*, 27 August, 29 October 1914.

52 Luddy, *Prostitution and Irish Society*, p. 179; CSORP 1914/22,394, NA (courtesy Sarah-Anne Buckley).

53 CI Report for April 1915, CO 904/96.

54 CI Report for October 1915, CO 904/97. The County Inspector reported, 'There is a good deal of drinking by women drawing separation allowances.'

55 Eileen Reilly, 'Women and Voluntary War Work', in Adrian Gregory and Senia Paseta (eds), *Ireland and the Great War: A War to Unite Us All?* (Manchester: Manchester University Press, 2002), pp. 58–64. For League of Honour details, see the *The Irish Times*, 4, 20, 28 November 1914, 2 June 1915.

56 WS 637, Muriel MacSwiney. She met with Louise Gavan Duffy, Jenny Wyse-Power and Min Ryan.

57 *Cork Free Press*, 24 June 1916; *CE*, 30 June 1916. The attendees included: Annie MacSwiney, Muriel Murphy, Josephine Coleman and Eileen Walsh.

58 *CE*, 30 June 1916.

59 Ibid., 6 July 1917.

60 Ibid., 29 May 1917, 2 June 1917; Connie Neenan Memoir. For MacSwiney's attendance and regrets, see the *CE*, 2 November 1916, 6 July, 17 August 1917 and the *Cork Free Press*, 26 August, 9 September 1916.

61 For examples, see the Cork Children's Milk Fund, *CC*, 30 October 1918; the Merchant Sailors' Widows and Orphans Fund, *CE*, 26 September 1918; the RIC Indemnity Fund, *CE*, 1 September 1919. Cork historian Antoin O'Callaghan explored the class implications of this kind of voluntary fundraising in a lecture at St Vincent de Paul Church (Sunday's Well), Cork, on 20 January 2009.

62 Sinn Féin Cork City Election Fund Treasurer's Accounts Received, 1 January 1918–6 February 1919, U271, Box 14, Item 11, CCCA.

63 *CE*, 6 July 1917.

64 Sinn Féin Cork City Election Fund Treasurer's Accounts Received.

65 *CE*, 29 April 1918, 15 January 1919.

66 Michael Collins to Terence MacSwiney, 4 August 1920, PR4/4/34, CCCA.

67 AOH County Secretary Thomas Hallinan to National Secretary J.D. Nugent, 7 February 1920, AOH Cork County Board Letter Book.

68 For examples, see the *CE*, 27 December 1918, 3 January 1919.

69 *CC*, 24 September 1917; *CE*, 24 September 1917.

70 *CE*, 26 November 1917. See also the *CE*, 15 November 1917.

71 Cumann na mBan, Poblachta na Éireann Branch Concert, circa January 1918, 2007-38-16, Cork Public Museum.

72 For another example, see John Borgonovo (ed.), *Florence and Josephine O'Donoghue's War of Independence* (Dublin: Irish Academic Press, 2006), p.47.

73 For examples see CDC Meeting Minutes, 2, 30 June, 4 August, 8 September 1918.

74 For examples see CDC Meeting Minutes, 4 August, 8 September 1918, 6 November 1919; Shandon Branch Meeting Minutes, 19 November, 3 December 1918, 21 January 1919, 2007-38-22, Cork Public Museum.

75 CDC Meeting Minutes, 30 June 1918.

76 *CE*, 18 April 1917, 27, 30 December 1918, 3 January 1919; Cumann na mBan Cork District Council Secretary's Report for 1919, CDC Meeting Minutes, 1918–20; RIC Inspector General's Report for January 1917.

77   *CE*, 27, 30 December 1918, 21 June, 2 August 1919; Cumann na mBan, Poblachta na hÉireann Branch Concert.
78   *CE*, 19 January 1917; *CC*, 23 April 1917.
79   *CC*, 23 April 1917.
80   Ibid., 8 December 1917.
81   *CE*, 19 October 1918; *II*, 19 October 1917.
82   *CE*, 20 October 1918; Lord Mayor Butterfield to Chief Secretary, 17 October 1917, CSORP 1917/25,855, NA.
83   WPB to Chief Secretary, circa 17 October 1917, CSORP 1917/25,855.
84   *CE*, 20 October 1917.
85   Finding of The King vs Mary Flynn, King's Bench Division, heard before the Cork Police Court Petty Sessions, 19 December 1918, CSORP 1919/1391, NA.
86   *CE*, 20 December 1918.
87   Finding of The King vs Mary Flynn; Crown Solicitor Jasper Wolfe to Undersecretary, Dublin Castle, 20 December 1918, CSORP 1919/1391; *CC*, 20 December 1918.
88   Solicitor General to Attorney General, 6 December 1918, CSORP 1919/1391.
89   *CC*, 1 February 1919. The fund was for impoverished students at the Christian Brothers' schools.
90   *CE*, 14 February 1919.
91   *CC*, 28 February, 28 March 1919; *CE*, 19 February, 7 March 1919.
92   *CC*, 28 March 1919.
93   'Irish Women, Do You Want Your Children Kidnapped?', leaflet and related notes, 2007-38-45, Cork Public Museum; Cumann na mBan Shandon Branch Minute Books, Meetings of 17 April and 13 May 1917, 2007-38-22, Cork Public Museum; *CC*, 15 May 1919; *CE*, 15 May 1919; de Róiste Diary, 14 May 1919. The 'Irish Women' leaflet was issued by the Cumann na mBan National Executive, in response to the RIC's arrest of an eleven-year-old child following the Soloheadbeg raid in Tipperary. See *The Irish Citizen*, May 1919.
94   *CE*, 15 May 1919.
95   Katherine Hayes to Lil Conlon, 16 May 1919, 2007-38-406, Cork Public Museum. The letter was written from Cork Women's Prison.
96   WS 1576, Peg Duggan; E. O'Donovan to May Conlon, 11 June 1919, 2007-38-393 (a), Cork Public Museum.
97   Maire Conlon to May Conlon, 30 May 1919, 2007-38-399. For another example of envy, see Birdie Conway to May Conlon, 29 May 1919, 2007-38-382 (a), Cork Public Museum.
98   Hannah Doody to Lil Conlon, 21 May 1919, 2007-38-408, Cork Public Museum.
99   CDC Inaugural Meeting, 3 February 1918. The represented branches were: Ballygarvan, Bishopstown, Blackpool, Blackrock, Blarney, Blarney St (later renamed Shandon), Clogheen, Cork, Douglas, Pouladuff, Poblacht na hÉireann, Riverstown, Rochestown, Whitechurch. Two other branches attended (Cobh, Passage West).
100   WS 1561, Margaret Lucy; WS 1576, Peg Duggan; CDC Secretary's District Report for 1919, 2007-38-21. See the CDC Meeting Minutes from 1918 to 1921 for a regular attendance of branches at the CDC. There were nominally twenty branches in the region in 1920–1, but five of those did not attend any CDC meetings during that period.
101   CDC Meeting Minutes, 1 December 1918, 30 May 1920 (Clogheen), 5 October 1920 (Eglinton Asylum).
102   Shandon Branch Meeting Minutes, 28 February, 14 March, 11, 18 April, 25 July, 15 August, 15, 31 October 1918, 4 February 1919.
103   Shandon Branch Meeting Minutes, 14, 28 February, 11 June, 11 July 1918.
104   Ibid., 6 February, 31 October, 12 November 1918, 27 March 1919, 4 April 1920.
105   Shandon Branch Meeting Minutes, 12 November 1918, 27 January 1919.
106   CDC Meeting Minutes, 2 June, 8 September, 3 November 1918; Shandon Branch

Meeting Minutes, 6 February, 18 April, 19 November, 3, 6, 11, 19 December 1918; *CC*, 19 November, 16 December 1918; *CE*, 11 June, 16 December 1918.

107   WS 1576, Peg Duggan; WS 869, P.J. Murphy.

108   WS 1576, Peg Duggan. The officer was Tadhg O'Sullivan, killed by police in 1921.

109   *CC*, 15 October 1917.

110   Report of RIC County Inspector, Cork East Riding, 9 December 1917, CO 904/199, de Valera, *Sinn Féin and Republican Suspects*; WS 1576, Peg Duggan.

111   CDC Meeting Minutes, 5 May 1918, 2007-38-21.

112   WS 805, Mrs Annie O'Brien (Cooney).

113   CDC Meeting Minutes, 5 May 1918.

114   Ibid., 8 September 1918.

115   *CE*, 23 August 1918; CCMM, 26 July 1918; de Róiste Diary, 17 May 1918.

116   *CE*, 26 June 1920; CDC Meeting Minutes, 1 July 1920.

117   *CE*, 21, 31 December 1920.

118   For examples see the CDC Meeting Minutes of 2 June 1918 (Sinn Féin general election), 30 June 1918 (National Defence Committee), 1 December 1918 (Sinn Féin general election), 5 May 1919 (American Delegation Reception Committee), 17 July 1919 (Young Ireland Sports Committee).

119   CDC Meeting Minutes, 30 June, 8 September 1918, 2 February 1919; Florrie O'Donoghue to Miss Murphy, Secretary, Republican Prisoners' Fund, Cork Brigade Adjutant's Notebook, MS 31,181, NLI; *CE*, 3 November 1917.

120   *CE*, 24–26 June, 13 August, 24 September, 26 November, 10 December 1917.

121   *CE*, 13 August 1917; *CC*, 13 August 1917.

122   *CE*, 2 July 1917.

123   Tomás MacCurtain Notes, Circa December 1917, L1966-141, Cork Public Museum; de Róiste Diary, 2 December 1917, 1 January 1918; Cork City/Tomás MacCurtain Chronology, MS 31, 398 (1), NLI.

124   CDC Meeting Minutes, 30 June 1918.

125   Ibid., 3 November 1918. The 19 November 1918 *Cork Constitution* reported that 'many women' attended the meeting.

126   *CE*, 24 April 1918.

127   *CC*, 29 April 1918.

128   *CE*, 4, 12 December 1918.

129   *CC*, 12 December 1918; *CE*, 12 December 1918.

130   CDC Meeting Minutes, 1 May 1921.

131   De Róiste Diary, 18 November 1917.

132   For example, Tomás MacCurtain and Terence MacSwiney clashed with Liam de Róiste over Sinn Féin policy; Seán O'Hegarty and Tomás MacCurtain fell out over the role of the IRB in the Irish Volunteers; Jerry Lane dropped out of Sinn Féin after he was accused of corruption.

133   Joanne Mooney Eichacker, *Irish Republican Women in America: Lecture Tours, 1916–1925* (Dublin: Irish Academic Press, 2003), pp. 92–137; *CE*, 4, 12 December 1918, 6 January, 7 May 1919, 5 July 1920; *CC*, 24, 29 April 1918.

134   Barry Egan to Father John, 19 August 1932, Egan Papers, U404 (3), CCCA.

135   WS 1576, Peg Duggan.

136   De Róiste Diary, 18 November, 10 December 1917. At the Cork Trades Council's Women's Anti-Conscription Meeting in 1918, Madge O'Leary and Mary MacSwiney represented the opposing wings of the Cumann na mBan split. See *CC*, 29 April 1918.

137   CDC Meeting Minutes, 3 February, 3 March, 5 May, 2, 30 June, 7 July, 4 August 1918; Conlon, *Cumann na mBan and the Women of Ireland*, p. 55.

138   De Róiste Diary, 12 October 1918; MacCurtain to MacSwiney, 13 April 1917, P48a/36/3.

139   Borgonovo, *Florence and Josephine O'Donoghue's War of Independence*, p. 37.

140   Seán Jennings to Mary MacSwiney, 6 April 1918, P48a/36/1, MacSwiney Papers.

141 MacCurtain to MacSwiney, 13 April 1917.
142 CDC Meeting Minutes, 8 September 1918.
143 CDC Meeting Minutes, 15 September 1918. The leaders were national vice-president Mrs Aine Ceannt and organiser Mimi Plunkett.
144 De Róiste Diary, 12 October 1918; Cumann National Executive to Cork No. 1 Brigade Adjutant, 8 January 1919, MS 31,152; Cumann na mBan Convention Minutes, 28–29 September 1918, Ceannt-O'Brennan Papers, MS 41,494 (1), NLI; CDC Meeting Minutes, 1 December 1918, 2 March 1919.
145 Department of Home Affairs Memo, 9 March 1920, DE 2/38, Dáil Éireann Collection, NA.
146 Cumann na mBan Headquarters (Dublin) to Mary MacSwiney, 14 May 1920, P48a/9/2, Mary MacSwiney Papers; O'Hegarty to P. Sheehan, 12 March 1920, DE 2/38; D. O'Hegarty to Secretary, Department of Home Affairs, 22 May 1920, DE 2/38.
147 CDC Meeting Minutes, 2 November 1920.
148 CDC Meeting Minutes, 29 January 1922; J.J. Walsh to May Conlon, 18 February 1922; J.J. Walsh to May Conlon, 21 February 1922, 2007-38-277, Cork Public Museum. See also John Borgonovo, *The Battle for Cork, July–August 1922* (Cork: Mercier Press, 2011), pp. 29–30, 48, 54, 109, 114; and Ann Matthews, 'Women and the Civil War', *The Irish Sword*, vol. XX, no. 82, Winter 1997, pp. 382–3.

CHAPTER IX: CORK LABOUR, ECONOMY AND THE ITGWU

1 C. Desmond Greaves, *The Irish Transport and General Workers' Union: The Formative Years* (Dublin: Gill & Macmillan, 1982), pp. 153, 156; *CE*, 21 November 1916.
2 ITGWU Acting General Secretary Thomas Foran to Alderman Lynch (Sligo), 5 December 1916, MS 27037 (3), NLI; *Southern Star*, 16 February 1917.
3 Stephen Broadberry and Peter Howlett, 'United Kingdom During World War One: Business as Usual?', in Stephen Broadberry and Mark Harrison (eds), *Economics of World War One* (Cambridge: Cambridge University Press, 2005), p. 219. Liam Kennedy reports that during the war Irish cost of living indexes more than doubled in all three indicators. See Liam Kennedy, 'The Cost of Living in Ireland, 1698–1998', in David Dickson and Cormac Ó Gráda (eds), *Refiguring Ireland: Essays in Honour of L.M. Cullen* (Dublin: The Lilliput Press, 2003), p. 262.
4 Kennedy, 'The Cost of Living in Ireland'.
5 Paul Halpern, *A Naval History of World War One* (London: University College London Press, 1994), p. 338.
6 At least ninety-six Cork sailors lost their lives during the sinking of the following City of Cork Steam Packet Company steamers: *Bandon*; *Lismore*; *Ardmore*; *Kenmare*; *Inniscarra*; and *Innisfallen*. See *CC*, 7 March, 8 June 1918; and *CE*, 15 March, 12, 25 June, 26 September 1918.
7 Halpern, *A Naval History of World War One*, pp. 341, 365; Elizabeth Greenhalgh, 'David Lloyd George, George Clemenceau and the 1918 Manpower Crisis', *The Historical Journal*, vol. 50, no. 2, June 2007, pp. 397–421.
8 E.J. Riordan, *Modern Irish Trade and Industry* (London: Methuen & Co., 1921), pp. 207, 214.
9 D.S. Jacobsen reports Cork's wartime wages as roughly two thirds of those in Manchester, which was decisive in attracting Ford Motors to Cork in 1917. See D.S. Jacobsen, 'The Political Economy of Industrial Location: The Ford Motor Company at Cork 1912–1926', *Irish Economic Social History*, vol. IV, 1977, pp. 36–55.
10 US Consul, Queenstown, Annual Report for Commerce and Industries for 1917 and 1918, US Consular Records, vol. 124, RG 84.
11 Letter to Cork Brewers and Distillers, 12 July 1916, Cork Coopers' Society Minute Book, U218/A/7, CCCA. See also the Society's special meeting to address inflation, 11 July 1916.
12 *CC*, 19 January 1918.

13 CI Report for May 1917.

14 *CC*, 1 June, 20–21 July 1917, 2 October 1918.

15 *CC*, 21 July, 3 August 1917; CPLGMM, 10 January 1918.

16 David Fitzpatrick, 'Home Front and Everyday Life', in John Horne (ed.), *Our War: Ireland and the Great War* (Dublin: Royal Irish Academy, 2008), pp. 131–56.

17 Riordan, *Modern Irish Trade and Industry*, pp. 303–7.

18 See the PLG letter to Lord Balfour, Cork CPLGMM, 18 September 1915; and *CC*, 26 February, 13 March 1916.

19 Quoted in Thomas Linehan, 'The Development of Cork's Economy and Business Attitudes, 1910–1939', MA thesis, UCC 1985, pp. 28–9.

20 CPLGMM, 15 August 1918.

21 Robert O'Connor and E.W. Henry, 'Estimates of Gross and Net Output and Income Arising in Agriculture in All Ireland in the Free State Area in Selected Years Between 1900/1901 and 1926/1927', *Irish Economic and Social History*, vol. XXIII, 1996, pp. 45–72; Cormac Ó Gráda, *Ireland: A New Economic History, 1780–1932* (Oxford: Clarendon Press, 1994), pp. 389–90.

22 CI Report, State of the City and Riding During the Year 1916, [handwritten report], 22 January 1917, pp. 496–509, PRO 903/19/part 2, TNA.

23 Colman O'Mahony, *The Maritime Gateway to Cork: A History of the Outports of Passage West and Monkstown, 1754–1942* (Cork: Tower Books, 1986), p. 114. For example, the bacon curer Lunham Brothers provided pork to navy ships. See the Cork Coopers' Society Minute Books, 26 August, 9 September 1914 and 21 January 1915. For a military contract for Denny's Bacon Curers, see Hansard, HC Debates, 02 April 1917, vol. 92, cc 929.

24 *Cork Industrial Development Association 14th Annual Report, 1916*; See also the *CC*, 13 March 1916.

25 Aeroplanes in this period were made out of wood and cloth. The factory saw a significant strike in July 1918 and shut down at the end of 1920. For details see *CE*, 1 July 1918, 5 January 1921; and Edward Lahiff, 'Industry and Labour in Cork, 1890–1921', MA thesis, UCC, 1988, p. 119.

26 *CC*, 17 December 1918.

27 Riordan, *Modern Irish Trade and Industry*, pp. 207–11.

28 *CE*, 14 December 1917.

29 *CC*, 20 September 1917. Timber milling and furniture production (both major employers) were affected. For an outline of the city's economy during this period, see the pamphlet 'Cork Past and Present, Handbook for the Irish Convention, September 1917', MP 855, UCC.

30 *Cork Industrial Development Association 17th Annual Report, 1920*, MP 580.

31 Cork IDA Quarterly Report, 8 November 1916, in the *Cork Industrial Development Association 14th Annual Report, 1916*, p. 48.

32 Ó Drisceoil and Ó Drisceoil, *The Murphy's Story: History of Lady's Well Brewery* (Cork: Murphy's Brewery, 1997), pp. 77, 79; Andrew Bielenberg, 'Irish Distilling Industry Under the Union', in Dickson and Ó Gráda, *Refiguring Ireland*, pp. 290–315. Bielenberg reports that Irish spirits output declined by half from 1914 to 1918.

33 Riordan, *Modern Irish Trade and Industry*, p. 152; CHCMM, 1 November 1916, 16 May 1917; Maurice Healy, MP to Chief Secretary, 16 July 1917; and District Inspector Swanzy Report of 13 July 1917, both found in CSORP 1917/24,053, NA; and the *Cork Industrial Development Association 14th Annual Report, 1916*, p. 48.

34 Waterford Harbour revenue declined from £13,600 in 1913 to £6,000 in 1917. See the Office of Public Works to Dublin Castle, 27 June 1918, CSORP 1918/18,303, NA.

35 Cork Harbour Commission Minutes, 25 July 1917, 14 January 1918.

36 CHCMM, 27 March 1918.

37 Cork IDA Quarterly Report, 8 November 1916, in the *Cork Industrial Development Association 14th Annual Report, 1916*, p. 48. See also *Cork Industrial Development Association 15th Annual Report, 1917*, p. 33.

38   Cork IDA Quarterly Report, 8 November 1916; Emmet O'Connor, 'Active Sabotage in Industrial Conflict, 1917–1923', *Irish Economic and Social History*, vol. XII, 1995, pp. 50–62.

39   Southern District Military Intelligence Report, April 1917; CI Reports for March and April 1917, CO 904/102; *CC*, 3, 6, 10, 25 April 1917.

40   Cork Coopers' Society Minute Books, 22, 31 August, 12, 22 September 1917, U218/A8, CCCA.

41   *CE*, 15, 19 October 1917; *CC*, 20 October 1917.

42   Niamh Puirséil, 'War, Work and Labour', in Horne, *Our War*, pp. 180–94; Emmet O'Connor, *Syndicalism in Ireland* (Cork: Cork University Press, 1988), pp. 23–38; Greaves, *The Irish Transport and General Workers' Union*, p. 183; Theresa Moriarty, 'Work, Warfare and Wages: Industrial Controls and Irish Trade Unionism in the First World War', in Adrian Gregory and Senia Paseta (eds), *Ireland and the Great War: A War to Unite Us All?* (Manchester: Manchester University Press, 2002), pp. 73–93. See also Emmet O'Connor, 'Agrarian Unrest and the Labour Movement in County Waterford, 1917–1923', *Saothar*, no. 6, 1980, pp. 40–58.

43   David Fitzpatrick, 'Strikes in Ireland, 1914–1921', *Saothar*, no. 6, 1980, pp. 26–39; O'Connor, *Syndicalism in Ireland*, pp. 25–27; Emmet O'Connor, 'Active Sabotage in Industrial Conflict'; Adrian Pimley, 'The Working-Class Movement and the Irish Revolution, 1896–1923', in G.D. Boyce, *The Revolution in Ireland*, p. 210.

44   Gerry Rubin, *War, Law and Labour: The Munitions Acts, State Regulation and the Unions, 1915–1921* (Oxford: Oxford University Press, 1987).

45   Emmet O'Connor, *A Labour History of Ireland* (Dublin: Gill & Macmillan, 1992), pp. 94–5; Greaves, *The Irish Transport and General Workers' Union*, p. 176; Moriarty, 'Work, Warfare and Wages', pp. 79–82.

46   *CE*, 15 January 1917.

47   Ibid., 16 March 1917; *CC*, 26 June 1917.

48   *CE*, 13 August 1917.

49   *CC*, 3, 17 October 1917; *CE*, 15, 20 October 1917.

50   *CC*, 19 December 1917; CHCMM, 14 January 1918.

51   Greaves, *The Irish Transport and General Workers' Union*, p. 184.

52   *Voice of Labour*, 19 January 1918; *CE*, 15 October 1917; Dan Bradley, *Farm Labourers: Irish Struggle, 1900–1976* (Belfast: Athol Books, 1988), p. 41; Greaves, *The Irish Transport and General Workers' Union*, pp. 183–4. Without a citation, Greaves puts union membership at 4,000 in mid-1918. See Greaves, *The Irish Transport and General Workers' Union*, p. 207.

53   Greaves, *The Irish Transport and General Workers' Union*, p. 191.

54   *CE*, 19, 21 December 1917; *Voice of Labour*, 5 January 1918.

55   *CE*, 1–2 July 1918; CI Report for June 1918, CO 904/105; CI Report for July 1918.

56   Moriarty, 'Work, Warfare and Wages', pp. 85–6; *CE*, 2 May 1919, 9 August 1920.

57   *Voice of Labour*, 22 December 1917, 15 February 1919; *CE*, 29 January 1918, 1 February 1918.

58   *CC*, 5 April 1918; *CE*, 2 May 1918.

59   *CC*, 24, 31 August, 5 October 1918; Assistant Inspector General RIC to Cork Town Clerk, 28 December 1918, CSORP 1919/5854, NLI; CPLGMM, 21 March 1918; Corporation Meeting Minutes, 13 December 1918, 23 January, 16 April 1919.

60   *CC*, 3 January, 27 February, 18 October 1919, 9 January 1920; John Borgonovo, *Spies, Informers and the Anti-Sinn Féin Society* (Dublin: Irish Academic Press, 2006), p. 93.

61   O'Connor, *Syndicalism in Ireland*, pp. 36–8; Moriarty, 'Work, Warfare and Wages', pp. 82–3.

62   Bradley, *Farm Labourers*, pp. 36–7; *Voice of Labour*, 16 March 1918. See also Thomas Neilan Crean, 'Labour and Politics in Kerry During the First World War', *Saothar*, no. 19, 1994, pp. 27–40.

63   Bradley, *Farm Labourers*, p. 40.

64   *Voice of Labour*, 16 November 1918.

65 CI Report for March 1917.

66 CI Report for April 1917.

67 CI Report for May 1917. See also the CI Report for June 1917.

68 *CE*, 16, 25 April 1917; *CC*, 21, 23 July, 11, 13 August; and Lahiff, 'Industry and Labour in Cork'.

69 John Horne, 'Labour and Labour Movements in World War One', in Jay Winter, Geoffrey Parker and Mary Harbeck (eds), *The Great War and the Twentieth Century* (New Haven: Yale University Press, 2000), pp. 187–227. For similar events in Australia, see Judith Smart, 'Feminists, Food and the Fair Price: The Cost of Living Demonstrations in Melbourne, August–September 1917', *Labour History*, no. 50, May 1986, pp. 113–31.

70 *CC*, 12, 22, 31 October 1917.

71 Southern District Military Intelligence Reports for March 1917 and July 1918; CI Reports for March, May, July 1918.

72 David Fitzpatrick, 'Strikes in Ireland', pp. 26–39.

73 Hughes Lagrange, 'Strikes and The War', in Charles Tilly and Leopold Haimson (eds) *Strikes, Wars and Revolutions in an International Perspective: Strike Waves in the Late 19th and Early 20th Century* (Cambridge: Cambridge University Press, 1989), pp. 473–99.

74 Ibid., p. 495.

75 *Voice of Labour*, 5, 19 January 1918.

76 Ibid., 19 January 1918.

77 Ibid., 30 March 1918.

78 O'Connor, *Syndicalism in Ireland*, p. 23.

79 *CC*, 31 October, 10 November 1917; *Voice of Labour*, 20 July, 14, 28 September 1918.

80 *CC*, 18 May, 31 October, 23 November 1917.

81 *CE*, 17 August, 18 September 1917.

82 Greaves, *The Irish Transport and General Workers' Union*, pp. 130, 175.

83 O'Shannon, Undated Memoir Draft and Notes, 93-12-12 (i), 93-12-12 (ii), O'Shannon Papers, Irish Labour History Museum [ILHM] Dublin; Translated Text Tomás MacCurtain's Diary, 11 July 1916, 21–22 July 1916.

84 See the extracts of two of his 1918 speeches, DMP Chief Secretary to Undersecretary, 5 February 1919, CO 904/211/334, Fr Michael O'Flanagan, *Sinn Fein and Republican Suspects*.

85 Florence O'Donoghue, Notes on a Manuscript Draft of Moiron Chavasse's Terence MacSwiney; Henry O'Mahony to Florrie O'Donoghue, 11 November 1942, MS 31,340 (11), NLI; Cathal O'Shannon, Undated Memoir Draft, 93-12-12 (i); Cathal O'Shannon Biography Summary, 93-12-12 (ii); *CE*, 19 November 1917, 23 January, 6 March 1918; CCMM, 14 December 1917; de Róiste Diary, 25 November 1917.

86 WS 637, Muriel MacSwiney; WS 1576, Peg Duggan; WS 1628, J.A. Busby; *CE*, 7 May 1919. In a Cumann na mBan concert programme, the Wallace's advertisement read, 'All Irish-Ireland and Labour Papers Stocked'. See the Cumann na mBan Poblachta na Éireann Branch Concert Programme.

87 WS 1576, Peg Duggan; Cumann na mBan Cork District Council Meeting Minutes, 6 July 1920, 2007-38/23; *Voice of Labour*, 29 June, 13 July 1918.

88 CCMM, 25 November 1918, 2 May 1919; *CE*, 19 May, 18 June 1919, 13 September 1920.

89 *Voice of Labour*, 15 December 1917; *CE*, 26 November 1917, 6 March 1918, 2, 22 May 1919.

90 WS 1628, James A. Busby. An ICA scout unit, Fianna Saoirse, appeared in Dublin during this period. See Manus O'Riordan, *James Connolly, Liberty Hall and the 1916 Rising* (Dublin: Irish Labour History Society, 2006), pp. 80, 83.

91 WS 1628, James A. Busby; *CE*, 24 September 1917, 22 January, 6 March 1918, 2, 7, 22 May 1919.

92 For example, see Michael Tobin, *CE*, 22 May 1919; and Seamus Quirke, *CE*, 13 September 1920. See also the de Róiste Diary, 23 October 1917.

93   Southern District Military Intelligence Report for March 1917; RIC Inspector General's Report for January 1919, CO 904/108.

94   WS 25, Pat Higgins; WS 89, Micheál Ó Cuill; WS 102, James Barry; Precis of Information, October 1914, RIC Crime Special Branch, CO 904/120, *British in Ireland Series*.

95   De Róiste Diary, 5 November 1917, 1 January 1918.

96   Cathal O'Shannon, Undated Article Draft, 93-12-12 (i), ILHM.

97   John Borgonovo (ed.), *Florence and Josephine O'Donoghue's War of Independence* (Dublin: Irish Academic Press, 2006), p. 48.

98   John Borgonovo, '"Codename G" and the Women Spies of Cork, 1920–1921', in Marti Lee and Ed Madden (eds), *Irish Studies: Geographies and Genders* (Boston: Cambridge Scholars Publishing, 2008), pp. 88–103.

99   The most prominent was Dominic O'Sullivan, brigade adjutant in 1921 and Cork ITGWU Branch secretary in the early 1920s. Second Battalion commander Connie Neenan was also a loyal ITGWU member. See Dominic O'Sullivan to Cathal O'Shannon, 5 May 1924, 93-12-71B; 'Mark My Greetings Well', Draft Cathal O'Shannon Memoir, 93-12-12 (ii), ILHM; Connie Neenan Memoir, CCCA. Speaking to the Irish Labour Party's annual Trade Union Congress in Cork during August 1920, Terence MacSwiney described prominent Irish Volunteers as 'tradesmen, clerks, etc.'. See *CC*, 3 August 1920.

100   *CC*, 26 November 1917; *CE*, 26 November 1917; Southern District Intelligence Report for November 1917; CI Report for November 1917.

101   *Voice of Labour*, 15 December 1917.

102   There were general strikes in 1920 after the deaths of both Lord Mayor Tomás MacCurtain and Terence MacSwiney. The motor permit strike continued for a month in January 1920, while the munitions strike affected the Cork dock and railways from July to November 1920.

CHAPTER X: PREVENTING ANOTHER BLACK '47: THE CORK PEOPLE'S FOOD COMMITTEE, 1917–18

1   *CE*, 29 January 1918.

2   David Lloyd George, *War Memoirs of David Lloyd George* (Boston: Little Brown and Co., 1937), p. 755.

3   Stephen Broadberry and Peter Howlett, 'United Kingdom During World War One: Business as Usual?', in Stephen Broadberry and Mark Harrison (eds), *Economics of World War One* (Cambridge: Cambridge University Press, 2005), pp. 206–31; Elizabeth Greenhalgh, 'David Lloyd George, George Clemenceau and the 1918 Manpower Crisis', *The Historical Journal*, vol. 50, no. 2, June 2007, pp. 397–421; Paul Halpern, *A Naval History of World War One* (London: University College London Press, 1994), pp. 338, 341, 365; Peter Stearns, 'Sharing Scarcity: Bread Rationing and the First World War in Berlin, 1914–1923', *Journal of Social History*, vol. 32, Winter 1998, pp. 371–93; Charles Bertrand (ed.), *Revolutionary Situations in Europe, 1917–1922: Germany, Italy, Austria-Hungary* (Montreal: Interuniversity Centre for European Studies, 1977); Linda Bryder, 'The First World War: Healthy or Hungry', *History Workshop*, no. 24, Autumn 1987, pp. 141–51; J.M. Winter, 'The Impact of the First World War on Health in Britain', *The Economic History Review*, vol. 30, 1977, pp. 487–507; Richard Wall and Jay Winter, *The Upheaval of War: Family, Work and Welfare in Europe, 1914–1918* (Cambridge: Cambridge University Press, 1988); Peter Dewey, 'British Farming Profits During the First World War', *Economic History Review*, vol. 37, August 1984, pp. 373, 390; Peter Dewey, 'Food Production and Policy in the United Kingdom, 1914–1918', *Transactions of the Royal Historical Society*, vol. 30, 1980, pp. 71–89; Peter Dewey, 'Nutrition and Living Standards in Wartime Britain', in Wall and Winter, *The Upheaval of War*, pp. 197–220; and Richard Wall, 'English and German Families and the War', in Wall and Winter, *The Upheaval of War*, pp. 43–100.

4   See the *Cork Examiner* editorial on 3 November 1916. See also the CCMM, 23

February, 23 March, 27 April, 8 June, 17 August 1917; CPLGMM, 25 May 1916, 9 August 1917, 6 September 1917. In November 1916, the corporation debated establishing municipal control over meat, fuel and milk supplies. See the *CC*, 2 November 1916.

5   CPLGMM, 25 September, 7, 23 October 1915.

6   Ibid., 1, 27 January 1916.

7   Ibid., 2 March 1916.

8   Cork Corporation Law and Finance Committee Meeting Minutes, 1 November 1916, CCCA.

9   *CC*, 2 November 1916.

10   *CE*, 20, 23 January 1916.

11   For some examples of famine stories, see the *Southern Star*, 18 March, 9 September, 11 November 1916, 6 January, 16 February, 2 June 1917. The British Information Ministry also produced the propaganda pamphlet, 'The Starvation of Germany'. See M.L. Sanders and Philip Taylor, *British Propaganda During the First World War* (London: Macmillan, 1982), p. 149.

12   Cork Corporation Meetings Minutes, 23 February, 23 March, 27 April, 8 June, 17 August 1917.

13   CI Report for February 1917.

14   For complaints about profiteering, see the *CC*, 20, 26 July, 19 September, 24 October 1917, 4 January 1918; *CE*, 18–19 September 1917, 4, 9 January 1918. For complaints about the failure to prosecute profiteers, see the *CC*, 10, 21 September 1917, 5, 19 January, 4 February, 1 March 1918.

15   *CE*, 15 February 1917.

16   Ibid., 16 February 1917.

17   Ibid., 5 March 1917.

18   Ibid., 26 February, 1–2, 5, 9, 12, 14, 16, 23, 26, 28 March 1917.

19   Cork Corporation Law and Finance Committee Meeting Minutes, 19 January 1917 (Allotment Scheme, Local Government Board Regulations). See also *CE*, 24 March 1917.

20   *CE*, 8, 9, 29 March 1917.

21   Ibid., 23 November 1917.

22   Ibid., 27 March 1917. See also 8, 15 March 1917.

23   *CC*, 22 February, 1 March 1918.

24   Hansard, HC Debates, 25 February 1918, vol. 103, cc 1080–1; HC Debates, 11 March 1918, vol. 104, cc 49; HC Debates, 28 October 1918, vol. 110, cc 1121–2W; *CE*, 16 February 1917.

25   *CC*, 5 September 1917.

26   *CE*, 3 September 1917.

27   *CC*, 10 September 1917.

28   *CE*, 18 September 1917.

29   *CC*, 31 October 1917.

30   Ibid., 10 September 1917.

31   *CE*, 23 October 1917.

32   *CC*, 23 November 1917; *CE*, 5, 28 December 1917.

33   *CE*, 23 November 1917.

34   *CC*, 18 May, 18 November 1916, 20, 26, 31 July 1917. For a proposed inquiry into the supply of milk to the workhouse, see the *CC*, 14 January 1914; and the CPLGMM, 1 and 27 January 1916.

35   *CC*, 4, 13–14 November 1916, 20 July, 10 September, 12 November 1917.

36   Ibid., 18 December 1917; *CE*, 11, 12, 18 December 1917.

37   *CE*, 11 December 1917.

38   *CC*, 26 July 1917; *CE*, 21 December 1917

39   *CE*, 3 September 1917.

40   CCMM, 9 November 1917.

41   *CC*, 10 November 1917, 12 January 1918; *CE*, 12 February 1918; *Voice of Labour*, 22 December 1917.

42   *Voice of Labour*, 22 December 1917.

43   See Michelle O'Mahony, *Famine in Cork City: Famine Life at Cork Union Workhouse* (Cork: Mercier Press, 2005).

44   *CE*, 3 November 1917.

45   Liam de Róiste Papers, U271/F1, CCCA.

46   *CC*, 24 September 1917.

47   *CE*, 26 November 1917; *CC*, 26 November 1917.

48   *CC*, 31 October 1917.

49   Sinn Féin Food Committee, 19 November 1917, Robert Barton Papers, MS 8786, NLI. See a reference to North East Ward Sinn Féin Club members working on 'the food problem' in Dinan vs Harrington.

50   'Notes from a Speech delivered by de Valera MP, Kanturk on 13.12.17', taken by Constable Daniel Donovan, CO 904/199, *Éamon de Valera, Sinn Féin and Republican Suspects*.

51   Report of Food Director Philip J. MacMahon, 20 August 1918, CO 904/203/172, J. Gregan, *Sinn Féin and Republican Suspects*.

52   Tomás MacCurtain's Notes on the Sinn Féin Convention, 19 December 1917, L1966-141, MacCurtain Collection, Cork Public Museum.

53   Florrie O'Donoghue Cork/Tomás MacCurtain Chronology, MS 31,398 (1), NLI.

54   De Róiste Diary, 1 January 1918; Tomás MacCurtain notes, circa 28 December 1917, L1966-141, Cork Public Museum.

55   De Róiste Diary, 2 December 1917.

56   Ibid., 28 December 1917.

57   Ibid., 5 January 1918. The Sinn Féin delegation was comprised of Liam de Róiste, Seán Ó Tuama and two republican labour activists, John Good and Tadhg Barry.

58   *CE*, 4 January 1918.

59   Cork Poor Law Guardians Meeting Minutes, 3 January 1918.

60   CHCMM, 9 January 1918. The delegation was comprised of de Róiste, MacCurtain, John Good and Seán Murphy (Irish Volunteer leader).

61   De Róiste Diary, 10 January 1918.

62   CCMM, 11 January 1918. See also *CC*, 12 January 1918.

63   *Voice of Labour*, 5 January 1918.

64   Report of Sinn Féin Food Director Philip MacMahon, 20 August 1918.

65   *II*, 18 January 1918.

66   Ibid., 15 January 1918.

67   Ibid., 18 January 1918.

68   Ibid., 21 January 1918.

69   Ibid., 2 January 1918.

70   RIC Inspector General's Report for January 1918; see also RIC county inspectors' (CI) Reports for January 1918 for Kilkenny, King's, Meath, Queen's, Galway East Riding, Roscommon, Sligo, Clare, Tipperary North Riding and Tipperary South Riding, CO 904/105, *British in Ireland Series*.

71   RIC CI Reports for January 1918 for Meath, Roscommon, Sligo and Clare.

72   *II*, 18 January, 14, 28 February 1918; *Meath Chronicle*, 26 January, 2 February 1918; *Anglo-Celt*, 12 January 1918; RIC CI Reports for January 1918 for Kilkenny, Mayo, County Dublin and Tipperary South Riding.

73   *II*, 2, 15 January 1918.

74   Ibid., 10, 24 December 1917, 15 January 1918.

75   Ibid., 10 January 1918.

76   Ibid., 12 January 1918.

77   Ibid., 11 February 1918.

78   *CC*, 12 January 1918; *CE*, 11, 14 January 1918.

79   *CE*, 9, 16, 20 February 1918; *CC*, 11, 12, 20 February 1918.

80 *II*, 12, 15 January 1918.

81 *CC*, 28 December 1917, 17 January 1918; *CE*, 4, 11 January 1918.

82 *CE*, 9 January 1918; *CC*, 27 July, 24 November 1917, 5, 19 January, 4 February, 1 March 1918.

83 *CC*, 6 February 1918.

84 Cork Corporation Meeting Minutes, 25 January 1918.

85 Cork County Club House Committee Meeting Books, 23 February 1918, U606 Box One, CCCA.

86 *Voice of Labour*, 5 January 1918.

87 Dewey, 'British Farming Profits During the First World War', p. 385.

88 *CE*, 19 January 1918. See also the *Cork Constitution* editorial, 16 July 1917.

89 *Southern Star*, 8 December 1917.

90 *CC*, 5 February 1918. The Department of Agriculture and Technical Instruction asked Cork Corporation to investigate the charges, and ordered the Cork Food Committee to assign two veterinarians to the case. Cattle Trader Paul O'Flynn likewise accused South of Ireland Cattle Traders with secretly slaughtering calves and dairy cows near the Cork docks. See his letter to the editor, *CE*, 20 February 1918.

91 *CC*, 7, 14 February 1918. See also *CE*, 19 January 1918; and *CC*, 16 February 1918.

92 *CC*, 11 February 1918.

93 *CE*, 12, 15, 18 March 1918.

94 *CE*, 19 January 1920; *CC*, 19 January 1920.

95 *Voice of Labour*, 28 December 1918.

96 *CC*, 29 January 1918; *CE*, 29 January 1918; CI Report for January 1918, CO 904/105; de Róiste Diary, 6 February 1918.

97 RIC Inspector General's Report for February 1918, CO 904/105; *CC*, 26 January, 7 February 1918.

98 *CC*, 4 February 1918.

99 CHCMM, 6, 13 and 20 February 1918. The Harbour Commission instead published the data in the Cork newspapers.

100 *CC*, 4 February 1918.

101 *CE*, 5 February 1918.

102 *CC*, 5 February 1918; *CE*, 5 February 1918.

103 *CE*, 6–7, 11, 16, 20 February 1918; *CC*, 6, 8, 11–12, 16, 20 February 1918.

104 *CE*, 5 February 1918.

105 RIC Inspector General's Report for February 1918; WS 719, E Company, 1st Battalion Joint Statement; *CE*, 5–7, 11, 18 February 1918.

106 *CE*, 7, 11 February 1918; *Southern Star*, 9 February 1918.

107 *CE*, 7 February 1918.

108 *CC*, 1 March 1918.

109 Cork Rural District Council to Prime Minister David Lloyd George, 12 February 1918, CSORP 1918/4489, NA.

110 *CC*, 14–16 February 1918.

111 Ibid., 2 March 1918.

112 Ibid., 23 February 1918. See also *CE*, 6 February 1918.

113 Ibid., 5 February 1918.

114 *CE*, 20 February 1918.

115 Ibid., 18 February 1918.

116 De Róiste Diary, 6 February 1918.

117 See the RIC CI Reports for February 1918 in Donegal, Dublin, Kildare, Kilkenny, King's, Longford, Meath, Queen's, Westmeath, Wexford, Carrick-on-Shannon, Galway East Riding, Mayo, Roscommon, Sligo, Clare, Limerick and Tipperary North Riding, CO 904/105. For additional references to the 1918 land agitation in the west, see Arthur Mitchell, *Labour in Irish Politics, 1890–1930* (Dublin: Irish Academic Press, 1974), pp. 86–7; and Tony Varley, 'Agrarian Crime and Social

Control: Sinn Féin and the Land Question in the West of Ireland in 1920', in Mike Tomlinson, Tony Varley and Ciaran McCullough (eds), *Whose Law and Order? Aspects of Crime and Social Control in Irish Society* (Belfast: Sociological Association of Ireland, 1988), pp. 54–75.

118   RIC Inspector General's Report for February 1918.

119   Ibid.; See RIC CI Reports for February 1918 in Donegal, Kildare, Queen's, Mayo, Roscommon, Sligo and Clare.

120   *CC*, 9 March 1918; RIC CI Report for February 1918 in Roscommon. For a landlord's perspective of the Roscommon trouble, see Patrick Buckland's *Irish Unionism. 1: The Anglo-Irish and the New Ireland, 1885–1922*, pp. 140–2. Buckland describes the experiences of Margaret and Maria Ffolliott, who were targeted for land seizure.

121   RIC CI Report for February 1918 in Galway East Riding.

122   *II*, 9, 26, 28 February, 2, 4, 14–16 March 1918; Michael Brennan, *The War in Clare, 1911–1921* (Dublin: Four Courts Press, 1980), p. 33; David Fitzpatrick, *Politics and Irish Life, 1913–1921: Provincial Experience of War and Revolution* (Dublin: Gill & Macmillan, 1977), pp. 62, 130–2, 220. See also Terence Dooley, *The Land for the People: The Land Question in Independent Ireland* (Dublin: UCD Press, 2004), pp. 33–9.

123   Irish Volunteer leader Michael Brennan. See Brennan, *The War in Clare*, p. 33. Tried for cattle driving (rather than cutting wood for trench building as Brennan claims), two dozen of his subordinates simply walked out of an Ennis courtroom amid a demonstration by Brennan and other Volunteers. Outside, the crowd shouted, 'Up the Cattle Drives', 'To Hell with England', and 'The Land for the People'. See the *II*, 9 February 1918.

124   See the RIC CI Reports for February 1918 in Kildare, Westmeath, Tipperary North Riding and Mayo.

125   *II*, 25 March 1918.

126   RIC Inspector General's Report for February 1918.

127   Ibid.; See also RIC CI Reports for February 1918 in Tyrone, Kilkenny, Meath, Westmeath and Wexford.

128   *CC*, 6 March 1918.

129   *II*, 22–23 February 1918 and 9 March 1918; Dorothy Macardle, *The Irish Republic, 1911–1925* (Dublin: Irish Press, 1951), pp. 240–2; Piaras Beaslaí, *Michael Collins and the Making of New Ireland, Vol. I* (Dublin: Phoenix Publishing Company, 1926), p. 181.

130   *II*, 9 March 1918.

131   Fitzpatrick, *Politics and Irish Life*, p. 132; Varley, 'Agrarian Crime and Social Control', p. 59; *II*, 26 February 1918.

132   RIC Inspector General's Reports for March and April 1918, CO 904/105; RIC CI Reports for March 1918 in Dublin, Kildare, Kilkenny, King's, Longford, Queen's, Galway East and West Riding, Roscommon and Sligo, CO 904/105. The inspector general reported disturbances in Clare, Galway, Kildare, King's, Queen's, Longford, Mayo, Roscommon and Sligo.

133   RIC Inspector General's Report for March 1918, CO 904/105; RIC CI Reports for March 1918 in King's, Queen's and Roscommon.

134   De Róiste Diary, 10 March 1918.

135   *CC*, 8, 11–12, 16, 20 February 1918; *CE*, 19 January, 5, 7, 11, 16, 18, 20 February, 12 March 1918. For the lack of a dead meat trade in 1919, see the Cork Chamber of Commerce, pp. 209–10; 'Cork Industrial Development Association 17th Annual Report, 1920', MP 580, UCC. In mid-March 1918, Cork's 120 journeymen butchers and boy assistants struck over the loss of overtime hours due to the ending of the dead meat export trade. See *CE*, 12, 15, 18 March 1918.

136   Cork veal traders were idle all of February. See *CC*, 2 March 1918.

137   *CE*, 1 October 1918.

CHAPTER XI: INSURRECTION: THE 1918 CONSCRIPTION CRISIS

1 Tadhg Barry, 'In Memorium', *Songs and Other (C)Rhymes of a Gaol-Bird*, MP, UCC. The poem was dedicated to a friend of Barry's who fought against the rebels during the Easter Rising and was then killed in France serving with the Dublin Fusiliers.

2 Southern District Intelligence Report for September 1916, CO 904/156.

3 CI Reports for March, May, June, September, October, November, December 1917.

4 CI Reports for January, February, April, July 1917.

5 CI Report for March 1917.

6 Southern District Intelligence Report for January 1917, CO 904/157.

7 Southern District Report for July 1917.

8 Southern District Intelligence Reports for September and October 1917.

9 Southern District Intelligence Report for November 1917, CO 904/157.

10 Provided in the Redmond Papers, MS 15,259. The last three figures listed in 1917 are 329, 306 and 234. The table does not include the figure for 15 December 1917 to 15 January 1918, which was 271.

11 *CE*, 24 April 1917.

12 *CC*, 1 November 1918.

13 *CE*, 16 October 1918.

14 Ibid., 4 December 1915, 3 November 1916, 29 August 1917.

15 *II*, 19 May 1916.

16 Thomas Johnstone, *Orange, Green and Khaki: The Story of the Irish Regiments in the Great War, 1914–1918* (Dublin: Gill & Macmillan, 1992), p. 213; Keith Jeffery, 'The Irish Military Tradition in the British Empire', in Keith Jeffery (ed.), *An Irish Empire? Aspects of Ireland and the British Empire* (Manchester: Manchester University Press, 1996), p. 106; *CE*, 19 May 1916; *CC*, 1 June 1916.

17 *UCC Official Gazette*, no. 21 (June 1916), no. 22 (December 1917), no. 23 (April 1918), Box 7, Boole Library, UCC.

18 *CE*, 1 September, 11 October 1917.

19 Report of the President of University College Cork, 1916–1917, Box 7, Boole Library, UCC; 'War Record of University College Cork 1919', CSORP 1919/10,879, NA; List of UCC fatalities, courtesy Michael Holland, UCC Curator. In 1911, Harper narrowly beat out the well-qualified Éamon de Valera for his faculty position.

20 *CE*, 7–22 July 1916.

21 Ibid., 10 November 1916.

22 Gerry White and Brendan O'Shea, *A Great Sacrifice: Cork Servicemen Who Died in the Great War* (Cork: Echo Publications, 2010), p. 297.

23 *CE*, 21, 28 June 1916.

24 Ibid., 2, 21 November 1916.

25 Johnstone, *Orange, Green and Khaki*, pp. 354–63.

26 Elizabeth Greenhalgh 'David Lloyd George, George Clemenceau and the 1918 Manpower Crisis', *The Historical Journal*, vol. 50, no. 2, June 2007, pp. 397–421; Adrian Gregory, 'You Might as well Recruit Germans', in Adrian Gregory and Senia Paseta (eds), *Ireland and the Great War: A War to Unite Us All?* (Manchester: Manchester University Press, 2002), pp. 113–32.

27 Keith Middlemas (ed.), *Thomas Jones Whitehall Diary, vol. I* (London: Oxford University Press, 1969), p. 58.

28 *CE*, 10 April 1918.

29 *CC*, 10 April 1918.

30 Ibid., 19 April 1918.

31 Corporation Meeting Minutes, 12 April 1918.

32 Ibid. (the motion was submitted to the corporation).

33 PLG Meeting Minutes, 11 April 1918.

34 CHC Meeting Minutes, 17 April 1918.

35   *CC*, 14, 18, 24 April, 6 May 1918; *CE*, 4, 21–22 April 1918.
36   Willie O'Connor to Lord Lieutenant Wimborne, 11 April 1918, CSORP 1918/2791, NA. O'Connor was informed on 17 April that he was legally bound to remain in office and would be fined if he refused to continue his duties.
37   *CC*, 23 April 1918.
38   *CE*, 17 April 1918.
39   Lieutenant General Bryan Mahon to Field Marshal John French, Commander-in-Chief Home Forces, 27 April 1918, CD 178/1/5, Roger McCorley Collection, MA. See also the War Cabinet Meeting Minutes, 19 April 1918, CAB/23/6.
40   Philip Harold Barry to US Consul, 24 April 1918, attached to letter from US Consul to American Ambassador Walter H. Page, 17 May 1918, US Consul Records, Cork, Ireland, RG 84, vol. 118.
41   *CC*, 18 April 1918.
42   *CE*, 19 April 1918.
43   Ibid., 4 May 1918; See also *CC*, 29 April 1918.
44   *CE*, 4 May 1918.
45   *CC*, 10 May 1918.
46   Ibid., 24 May 1918.
47   De Róiste Diary, 16 April 1918.
48   Corporation Meeting Minutes, 12 April 1918.
49   *CE*, 17 April 1918.
50   Ibid., 22 April 1918.
51   Ibid., 19 April 1918.
52   Ibid., 16, 19 April 1918.
53   Ibid., 16 April 1918.
54   *CC*, 11 May 1918.
55   *CE*, 17 April 1918.
56   Ibid., 11 May 1918.
57   Ibid., 15 May 1918.
58   CHCMM, 17 April 1918.
59   J.J. Horgan, *From Parnell to Pearse: Some Recollections and Reflections* (Dublin: Browne & Nolan, 1948), p. 328.
60   AOH Annual Convention Report, 9 February 1919, U389a/25, CCCA.
61   Southern District Military Intelligence Report for April 1918; BMH WS 566, Charles O'Connell; WS 719, E Company, 1st Battalion Joint Statement; WS 1568, James Coughlan; WS 1584, Patrick Murray; WS 1639, Captain Laurence M. Neville, WS 1656, Daniel Healy; John Borgonovo (ed.), *Florence and Josephine O'Donoghue's War of Independence* (Dublin: Irish Academic Press, 2006), p. 47; Connie Neenan Memoir.
62   *CC*, 17 April 1918.
63   *CE*, 15 April 1918.
64   Ibid., 22 April 1918.
65   Ibid., 15 April 1918.
66   De Róiste Diary, 16–17 April 1918.
67   *CE*, 16 April 1918.
68   *Cork Free Press*, 22 July 1916; *CC*, 25–26 June, 4, 28 September 1917, 16 April 1918.
69   CI Report for April 1918; *CC*, 22 April 1918; *CE*, 22 April 1918.
70   *CE*, 22 April 1918.
71   CI Report for April 1918.
72   *CE*, 22 April 1918.
73   *CC*, 24 April 1918; *CE*, 24 April 1918; CI Report for April 1918.
74   *CE*, 24 April 1918.
75   *CC*, 24 April 1918.
76   De Róiste Diary, 22 April 1918.
77   *CE*, 24 April 1918; WS 1561, Margaret Lucy.

78 Paraphrase of telegram to American Ambassador, London, from American Consul, Queenstown, 23 April 1918, US Consul Records, Cork, Ireland, RG 84, vol. 118.

79 *CC*, 24 April 1918.

80 *CE*, 24 April 1918.

81 De Róiste Diary, 23 April 1918.

82 *CC*, 29 April 1918.

83 Thomas Foran, ITGWU Executive Memorandum, 18 April 1918, MS 17,115 (ii), NLI.

84 *Watchword of Labour*, 13 April 1918.

85 Ibid., 20 April 1918.

86 Cathal O'Shannon, Chronology, Memoir Draft, MS 93-12-12 (i), Cathal O'Shannon Papers, Irish Labour History Museum, Dublin.

87 *CE*, 29 April 1918; CI Report for April 1918.

88 The *Cork Examiner* and British Military Intelligence (Southern District Report for April 1918) reported £5,000, while police claimed £6,000.

89 *CE*, 29 April 1918.

90 Southern District Military Intelligence Report for April 1918.

91 *Watchword of Labour*, 17 August 1918; Cathal O'Shannon Report to Mansion House Committee, 7 May 1918, 93-12-84(A), Irish Labour History Museum.

92 Undated Mansion House Committee Memorandum, MS 17,115 (iv), NLI.

93 'Memorandum of Labour Representatives', Undated Mansion House Committee Report, MS 17,115 (ii), NLI.

94 *CC*, 20 April 1918.

95 Executive Memorandum, 24 June 1918, Irish Trades Union Congress and Labour Party, MS 17,115 (ii).

96 'Suggestions to Local Defence Committees', MS 17,115 (iii), NLI.

97 De Róiste Diary, 14 May 1918.

98 *CE*, 23 August 1918; de Róiste Diary, 14 May 1918; Cumann na mBan CDC Meeting Minutes, 30 June 1918.

99 Cork Coopers' Society Meeting Minutes, 3 July 1918.

100 *CE*, 23, 30 August, 16 November 1918, 6, 15, 20 January, 5, 7 February 1919; *CC*, 2 September, 6 November 1918. Seán O'Hegarty later characterised the bishop's actions as 'of doubtful morality'. See *CE*, 29 September 1923.

101 Tim Healy to Maurice Healy, 7 November 1918, Mrs T.M. O'Sullivan Collection, BMH CD 21, Cathal Brugha Barracks.

102 CI Report for May 1918, CO 904/106.

103 WS 1547, Mick Murphy; WS 1568, James Coughlan; WS 1579, Seán Lucey; WS 1708, William Barry; WS 1584, Pa Murray; Seán Healy to Florrie O'Donoghue, 29 October 1965, MS 31,342 (2), NLI. A third battalion briefly encompassed the southside 'liberties' (suburbs beyond the city boundary). It was broken up, probably owing to unauthorised robberies by the 3rd Battalion staff investigated by Richard Mulcahy of GHQ. See WS 446, Frank Haynes; WS 1656, Dan Healy; and Connie Neenan Memoir, CCCA.

104 Borgonovo, *Josephine and Florence O'Donoghue's War of Independence*, pp. 35–7; Cork City Chronology, MS 31,398 (1); 9, 17, 24 July 1918, Brigade Communication Officer's Notebook, MS 31,181, NLI.

105 Headquarters Cork Brigade to Adjutant T. Barry, 3 July 1918, MS 31,181.

106 WS 558, B Company, 1st Battalion Joint Statement; WS 1657, Jeremiah Keating; WS 1707, Patrick Collins; Borgonovo, *Florence and Josephine O'Donoghue's War of Independence*, p. 80; Robert Graves, *Good to All That* (London: Penguin Books, 1960), p. 222.

107 Cited order dated 25 February 1918, in Deputy Chief of Staff GHQ Order to All Brigades, 19 January 1920, MS 11, 410 (ii), NLI; CI Report for May 1918; *CE*, 28 May, 14 November 1918; *CC*, 9, 11 May 1918; 'Returns of Outrages Attributed to the Sinn Féin Movement', Judicial Division to Chief Secretary's Office, CSORP

1919/1957, NA. See Borgonovo, *Florence and Josephine O'Donoghue's War of Independence*, pp. 27–8 for an account of one such unauthorised raid.

108   WS 1521, Michael Walsh; WS 1584, Pa Murray; WS 1654, Cornelius Kelleher; WS 1656, Dan Healy. See also Hansard, HC Debates, 11 July 1918, vol. 108, cc 481.

109   Connie Neenan Memoir.

110   Thomas Barry (Blackrock Road) Undated Statement to Florrie O'Donoghue, MS 31,222, NLI.

111   WS 719, E Company, 1st Battalion Joint Statement; WS 1641, Tim Buckley; WS 1656, Dan Healy; WS 1675, Joe O'Shea; Seán Breen in the Ernie O'Malley Notebooks, P17B/125, UCD Archives.

112   WS 719, E Company, 1st Battalion Joint Statement; WS 746, Seán Culhane; WS 1521, Michael Walsh; WS 1547, Mick Murphy; WS 1675, Joe O'Shea; WS 1676, Robert Ahern; Connie Neenan Memoir; Ray Kennedy in the O'Malley Notebooks, P17b/111.

113   Connie Neenan Memoir; WS 1741, Michael O'Donoghue.

114   WS 746, Seán Culhane.

115   WS 746, Seán Culhane; WS 1584, Pa Murray.

116   WS 1568, James Coughlan; WS 1579, Seán Lucey; WS 1639, Laurence Neville; WS 1675, Joe O'Shea; WS 1676, Robert Ahern; WS 1708, William Barry; WS 1751, Michael O'Donoghue; Ray Kennedy in the O'Malley Notebooks.

117   WS 1676, Robert Ahern.

118   *CE*, 29–30 April, 19, 21–22 May 1919; Connie Neenan Memoir; CI Report for April 1919, CO 904/108; WS 561, Matt O'Callaghan; WS 1631, Charles Meaney.

119   Borgonovo, *Florence and Josephine O'Donoghue's War of Independence*, pp. 46–7.

120   Florrie O'Donoghue to Pat Higgins, 30 July 1918, Brigade Communication Officer's Notebook; WS 1654, Cornelius Kelleher; WS 1726, Cornelius Cronin; Robert Langford Draft BMH Statement. MacCurtain equipped his outdoor headquarters at Ballingeary with folding beds and a tent.

121   Denis Kennedy to Florrie O'Donoghue, 18 November 1945, MS 31,340 (8), NLI.

122   WS 739, Felix Doherty.

123   WS 446, Frank Haynes; WS 739, Felix Doherty.

124   Borgonovo, *Florence and Josephine O'Donoghue's War of Independence*, p. 47.

125   Ibid., p. 40.

126   Mahon to Lord French (Commander in Chief, Home Forces), 16 April 1918, F48/6/7, Parliamentary Archives, London.

127   Walter Long, Colonial Office, Memorandum to the War Cabinet, 29 May 1918, CAB 24/52, TNA.

128   French to Lloyd George, 19 April 1918, F48/6/8, Parliamentary Archives.

129   French to King George V, 13 July 1918, F48/6/17, Parliamentary Archives.

130   French to Prime Minister Lloyd George, 18 April 1918, F48/6/4. See also the CI Report for January 1919, CO 904/108; *CC*, 11–14 January 1919.

131   French to Lloyd George, 18 April 1918, F48/6/4.

132   French to Lloyd George, 18 April 1918; Lord French Report to the War Cabinet, 19 April 1919, F48/6/10; Undated 'Scheme for Dispositions and Organisation in Ireland during the Enforcement of the Military Service Act', F48/6/8; Lieutenant General Bryan Mahon to French, 26 March 1918, 'Memorandum of the Enforcement of Conscription in Ireland', CD 178-1-5, Cathal Brugha Barracks.

133   French Report to the War Cabinet, 19 April 1918.

134   French to Lloyd George, 19 May 1918, F48/6/12.

135   CI Report for June 1918; Southern District Intelligence Report, May 1918, CO 904/107.

136   *CE*, 20 May, 10 June 1918; WS 666, Bill Hales; de Róiste Diary, 18–19 May 1918; List of Suspects Ordered Interned but Still at Large, 17 May 1918, CSORP 1919/8435; 'Sinn Féin Leaders Arrested and Deported, 1918', PRO 904/24/1, Kew. The missed Volunteer leaders were Tomás MacCurtain, Seán Murphy, Seán O'Sullivan and Donal Óg O'Callaghan.

137 De Róiste Diary, 19 May 1918.
138 *CE*, 24 May 1918.
139 J.J. Horgan, 'Precepts and Practice in Ireland, 1914–1919', *Studies*, vol. VIII, no. 30, June 1919, pp. 210–26.
140 *CC*, 20 May 1918; *CE*, 20, 27 May 1918.
141 American Consul to Ambassador Walter H. Page, 21 May 1921, RG 84, vol. 118.
142 CPLGMM, 30 May 1918.
143 CCMM, 14 June 1918.
144 *CE*, 24, 27 May, 15 June 1918.
145 Ibid., 15 June 1918.
146 CI Report for June 1918, CO 904/105; *CC*, 15 June 1918; *CE*, 15 June 1918.
147 *CC*, 29 April, 1–4, 6–7, 9–11 May 1918; *CE*, 30 April, 1, 10–11 May 1918; US Consul, Cork to US Ambassador Walter H. Page, 9 May 1918, RG 84, vol. 118; *The Irish Times*, 2–4, 6–8, 10 May 1918.
148 US Consul, Cork, 'The Political Situation in the South of Ireland', 12 May 1918, RG 84, vol. 118. See also the *CC*, 6–10 May 1918; CHC Meeting Minutes, 8 May 1918; Southern District Military Intelligence Report for June 1918; Hansard, HL Debates, 20 June 1918, vol. 30, cc 28.
149 *CE*, 30 April 1918.
150 *CC*, 2 May 1918.
151 Ibid., 29 April, 1–2, 6 May 1918; *CE*, 30 April, 1 May 1918; CHCMM, 22 May 1918; CPLGMM, 2 May 1918.
152 *CE*, 1 May 1918; *CC*, 2 May 1918.
153 *CC*, 3–4 May 1918.
154 CHCMM, 22 May 1918; CPLGMM, 2, 16 May, 20 June 1918.
155 De Róiste Diary, 23 April 1918. See also Lionel Caplan, '"Bravest of the Brave": Representatives of the Gurkha in British Military Writings', *Modern Asia Studies*, vol. 25, July 1991, pp. 571–97.
156 Governor General Ferguson to the Colonial Office, 27 July 1918; Henry Lambert (for Walter Long) to the Irish Chief Secretary, 27 July 1918, both found in CSORP 1918/20,554, NA.
157 WPB to Chief Secretary and Lord Lieutenant, circa 27 July 1918, CSORP 1918/20,554.
158 Michael Wheatley, *Nationalism and the Irish Party: Provincial Ireland, 1910–1916* (Oxford: Oxford University Press, 2005), p. 231.
159 *CC*, 23 September 1916.
160 CPLGMM, 18 May 1916.
161 As reported in the *Cork Constitution*, 8 May 1917.
162 Lord French to Prime Minister Lloyd George, 19 May 1918, F48/6/12, Parliamentary Archives.
163 *CE*, 19 July 1918.
164 Ibid., 20 July 1918.
165 Ibid., 25 July 1918.
166 Joseph Hurry to Chief Secretary Shortt, 20 July 1918, CSORP 1918/20,105, NA.
167 Northern Command Military Intelligence Report for February 1918, CO 904/157, *British in Ireland Series*.
168 Manus O'Riordan, *James Connolly: Liberty Hall and the 1916 Easter Rising* (Dublin: Irish Labour History Society, 2006), pp. 28–9.
169 John Borgonovo, *The Battle for Cork, July–August 1922* (Cork: Mercier Press, 2011), pp. 105–6.
170 Memo to the Lord Lieutenant and Chief Secretary, 15 June 1918, PRO 904/169/2, TNA.
171 CCMM, 12 July 1918, CCCA.
172 *CE*, 8, 11–12 July, 3 August 1918. Quotation comes from *CE*, 4 July 1918.
173 *CE*, 8 July 1918.

174 Ibid., 10 July 1918.
175 Ibid., 8 July 1918.
176 Ibid., 9 July 1918.
177 Ibid., 26 June, 10 July 1918. St Nick's players engaged in a team-wide brawl, started by Dan 'Sandow' O'Donovan, later a senior IRA officer.
178 Ibid., 13 July 1918.
179 Ibid., 16–17 July 1918.
180 Ibid., 15 July 1918.
181 Ibid., 17 July 1918.
182 Ibid.
183 Pádraig Purséil, *The GAA In Its Time* (Dublin: Ward River Press, 1984), p. 175; Maura Cronin, 'Work and Workers in Cork City and County, 1800–1900', in Cornelius Buttimer and Patrick O'Flanagan (eds), *Cork: History and Society. Interdisciplinary Essays on the History of an Irish County* (Dublin: Geography Publications, 1993), p. 108.
184 *CE*, 17 July 1918.
185 *CE*, 22 July 1918.
186 Hansard, HC Debates, 25 July 1918, vol. 108, cc 1978–9.
187 Hansard, HC Debates, 01 August 1918, vol. 109, cc 599–600.
188 *CE*, 15 July 1918.
189 Ibid., 22 July 1918.
190 *CC*, 22 July 1918; *CE*, 22 July 1918; *Freeman's Journal*, 22 July 1918.
191 For examples of prohibited fixtures see the RIC CI Reports for July 1918 in Belfast, Dublin, Galway East, Galway West, Kildare, Kilkenny, King's County, Limerick, Monaghan, South Tipperary, Tyrone, Waterford and Wexford, CO 904/106.
192 *CE*, 22 July 1918.
193 Southern District Military Intelligence Report for July 1918.
194 US Consul, Cork to Irwin Laughlin, Charge d'Affaires, American Embassy, London, 12 June 1918, RG 84, vol. 118; *CE*, 12 June 1918, 28 March 1919; WS 1567, James McCarthy.
195 This seems to be the Fitzgerald Park band promenade referenced above.
196 Frank O'Connor, *An Only Child* (London: Macmillan & Co., 1961), p. 185.
197 *CC*, 29 July 1918. Meetings were held at Knockraha, Bearings and Mallow. See also the report of Sergeant J. O'Malley, Farran, 13 August 1920, PRO 904/24/2.
198 WS 810, 3rd Battalion Joint Statement. Herlihy was captain of the IRA's Strelane Company. The officers date this event as May 1918, but mention the arrest of two city IRA officers, who were detained during the 21 July meeting held in the same location.
199 CDC Meeting Minutes, 4 August 1918. Meetings were held at Pouladuff, Riverstown, Blackpool, Bishopstown and Ballygarvan. The US Consul at Queenstown reported that government authorities had banned further mention of these illegal gatherings in Irish newspapers. See the US Consul Report, 'Political Situation in the South of Ireland', 12 September 1918, US Consul Records, Cork, RG 84, vol. 119.
200 US Consul Charles Hathaway to US Ambassador Walter H. Paye, 31 July 1918, US Consul Records, Cork, RG 84, vol. 119.
201 *CE*, 26 September 1918.
202 Ibid., 29 July 1918; *CC*, 29 July 1918.
203 *CE*, 30 July 1918.
204 Ibid., 3 August 1918.
205 Hansard, HC Debates, 01 August 1918, vol. 109, cc 599–600.
206 *CE*, 30 July 1918.
207 Hansard, HC Debates, 29 July 1918, vol. 109, c. 116.
208 *CE*, 30 July 1918; 5 August 1918.
209 *Freeman's Journal*, 5 August 1918.

210 *CE*, 5, 8 August 1918.
211 Ibid., 8 August 1918.
212 Sinn Féin Headquarters to All Comhairlí Ceanntair, 3 August 1918, CO 904/203/172, J. Gregan, *Sinn Féin and Republican Suspects*.
213 *CC*, 16 August 1918; *CE*, 19, 24 August 1918.
214 CI Report for August 1918, CO 904/106.
215 Edward Shortt to Prime Minister Lloyd George, 4 July 1918, F45/6/6.
216 *CC*, 10 October 1918.
217 Ibid., 15 October 1918.
218 Ibid.
219 Delaney to Chief Secretary, 2 September 1918, CSORP 1917/34,525, NA.
220 Corporation Meeting Minutes, 26 July 1918; CPLGMM, 15 August 1918; *CC*, 23 July, 16, 30 August 1918.
221 Horgan, *From Parnell to Pearse*, p. 329. See also his letter to Denis Gwynn, *From Parnell to Pearse*, p. 332.
222 Adrian Gregory, '"You might as well recruit Germans": British Public Opinion and the Decision to Conscript the Irish in 1918', in Adrian Gregory and Senia Paseta (eds), *Ireland and the Great War: A War to Unite Us All?* (Manchester: Manchester University Press, 2002), p. 129; Adam Seipp, *The Ordeal of Peace: Demobilisation and the Urban Experience in Britain and Germany, 1917–1921* (Surrey: Ashgate, 2009), p. 138.
223 CI Report for August 1918. Adrian Gregory reports that during the last three months of the war, 56 per cent of Irish recruits joined the RAF. See 'You Might as Well Recruit Germans', p. 129.
224 *CC*, 10–11, 15, 21 October 1918; *CE*, 13–14 September, 3, 11, 21–22 October 1918.
225 *CE*, 3 October 1918.
226 *CC*, 11 November 1918. Ireland generated just 11,781 of the targeted 50,000 enlistments. The Irish Recruiting Council stopped issuing enlistment totals following the Armistice. The last total was: All Ireland, 11,781; Dublin, 2,694; Belfast, 4,448; Cork, 840; Limerick, 623; Wexford, 869; Omagh, 1,032; Galway, 271; Armagh, 391; Mullingar, 366; Sligo, 198.
227 Jeffery, 'The Irish Military Tradition and the British Empire', p. 100. See also David Fitzpatrick, 'The Logic of Collective Sacrifice: Ireland and the British Army, 1914–1918', *Historical Journal*, no. 38, December 1995, p. 1030.
228 *CC*, 10 October 1918.
229 Ibid., 21 October 1918; *CE*, 21 October 1918.
230 CI Report for October 1918, CO 904/107.
231 *CC*, 21 October 1918.
232 *CE*, 21 October 1918.
233 CI Report for October 1918.
234 *CC*, 1, 7–10, 12 October 1918; *CE*, 7, 11, 29–31 October 1918.
235 *CC*, 23, 28–30 October 1918.
236 Cork Corporation Public Health Committee Meeting Minutes, 29, 31 October, 12, 26 November 1918, CP/C/CM/PH/A26, CCCA; CCMM, 25 November 1918; PLG Meeting Minutes, 31 October, 14 November 1918; *CC*, 23, 28–29 October 1918.
237 *CC*, 12 November 1918.
238 Ibid., 5 November, 13 December 1918.
239 For details see Borgonovo, *Florence and Josephine O'Donoghue's War of Independence*, pp. 50–3; and Florrie O'Donoghue's more detailed account in *Sworn To Be Free: The Complete Book of IRA Jail Breaks* (Tralee: Anvil Books, 1971).
240 For some local reactions, see the *CE*, 12, 14 November 1918; and the *CC*, 12 November 1918. Dublin Castle fired Warder J.J. Keane, incorrectly assuming he assisted the escape. See CO 904/204/214, J.J. Keane, *Sinn Féin and Republican Suspects*.
241 *CC*, 12 November 1918; *CE*, 12 November 1918; WS 1741, Michael O'Donoghue; de Róiste Diary, 12 November 1918.
242 *CC*, 12 November 1918.

243　De Róiste Diary, 11 November 1918.

Chapter XII: The Victory of Sinn Féin: The 1918 General Election

1　This chapter first appeared in the collected edition, *From Parnell to Paisley: Constitutional and Revolutionary Politics in Modern Ireland* (Dublin: Irish Academic Press, 2010), edited by Caoimhe Nic Dháibhéid and Colin Reid.

2　For an interesting discussion of Cork politics and the 1918 general election, see Micheál Martin, *Freedom to Choose: Cork and Party Politics, 1918–1932* (Cork: The Collins Press, 2009), Chapter 1.

3　Tom Garvin, *The Evolution of Irish Nationalist Politics* (Dublin: Gill & Macmillan, 1981), p. 99; F.S.L. Lyons, *The Irish Parliamentary Party, 1890–1910* (London: Faber & Faber, 1951), p. 10.

4　*CE*, 12 April 1918; Southern District Intelligence Report for April 1918. See the Robert Barton Papers, Sinn Féin Executive Papers, Summary of Monies Received up to 12 August 1921, MS 8062 (2), NLI.

5　RIC 1918 Intelligence Notes, CO 903/19, Part IV, Kew.

6　For a discussion on its impact in Ireland, see James McConnell, 'The Franchise Factor in the Defeat of the Irish Parliamentary Party, 1885–1918', *The Historical Journal*, vol. 47, no. 2, June 2004, pp. 355–77; and Brian Farrell, *The Founding of Dáil Éireann* (Dublin: Gill & Macmillan, 1971), pp. 45–50.

7　*CE*, 11 June 1918; de Róiste Diary, 29 June 1918; Cumann na mBan CDC Meeting Minutes, 3 March, 5 May 1918.

8　*CE*, 1 July 1918.

9　Ibid., 2 October 1918; *CC*, 16 November 1918.

10　Cork Poor Law Guardians (PLG) Clerk's Memo, 16 April 1918; PLG Clerk to Rate Collectors, 27, 29 April 1918; PLG Clerk to Crown Clerk Henry Wright, 24 April, 1, 9, 2 May 1918, Cork Poor Law Guardian Clerk's Letter Book, BG/69/B9, CCCA.

11　Denis Tobin to the Dáil Éireann Department of Home Affairs, 7 October 1921, DE 10-6, NA.

12　PLG Clerk to Officer Commanding Naval Station Queenstown, 24 June 1918; PLG Clerk to Henry Wright, 27 June 1918, both found in Poor Law Guardian Clerk's Letter Book.

13　Tobin to the Department of Home Affairs.

14　*CC*, 3, 8, 9, 10, 12–14, 17, 22 August 1918.

15　Ibid., 17 August 1918.

16　See ibid., 1, 19 August 1918.

17　Ibid., 3, 14 August 1918.

18　Tim Healy wrote of O'Brien's decision on 17 February 1918: see Healy, p. 591. O'Brien claimed his decision came after the 1916 Bantry election. See William O'Brien's 'An All for Ireland Memento' dated Christmas 1918, P150/628, Éamon de Valera Papers, UCD Archives.

19　Tim Healy to Maurice Healy, Transcribed Letter, 15 October 1918, CD 21-1, Mrs T.M. O'Sullivan Collection, Bureau of Military History. See also Tim Healy to Maurice Healy, 12 October 1918, CD 21-1. Tim Healy reported in September that O'Brien had told him he would not stand again: 'My mind was made up long ago.' See Tim Healy to Maurice Healy, 6 September 1918.

20　J.J. Horgan to Miss O'Brien, 18 November 1918, 6772/273, TCD.

21　*CC*, 17 October, 19 November, 2 December 1918; *CE*, 31 October 1918. See also William O'Brien, *The Irish Revolution and How It Came About* (London: George Allen & Unwin Ltd, 1923), p. 385.

22　William O'Brien to Frank Gallagher, 3 January 1918, UC/UOB/PP/AS/161, UCC.

23　J.J. Horgan to Miss O'Brien; J.J. Horgan to John Dillon, 19 June 1918, 6772/270, TCD.

24　Cork All-For-Ireland Club to O'Brien, 26 November 1918, UC/UOB/PP/AS/169, UCC.

25　Tim Healy to Maurice Healy, 21 May 1918, CD-21.

26 'All for Ireland Memento'; *CC*, 25 November 1918; *II*, 25 November 1918.
27 Arthur Norway to Undersecretary, Dublin Castle, 12 November 1914, CO 904/212/351, *Sinn Féin and Republican Suspects*; John Power, *A Story of Champions* (Cork: Lee Press, 1941), pp. 93–6; *Evening Echo*, 4 November 1954; WS 91, J.J. Walsh; WS 89, Michael O'Cuill; WS 77, Harry Lorton.
28 *CE*, 7 April 1918.
29 Transcribed Tomás MacCurtain Diary, 21–22 July 1916; MacCurtain Notes, 19, 28 December 1917; WS 153, Éamon Dore; O'Shannon draft memoir.
30 *CE*, 8 August, 11 October 1918; *Voice of Labour*, 2 March, 17 August 1918.
31 Cathal O'Shannon to Liam de Róiste, 21 August 1918, F15, CCCA; de Róiste Diary, 5–6 September 1918.
32 De Róiste Diary, 10 September 1918; *CE*, 5 February 1918.
33 For examples, see letters from 'A disgusted worker' and 'Plain Worker', *CE*, 6 November 1918.
34 De Róiste Diary, 15, 18 September, 12 October 1918.
35 William O'Brien (ITGWU leader) Diary, 9, 19 October 1918, MS 15,705, NLI; de Róiste Diary, 28 October 1918.
36 Éamon O'Mahoney to Liam de Róiste, 24 and 28 September 1918, 10539/426; Seán Ó Tuama to de Róiste, 2 October 1918, 10539/439; Patrick Brady to de Róiste, 11 October 1918, 10539/431; Tom O'Donovan to de Róiste, 1 October 1918, 10539/432; Patrick Brady to de Róiste, 12 October 1918, 10539/433, all found in the de Róiste Papers, TCD.
37 De Róiste Diary, 10, 28 September, 22 October 1918; William O'Brien's (ITGWU leader) diary, 8 September, 1918; *CE*, 27 September 1918; *Voice of Labour*, 28 September 1918.
38 De Róiste Diary, 28 September, 22, 25 October 1918; Cork Coopers' Society Meeting Minutes, 9 October 1918.
39 *CE*, 22, 30 October 1918.
40 De Róiste Diary, 5 November 1918.
41 *CE*, 11 November 1918.
42 Henry Donegan to John Dillon, 3 January 1919, 6775/87/1878, TCD.
43 John Dillon to J.J. Horgan, 11 November 1918, MS 18,271, NLI.
44 Ibid., 20 November 1918, MS 18,271; Horgan to Miss O'Brien.
45 Henry Donegan to John Dillon; de Róiste Diary, 1 December 1918. See also the *CE*, 21 November 1918, 1 February 1919.
46 See the *CE*, 1, 10, 11, 16, 18, 20–23 November 1918.
47 M. O'Leary to Considine O'Donovan, 2 December 1918, Postal Censorship Reports, CO 904/164, *British in Ireland Series*.
48 The meetings occurred on 20, 21 and 22 November. For accounts, see the *CE*, 20–23 November.
49 Tadhg Barry to Liam de Róiste, 24 November 1918, de Róiste Papers, C15, CCCA.
50 W.F. O'Connor to Lord Lieutenant, 23 November 1918; J.J. Taylor (secretary to the lord lieutenant), 25 November, 1918; W.F. O'Connor to Lord Lieutenant, 29 November 1918, all found in CSORP 1918/2791, NA.
51 *CE*, 2 December 1918.
52 De Róiste Diary, 1 December 1918.
53 *CE*, 2 December 1918; Gerry White and Brendan O'Shea, *Baptised in Blood: The Formation of the Cork Brigade of the Irish Volunteers, 1913–1916* (Cork: Mercier Press, 2005), p. 34.
54 He had recently challenged Éamon de Valera to a public debate. See the *Southern Star*, 19 January 1918. He also wrote a letter to the *CE*, 16 August 1917.
55 Tadhg Barry to Seán Courtney, 8 December 1918, CD 75-3-4, BMH.
56 *CE*, 15, 19, 20, 23, 28 and 30 November 1918.
57 *CC*, 2 December 1918.
58 *CE*, 2 November, 6 December 1918.

59 *CE*, 7 April 1919. Sixty followers of Lord Midleton left the Irish Unionist Alliance in January 1919. See *CE*, 25 January 1919.

60 *CC*, 5 December 1918.

61 Ibid., 12 April 1918. See also *CE*, 24 May 1918; *CC*, 23 June 1917, 16 November 1918.

62 *CC*, 1 August 1918.

63 Ibid., 3, 4, 13 December 1918, 19 June 1919.

64 Bishop Cohalan to Liam de Róiste, 30 November 1918, U 271/F21, CCCA.

65 *CE*, 19 November 1918.

66 De Róiste Diary, 2 December 1918.

67 *CE*, 19 November 1918.

68 De Róiste Diary, 2 December 1918.

69 Florrie O'Donoghue to 'Seán', undated, regarding the Election Committee, MS 31,172, NLI. From the subject matter this can only refer to the General Election Committee meeting described by both Liam de Róiste in his diary and O'Donoghue in his memoir. It seems highly likely the recipient was Seán O'Hegarty, who was the acting Cork No. 1, as Tomás MacCurtain was in Dublin recovering from a bout of influenza, as noted below. The timing and threatened withdrawal matches Seán Scannell's letter to Liam de Róiste. O'Donoghue also refers to the dispute with Walsh occurring at a meeting on Monday evening, which again matches de Róiste's timing of the incident.

70 De Róiste Diary, 2 December 1918.

71 MacCurtain was recovering from the Spanish Influenza. See John Borgonovo (ed.), *Florence and Josephine O'Donoghue's War of Independence* (Dublin: Irish Academic Press, 2006), p. 55.

72 De Róiste Diary, 2 December 1918.

73 Florence O'Donoghue, *Tomás MacCurtain: Soldier and Patriot* (Tralee: Anvil Press, 1971), p. 136.

74 Seán Scanlan to Liam de Róiste, 28 November 1918, C215, de Róiste Papers, CCCA.

75 De Róiste Diary, 2 December 1918.

76 For examples, see the *CC*, 2, 4, December 1918; *CE*, 3, 6–7 December 1918.

77 Tom Garvin, *Nationalist Revolutionaries in Ireland* (Oxford: Clarendon Press, 1987), pp. 118–19.

78 Tomás MacCurtain 'Davis, Lalor and Sinn Féin', Lecture, circa January 1919, L1945-245-4, Cork Public Museum.

79 *CE*, 10 December 1917, 6 December 1918.

80 Ibid., 13 December 1918.

81 *CC*, 5 December 1917, 21 November 1918, 7 December 1918.

82 Ibid., 9, 10 and 13 December 1918; *CE*, 25 November 1918 and 3, 7, 12 and 13 December 1918.

83 *CE*, 3 December 1918.

84 Ibid., 11 December 1918.

85 Ibid., 19 November 1918.

86 Ibid., 12 December 1918.

87 *CC*, 7 December 1918.

88 For example, see John Ellis, 'The Degenerate and the Martyr: Nationalist Propaganda and the Contestation of Irishness', *Éire-Ireland*, Fall/Winter 2000/2001, pp. 11–18.

89 *CE*, 2, 6, 9, 14 December 1918.

90 John Good spoke at election rallies on 19, 25 November, 2, 4, 6, 9 December; Éamon O'Mahoney, president of the Cork Trades Council, spoke on 2 December (at three separate meetings), 4, 5 and 14 December; Michael Lynch of the Queenstown Trades Council spoke on 2, 5 and 11 December; Tom Donovan, Secretary of the Cork ITGWU, spoke on 2 December 1918.

91 *CE*, 19 November, 4 December 1918.

92 Ibid., 13 December 1918.

93   Ibid., 19 November 1918
94   Cumann na mBan CDC Meeting Minutes, 2 June 1918.
95   *CE*, 12 December 1918
96   Ibid., 21 November, 3, 9 December 1918.
97   Ibid., 25 November 1918.
98   Ibid., 2 December 1918.
99   Ibid., 13 December 1918.
100 Ibid.
101 Ibid., 25 November, 9 December 1918.
102 Ibid., 9 December 1918.
103 Ibid., 6 December 1918.
104 William Murphy to John Dillon, 20 September 1918, 6775/87/1776, TCD.
105 *CC*, 6 December 1918.
106 *CE*, 6 December 1918.
107 Ibid., 13 December 1918.
108 Ibid., 3 December 1918.
109 Ibid., 9 December 1918
110 Ibid., 2 December 1918
111 *CC*, 4 December 1918; *CE*, 19, 25 November, 6, 9, 14 December 1918.
112 *CE*, 6 December 1918.
113 Ibid., 15 October 1918.
114 Ibid., 19 November, 4 December 1918.
115 Sinn Féin Election Fund Treasurer's Report, CCCA.
116 *CE*, 16 December 1918.
117 *CC*, 16 December 1918.
118 Ibid., 1, 3, 10, 13–14, 17 August 1918.
119 Henry Donegan to John Dillon, 3 January 1919, 6775/87/1878, TCD.
120 *CE*, 16 December 1918.
121 De Róiste Diary, 15 December 1918.
122 *CC*, 25 November 1918. See also the *CE*, 25 November 1918; Henry Donegan to John Dillon.
123 The boy spoke from a podium set up for the Irish Party candidates. During his speech he amused the crowd when he theatrically paused to pour himself a glass of water, drank it and then resumed his denunciation of the Redmondites.
124 Henry Donegan to John Dillon.
125 For outdoor UIL meetings, see *CE*, 7, 9, 11 December 1918.
126 *CC*, 16 December 1918; *CE*, 16 December 1918.
127 *CE*, 11 December 1918. See also *CE*, 6 December 1918 ('The Cork City Election campaign is proceeding without incident of note and promises to be one of the most quiet and yet most interesting in modern records'); and *CE*, 30 December 1918 ('It was the most quiet election in the political records of Cork').
128 *CC*, 30 December 1918.
129 Ibid., 30 December 1918.
130 Fr Augustine, Capuchin Monastery, Dublin, to Liam de Róiste, 2 January 1919, U271/C12, CCCA.
131 J.J. Walsh to Tadhg Barry, 7 January 1919, Postal Censorship Third and Fourth Report, CO 904/164.
132 AOH Annual County Convention Report, 9 February 1919.
133 *CC*, 30 December 1918.

CONCLUSION

1   *CE*, 13 December 1918.

Index